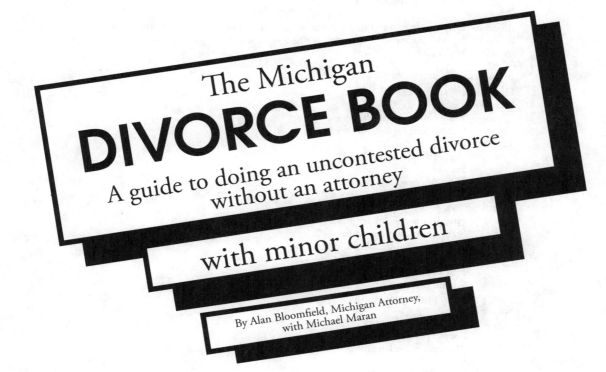

The Michigan
DIVORCE BOOK
A guide to doing an uncontested divorce without an attorney

with minor children

By Alan Bloomfield, Michigan Attorney,
with Michael Maran

Thunder Bay Press

Holt, Michigan

The Michigan Divorce Book: A Guide to Doing an Uncontested Divorce without an
Attorney (with minor children)
by Alan Bloomfield with Michael Maran

Published by
Thunder Bay Press
Holt, MI 48842

Printing history:
First edition: January 1986
Second edition:
      First printing: June 1989
      Second printing: September 1990
Third edition:
      First printing: May 1993
      Second printing: October 1994
      Third printing: January 1996
      Fourth printing: June 1997
Fourth edition:
      First printing: February 1998
      Second printing: November 1999
      Third printing: October 2000
Fifth edition:
      First printing: March 2001
      Second printing: March 2002
      Third printing: June 2003
Sixth edition:
      First printing: January 2004
      Second printing: January 2005
      Third printing: January 2006
Seventh edition:
      First printing: March 2007
      Second printing: December 2007
Eighth edition:
      First printing: January 2009
      Second printing: December 2009
      Third printing: November 2010
Ninth edition: March 2013
Tenth edition: January 2016

ISBN: 978-1-933272-57-3
Library of Congress Control Number: 2015959624

Printed in the United States of America

Illustrations: Patric Fourshé

Contents

Preface

Chapter 1

PART I: Introduction to Divorce

PART II: Uncontested Divorce

PART III: Doing an Uncontested Divorce Yourself

Chapter 2

PART I: Starting Your Divorce

PART II: Finishing Your Divorce

Appendices

Preface

Do your own divorce? The idea may sound crazy to many people. After all, doesn't everyone need a lawyer to get a divorce?

The fact is, you have the right to do your own divorce, just as you have the right to represent yourself in any legal matter. The right of legal self-representation is so important it's protected by the Bill of Rights in the U.S. Constitution (it falls under the First Amendment's right of petition for redress of grievances). In Michigan, legal self-help is also guaranteed by Sec. 13 of Art. 1 of the Michigan Constitution of 1963, which says: "a suitor in any court of this state has the right to prosecute or defend his suit, either *in his own proper person* or by an attorney." (Emphasis added.)

Despite these guarantees, the right to represent yourself in court doesn't mean very much if you don't know what you're doing once you get there. That's where this book comes in.

Chapter 1 describes divorce, tells you what an uncontested divorce is and helps you decide whether you can handle it yourself. Chapter 2 has instructions and sample forms to guide you through a divorce. And last but not least, blank forms are included in the back of the book which you can tear out and use to file your own divorce case.

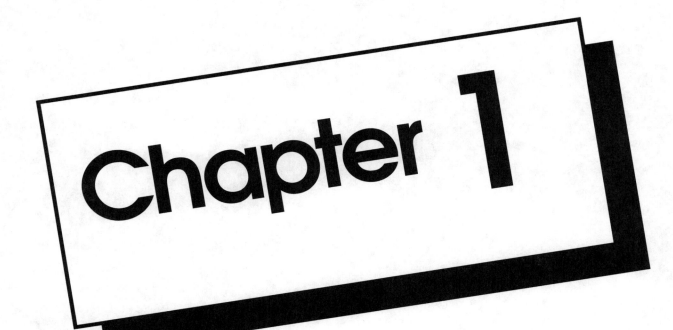

PART I: Introduction to Divorce

PART II: Uncontested Divorce

PART III: Doing an Uncontested Divorce Yourself

PART I: Introduction to Divorce

Asked about the origin of divorce, the French philosopher Voltaire said he didn't know exactly, but assumed that divorce was invented a few weeks after marriage. His reasoning? A couple married, quarreled and were ready for divorce a few weeks later.

Although it was meant as a joke, Voltaire's remark wasn't that far from the truth. Divorce *has* been around almost as long as marriage. The Babylonian Code of Hammurabi, the oldest known code of law, authorized divorce on several grounds, including a wife's barrenness, disloyalty, neglect or disease. According to the Bible, a Hebrew husband could divorce his wife for "uncleanness" by handing her a "bill of divorcement" and sending her away.

It was this law that Jesus was quizzed about by the Pharisees when they asked him: "Is it lawful for a man to divorce his wife?" The Gospel of St. Mark says Jesus condemned the practice, adding: "What therefore God hath joined together, let not man put asunder." Yet St. Matthew's account of this incident is different. It says that Jesus permitted divorce on grounds of wives' "fornication." Other New Testament scripture is also contradictory; some passages are hostile to divorce, while others seem to tolerate it.

With all this confusion, the Bible can be interpreted to either allow or disallow divorce. Catholic countries sided with the Mark Gospel and forbade divorce. But Protestant countries—with the notable exception of England—followed Matthew and allowed divorce on grounds of adultery and sometimes desertion.

When it came to law, America usually took its cue from England, so it should have observed the English ban on divorce. But divorce became firmly established in this country after the first American divorce was granted in 1639 by the Massachusetts Bay Colony to Mrs. James Luxford for her husband's bigamy.

There were several reasons for that. In a way, America itself was the child of divorce: the "divorce," in the guise of the American Revolution, from England. It's even possible to read the Declaration of Independence as the petition for that divorce. This interpretation isn't as far-fetched as it seems. Thomas Jefferson, the author of the Declaration of Independence, had handled divorce cases as a young lawyer, and the catalog of grievances and wrongs found in the declaration echoed those from his divorce practice.

There were also practical reasons for the American love affair with divorce. During the colonial era, divorce was forbidden in England, France, Italy and several other European countries. Many immigrants to America were fleeing these repressive divorce laws as much as religious or political persecution. Once here, they were in no mood for tough European-style divorce laws.

By the mid-19th century, almost all the states had divorce laws. Typically, these laws permitted divorce on a variety of fault grounds. According to this fault system, divorce was available only when one spouse had committed marital misconduct. This gave the faultless spouse grounds for a divorce.

On the other hand, an at-fault spouse wasn't entitled to get a divorce. A peculiar divorce doctrine called recrimination prevented anyone with "unclean hands" from asking for a divorce. Recrimination effectively barred an at-fault spouse (who often wanted out of the marriage the most) from getting a divorce, unless the faultless spouse was willing to excuse the marital misconduct. By using this divorce veto, the faultless spouse could blackmail the at-fault spouse—by demanding extra property, support or other concessions—as the price for the divorce.

During this era, Michigan divorce law was typical of the fault divorce laws. The 1846 divorce law had seven fault grounds for divorce: 1) adultery 2) physical incompetence 3) imprisonment 4) desertion 5) husband's drunkenness 6) extreme cruelty 7) husband's neglect. It also had a strict recrimination doctrine.

But not every state was as generous with divorce grounds as Michigan. Before 1967, New York had a notoriously tough divorce law, which allowed divorce only on grounds of adultery. South Carolina was even worse. Divorce was legalized in that state after the Civil War and then abolished in 1878. Divorce was finally re-established in South Carolina in 1949, after an absence of 71 years!

When people were frustrated by strict divorce laws in their home states, they often fled to other states with better laws. This so-called migratory divorce was possible because the United States, unlike most countries, doesn't have a uniform national divorce law. Instead, divorce is regulated by each state. With 50 different divorce laws, it's no wonder that migratory divorce has been a problem in America since colonial times.

Many states tried to stop migratory divorce by adopting divorce residence requirements or erecting other barriers. But a handful of states encouraged divorce migration as a boost to local tourism. Nevada even managed to make migratory divorce its largest industry for a while. In 1907, William Schnitzer, a sharp New York lawyer, noticed that Nevada had a lax divorce law, with a short residence period, seven grounds for divorce and no recrimination doctrine. Schnitzer opened an office in Reno and soon divorce migrants flocked there. Other lawyers followed in Schnitzer's footsteps and migratory divorce flourished in Nevada.

As easy as migratory divorce was, it was still very expensive. There was the cost of getting the divorce, not to mention the expense of traveling to another state and living there during the residence period. As a result, migratory divorce was a luxury only the wealthy could afford.

Among those making the trek to Nevada was Nelson Rockefeller, then governor of New York. Millionaire Rockefeller got a Nevada divorce in 1962 while thousands of his fellow New Yorkers were stuck at home without a divorce remedy. Rockefeller's divorce caused a furor, and many think it cost him the Republican presidential nomination in 1964.

By the 1960s, all the controversy over migratory divorce had created the mood for change. California took the first step in 1969 when it adopted a "no-fault" divorce law. Previously, California had had a fault divorce law with several fault grounds (adultery, extreme cruelty, willful neglect, etc.). It replaced these with two no-fault grounds: incurable insanity and irreconcilable differences. What's more, the new California law banished fault from the other divorce issues of alimony, child support and property division.

The California no-fault law revolutionized divorce in America, as other states rushed to enact similar no-fault laws. Within five years, 45 states had adopted no-fault divorce. By 1986, when final holdout South Dakota gave in, every state had some type of no-fault divorce.

Michigan was among the first states to adopt no-fault divorce in the early 1970s. But in Michigan the transition from fault to no-fault divorce wasn't as smooth as it was in other states. At first, Michigan lawmakers were poised to adopt a sweeping California-style no-fault divorce law removing fault from divorce entirely. Michigan lawyers were horrified at this idea because they feared that no-fault divorce meant no-lawyer divorce. The lawyers lobbied furiously against the no-fault proposal. Ultimately, a deal was reached providing for no-fault divorce grounds, but with fault left intact for most of the other divorce issues. This no-fault divorce law took effect on Jan. 1, 1972, and is still the law today.

In the last few years, no-fault divorce has stirred up new controversy. Feminists have complained that no-fault divorce can be unfair to women. Their reasoning: no-fault destroyed the divorce leverage women once had, leading to smaller property division and support settlements for them. Some conservatives argue that no-fault divorce actually encourages divorce, bringing more of the social problems associated with divorce.

In Michigan, no-fault critics have introduced bills in the legislature to repeal parts of the no-fault law, and re-introduce fault into divorce grounds. These proposals got a lot of press, but haven't gone anywhere as legislators have shied away from re-opening the debate on no-fault divorce.

Do-It-Yourself Divorce

During the era of fault divorce, few dared to do their own divorces because they were hard to handle. But a no-fault divorce is really just a clerical task, which even a nonlawyer can manage. As soon as no-fault laws were adopted, nonlawyer entrepreneurs set up do-it-yourself divorce services to help people do their own divorces.

In Michigan, two such operations sprang up in 1972 after the no-fault divorce law went into effect: Harry Gordon Associates in Oak Park and Gordon, Graham and Cramer in Detroit. Harry Gordon Associates sold a divorce kit with forms and instructions. Gordon, Graham and Cramer offered personalized services, including preparation of papers, filing and help with court appearances.

Alarmed at this threat to their business, Michigan lawyers sought to enforce the unauthorized practice of law statute against their new rivals. Like most states, Michigan has an unauthorized practice law barring nonlawyers from practicing law. This law permits you to represent yourself, but you must be a lawyer to represent others.

In 1972, courts invoked this law and ordered Harry Gordon Associates and Gordon, Graham and Cramer out of business. Facing jail if they disobeyed, most of the firms' operators reluctantly closed. But Virginia Cramer, one of the partners in Gordon, Graham and Cramer, refused to be intimidated. She re-emerged with a new divorce service similar to her old one. Just like before, lawyers tried to stop her claiming that she was engaged in the unauthorized practice of law.

After battling in court for several years, the parties ended up before the Michigan Supreme Court in the case known as *State Bar of Michigan v. Cramer*. The issue in the case was whether Cramer had violated the unauthorized practice law by providing personalized legal services. The court decided that she had when she gave clients *specific* legal information (telling them what to do in their particular situations). On the other hand, the court said that nonlawyers like Cramer could offer *general* legal information in the form of books or legal kits.

Thanks to the apparent ban on nonlawyer divorce services, few such firms exist in Michigan. Without this option, most divorce do-it-yourselfers have had to rely on self-help divorce books or kits. Since the 1970s, several legal aid organizations and women's groups have offered do-it-yourself divorce kits. This book has its genesis in one such kit published in 1981. It was enlarged into book form in 1986, and has been revised several times since then.

PART II:
Uncontested Divorce

Before you start your divorce, it's important to talk with your spouse and see if you agree on the divorce issues. This will determine whether your divorce will be contested or uncontested.

A disagreement over the divorce issues usually means a contested divorce. You are entitled to represent yourself in a contested divorce. But your spouse would probably get a lawyer, providing an edge over you during the divorce. That's why you shouldn't represent yourself in a contested case.

On the other hand, if you and your spouse agree on all the divorce issues, you have an uncontested divorce. You ought to be able to handle this kind of divorce yourself without a lawyer. But see Part III for several situations in which even an uncontested divorce may be too complicated for you to do yourself.

What sort of agreement do you need for an uncontested divorce? A formal written agreement—called a separation or settlement agreement—won't be necessary. Michigan doesn't require these in uncontested cases, as some states do. Instead, an informal agreement or understanding should be enough.

Sometimes you may not need an agreement at all. Needless to say, it's impossible to discuss divorce with a spouse who has disappeared. In that case, the spouse's absence should permit you to go ahead and get an uncontested divorce just as if s/he were agreeing to it.

Divorce Issues

During your talk, you and your spouse may quickly agree that your marriage must end. But a divorce is far more than simply ending a marriage. That's especially true when you have minor children. With that type of divorce, there are no less than seven important divorce issues:

- end of marriage
- custody
- parenting time
- residence of children
- child support
- property division
- alimony

These are the issues you and your spouse must agree on to have an uncontested divorce. To help you reach agreement, the rest of this chapter examines these issues in detail.

End of Marriage

Above all else, a divorce means ending your marriage. To accomplish that, you need specific grounds (reasons). As explained in Part I, Michigan once had fault grounds, such as adultery, desertion, extreme cruelty, etc., for divorce. But in 1972, Michigan adopted these no-fault grounds for divorce:

> There has been a breakdown of the marriage relationship to the extent that the objects of matrimony have been destroyed and there remains no reasonable likelihood that the marriage can be preserved.

If you look at these grounds closely, you see that three things must exist to get a divorce: 1) a marital breakdown ("breakdown of the marriage relationship") 2) that is serious ("to the extent that the objects of matrimony have been destroyed") 3) and permanent ("there remains no reasonable likelihood that the marriage can be preserved").

At first, when the no-fault law was new, courts had trouble applying the no-fault grounds. Judges continued to probe into the reasons for marital breakdowns, as they had under the old fault law. Some judges even denied divorces when they felt that a marriage hadn't really broken down or could be saved. By the late 1970s, courts were applying the no-fault law more liberally. These days, courts don't investigate the marital breakdown very much, and divorces are granted for almost any reason. As a result, the end-of-marriage issue is seldom contested in divorces any more.

Glossary

Uncontested divorce—divorce where spouses agree on all the divorce issues.

No-fault divorce—all Michigan divorces, whether contested or uncontested, are no-fault divorces since they must use no-fault grounds.

Custody

If end of marriage is the easiest divorce issue, custody is the most difficult because it's so emotional for parents. Fairly or not, parents regard custody as a test of their worth as parents. With the stakes so high, courts have struggled to find a custody formula that satisfies parents while looking out for children.

In the beginning, custody was simple. According to old English law, children were the property of their fathers and they could do with them what they liked. As for mothers, they were "entitled to no power [over their children] but only to reverence and respect," according to Blackstone's influential *Commentaries on the Law of England.*

In America, courts were more sympathetic to mothers, and seldom gave custody to fathers as easily as the English did. By the 19th century, that sympathy had evolved into an actual preference for maternal custody, known as the tender years doctrine. This doctrine gave custody to mothers of young children (of "tender years") unless they were unfit parents.

Michigan once had a tender years doctrine that gave mothers custody of children under the age of 12, except when they were unfit. This preference put fathers at a severe disadvantage when they sought custody. According to a 1948 Michigan custody survey, mothers got custody 95% of the time when the issue was contested.

By the 1960s, the unfairness of Michigan's custody law was plain, leading to adoption of a new law in 1970. The child custody act of 1970 abolished the tender years doctrine and assigned custody according to the "best interests of the children." These best interests were defined as the sum of several factors listed in the act (see below).

The new custody law may have changed how custody was awarded, but it didn't alter the type of custody courts ordered. The one-parent custody known as sole custody remained the favorite type of custody after passage of the act in 1970.

But by the 1970s, families were changing rapidly and many parents had become dissatisfied with sole custody. Many fathers disliked sole custody because it confined them to a limited weekend-daddy role. Some working mothers found it difficult to cope with sole custody and new-found job responsibilities. And most children wanted more contact with their noncustodial parents than sole custody provided.

Parents displeased with sole custody wanted more flexible arrangements, such as joint custody. There are several forms of joint custody, also known as shared custody or coparenting. But whatever the form, joint custody tries to give parents control of their children in many of the same ways they had before the divorce.

More Information

Regardless of which type of custody you choose, divorce is hard on children. To help them adjust, some schools have divorce support groups for students.

Family counselors and therapists can also provide support. Look under "Marriage, Family, Child & Individual Counselors" in the yellow pages for one near you.

Or call the **American Association for Marriage and Family Therapy** at (703) 838-9808 for a list of counselors in your area, or use the association's online referral service at www.TherapistLocator.net.

Books about divorce and children:

Helping Your Kids Cope with Divorce the Sandcastles Way, M. Gary Neuman, New York: Times Books, 1998

What About the Kids?, Judith Wallerstein and Sandra Blakeslee, New York: Hyperion, 2003

Parents and children arranging custody amicably? You would think that the legal system would have encouraged joint custody. On the contrary, most legal experts were against the idea. Judges feared joint custody because they were convinced that it would disrupt families. Lawyers dreaded it because they thought that it would hurt business. Custody cases produced big fees for lawyers, so the idea of joint custody made many nervous.

Despite the hostility, by the late 1970s parents were seeking and winning joint custody in isolated cases, including several landmark cases in Michigan. But the event that really turned the tide was California's passage of the first comprehensive joint custody law in 1979. Not only did this law permit joint custody, it created a legal presumption in favor of it.

During the next several years, most states followed California's example and adopted similar joint custody laws. Michigan joined their ranks when it added joint custody provisions to its custody law in 1980.

Types of Custody

Before the introduction of joint custody, custody was all or nothing. One parent got it, leaving the other parent with nothing except a custody substitute in the form of visitation (now called parenting time). The 1980 joint custody law redefined custody by dividing it into two parts: legal custody and physical custody. These two elements can be combined in various ways to provide for several types of custody:

Glossary

Legal custody—the right and responsibility to make *important* decisions affecting children.

Physical custody—allows a parent to have the children live with him/her. It also includes the right and responsibility for making routine decisions about the children while they are living with the parent.

Sole custody. Sole custody assigns both legal and physical custody of the children to a custodial parent. Since the custodial parent has physical custody, the children live with him/her. The noncustodial parent ordinarily has periodic parenting time.

As the children's legal custodian, the custodial parent makes all important decisions about the children. Routine decisions are made by the parent in whose care the children are when the routine decision has to be made (usually this is the custodial parent, but it could be the noncustodial parent during a period of parenting time).

Joint legal custody. With this arrangement, one parent has physical custody of the children, but both parents share legal custody. Like sole custody, the children live with the custodial parent (parent with physical custody); the noncustodial parent ordinarily has parenting time.

Because legal custody is joint, both parents must agree about important aspects of the children's health care, education, religion, etc. For example, if a child wanted to transfer from a public to a private school, both parents must consent to the transfer. But if the child needed a routine school permission form signed, the parent taking care of the child at the time could sign the form.

Joint physical custody. When parents have joint physical custody, they share physical and usually legal custody of the children. As joint legal custodians, the parents share decision-making for the children, as described above. And as joint physical custodians, both parents also share physical control of the children. But how can that be accomplished? After all, you can't physically divide the children in two as King Solomon proposed in the Bible story. As it happens, there are several ways for parents to share physical custody of children:

¶ *Split-time custody.* With split-time custody, the children live with each parent for fairly short periods of time. For example, the children might reside with one parent for a week, then move to the other for the next week, and so on. Parents of young children have been known to exchange custody every few days or even every other day.

¶ *Block-time custody.* Block-time custody allows the children to spend large amounts of time with the parents. Typically, block-time custody is scheduled around the children's school year. In this arrangement, the children might reside with one parent for the nine-month school year and with the other parent during the three-month summer vacation.

¶ *"Bird's nest" custody.* Just as birds tend to their young in the nest, the children can stay in the home and the parents take turns moving in and out. Each parent exercises physical custody while living in the home with the children.

Split custody. Split custody divides the children between the parents so that each parent has custody of one or more. You can split sole custody or joint legal custody by assigning physical custody of the children to different parents. In a way, joint physical custody is already split because the parents share custody of the children. But you can split joint physical custody even more by putting the children on different custody schedules, so they don't move together as their physical custody changes.

Mixed custody. Ordinarily, parents get one type of custody for all their children. But it's possible to mix custody so there are different types of custody for the children of a family. For example, one parent might have sole custody of two children and joint physical custody of a third child with the other parent.

Third-party custody. When you divorce, you lose natural custody of your children to the court, which becomes their guardian. Ordinarily, the court gives custody back to you or your spouse. As a matter of fact, Michigan custody law favors parental custody (see below for more about this so-called parental presumption). Nevertheless, a court can award custody to a third party, instead

More Information

About custody for fathers, contact one of these fathers' rights groups:

Dads & Moms of Michigan "Kids Need Both Parents"
6443 Inkster Road, #290
Bloomfield Twp, MI 48301
(248) 559-3237
www.dadsandmomsofmichigan.org

National Center for Men
117 Pauls Path #531
Coram, NY 11727
(631) 476-2115
www.nationalcenterformen.org

There are several excellent books about joint custody:

Joint Custody and Co-Parenting, Miriam Galper, Philadelphia: Running Press, 1980

The Disposable Parent, Mel Roman and William Haddad, New York: Holt, Rinehart & Winston, 1978

Sharing Parenthood after Divorce, Ciji Ware, New York: Bantam Books, 1984

of parents, when the parents aren't fit to care for the children. Parents can also agree to turn over custody to third parties. Third-party custodians might be relatives, such as grandparents, or even nonrelatives like a foster parent or child welfare agency.

After its debut in 1980, joint custody quickly became established in Michigan. A 1984 survey of Michigan judges found that they were routinely ordering joint legal custody, although many were still skeptical about joint physical custody. Nationally, it's been estimated that joint legal custody is awarded in 81% of cases.

Despite this popularity, joint custody has critics. They complain that joint legal custody gives noncustodial parents mostly symbolic power, but no real parental authority. They also cite studies showing that joint legal custody doesn't seem to improve compliance with parenting time or child support orders.

Joint physical custody poses practical problems. Split-time custody, particularly for short intervals, is disruptive for parents and children alike. Block-time custody is more sensible because it can be scheduled around work and school schedules. Bird's nest custody offers even greater stability for children, although not for parents. Yet all these types of joint physical custody are expensive, as the parents must have separate living accommodations, clothing, toys, etc., for the children.

Split custody is often perceived as unfair or even cruel, because it separates children. For this reason, courts normally frown on split custody of young children. But they may allow it for adolescents, particularly when they have strong custody preferences.

What all this shows is that there is no magic custody formula. Each type has its pluses and minuses. You must be aware of these and choose the type of custody that is best for you.

Court-Ordered Custody

Because all children must have caretakers, a court can make a preliminary custody order during a divorce to settle the custody issue until the end of the divorce (see "Do I Need 'Preliminary Relief'?" on page 60 for more about preliminary custody). With or without a preliminary custody order, the court always makes a final custody order in the Judgment of Divorce at the end of the divorce. This order continues, subject to future modification, until the children reach the age of 18.

When custody is contested during a divorce, the court must decide the issue according to the best interests of the children. The child custody act of 1970 defines children's best interests as the sum of the following factors:

- love, affection and other emotional ties existing between the parties involved and the child
- capacity and disposition of the parties involved to give the child love, affection and guidance, and to continue the education and raising of the child in his or her religion or creed, if any
- capacity and disposition of the parties involved to provide the child with food, clothing, medical care or other remedial care recognized and permitted under the laws of this state in place of medical care, and other material needs
- length of time the child has lived in a stable, satisfactory environment, and the desirability of maintaining continuity
- permanence, as a family unit, of the existing or proposed custodial home or homes
- moral fitness of the parties involved
- mental and physical health of the parties involved
- home, school and community record of the child
- reasonable preference of the child, if the court considers the child to be of sufficient age to express preference
- willingness and ability of each of the parties to facilitate and encourage a close and continuing parent-child relationship between the child and the other parent or the child and the parents
- domestic violence, regardless of whether the violence was directed against or witnessed by the child
- any other factor considered by the court to be relevant to a particular child custody dispute
- when joint custody is also at stake, the judge must also consider an extra factor: whether the parents will be able to cooperate and generally agree concerning important decisions affecting the welfare of the child

Note: In most cases, custody must be withheld from a parent who has committed criminal sexual conduct against any children in the family.

During a custody trial, the judge must address *all* of these best interest factors. The judge must make specific factual findings and reach legal conclusions about each factor, even when it doesn't seem to apply.

Besides the best-interest factors, courts deciding custody are guided by two legal presumptions: custodial presumption and parental presumption.

To provide stability for children, the custodial presumption gives current custodians of children preference over noncustodians seeking custody. The presumption applies when children are living in an "established custodial environment." According to the custody law, a custodial environment exists when "over an appreciable time the child naturally looks to the custodian in that environment for guidance, discipline, the necessities of life, and parental comfort."

The custodial presumption doesn't always figure in contested divorce cases because usually not enough time has passed to establish a custodial environment. But it may apply when the parents have been separated awhile and one parent alone has cared for the children.

Glossary

Legal presumption—a rule of evidence helping a party to prove something, or which makes it more difficult for another party to prove something.

Sometimes, two custodial environments coexist. Michigan courts have ruled that joint physical custody can establish custodial environments with both parents, and each may invoke the custodial presumption. This creates a kind of custody stalemate that is difficult to change.

The parental presumption gives parents a custody edge over nonparents. The parental presumption seldom applies in divorce cases because it's usually the parents who are vying for custody. Nevertheless, third parties can sometimes intervene in divorces and seek custody. And in some divorce cases, the custody of children may already be in the hands of third parties, such as relatives, foster parents or child welfare agencies. In these situations, parents can invoke the parental presumption to get custody away from third-party custodians, or fend off custody claims of intervening third parties.

Even when these custody presumptions apply, contesting custody is still painful and messy. To begin with, a custody battle is expensive. Lawyer fees for each spouse may be $5,000 or more. Added to this is the cost of having child psychologists or other expert witnesses testify during the custody hearing. What with lawyers, expert witnesses and other fees, a custody fight can cost many thousands of dollars.

Fighting over custody can also take a huge emotional toll. As explained in Part I, when Michigan's no-fault divorce law was adopted, fault was removed from the grounds for divorce, but left intact for all the other divorce issues. In custody law, fault appears in the guise of the "moral fitness of the parties." This leaves the door open for evidence of many kinds of marital misconduct.

As bad as a custody fight is for parents, it can be even worse for children. Contesting custody pits parent against parent, and can be extremely upsetting for children. The custody law also requires most children to declare their parental preference, forcing them to make a painful choice about which parent they like best.

A custody fight can also jeopardize joint custody. When joint custody is at stake, the court must consider the 13th custody factor of parental cooperation. Rightly or wrongly, some courts believe a custody battle shows a lack of parental cooperation, ruling out joint custody. As a result, custody contests often become winner-take-all, with the victors getting sole custody as the prize.

Uncontested Custody

If you and your spouse agree on custody, the court should approve your custodial arrangement. If you've chosen some form of joint custody, your agreement will carry even greater weight, because the custody law says that there is a presumption in favor of joint custody when both spouses have agreed to it. The forms in this book have provisions for sole custody, several forms of joint custody, split, mixed and third-party custody (see "Custody Provisions" in Appendix H for more about these custody choices and how to provide for them).

Whatever you and your spouse agree to, keep in mind that the court always has the final say on custody. In an uncontested divorce, you have a lot of room to bargain over property division and alimony. But the court keeps more control over the divorce issues directly affecting the welfare of minor children: custody, parenting time and child support. Therefore, the court has the right to reject your custody agreement when it isn't in your children's best interests.

Parenting Time

Until 1996, when the terminology changed, parenting time was known as visitation (some older divorce forms may still use this name). Whichever name it goes by, parenting time gives the children access to the noncustodial parent so the parent-child relationship can continue after the divorce. Parenting time is actually a right possessed by children. This fact often gets lost when parents fight over it, trying to assert their parenting time "rights."

Ordinarily, parenting time is given to noncustodial parents whenever sole custody or joint legal custody is ordered. But parenting time might be necessary for custodial parents in some long-term joint physical custody arrangements. For example, parents with split- or block-time custody where custody is exchanged infrequently might need parenting time. On the other hand, frequent split-time or bird's nest custody probably doesn't require parenting time.

Courts can order parenting time during a divorce as a form of preliminary relief, settling the issue until the end of the divorce (see "Do I Need 'Preliminary Relief'?" on page 60 for more about preliminary parenting time orders). At the end of the divorce, the court will make a final parenting time order in the Judgment of Divorce. This order will continue, subject to future modification, until the children reach the age of 18.

Types of Parenting Time

Many states have just one kind of parenting time: specific parenting time. In Michigan, you can choose from several types of parenting time:

Reasonable parenting time. Reasonable parenting time is a flexible arrangement allowing parents to schedule parenting time as they please, at times and on terms that are convenient for them.

Specific parenting time. Specific parenting time fixes parenting time according to specific times, terms and conditions.

Supervised parenting time. If a parent is irresponsible, the parenting time can be supervised by a responsible third party, such as a grandparent.

Long-distance parenting time. When face-to-face contact is too risky (for an irresponsible parent) or impossible (for a faraway parent), courts are allowing long-distance parenting time by telephone, video-conferencing or the Internet.

Court-Ordered Parenting Time

When one parent contests whether the children should have parenting time with the other parent, the court must decide the issue during a trial or hearing. Since parenting time is really a right of children, it's provided to them according to their best interests. That's determined by the same 12-factor test used to decide custody cases (see above for the full list).

Michigan law presumes that parenting time is in the best interests of children, and can only be taken away from them when parenting time endangers their mental, emotional or physical health. Judges also favor parenting time and are reluctant to withhold it. Even when a noncustodial parent is irresponsible, a court will often order supervised or long-distance parenting time, rather than deny it completely.

Thanks to this preference for parenting time, contesting parenting time should be ordered is unusual. Instead, most parenting time battles are fought over the type, frequency or duration of parenting time. In these disputes, the parenting time law says that the court may consider the following factors in making a parenting time order:

- existence of any special circumstances or needs of the child
- whether the child is a nursing child less than six months of age, or less than one year of age if the child receives substantial nutrition through nursing
- reasonable likelihood of abuse or neglect of the child during parenting time
- reasonable likelihood of abuse of a parent resulting from the exercise of parenting time
- inconvenience to, and burdensome impact or effect on, the child traveling to and from the parenting time
- whether the noncustodial parent can reasonably be expected to exercise parenting time in accordance with the court order
- threatened or actual detention of the child with the intent to retain or conceal the child from the other parent or from a third person who has legal custody. A custodial parent's temporary residence with the child in a domestic violence shelter may not be construed as evidence of the custodial parent's intent to retain or conceal the child from the other parent
- any other relevant factors

Michigan law says that a court must order specific parenting time when a party asks for it. Even without such a request, courts often order specific parenting time in contested cases. Reasonable parenting time demands a good deal of give-and-take, making reasonable parenting time unsuitable for feuding parents.

Uncontested Parenting Time

If you and your spouse agree on parenting time, the court will almost always approve your arrangement. In fact, the parenting time law says that parental agreements about parenting time carry great weight. The forms in this book have provisions for both reasonable and specific parenting time (see "Parenting Time Provisions" in Appendix H for suggestions about specific parenting time choices). But like other divorce issues affecting child welfare, courts get the final word on parenting time, and they can reject your parenting time agreement when it isn't in your children's best interests.

Residence of Children

The residence (also known as domicile) of minor children used to be a minor issue during divorce. Divorce judgments did bar custodial parents from taking children out of state without court approval. But otherwise, divorced parents were free to move around the state with their children as they pleased.

This freedom of movement worked all right in an era when sole custody was the norm. But as joint custody became more common, it was difficult to reconcile freedom of movement with joint custody rights. Imagine a parent moving with children from Detroit to Copper Harbor in the Upper Peninsula (a distance of over 600 miles), and the effect this move would have on the other parent's joint custody or parenting time back in Detroit.

As a result, in 2001 Michigan adopted a new law governing children's residence. The law tries to harmonize—not always successfully—parents' rights of movement and custody and parenting time arrangements for children.

Establishing Residences of Children

The 2001 residence law establishes local residences of minor children during divorce. These residences are created when a case is filed. A divorce-filing actually establishes two local residences of the children: one with each parent, at the parental homes (the Summons and Complaint (MC 01) will list these addresses). The local residences established at divorce will become a permanent reference point, or "home base," for applying several important exceptions to the 2001 law explained below.

It's also important to keep in mind that dual residences exist with both parents even if one parent ends up with most, or all, custody during the divorce. At this point, residence is a totally separate issue from custody and is fixed without regard to custody.

Like a custody or parenting time order, a divorce judgment's residence-of-children order covers the minor children until they reach the age of 18, and then expires for each of them. On its face, the residence order applies to the children only. But it also applies indirectly to the parents, since the parents mustn't move the children's residences, which are also their own.

All this may sound rather restrictive and confining. But in fact, parents have quite a lot of freedom to move, thanks to an elaborate system of exclusions and exceptions under the 2001 law.

Exclusions

Some kinds of moves are excluded outright from the 2001 residence law. Parents covered by these exclusions are free to move without prior court approval. These moveaways are excluded from the residence law:

- move when a parent has received sole custody (sole legal and sole physical custody) *
- move by a parent when the other parent consents to the move
- move caused by a flight from domestic violence

Exceptions

Besides excluded moves, other moves are excepted from the residence law. Moveaways covered by these exceptions are based on distance, so you must know the children's two local residences established at divorce-filing (see above for more about these). It's also helpful to have a good map (such as a road map or atlas) and an inexpensive compass, like the ones geometry students use. Incidentally, distances are measured not by road miles (as you would drive on a road), but in a straight line on the map as a "crow flies."

Like excluded moves, these moves are exempted from the 2001 residence law and may take place without court review:

- move if the children's local residences are more than 100 miles apart

On your map, you can use the scale to measure the distance in miles from the children's two residences. If these residences are more than 100 miles apart, you can move anywhere.

> *Example #1:* A wife living in Lansing files for divorce there against her husband in Traverse City. Because Lansing is more than a 100 miles from Traverse City, the parents can move anywhere.

- move by a parent inside his/her own 100-mile local residence zone

The exception above can be a little difficult to judge. On your map, find the local residence of the relocating parent. Using the map scale, measure a 100 miles on the compass and lock it. Put the pointed end on the residence and draw a 100-mile circle around this point. A move within this circle or zone is permissible under this exception.

---

*   Curiously, the 2001 law only mentions sole legal custody. But since sole legal custody is incompatible with any kind of joint custody, this limits the exclusion to sole custody cases; and by implication, this exclusion also makes the 2001 law apply to joint custody cases only.

Example #2: A wife files for divorce in Lansing against her husband, a resident of Mt. Pleasant. Dual residences for the children exist in both cities. According to this exception, the wife could move inside a zone of 100 miles radius around Lansing (or the husband, if he wished to move, could move within a 100-mile zone around Mt. Pleasant).

- move if the move actually brings the local residences closer together; a move creating more distance is barred

This final exception is even harder to visualize. Using a map and compass, place the two ends (pointed and pencil) of the compass on each parent's residence, and lock the compass. Then, put the pointed end on the stay-behind parent's residence and draw a circle around this residence. This is the area in which the relocating parent can move under this exception.

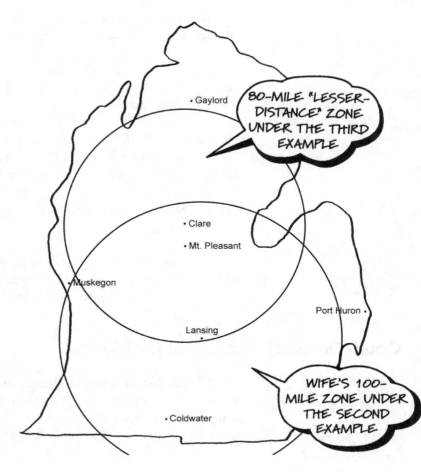

Example #3: A wife files for divorce in Lansing against her husband in Clare. The distance between these local residences is 80 miles. The wife could move into a zone 80 miles around Clare, because this move wouldn't create more distance than existed before. Similarly, the husband could move into an 80-mile zone around Lansing.

Moving out of State

Before the 2001 residence law was adopted, Michigan had a court rule preventing a custodial parent from moving out of state with the children except with court approval. This gave the noncustodial parent a chance to oppose the move and possibly convince the court to keep the children in Michigan.

It was unclear how the 2001 residence law and the old court rule meshed. Had the 2001 law replaced the court rule or was the rule a separate and extra requirement for all out-of-state moveaways? Recently, Michigan courts have ruled that the 2001 residence law overrides the old court rule in many respects.

As a result, the system of exclusions and exceptions in the 2001 law also applies to moves outside the state of Michigan.

Example #4: A couple divorces in Lansing and the wife gets sole custody of the children. She could move to California because of the 2001 law's sole custody exclusion.

Example #5: A couple gets divorced in Monroe, Michigan, and they receive joint custody of the children. The mother (or father) could move the 25 miles to Toledo, Ohio, because the move falls inside her 100-mile local residence zone allowed by the 2001 law. Had the wife wanted to move more than 100 miles away to, say southern Ohio, she would need court permission.

In either example, the relocating *custodial* parent would need court approval of the out-of-state move, as required by the court rule. But this would be just a formality since the move would be permissible under the 2001 law.

Court-Ordered Change of Residence

When a parent wants to change the children's residence and none of the exclusions or exceptions applies, s/he must file a change-of-residence motion asking for court approval of the move. The motion must be granted before the move takes place; you can't move first and seek approval later. * At the hearing on the motion, the court must consider the following factors:

- whether the legal residence change has the capacity to improve the quality of life for both the child and the relocating parent
- the degree to which each parent has complied with, and utilized his or her time under, a court order governing parenting time with the child, and whether the parent's plan to change the child's legal residence is inspired by that parent's desire to defeat or frustrate the parenting time schedule
- the degree to which the court is satisfied that, if the court permits the legal residence change, it is possible to order a modification of the parenting time schedule and other arrangements governing the child's schedule in a manner that can provide an adequate basis for preserving and fostering the parental relationship between the child and each parent; and whether each parent is likely to comply with the modification
- the extent to which the parent opposing the legal residence change is motivated by a desire to secure a financial advantage with respect to a support obligation
- domestic violence, regardless of whether the violence was directed against or witnessed by the child

---

*   There is an exception to this rule when the relocating spouse is fleeing the threat of domestic violence. In that case, the spouse can move while the motion is pending.

When parents want to take children outside the country, extra factors must be considered. For international moves, courts look at international relations between the U.S. and the destination foreign country, cultural factors, the severe impact the move will likely have on joint custody and parenting time and the enforceability of custody orders in the foreign country.

Whether the move is intrastate, interstate or even overseas, courts frequently allow changes of residence for children. After all, parents often have good reasons for moving—to remarry, take a new job, return to school to acquire new job skills—and courts don't want to stand in the way of these opportunities.

Uncontested Change of Residence

You may want to change the residence of children around the time of the divorce. The moveaway may be permissible without the approval of the defendant and the court, or you may need the consent of both to move.

The timing of your move is important. If you want to move early in the divorce, consider moving before you file the case. Remember, the residence of children is established at divorce-filing. So if you move to where you want to go beforehand, you won't have to deal with the issue during the divorce. *

After divorce-filing, when children's residences have already been established, a local residence can be changed if covered by one of the exclusions and exceptions. One exclusion allows a change of residence with the consent of a defendant-joint custodian. The trouble is, you need a special change-of-residence order for a pending-divorce moveaway. The defendant must also consent to the order, which is legally awkward if s/he has defaulted and is out of the case. As a result, the forms in this book don't provide for a pending-divorce move with the consent of the defendant. In addition, out-of-state moves during this time are discouraged since courts want children nearby while the case is pending.

You have more flexibility at the end of the divorce. Sometimes, parents want to finish their divorce and then move, perhaps even out of state. Once again, an intrastate end-of-divorce move may be permissible without court review if covered by one of the exclusions or exceptions. Custodial parents wishing to move out of state at this time may also be covered by the 2001 residence law's exclusions or exceptions (see "Moving out of State" above), but they still need formal court permission for any move.

One move exclusion is based on the defendant's consent, which must be recorded with the court. To obtain the defendant's consent and get court approval when necessary, see "Change of Children's Residence Provisions" in Appendix H.

---

*   This kind of maneuver may not possible if the children's residences have already been established by a prior family law case, such as a family support or paternity case.

Child Support

No divorce issue is more controversial than child support. Child support recipients—women usually—and child support payers—ordinarily men—have organized into opposing camps and each feels victimized by the present system of child support.

Child support recipients have been faced with massive nonpayment of support. According to federal figures, in more than a half of child support cases nationally no child support is paid at all (other studies put this percentage even higher). And according to recent figures, Michigan child support recipients are owed a staggering $9 billion in overdue support.

What makes this payment record even more dismal is that it comes after decades of child support reform. For years, states were notoriously lax in collecting child support. Soaring welfare costs in the 1970s signaled that many payers were avoiding their child support obligations. In 1975, the federal government passed new laws encouraging states to enforce child support orders.

In 1985, yet another federal law was enacted to strengthen child support enforcement. The new law also expanded the definition of child support to include more than just payments for food, clothing and shelter. According to the new law, child support may include payment of the costs of children's medical, dental and other health care, as well as child care and educational expenses.

In spite of these efforts, child support payment is still spotty. Believe it or not, Michigan has had a better-than-average enforcement system, with a "collection rate" (where at least one payment is received) of 60% in 2001. But that only looks good compared to the 44% national average.

Child support payers also have an ax to grind. One of their chief complaints has been that child support orders are unpredictable, varying almost at the whim of judges. Some studies agree. One in Denver found that the amount of child support depended on the skill of one's lawyer, the judge in the case and even the season of the year! In Michigan, state officials surveyed child support in the mid-1980s by sending two fictional child support cases to 69 Michigan counties, asking them to figure child support. To their shock, the surveyors got back almost as many different answers as they sent questionnaires.

The Michigan survey revealed that many counties figured child support as a flat percentage of the payer's income. Typically, 20% was charged for one child, 30% for two children and 40% for three or more. Other counties used a modified flat-rate method, while a few counties seemed to have no method at all.

More Information

About Michigan child support, ask for the booklet "Understanding Child Support: A Handbook for Parents" from:

Michigan Department of Health and Human Services (DHHS)
Office Services Division
P.O. Box 30037
Lansing, MI 48909

The booklet is also accessible at www.michigan.gov/mdhhs, then to Forms and Publications, to Child Support.

About child support enforcement, contact:

National Child Support Enforcement Association (NCSEA)
7918 Jones Branch Drive
Suite 300
McLean, VA 22102
(703) 506-2880
www.ncsea.org

For more about the Michigan child support formula, see "Michigan Child Support Formula" on page 257 in Appendix H.

Contact the fathers' rights groups cited on page 12 for information about fathers and child support.

Not only did those customary methods of figuring child support produce variable orders, they were actually contrary to Michigan law. The law says that child support must be based on three primary factors: 1) the noncustodial parent's income 2) the custodial parent's income 3) the needs of the children. The customary methods for figuring child support failed to account for all these factors. The flat-rate method, for example, considered the noncustodial parent's income only and ignored the resources of the custodial parent. And none of the customary methods took the needs of the children seriously into account.

Michigan Child Support Formula

What this suggested was that Michigan needed a uniform child support formula, based on the three child support factors. A few Michigan counties had had these formulas for years. Nevertheless, many judges opposed any child support formulas or guidelines because they wished to preserve their right to set child support on a case-by-case basis.

Like it or not, Michigan was forced to adopt a uniform child support formula by the 1985 federal child support law. This law required states to adopt such guidelines by Oct. 1, 1987, or risk losing valuable federal aid. Michigan dutifully complied and put its child support formula into effect in May 1987.

The child support formula assumes that the needs of children can be fixed as a percentage of a family's total income, which varies with the amount of family income and the number and ages of the children. According to the formula, these needs must be shared by the parents in proportion to their income. The child support recipient pays his/her share by direct spending on the children, while the payer-parent contributes in the form of child support. By using this method of figuring child support, the formula employs all three child support factors, as required by law.

At first, the Michigan child support formula was merely an optional guideline which judges could follow as they wished. But in 1991, the formula became mandatory, with a few exceptions. Now, all Michigan child support is supposed to be set by the formula.

Adjusting or Departing from the Formula

Not every divorce case fits neatly within the Michigan child support formula. The designers of the formula anticipated many of these exceptional cases and provided for adjustments to the formula.

When parents have low incomes, the formula adjusts so their modest income isn't consumed by child support. There are also adjustments for third-party custody (when a third party, not the parents, has custody of the children), in which the parents pay child support to the third-party custodian. These exceptional cases are described on page 258 and page 262 in Appendix H.

If simple adjustment isn't enough, it's possible to depart from the Michigan child support formula and set child support at a nonformula amount. You can depart by agreement with the defendant or upon your request alone. Either way, you must have a good reason for departure and the court must approve. For more about departure, see "Departing from the Formula" on page 262 in Appendix H.

Other Kinds of Child Support: Health Care, Child Care and Educational Expenses

In recent years, the concept of child support has been expanded to pay for more than the basic needs of children (food, clothing and shelter). Today, child support also covers children's health care, child care and educational expenses.

With its ever-increasing cost, health care is naturally the greatest concern. Court orders like divorce judgments require parents to maintain health care coverage (health insurance, HMO, PPO, etc.) reasonably available to them. Parents must also share the cost of out-of-pocket health care coverage premiums and medical expenses not paid for by primary coverage. See "Health Care" on page 259 in Appendix H for more about the knotty problem of health care for children.

Similarly, parents can be ordered to pick up the cost of child care and educational expenses of their children. The Michigan child support formula provides for the addition of a child care supplement to the base child support amount. Educational expenses can be assigned to one or both parents. For more about these topics, see page 261 and page 262 in Appendix H.

Payment of Child Support

Method of Payment

In 1991, Michigan also adopted a new method of collecting child support. Previously, child support was typically paid under the honor system, with payers voluntarily making support payments to the friend of the court. Only when payers got behind was an income withholding order issued directing their source of income (usually employers) to withhold money and pay it to the friend of the court.

As child support debts began piling up, it became apparent that the honor system of payment wasn't working. In 1991, this system was replaced by immediate income withholding. Under the new method, income withholding normally starts when a child support order goes into effect. At that time, court officials contact the payer's employer or other source of income and set up withholding.

Immediate income withholding is designed for the bulk of cases. Courts and child support recipients prefer this method of payment because it's reliable. On the other hand, some child support payers dislike the payment method since it means extra paperwork for their employers.

In some cases, you can bypass immediate income withholding and choose another method of payment. You can do this by opting out of the friend of the court system, either totally, partially or in a limited way. See Appendix C for more about the types of opt-outs and whether you qualify.

After opting out of immediate income withholding, the new method of payment continues as long as the payer makes regular payments. But if the payer falls behind by a month's worth of payments, the friend of the court must act to put immediate income withholding back in effect. The friend of the court will schedule a hearing on the payment issue and the court will decide which method of payment should be used.

When child support recipients are getting Family Independence Program (FIP) payments, they must assign their child support to the state. After assignment, the child support is transferred to the Michigan Department of Health and Human Services (DHHS), instead of the recipient, to offset the cost of the FIP grant.

Whichever method of payment is in force, child support usually takes the form of periodic cash payments. Child support was typically paid weekly. Since 2002, child support has been computed and paid by the month.

Full Payment of Child Support

One of the worst things about the old child support collection system was cancellation of unpaid child support. When delinquent payers were brought into court, judges often allowed them to pay just a percentage of the debt, canceling the rest.

This kind of cancellation, or retroactive modification, of child support is now generally forbidden by law. These days, each child support payment becomes a separate judgment when due and full payment is expected. There are a few exceptions to this rule. Past-due child support can be modified or even canceled when: 1) there is a court-approved retroactive modification agreement between the parties 2) one party has hidden income, allowing modification of the debt to compensate for the fraud. A child support debt relief law provides relief in special cases.

Duration of Child Support

When a divorce with minor children is filed, the court can order child support during the divorce as a form of preliminary relief (see "Do I Need 'Preliminary Relief'?" on page 60 for more about preliminary child support). With or without a preliminary child support order, the court normally orders final child support in the Judgment of Divorce at the end of the divorce.

The divorce judgment makes child support payable until the children are 18 * or 19½ as long as they are 1) regularly attending high school on a full-time basis with a reasonable expectation of completing sufficient credits to graduate from high school 2) residing on a full-time basis with the recipient of the support or at an institution.

---

*   Sometimes child support can end *before* age 18 if the minor child becomes emancipated by: 1) marriage 2) enlistment in the military 3) court order.

Michigan used to stop child support when children turned 18, even if they were still attending high school. But in 1990 the child support law was amended, and over-18 children became entitled to child support while attending high school as described above. What's more, child support payers can *voluntarily* agree to pay support for even longer periods. For example, they might agree to provide child support while their children attend college.

Centralization of Child Support Services

For years, county friends of the court were the primary collectors and distributors of support (both child support and alimony). Today, a state agency in Lansing, the state disbursement unit (SDU), has taken over these duties.

Under the centralized system, support payers (employers deducting support under immediate income withholding or payers paying support themselves) send all payments to the SDU. The SDU is supposed to distribute these payments to support recipients across the state within two days after arrival in Lansing. More and more, SDU support distributions are transmitted electronically to recipients' personal checking, savings or debit card accounts.

The aim of the SDU is quicker payment, more accurate record-keeping and ultimately better enforcement. Right now, most enforcement stays with local friends of the court, but some enforcement responsibility is being transferred to the state.

Court-Ordered Child Support

Child support can be ordered during a divorce, as a form of preliminary relief (see "Do I Need 'Preliminary Relief'?" on page 60 for more about preliminary child support), and/or at the end of the divorce in the judgment of divorce. Either way, the order will make the support payable until each child is 18 or 19½ if still attending high school.

When child support is contested, the court must set the support according to the Michigan child support formula, unless it's "unjust or inappropriate" to do so. In that exceptional case, the court can depart from the formula and order a different amount of child support. With the parents battling over child support, the court will almost certainly order payment by immediate income withholding.

Uncontested Child Support

Ordinarily, child support for your case will be set by the Michigan child support formula. "Child Support Provisions" in Appendix H tells how support is determined under the formula. But in exceptional cases, you and the defendant can agree to set child support outside the formula. See "Departing from the Formula" on page 262 for when and how to do this.

Your child support will probably be paid by immediate income withholding, since this is now the normal method of payment. Nevertheless, sometimes it's permissible to avoid immediate income withholding and choose another payment method. As Appendix C explains, you can do this by opting out of the friend of the court system totally, partially or in a limited way.

By law, child support must continue until each child is 18 or 19½ if still attending high school. Child support payers can voluntarily pay support even longer, such as while a child attends college. But this takes a special agreement between the parents, which is difficult to prepare. If you want to provide for long-term child support, contact a lawyer for help.

Property Division

Years ago, divorce property division was little more than divvying up pots, pans and clothing. But today a lot more may be at stake. Wendy McCaw, wife of cellphone magnate Craig McCaw, may have received the largest ($460 million) divorce property division. Other big winners include wives of Hollywood celebrities like Mel Gibson's first wife Robyn ($425 million) and Maria Shriver, Arnold Schwarzenegger's ex ($250-375 million).

What all these divorces have in common is that they happened in western states with community property laws. In these states, marriage is considered an equal financial partnership, so most property acquired during a marriage belongs to the spouses equally, regardless of which spouse earned or owned it. And when a marriage ends—by death or divorce—each spouse gets one-half of the marital property.

Only nine states, mostly in the South and West, have community property. The rest, including Michigan, have a different system of property ownership and division. At one time, Michigan divided property during divorce strictly according to ownership: Each spouse got whatever they owned. This system was simple and neat, but it discriminated against wives because husbands usually owned most property.

Accused of unfairness, Michigan adopted an equitable distribution system of property division in divorce cases. Like community property law, equitable distribution recognizes that marriage is a financial partnership, giving each spouse a share of the property regardless of ownership.

Despite that similarity, community property and equitable distribution divide property very differently. Spouses always get equal shares of community property. In equitable distribution, the shares can be equal or unequal. All the law asks is that the division be "just and reasonable" or "equitable" under the circumstances.

The flexibility of equitable distribution shows up in court decisions. For example, in Michigan divorces wives have gotten as much as 90% or as little as 10% of the property. Under equitable distribution, such lopsided divisions are permissible if justified by the facts of the case. Nevertheless, these are exceptional cases. In the vast majority of divorces, a 50-50 split, or something close to it, is the equitable division.

Court-Ordered Property Division

When spouses wrangle over property, the court must divide it for them during a trial. According to equitable distribution, the division must be "just and reasonable" or "equitable." But since these general principles don't give enough guidance, courts have developed nine specific factors for property division:

- duration of the marriage
- contribution of the parties to the marital estate
- age of the parties
- health of the parties
- life status of the parties
- necessities and circumstances of the parties
- earning abilities of the parties
- past relations and conduct of the parties
- general principles of equity

In many states, property divisions are based solely on economic factors. If fault is taken into account, it's only to the extent that fault has had an impact on the property. For example, California ignores fault in property divisions except when one spouse has squandered the community property. In that case of "economic fault," the other spouse gets a greater share of the property.

Most of Michigan's property division factors are also economic. But fault creeps into divorce when the property division is contested through the "past relations and conduct of the parties" factor. And in Michigan, this fault isn't confined to misuse of property. It can include almost any type of marital misconduct, no matter how embarrassing or lurid.

Since equitable distribution is designed to be flexible, courts can weigh the property division factors much as they wish. They can focus on the important factors in the case, while disregarding others that don't apply. Courts may also consider other things through the catch-all "general principles of equity" factor.

Courts can avoid all that if the parties have a prenuptial agreement, since the agreement will normally control the division of property. Prenuptial agreements (also called antenuptial agreements or marital contracts) are contracts between spouses-to-be spelling out how property shall be divided when the marriage ends by death or divorce.

Michigan courts weren't always willing to use prenuptial agreements during divorce. For years, they refused to enforce these agreements believing that they encouraged divorce. But in 1991, the Michigan Court of Appeals reversed that rule and decided that prenuptial agreements are enforceable when: 1) the agreement was fairly entered into before the marriage 2) the agreement itself was fair at the time it was signed 3) facts and circumstances haven't changed enough since the agreement was signed that would make it unfair to enforce the agreement.

Uncontested Property Division

Before you and your spouse agree on a property division, you must know the extent and value of your property. "Can I Get a Fair Property Division?" on page 53 has important information about that. It tells which property is divisible in a divorce, and how to value it.

After you agree on a property division, the court should approve it because you have more control over property division than other divorce issues. If you happen to have a prenuptial agreement dealing with divorce, you should be able to use it to divide your property, unless the agreement is "unfair" (see above for the fairness requirements for prenuptial agreements). Whatever you decide about property division, see "Property Division Provisions" in Appendix H for information about providing for and carrying out the division.

Alimony

From the start, American courts awarded support in the form of alimony to wives. In 1641, just two years after the first American divorce, Massachusetts Bay Colony passed a law giving wives a right to alimony.

During this era, courts regarded alimony as wife-support, and husbands never got it. But in the 1960s, states revised their alimony laws to make it payable to either men or women. Michigan amended its alimony law in 1970 to permit alimony for men.

Since then, there have been some well-publicized cases of women paying alimony to men. Actresses Jane Seymour and Roseanne Barr reportedly paid their former husbands alimony. And even among the less famous, men are receiving alimony more often as women achieve financial parity with men. But typically, men are the alimony payers and women are the recipients.

Despite all the attention it gets, alimony has never been very common. At the beginning of the twentieth century, alimony was awarded in a scant 9.3% of divorces. Although exact figures are hard to come by, that percentage seems to have increased during the next 50 years. One study of California divorces in 1968 found that wives received alimony in 20% of divorces. But by 1975, only 14% of divorce cases included alimony.

As the number of alimony orders declined, the duration of alimony also shrank. Years ago, alimony was usually an open-ended award which continued indefinitely until the wife remarried or died. Nowadays, alimony is likely to be for a limited time—maybe a year or two—to help the recipient get back on his/her feet after divorce. This kind of short-term alimony is sometimes referred to as rehabilitative or transitional alimony.

In Michigan, alimony can be paid during a divorce or afterward. Alimony during a divorce is available as preliminary relief, but only through a temporary order issued after a motion and hearing. See "Do I Need 'Preliminary Relief'?" on page 60 for more about preliminary alimony.

Whether or not preliminary alimony has been ordered, alimony can be granted in the Judgment of Divorce at the end of the divorce. In most cases, alimony takes the form of cash payments payable periodically (weekly, monthly, etc.). These payments won't last forever because judgments usually make alimony subject to conditions ending it. These conditions are negotiable, but most judgments contain several of the following:

Death.   Alimony is almost always terminated when the recipient dies (as explained below, there are sound tax reasons for making such a provision). Alimony doesn't automatically end when the payer dies, and it can survive and become a debt of his/her estate. Nevertheless, judgments often terminate alimony when payers die.

Remarriage.   Alimony often ends when the recipient remarries, but seldom ends if the payer remarries.

Cohabitation.   To prevent recipients from choosing cohabitation over remarriage as a way to keep alimony, the alimony may end if the recipient cohabitates with a member of the opposite sex.

Date.   Alimony may end on a specific date.

Modification.   In Michigan, true alimony has customarily been open to modification when there has been a change in the parties' circumstances. A modification could result in an increase, decrease or even termination of the alimony.

Michigan law does allow divorce parties to designate alimony as non-modifiable. However, this has to be done carefully in a negotiated divorce settlement; you can't do it in an uncontested divorce without input from the defendant. Thus, all alimony described in this book remains modifiable.

Types of Alimony

Alimony is a slippery word because Michigan law and federal law define alimony differently. Adding to complications, Michigan court rules use the phrase "spousal support" instead of alimony. Because of this, the forms in this book also use spousal support to mean alimony, although the text will continue to use the familiar term alimony.

Michigan divorce law regards as alimony any divorce-related payments of money or other property from one (ex)spouse to the other for purposes of support. As explained before, alimony usually takes the form of cash payments paid periodically (weekly, monthly, etc.). There is another kind of so-called alimony, alimony-in-gross, which is often paid in several lump-sum payments. Despite its name, alimony-in-gross is really division of a liquid asset: money. Thus, alimony-in-gross is really property division and not true alimony.

The federal tax code has its own rules for defining alimony. The tax law generally disregards what parties call their payments. Instead, it considers support payments as alimony if they are:

- paid in cash (including checks or money orders)
- made to a spouse or to someone on his/her behalf
- made in a divorce document (such as a divorce order or judgment)
- made when the spouses are living apart (subject to several exceptions, including payment of temporary alimony)
- end on the death of the recipient-spouse
- not provided as child support
- not designated as something other than alimony

These tax rules are important because payments that qualify as alimony get special tax treatment. The payments are deductible by the payer and counted as income for the recipient.

Payment of Alimony

Like child support, alimony is normally paid by immediate income withholding to the state disbursement unit (SDU). But it's possible to set up other payment methods, and have alimony paid to the SDU without immediate income withholding or directly to the payee. See "Choosing an Alimony Payment Method" in Appendix H for more about these other payment options.

Court-Ordered Alimony

When spouses contest the issue of alimony, the court must decide the issue in a trial. To determine whether alimony is payable, the court considers the following factors:

- length of the marriage
- ability of the parties to work
- source of and amount of property awarded to the parties
- age of the parties
- ability of the parties to pay alimony
- present situation of the parties
- needs of the parties
- health of the parties
- prior standard of living of the parties and whether either is responsible for the support of others
- past relations and conduct of the parties
- general principles of equity

Like property division, the procedure for deciding alimony is flexible, so a court may apply these factors as it chooses. It can weigh the factors unequally, disregard ones that don't apply or add others that seem important through the catch-all "general principles of equity" factor.

Most of the alimony factors are economic. This makes sense because what alimony is really about is the need of one spouse for support and the ability of the other to pay it. But fault can creep in through the "past relations and conduct of the parties" factor. As with property division, fault in contested alimony cases may include almost any evidence of marital misconduct.

After a court decides that alimony is due, it must then determine the amount. In Michigan, there are no uniform alimony guidelines as there are for child support. So most judges set alimony on a case-by-case basis using the following factors:

- length of the marriage
- contributions of the parties to the joint estate
- age and health of the parties
- parties' stations in life
- necessities of the parties
- earning ability of the parties

In 1983, Washtenaw County rejected the case-by-case approach and adopted an alimony formula. It judges the strength of an alimony claim (length of the marriage, age, income and job skills are the most important factors), adjusts the claim for other factors and then provides for a mathematical computation of alimony. Recently, other counties have begun using Washtenaw's alimony formula or adaptations of it. This suggests a need for a uniform state-wide alimony formula, which may be developed in the future.

Uncontested Alimony

Since alimony isn't ordered in most divorces, divorce judgments usually waive (surrender) alimony. Sometimes it's possible to reserve alimony, allowing you to ask for it after the divorce. Or you and your spouse can agree to have alimony granted by including an alimony order in your divorce judgment.

"Alimony Provisions" in Appendix H has more information about all those methods of dealing with alimony. It also includes two basic alimony orders for short- and long-term alimony, which you can adapt to your situation.

Other Divorce Issues

Ending the marriage, custody, parenting time, residence of children, child support, property division, and alimony aren't the only divorce issues. But any other divorce issues are relatively minor and seldom contested.

Name Change

Name change for women and minor children is another minor divorce issue. After a divorce, women often want to drop their married names and resume maiden or former names. For them, Michigan law offers two name change methods: 1) common law name change by usage 2) court-ordered name change from: (a) the court when the divorce is granted (b) a separate name change case later.

The usage method is the easiest because all you do is choose a new name and begin using it regularly. No court order is necessary. The name change is legal as long as you're not adopting a new name for a fraudulent or improper purpose.

The trouble with the usage method is that it's no longer very effective. These days, with the general anxiety about security and special concern about identity theft, authorities want official proof of name changes; informal name changes aren't acceptable any more. As a result, most women choose formal court-ordered name changes.

It's easy for a woman to change her name during divorce. When the divorce is final, the court can allow the wife, whether she is plaintiff or defendant, to adopt a different surname (last name). She may resume a maiden or former married name, or choose any other surname. The only restriction is that the name change mustn't be sought with "any fraudulent or evil intent" (to avoid past debts, hide from law enforcement officers, etc.). The divorce papers in this book have provisions for women to ask for name changes (in the divorce complaint) and receive name changes (in the divorce judgment).

Some women who ultimately want to change their names aren't ready for name changes during divorce. They may want to keep their married names so they match the names of their young children. Then later, when the children are older, they may be ready to change their names.

Women seeking name changes postdivorce must file separate name change cases. Before filing, they must satisfy a one-year county residency requirement. They must be fingerprinted by the police and submit to a criminal background check. After publishing a legal notice in the newspaper, they must attend a court hearing to get the name change.

Needless to say, this procedure takes much more effort than a divorce name change. That's why most women, if they have a choice, choose a name change during divorce.

Michigan name change law doesn't say that children can change their names during divorce. Nevertheless, some courts have allowed name changes for minor children during divorce. If the parents disagree about the child's name change, the issue is decided by the court according to the same best interests test used in custody and parenting time disputes.

Name change at divorce is seldom an issue for men, because men don't customarily change their names at marriage. However, today some men add their wives' surnames to their own, by hyphenation, at marriage, and may then want to drop the addition at divorce.

Michigan divorce law isn't very helpful for men in this predicament. The law has no provision for male name changes during divorce. To change their names at divorce, men must do it by custom and usage under the common law method, or file a separate name change case, outside of divorce, to get a formal a court-ordered name change.

Dependency Exemptions

When parents do their income taxes, they can claim extra exemptions for dependent children. These exemptions are valuable because they act like deductions and reduce income tax.

After a divorce, the custodial parent is entitled to the dependency exemptions for the children. However, these exemptions can be assigned to the noncustodial parent by the agreement of the parties or by the court if they contest the issue. Either way, the divorce judgment must make the assignment. "Assigning Dependency Exemptions" in Appendix H has more about assignment and sample assignment provisions.

PART III: Doing an Uncontested Divorce Yourself

Most uncontested divorces go smoothly. But divorce remains a difficult legal procedure, and can sometimes get complicated. There may be a problem with jurisdiction, trouble serving the divorce papers, difficulty dividing the property or the danger of spouse abuse. All these problems and more can make your divorce—although it's uncontested—too difficult for you to do yourself.

Am I Married?

It may seem silly, but the first thing you should do before a divorce is make sure you are really married. If you discover that you aren't married, you won't need a divorce to split up.

The legality of a marriage is typically judged by the law of where it began, not where it ends. If you were married in Michigan, you look at Michigan marriage law. Those married out of state must consider the marriage law of that place.

Michigan authorizes two types of marriage: 1) ceremonial marriage, performed by most clergymen and some government officials 2) secret marriage, a rather obscure form of marriage before a probate judge for the benefit of: (a) people with a good reason to keep their marriage secret (b) children under the age of 16 in certain circumstances. Other states have different types of ceremonial marriage, which are valid in Michigan.

Most states have abolished common law marriage, in which couples informally agree to live together as husband and wife. However, many states had it in the past. Michigan recognized common law marriage until Jan. 1, 1957. Today, only the District of Columbia and the following states permit common law marriage:

- Alabama
- Colorado
- Iowa
- Kansas
- Montana
- Rhode Island
- South Carolina
- Texas
- Utah

If your common law marriage began in one of these states, it's legal in Michigan. Or if it began in Michigan before Jan. 1, 1957, or in other states while they recognized the institution, it's also valid here.

More Information

To obtain Michigan marriage, divorce and death records, contact Michigan's vital records office:

Department of Health and Human Services
Vital Records Office
201 Townsend St.
Capitol View Bldg. 3rd Floor
Lansing, MI 48933
(517) 335-8666

Or order Michigan vital records online at www.michigan.gov/mdhhs, then to Birth, Death, Marriage and Divorce Records.

To find vital records offices in other states, go to www.vitalrec.com. This Web site can also help you find vital records in foreign countries. Or get the *International Vital Records Handbook*, 6th ed., Thomas Kemp, Baltimore: Genealogical Publishing Co., 2013.

The SSA's death index lists deceased people whose survivors have received social security death benefits. Not everyone applies for or receives these benefits, so the index isn't 100% complete, but it's a good place to start. The index is available at www.familysearch.com for free.

If you doubt whether you are really married, check with the official of the office where you believe your marriage license is filed. In Michigan, that official is the county clerk who issued the license to you; in other states it might be someone else.

Another way to trace marriage records is through a state vital records office. Every state has an office that compiles records of marriages, divorces, births and deaths. By writing to the vital records office of the state in which you think you were married, you can get a copy of your marriage license, if one exists.

After you confirm that you are married, you should also make sure that your marriage hasn't already ended by a divorce or annulment. Unlike common law marriage, there is no such thing as informal "common law" divorce. So despite what some people think, tearing up your marriage license, giving back wedding rings, etc. will not make you divorced. Therefore, any divorce that your spouse may have gotten must have been court-ordered.

If you think that you may have been involved in a prior divorce, investigate and see whether a divorce judgment (also known as a decree or order in some states) was ever issued in the case. The court where the divorce was filed will have record of the judgment. If you don't have much information about the divorce, use the procedure described above to contact the vital records office of the state where the divorce was filed. It should have a record of the divorce judgment, if in fact one was issued.

Naturally, your spouse's death also ends your marriage. You might not know about this if you've separated from your spouse and remained out of touch. If you suspect that your spouse has died, you can confirm that by checking to see if a death certificate was filed. In Michigan, death certificates are filed with the county clerk of the place of death. If you don't know the county, use the state vital records office. A quicker way to check on the death of anyone is through the Social Security Administration's (SSA) death index.

It's also possible to have your spouse legally declared dead after a long disappearance. Like most states, Michigan has an Enoch Arden law (so called after the shipwrecked sailor of the Tennyson poem who returned from ten years at sea to find his wife remarried), which allows a person to be declared dead after seven years of complete absence.

Do I Really Want to End My Marriage?

When you get a divorce, the marriage between you and your spouse is ended finally and irrevocably. This allows each of you to remarry, if you wish. As someone divorce-bound, you're probably well aware of these and other benefits of divorce.

But as you prepare to divorce, don't forget the many advantages of remaining married. Recently, when Vermont lawmakers were debating their controversial same-sex civil union law, legal experts there counted around 300 benefits of marriage offered by state law. Michigan law certainly provides as many or more. All in all, marriage offers many valuable rights, such as: 1) support 2) property rights 3) estate and will rights 4) private benefits 5) public benefits 6) miscellaneous rights.

To be sure, some of these rights can be continued or compensated after a divorce. You can sometimes get post-divorce support in the form of alimony, and your property rights, including rights in retirement plans, can be recovered in the property division of the divorce.

But many marital rights are lost forever by a divorce. After a divorce, you lose all rights to your spouse's estate, including: 1) the right to inherit a share of his/her estate if s/he dies without a will 2) the right to take a minimum share of the estate, if the will slights you 3) dower (an estate that widows have in their husbands' real property) 4) miscellaneous allowances from your deceased spouse's estate. Divorce also automatically revokes all distributions of property and some appointments in your spouse's will which benefit you.

You may also lose valuable private benefits, often provided by an employer, available through your spouse, such as retirement, fringe, life and health plan benefits. There are substitutes for some of these, such as COBRA-provided health care coverage (see "Coverage for Spouse" on page 147 for more about this coverage), but never completely and usually at a higher cost.

The death of your spouse after your divorce will leave you without public benefits, such as wrongful death claims or survivor's benefits from worker's compensation or no-fault automobile insurance, that you might have enjoyed had you remained married. What's worse, if you happen to divorce before the

More Information

On divorce and social security, get "What Every Woman Should Know" (SSA Pub. No. 05-10127) from your local social security office, by calling the SSA at (800) 772-1213 or at www.ssa.gov/pubs/EN-05-10127.pdf.

See "Can I Get A Fair Property Division?" on page 53 for resources about retirement benefits.

Good information about these and other topics:

Divorce & Money, 10th ed., Violet Woodhouse and Dale Fetherling, Berkeley: Nolo, 2011

The Dollars and Sense of Divorce, Judith Briles, et al., Chicago: Dearborn Financial Publishing, 1998

More Information

Some non-profit counselors are listed in the yellow pages under "Social Service Organizations." For-profit counselors appear under the "Marriage, Family, Child & Individual Counselors" category.

See page 10 about obtaining a referral to a counselor from the **American Association for Marriage and Family Therapy.**

tenth anniversary of your marriage, you may lose the right to get social security benefits based on your spouse's earnings record.

Divorce also jeopardizes other miscellaneous marital rights that you may have never thought about. For example, aliens (noncitizens) can lose entrance or residence rights when they divorce U.S. citizens. After a divorce, you cannot file a joint income tax return, and may face a bigger tax bill. Marriage also entitles you to discounts on airplane tickets, hotels, etc., which single people don't always enjoy.

After considering all that marriage offers, you may decide that it isn't so bad after all. If you think that your marriage can be saved, you may find marriage counseling helpful. Many religious and human service organizations provide counseling, usually without charge. Private marriage and family counselors offer similar services. These private counselors charge fees for their services, but some health plans pay for the cost.

Is Divorce the Best Way to End My Marriage?

Divorce isn't the only cure for a bad marriage. By declaring a marriage non-existent, an annulment also ends the marriage. A legal separation—known as separate maintenance in Michigan—ends a marital relationship, although the marriage itself is left intact. Like divorce, an annulment or separate maintenance allows the court to decide the issues of custody, parenting time, residence of children, child support, property division and alimony. Before you choose a divorce, consider whether an annulment or separate maintenance might be better for you.

Annulment

Many people don't really understand annulment. For one thing, they often confuse legal annulments with religious annulments. Legal annulments are granted by courts of law, and affect one's legal rights. Some religious denominations, notably the Roman Catholic Church, offer religious annulments. These end marriages in the eyes in the church, restoring various religious privileges. A religious annulment is obtained from the religious organization and has absolutely no effect on legal rights.

Another misunderstanding about annulments is that they are routinely available for spouses who have been married for a short time and simply want to "call the whole thing off." The fact is, the length of a marriage is often insignificant: A marriage of a few days may not be annullable, just as a marriage of many years can be annulled. The real distinction between divorce and annulment is that a divorce ends a valid marriage, while an annulment is a legal declaration that no marriage ever existed because of a serious legal defect in the marriage at the time it was performed.

Like most states, Michigan presumes that marriages are legally valid. As a result, minor legal defects in a marriage, such as irregularities in the marriage ceremony, lack of authority of the person who performed the ceremony, etc., are excusable. But if the legal defect is serious, the marriage is subject to annulment. In Michigan, the serious legal defects providing grounds for an annulment concern whether the spouses: 1) had the legal capacity to marry 2) properly consented to marriage. *

Legal capacity. One must satisfy several requirements to marry in Michigan. If a spouse failed to meet any of these requirements when the marriage was performed, the spouse lacked the legal capacity for marriage. This defect can provide grounds for annulment:

¶ *Bigamy.* A spouse marries while already married to someone else.

¶ *Incest.* The spouses are related too closely by blood (you cannot marry a parent, child, grandchild, grandparent, brother or sister, aunt or uncle, niece or nephew or first cousin) or marriage (a stepparent, stepchild, step-grandchild, son- or daughter-in-law, father- or mother-in-law, spouse of a grandchild or grandparent-in-law are all not marriageable).

¶ *Underage.* Eighteen is the age of consent to marry in Michigan. Men and women 16-18 can marry if they obtain the proper parental consent. Under some circumstances, children under 16 can marry with parental consent in a secret marriage in probate court. Anyone who marries while underage and/or without the proper parental consent, lacks the legal capacity to marry.

¶ *Mental incompetency.* Mental incompetency of a spouse at the time of a marriage is an additional legal incapacity. Onset of mental incompetency after marriage doesn't affect the marriage.

¶ *Physical incapacity.* Sterility and some kinds of sexual dysfunction, which exist at the time of the marriage, are also recognized as incapacities.

Consent. According to Michigan law, both spouses must give proper consent to their marriage. If a spouse's consent is absent or defective, for any of the reasons below, the marriage may be annulled:

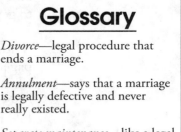

Glossary

Divorce—legal procedure that ends a marriage.

Annulment—says that a marriage is legally defective and never really existed.

Separate maintenance—like a legal separation, allowing the spouses to live apart with the marriage still intact.

---

* As mentioned before, the legality of a marriage is judged by the law of the state where it began. These annulment grounds apply to Michigan marriages only. There may be different annulment grounds for out-of-state marriages.

¶ *Force.*   A spouse's consent to the marriage is obtained forcibly. Ordinarily, the force must be the use or threat of physical force, but in some cases extreme psychological duress will qualify as force.

¶ *Intoxication.*   A spouse's consent to the marriage might be defective if s/he is under the influence of alcohol or drugs when the marriage is performed.

¶ *Fraud.*   Fraud is a misrepresentation that causes someone to do something. If fraud is used to obtain consent to a marriage, the fraud can invalidate the marriage. Michigan law is clear that the fraud must affect an essential part of the marriage. For example, a spouse's misrepresentation about his/her ability to have or want children, or about an intention to engage in cohabitation or sexual relations, may be important enough to annul the marriage. But misrepresentations by a spouse about character, wealth, family background or premarital life don't provide fraud grounds for an annulment.

¶ *Sham marriage.*   Even when consent to a marriage is given voluntarily and knowingly, the consent might be defective if it wasn't seriously intended. Marriages based on such false consent are regarded as sham marriages, making them subject to annulment. An example of a sham marriage is a marriage by an alien (noncitizen) who marries a U.S. citizen solely to obtain permanent residence in this country. In that case, the alien's marriage may appear to be proper, but it is really nothing more than a ruse to obtain residence in this country.

If you possess any of these grounds for annulment, you may be able to end your marriage by annulment. Or you can disregard the annulment grounds, file for divorce and end your marriage that way. Which is the better choice?

There is no simple answer to this question because divorces closely resemble annulments. Both procedures end marriages and free spouses to remarry. They both settle custody, parenting time, residence of children, child support and property division. But alimony, especially long-term alimony, is difficult to get in an annulment.

An annulment may be quicker than a divorce. Annulments don't have waiting periods as divorces do (see "How Long Will My Divorce Take?" on page 48 for information about divorce waiting periods). And there are no state or county residence requirements for annulments as there are in divorce cases (see "Can I Get a Divorce in Michigan?" on page 43 and "Can I File the Divorce in My County?" on page 45 for more on state and county divorce residence requirements).

On the other hand, the grounds for annulment are harder to prove and easier to defend against than the no-fault divorce grounds. What's worse, most annulment grounds are based on fault. This means that an annulment can be messy, like divorce was under the old fault law.

If you believe that you have grounds for an annulment and cannot decide whether to file for divorce or annulment, talk with a lawyer about which procedure to use. Act quickly because it's possible to lose annulment grounds by waiting too long. If you decide to seek an annulment, have the lawyer represent you because this book doesn't have instructions or forms for annulment.

Separation

Unlike divorce or annulment, separation doesn't end a marriage. It merely ends the marital relationship between the spouses, leaving the marriage itself intact. Despite that fact, there may be sound reasons for choosing separation over divorce or annulment.

Years ago, people often separated to avoid the social stigma of divorce. With divorce more common now, this stigma has faded. Nevertheless, some people may still want to separate and remain married for social or religious reasons.

Some couples choose separation for more practical reasons. As explained before, spouses can lose valuable marital rights when their marriage ends. Since separation doesn't break the legal bond of marriage, it preserves these marital rights. With this in mind, spouses may decide to separate temporarily, and divorce later when losing these rights isn't so important. For example, spouses married eight or nine years might agree to separate for a few years, and then divorce, so they can qualify for social security benefits based on each other's earnings under the ten-year rule mentioned above. Or they may remain married to preserve benefits like health plan coverage.

Informal Separation

You don't need to go to court to separate. As a matter of fact, spouses can separate informally and live apart indefinitely. Separated spouses usually work out arrangements for custody, parenting time, residence of children, child support, property division and sometimes alimony. To avoid disputes, some estranged spouses enter into written separation or settlement agreements. These agreements spell out how custody, parenting time, residence of children, child support, property division and alimony are handled during the separation. In addition, the agreement can settle these issues for any divorce following the separation.

When separated spouses disagree about those issues, a court can step in to provide child support and alimony. Michigan's family support act allows a custodial spouse to get child support and/or alimony from the noncustodial spouse when s/he has failed to contribute any family support. For more information about family support, contact a support specialist at the DHHS. In many cases, the DHHS will file the family support claim for you.

An informal separation—even one with a written separation agreement—is difficult to maintain. If the spouses disagree about something, they have no place to resolve their dispute. As a result, some separated spouses seek a formal, court-ordered separation, which is popularly known as a legal separation.

Michigan Divorce Jurisdiction

	Defendant is a Michigan resident (and has been for at least 180 days immediately before the divorce is filed)	Defendant once resided with plaintiff in Michigan during their marriage, then moved out of state	Defendant never resided with plaintiff in Michigan during their marriage
Plaintiff is a Michigan resident (and has been for at least 180 days immediately before the divorce is filed)	Full jurisdiction immediately*	Full jurisdiction immediately**	Limited jurisdiction immediately **
Plaintiff once resided with defendant in Michigan during their marriage, then moved out of state	Full jurisdiction immediately	No jurisdiction until plaintiff (or defendant) moves back to Michigan and has resided there at least 180 days immediately before the divorce is filed, then full jurisdiction**	
Plaintiff never resided with defendant in Michigan during their marriage	Full jurisdiction immediately		No jurisdiction until plaintiff (or defendant) moves to Michigan and has resided there at least 180 days immediately before the divorce is filed, then limited jurisdiction**

* In fact, either plaintiff or defendant can satisfy the 180-day residence requirement by having resided in Michigan at least 180 days immediately before the divorce is filed.
** Full jurisdiction can also be obtained on a nonresident defendant by serving him/her while present in Michigan, such as during a visit to the state.

Legal Separation: Separate Maintenance

Michigan law provides for a special type of legal separation called separate maintenance. Separate maintenance doesn't end the marriage. But it settles the issues of custody, parenting time, residence of children, child support, property division and alimony, while the spouses live apart.

The procedure for getting a separate maintenance is like that for a divorce. Even the same no-fault grounds are used. Despite the resemblance, it's much harder to get a separate maintenance because Michigan law allows a defendant in a separate maintenance case to ask for a divorce instead. After the request, the court must grant a divorce if the marriage is broken. Therefore, it's impossible to get a separate maintenance without the approval of the other spouse. All this makes separate maintenance difficult, so see a lawyer if you want one.

Can I Get a Divorce in Michigan?

After deciding that a divorce is what you want, you must then determine whether you can get one in Michigan. Not everyone is entitled to divorce in Michigan. To get a divorce in this state, Michigan courts must have jurisdiction to hear your divorce case. Jurisdiction is based on the residences of you, your spouse and children.

Residence

Residence is important to your case as the basis for jurisdiction. But what is it really? Residence has several different legal meanings. For the purposes of divorce, residence means your permanent home, or the place where you intend to stay.

Long-time residents of Michigan don't have to worry about residence. But if you've moved to the state recently, you can establish residence by: 1) registering to vote here 2) getting a Michigan driver's license and/or registering a vehicle in the state 3) owning or leasing real property here (it's even better if you file for a homestead property tax credit at your Michigan address) 4) working and filing income tax returns here 5) maintaining financial accounts here 6) joining church, trade, professional or social organizations in Michigan.

Once established in Michigan, residence isn't lost by temporary absences out of state, such as vacations or business trips. Nor is it disturbed by leaving the state under military or government orders. For example, a resident of Michigan who enters U.S. military or foreign service usually remains a Michigan resident during active duty wherever assigned.

Residence may be important for the purposes of jurisdiction before you file for divorce, but it fades in significance afterward. After filing, you won't lose jurisdiction (or county venue, which is explained below) by changing your residence. Your ability to move post-divorce-filing may however be restricted by Michigan's residence-of-children law (see "Residence of Children" on page 17 for more about this law).

> ## Glossary
>
> *Plaintiff*—spouse who files for divorce.
>
> *Defendant*—spouse against whom divorce is filed.
>
> *Jurisdiction*—power of a court to decide a divorce case.
>
> *Venue*—in divorce cases, the correct county for divorce-filing.

Divorce Jurisdiction

Michigan divorce jurisdiction is based on the past and present residences of the spouses. These residences determine whether there is either full or limited jurisdiction for the case. A court can take full jurisdiction when at least the defendant-spouse is residing in Michigan (the plaintiff-spouse may be residing here as well), or when the spouses resided together in Michigan at some time during their marriage. Limited jurisdiction exists when only the plaintiff-spouse resides in Michigan and the defendant never resided here with him/her during their marriage.

Michigan Custody Jurisdiction

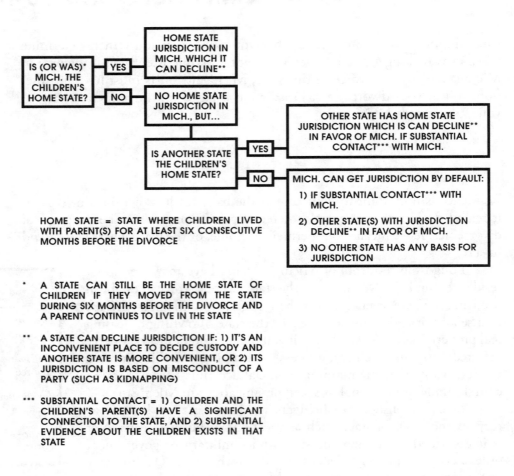

HOME STATE = STATE WHERE CHILDREN LIVED WITH PARENT(S) FOR AT LEAST SIX CONSECUTIVE MONTHS BEFORE THE DIVORCE

* A STATE CAN STILL BE THE HOME STATE OF CHILDREN IF THEY MOVED FROM THE STATE DURING SIX MONTHS BEFORE THE DIVORCE AND A PARENT CONTINUES TO LIVE IN THE STATE

** A STATE CAN DECLINE JURISDICTION IF: 1) IT'S AN INCONVENIENT PLACE TO DECIDE CUSTODY AND ANOTHER STATE IS MORE CONVENIENT, OR 2) ITS JURISDICTION IS BASED ON MISCONDUCT OF A PARTY (SUCH AS KIDNAPPING)

*** SUBSTANTIAL CONTACT = 1) CHILDREN AND THE CHILDREN'S PARENT(S) HAVE A SIGNIFICANT CONNECTION TO THE STATE, AND 2) SUBSTANTIAL EVIDENCE ABOUT THE CHILDREN EXISTS IN THAT STATE

Like other states, Michigan also imposes a residence requirement on divorce to discourage migratory divorce. In Michigan, the residence period is 180 days. The chart on page 42 depicts Michigan divorce jurisdiction with the residence requirement added.

The concept of jurisdiction is difficult, but it's important because it determines how much of your case the court can decide. As explained in Part II, divorce is divisible into several issues: end of marriage, custody, parenting time, residence of children, child support, property division and alimony. For reasons that are too complicated to explain here, certain divorce issues may need a particular type of jurisdiction. For example, child support, property division and alimony require full jurisdiction. Ending a marriage can use either limited or full jurisdiction.

Custody Jurisdiction

What about custody and the related issues of parenting time and residence of children? As it happens, these divorce issues have their own jurisdiction rules, imposed by the Uniform Child Custody Jurisdiction and Enforcement

Act (UCCJEA). In essence, this law, which all states have adopted, says that custody jurisdiction should usually be in the "home state" of children. A home state is similar to residence, or a permanent home. The chart on the opposite page illustrates.

When a court has full jurisdiction, with proper custody jurisdiction, it can do a divorce completely. It can end the marriage, order child support and alimony, divide the property and award custody and parenting time.

But with only limited jurisdiction, without power over custody, a court can do little. It can always end the marriage, and may be able to decide custody and parenting time. But it cannot order child support, divide property or award alimony.

If you have only limited jurisdiction in your case, seek legal advice. The lawyer can advise whether you can get by with that. If not, the lawyer could tell you how to get full Michigan jurisdiction or file for divorce in your spouse's state.

Can I File the Divorce in My County?

Assuming Michigan courts have some type of jurisdiction for your divorce, you must then file in the Michigan county with proper venue. In divorce cases, venue exists in the county where either you have or your spouse has resided at least 10 days immediately before the divorce is filed. Incidentally, residence for venue purposes is a place of permanent habitation, just as it is for jurisdiction. Naturally, when you both reside in the same county, the divorce must be filed there. But when you reside in different Michigan counties, venue is proper in either county. For the sake of convenience, most people choose to file in their own counties.

If the defendant resides out of state, venue will be in the Michigan county where the plaintiff resides. In those rare cases with out-of-state plaintiffs, venue will be in the Michigan county where the defendant resides. There is also a special venue rule for plaintiffs married to foreign-born or alien defendants, when there is a reasonable fear that the defendant may take the parties' children outside the U.S. In that case, the plaintiff may file in any Michigan county without regard to the 10-day residence rule. These special circumstances must be described in the divorce complaint.

What If My Spouse and I File for Divorce at the Same Time?

This is the dueling divorces problem: You and your spouse file for divorce around the same time, perhaps even before the divorce papers are served on each other. If both cases were filed in Michigan, the one filed first has priority and the later one must be dismissed (to dismiss the second case, see Appendix G about voluntary dismissal of divorce cases).

When the divorces are filed in different states, the situation is more complicated. If both states really have full jurisdiction, the first case filed usually has priority. But typically, only one state will be the home state of the minor children, giving this state custody jurisdiction under the Uniform Child Custody Jurisdiction and Enforcement Act (UCCJEA) (see "Can I Get a Divorce in Michigan?" on page 43 for more about using the children's home state as the basis for custody jurisdiction). As a result, the state qualifying as the children's home state will be the only one with full jurisdiction, and will have priority over the other state. The divorce case filed in the home state/full jurisdiction state will have priority even if it was filed second.

Can My Spouse Be Served with the Divorce Papers?

Regardless of the type of jurisdiction for a divorce, the defendant must get notice of the divorce. Like other lawsuits, notice in divorce cases is provided by serving the initial divorce papers on defendants. Service is explained in detail in Chapter 2.

At this point, you should know that service is easy and cheap if your spouse is available to receive the divorce papers. In that case, you can obtain service by any of three methods: 1) acknowledgment 2) mail 3) delivery. It doesn't matter where your spouse lives, because these service methods can be used anywhere in or outside Michigan.

Service can be difficult if a defendant is elusive (you know where the defendant is, but s/he is eluding or avoiding you). It's even more difficult if the defendant has disappeared (you don't know the whereabouts of the defendant). Luckily, the court rules provide for forms of alternate service to give hard-to-find defendants some type of notice (Appendix D has more about obtaining alternate service on elusive or disappeared defendants).

Thanks to this wide choice of service methods, you can be confident that when there is jurisdiction for your divorce there will be a way to serve the defendant.

What If My Spouse or I Am Imprisoned?

Incarceration of a spouse naturally puts a great strain on a marriage. If the marriage should break, the imprisonment also creates special problems for the divorce, whether the prisoner is plaintiff or defendant.

Divorce by an Imprisoned Plaintiff

Before filing, an imprisoned plaintiff must choose the correct county for filing. Choice of county is called venue and is controlled by the county residence of the divorce parties.

Prisoners are subject to special residence rules for venue. According to Michigan law, prisoners are presumed to remain residents of the county they resided in immediately before imprisonment. However, prisoners can become residents of the county of imprisonment if they can prove that they intend to reside there after release. Keep these residence rules in mind as you choose venue as directed in "Can I File the Divorce in My County?" on page 45.

Prisoners shouldn't have any difficulty serving their non-institutionalized spouses with divorce papers. The three regular methods of service (acknowledgment, mail, delivery), plus alternate service methods, are available to prisoners. Service by mail is probably easiest and cheapest. All these service methods and rules are explained in "Service" on page 99.

Plaintiff-prisoners do face a special problem at the end of divorce, during the final hearing. Ordinarily, divorce plaintiffs must appear personally in court and give some brief testimony for the Judgment of Divorce. To satisfy the court appearance requirement, some counties transport prisoners to court for final hearings in divorce. But transportation is expensive, especially for counties with large prison populations.

As an alternative, many counties allow and encourage prisoners to give their testimony in written or electronic form. The court rules permit this because they excuse court appearances in exceptional cases. Prisoners should contact prison legal services for help with giving final hearing testimony without a court appearance.

> ## More Information
>
> About divorce problems for prisoners, including giving final hearing testimony from prison, contact:
>
> **Prison Legal Services of Michigan**
> P.O. Box 828
> Jackson, MI 49204

Filing against a Defendant-Prisoner

There are special rules for divorces against defendants incarcerated in a Michigan prison (the prisoner must be in a state facility (prison, correctional facility, camp, etc.) operated by the Michigan Department of Corrections; inmates in county jails, prisons in other states or federal prisons aren't protected by these special rules) when minor children are involved. These rules try to make sure the inmate gets full due process (notice and opportunity to respond) during the divorce.

Before filing, the plaintiff must consider the choice-of-county, or venue, rules when choosing where to file (see "Can I File the Divorce in My County?" on page 45 for more about venue). Typically, plaintiffs file in their home counties, so the residence of a defendant-prisoner isn't an issue. But if you want to file where a defendant-prisoner resides, see the section above about how the residence of prisoners is determined.

You must know where the defendant is imprisoned and have his/her prisoner identification number. You may already know these things; if not, use Michigan's prison locator service to find out. After you have this information, you must take several special steps:

¶ In the caption of the Summons and Complaint (MC 01), add the following items in the defendant's box:

1) "Defendant is an inmate at [name of Michigan correctional facility] with prisoner identification number [prisoner identification number]."

2) "A telephone hearing with defendant must be held as provided by MCR 2.004."

¶ Later, after filing and service, the court will issue an order scheduling a hearing or conference with the defendant, by telephone, at his/her correctional facility.

During the telephone hearing, court officials must confirm that the defendant was served with the divorce papers, has access to a lawyer, if one is wanted, how s/he can communicate with the court and set any future hearings in the case.

¶ After the telephone hearing, the defendant will probably default and the case will proceed normally like other uncontested cases.

> ## More Information
>
> To locate a prison inmate for service and/or obtain the inmate's prisoner identification number, use a prison locator service.
>
> You can locate Michigan prisoners through the **Michigan Department of Corrections'** Offender Tracking Information System (OTIS). Do an internet search using the terms MDOC OTIS.
>
> For prisoners in other state prisons, see the Johnson and Knox book cited on page 211. It lists prison locator services nationwide.
>
> The federal **Bureau of Prisons** has a federal prison locator at http://www.bop.gov/inmateloc/.

The easiest way to serve a defendant in prison is by mail. Service by mail is described in "Service" on page 99, along with the other service methods. When your service-helper mails the service papers to the defendant, make sure the defendant's prisoner identification number appears next to his/her name in the address on the envelope. Many prisons require this number for delivery of mail to prisoners. If the defendant refuses to take and sign for the mailing, you can always use service by delivery, through the sheriff's office in the county where the prison is located.

What If My Spouse or I Am in the Military?

Military service adds both practical and legal problems to a divorce. As a practical matter, it may be difficult to find and serve papers on a defendant-servicemember stationed at a faraway military base. There are also state and federal military relief laws protecting active-duty servicemembers from hard-to-handle lawsuits. The federal law, the Servicemembers Civil Relief Act (SCRA), can be an especially stiff challenge when the servicemember is a defendant who is uncooperative or unresponsive.

Appendix F has complete information about dealing with military servicemembers whether as divorce plaintiffs or defendants.

How Long Will My Divorce Take?

Uncontested divorces take longer to complete than most uncontested lawsuits because Michigan law imposes two statutory waiting periods on divorces:

- 60 days in cases without minor children
- six months in cases with minor children

The waiting periods serve to delay divorces. The reason for the delay is two-fold. It gives the parties a chance to cool off, and possibly reconcile, after the heat of the divorce filing has passed. And in divorces with minor children, the delay also gives the friend of the court time to investigate the case (more about this later).

In your case, the six-month statutory waiting period applies. This means that at least six months must elapse between the day you file your divorce and the day you finish it in court at the final hearing.

The law says that the waiting period can be shortened to no less than 60 days in cases of "unusual hardship or compelling necessity." These cases might include divorces in which there has been physical abuse or violence, or divorces between spouse who have been separated for a long time. The trouble is, you must file a motion and get the judge's permission to shorten the waiting period. Because this book lacks the instructions and forms for such a motion, see a lawyer if you want to do that.

In addition to the statutory waiting period, there may also be unpredictable court-caused delays. Some courts are very busy and may not be able to hear your divorce immediately after the statutory waiting period expires. As a result, your divorce will take at least six months, and maybe a while longer if the court is busy.

How Much Will My Divorce Cost?

Doing your own divorce saves you lawyer fees, but not the court fees of the case. These court fees are due in all divorces—with or without lawyers. The court fees for uncontested divorces with minor children include:

Filing fee.   The fee for filing a divorce is $150.

Service fee.   You can expect to pay $0-50 to have the divorce papers served. The amount of the service fee depends on the method of service you use. Service by acknowledgment is usually available for free. Service by mail is around $10. Service by delivery is usually $23-50. If you use a sheriff for service by delivery, the sheriff charges a base service fee, currently $23, plus mileage (billed at a state government rate) to and from the defendant. Commercial process servers' fees for service by delivery may be slightly higher.

Motion fee.   You must pay a $20 fee whenever you file a motion. You must file at least one motion in an uncontested divorce: a motion for a default judgment in the middle of the case. You probably won't have to file another motion, unless you have to ask for something extraordinary, like alternate service.

Divorce Children

	Children included in divorce	Comments/exceptions
Children born during plaintiffs and defendant's current marriage	Yes	But paternity of children born during a marriage can be disproved by evidence that the father is not really the father. If paternity is disproved, the child would usually not be included in the divorce.
Unborn children of the marriage (= wife's pregnancy)	Yes	
Children born during a previous marriage of plaintiff and defendant	Yes	
Children born to plaintiff and defendant outside of their marriage	Yes, if…	Paternity has been established before the divorce or if it can be proved during the divorce.
Children legally adopted by plaintiff and defendant during their marriage	Yes	
Stepchildren of plaintiff or defendant	No	But, if a stepchild was adopted by plaintiff or defendant in a stepparent adoption, it will be a legally adopted child of theirs.
Children given up for adoption, or children over whom both plaintiff and defendant have lost parental rights	No	But if only one parent has lost parental rights, include the children in the divorce and explain the circumstances of the parent's loss of parental rights.

Judgment fee. In divorces with minor children, a $80 judgment fee must be paid. The law seems to require payment at the end of a divorce, but some counties may charge the fee up front.

Adding up these fees, you can expect to pay at least $250 ($150 filing, $20 motion and $80 judgment fees). The cost of service ($0-40) varies with the type of service you choose and must be added to the $250 amount.

Thanks to a landmark U.S. Supreme Court decision, poor people don't have to pay these court fees. In *Boddie v. Connecticut*, the supreme court decided that states must give everyone access to divorce, since they alone have the power to grant divorces. This means that those who can't afford divorce court fees are entitled to exemptions from payment. After the *Boddie* decision in 1971, Michigan adopted fee exemption rules for all types of cases, including divorce. See Appendix A for information about qualifying and applying for a fee exemption.

Which Children Must Be Included in My Divorce?

The children of your divorce ("divorce children") must include all the minor children of you and your spouse. In some cases, your adult children must also be included in the divorce for the purpose of support only.

Minor Children

The minor divorce children are the children you and your spouse have had together who are minors (under age 18) on the day you file for divorce. These children must be listed in your divorce papers, and shall be the subject of the custody, parenting time, residence of children and child support orders in the divorce.

If you have a blended family, with children of you and your spouse and children from other marriages or relationships, include only the children of you and your spouse in the divorce; leave out the other children.

In most cases, the divorce children are simply the minor children born during the spouses' current marriage. But in some cases, the divorce children are defined differently, as the chart on the opposite page shows. Include minor children in these exceptional categories (adoptees, out-of-wedlock children after proof of paternity, etc.) as you would other minor children.

You ought to be able to handle some of the exceptional cases without much problem. If you adopted children during your marriage, just include them in your divorce as you would biological children. When the wife is pregnant, mention her pregnancy in paragraph #7 of your divorce complaint. Then at the end of the divorce, list the child in the divorce judgment as follows: 1) by name and the date of birth if born during the divorce 2) as "unborn child" with the due date as the date of birth if still unborn.

Things aren't as simple when the paternity of children is at stake. Paternity is a legal judgment that a suspected father of a child really fathered the child. These days, paternity can be proved or disproved with almost 100% accuracy by genetic testing of blood or tissue samples from the child and suspected father.

Paternity can be decided as an extra issue during divorce. The trouble is, adding paternity to a divorce makes the case too complicated to do yourself. That's why you should consider dealing with paternity pre-divorce, in a separate paternity case. If you can do that, paternity will be settled before you file, keeping the divorce simple enough to do yourself.

According to Michigan paternity law, you can deal with paternity pre-divorce for children you and your spouse had together before marriage (out of wedlock). If the husband's paternity is proved, include the out-of-wedlock

---

To Obtain

Help with establishing paternity of out-of-wedlock children, mothers can call the Michigan Department of Health and Human Services at (866) 540-0008 or (866) 661-0005. You don't have to be on public assistance to receive help.

The DHHS also has two booklets about establishing paternity:

1) "What Every Parent Should Know About Establishing Paternity"

2) "DNA-Paternity Testing: Questions and Answers," available from:

Department of Health and Human Services
Office Services Division
P.O. Box 30037
Lansing, MI 48909

Both booklets are also accessible at www.michigan.gov/mdhhs, then to News, Publications & Information, to Publications, to Child Support.

children among your divorce children; exclude these children if paternity is disproved.

It used to be impossible to challenge the paternity of children born during marriage (in-wedlock children). This rule promoted the legitimacy of children even when it led to absurd results. So, for example, a child was regarded as the child of the husband even if he and the mother were separated and had no sexual contact for years before the child's conception and birth.

Since the 1970s, the old paternity rules have been relaxed and now it's possible for a wife, husband, alleged (biological) father or the DHHS to disprove paternity of in-wedlock children pre-divorce. The law allowing these paternity challenges is complicated, with many exceptions and time limits.

Whatever you do, don't ignore paternity until after the divorce. By waiting that long, you may lose the right to deal with the issue at all.

Adult Children

In some cases, you must include certain dependent adult children in your divorce case. According to Michigan law, adult children between the ages of 18 and 19½ are entitled to support if they are: 1) regularly attending high school on a full-time basis with a reasonable expectation of completing sufficient credits to graduate from high school 2) residing on a full-time basis with the recipient of the support or at an institution.

You must add these children to your divorce papers, if they qualify as divorce children in the chart. Paragraph #5b of the Complaint for Divorce (form TBP 1a) has a special place for them. They will receive child support while they remain in high school. But adult children won't be covered by the custody, parenting time or residence orders, since these stop at age 18.

What If a Third Party Is Involved or Intervenes in the Divorce?

Divorces are normally between parent-parties only. But sometimes so-called third parties, who could be grandparents, siblings, foster-parents or others, may already be present or appear in the case. These nonparent third parties may have or seek custody, parenting time, control of the children's residence or even child support * in several situations:

Involvement.   When a divorce is filed, a third party may already have court-ordered custody from a pre-divorce case or possess custody informally after a voluntary transfer from the parents.

---

*   Third parties cannot get child support without custody; but they may have child support redirected to them after becoming custodians of the children.

Intervention. A third party may not have custody or parenting time, but wants it. Ordinarily, Michigan law makes it very difficult for a third party to seek custody or parenting time from an intact family. But a divorce opens the door to some third-party claims for these things, allowing the third party to intervene in the divorce and ask for custody or parenting time. After intervention, the third party faces more difficulty because Michigan law strongly favors parents over third-party claimants.

Whichever way third parties appear—by prior involvement in your case or current intervention—they make a divorce case more complicated. Appendix E has more about a special notice due third-party custodians already involved in your case, and possibly, another notice to a court issuing a pre-divorce custody or parenting time order. Appendix H has information about granting custody to third parties during a divorce.

Must I Have the Friend of the Court in My Case?

Ordinarily, the friend of the court, who is a family court official, must participate in all divorces with minor children. The friend of the court performs a number of functions in divorce cases, including investigation and recommendation to the judge on divorce issues, refereeing, mediation, and review, modification and enforcement of orders (see "Court System" on page 71 for more about the friend of the court and its duties).

In most cases, the friend of the court's participation is beneficial. The friend of the court is a neutral third party who can help settle any disputes that break out. Its bookkeeping function for support is particularly helpful. Nevertheless, some divorces are completely amicable and the parties don't need or want friend of the court services.

According to a 2002 law, it's now possible to "opt out" of the friend of the court system—totally, partially or in a limited way—and manage the case yourself. This isn't always wise, and many cases are ineligible for opt-out. Appendix C has lots more about the pluses and minuses of opting out, the three types of opt-outs, opt-out restrictions and instructions and forms for opting out.

Can I Get a Fair Property Division?

As explained in "Property Division" on page 27, you are entitled to an equitable division of your property in a divorce. But exactly which property is subject to division?

Some states have rigid schemes for dividing property in divorces. They classify property as either marital-community property or nonmarital-separate property. In these states, only marital-community property is divisible during divorce.

In Michigan, by contrast, divorce property division is more flexible. Everything the spouses own is potentially subject to division. Despite what many people believe, this may include property the spouses brought into their marriage. It can also reach inheritances, will gifts or other gifts (including wedding gifts) received before or during the marriage.

Ordinarily, premarital property, inheritances and gifts are left out of divorce property division, and the spouse who owns this property keeps it. But the nonowner-spouse may claim a share of this property when: 1) s/he or the parties' children need the property for support 2) s/he has contributed to "acquisition, improvement or accumulation" of the property.

Saying that all property is potentially divisible in a divorce begs the question of what is property? Does it include everything the spouses possess or only those things with a definite market value?

It used to be that divisible property was confined to real property (land and buildings) and personal property, such as cash, bank accounts, stocks, bonds, household goods, motor vehicles, tools, etc., with a definite market value. But the definition of property has steadily expanded to include almost anything of value, regardless of whether it has a market value. So besides the familiar old property that has always been divided in divorces, there are several types of "new property" that may also be divisible:

Retirement benefits.   For years, courts refused to divide retirement benefits, such as pensions, despite the fact that these benefits are often the most valuable things spouses own. Ultimately, courts realized the unfairness of that position and now nearly all states permit the division of pensions and other retirement benefits.

Today, Michigan courts divide almost any type of retirement benefit provided by public- or private-sector employers, including pensions, 401(k), profit-sharing, employee stock ownership (ESOP), and saving/thrift plans. Also divisible are individual retirement benefits, such as individual retirement arrangement (IRA), simplified employee pension (SEP) and Keogh (HR-10) plans. The only type of retirement benefit immune from division is social security because it already has a built-in means of paying benefits to divorced spouses (see "Do I Really Want to End My Marriage?" on page 37 for more about obtaining social security off your spouse's earnings record).

Employee benefits.   Employees are often eligible for valuable fringe benefits, such as health plan coverage, sick and vacation pay, expense accounts, club memberships, meal allowances, lodging, discounts, etc. Some of these benefits, such as banked sick and vacation pay, have been divided in divorce cases in Michigan.

Life insurance.   Life insurance is often overlooked during property division, but it's divisible if it has a cash value. Whole life insurance policies usually have a cash value; term insurance policies ordinarily don't.

More Information

About the treatment of retirement benefits during divorce, see *Your Pension Rights at Divorce: What Women Need to Know* (3rd ed.) by Anne E. Moss, 2006, available for viewing online (the print edition has been discontinued) at www.pensionrights.org, then to Get the Facts, to Books.

Businesses.   Businesses, such as a sole proprietorship (one-person business) or an interest in a partnership or a small corporation whose stock is not traded publicly, are also divorce property.

Education.   Michigan was one of the first states to include education in divorce property divisions. According to Michigan law, education leading to an advanced degree (graduate, law, medicine, etc.) is divisible when the degree was the result of a "concerted family effort." What this means is that the nondegree-spouse contributed financial or other support to the spouse earning the advanced degree. If so, the nondegree-spouse's contribution can be valued and awarded to him/her.

Legal claims.   Some legal claims that a spouse has against third parties, such as personal injury or workers' compensation claims, are property that can be divided in divorces. For example, in one Michigan case a husband was awarded $700,000 for a libel claim, and the divorce court ruled that his wife was entitled to about half of the money.

    Spouses may also have legal claims against each other that can be decided in a divorce. At one time, it was impossible for spouses to sue each other for personal injuries. This immunity has been abolished and spouses are adding personal injury claims to divorces more often.

Debts.   Although it's hard to think of debts as property, they should be weighed during the property division because debts influence the overall fairness of the division.

    Whether your property is old, new or a mixture of both, you must have a good grasp of the extent and value of your property. Otherwise, you and your spouse risk agreeing to an inequitable property division. In all, you should do three things before you agree to a property division: 1) *inventory* your property 2) *value* it 3) find a way to *divide* it.

Inventorying Property

Property division begins with a complete inventory of all the property you and your spouse own. Ordinarily, only property owned when the divorce is filed will be divided. Property transferred before the divorce* or acquired during the divorce is normally left out of the division. So take your inventory just before you file.

    As you inventory your property, you may find that you don't know very much about it. In many marriages, one spouse handles the finances, leaving the other spouse in the dark. Luckily, there are several informal ways to get the financial information you need for the inventory.

---

*   But see "Does My Property Need Protection?" on page 58 for how courts can stop a spouse from transferring property to keep it out of the divorce.

Start with documents around the house, such as paycheck stubs, bank statements and retirement plan booklets. If you and your spouse have a joint safe deposit box, go through the box. You might find deeds, land contracts, stocks, bonds and life insurance policies hidden there.

Your recent joint personal tax returns, especially any schedules attached to these returns, can reveal valuable information about real property (schedules D and E), bank accounts (schedule B), and businesses (schedules C and F). Likewise, joint business income tax returns have important information about businesses. If you have discarded these returns, you can order copies by submitting Form 4506 to your IRS filing center.

Have you and your spouse applied for a loan recently? If so, you probably prepared a financial statement as part of the loan application. Since federal law makes it a crime to submit false information in the statement, it can be a reliable source of financial information.

If these informal methods fail to give you the financial information you need, there is a formal fact-finding device called discovery. Discovery comes in several forms, including depositions (oral interrogation out of court), interrogatories (written questions) and requests for documents. All these discovery methods are available during divorce to get you the financial information you need. The trouble is, discovery is difficult for nonlawyers to use. If you think you need it, contact a lawyer for help.

Valuing Property

There are many methods of valuing property. Michigan law doesn't say which method must be used, but fair market value seems to be the accepted measure of value.

Fair market value is usually defined as the price property would bring in a sale between a willing buyer and willing seller. When the property is subject to a debt, an adjustment may be necessary. For indebted property, the equity value of the property—its fair market value minus the debt against it—is often used instead of gross fair market value.

To value real property, you can either: 1) compare your property to the sale prices of other similar property sold recently in your neighborhood 2) double the amount of your property's tax assessment, since assessments are usually around 50% of market value.

You should be able to establish the fair market value of most kinds of personal property informally without going to the trouble and expense of getting formal appraisals.

Cash or near-cash assets (bank accounts, certificates of deposit, money market funds, etc.) are worth their present account balances. The value of stocks, corporate bonds and other securities are listed daily in the *Wall Street Journal*. Use the current redemption value for series E/EE and I U.S. savings bonds. You can value whole life insurance by figuring the cash surrender value on the policy chart, or by asking the insurance company or your insurance agent for this value.

The value of motor vehicles can be obtained from National Automobile Dealer Association (NADA) bluebooks. There are also price guides for stamps, coins, jewelry and antiques. You can estimate the value of household goods and tools by comparing them to similar used items.

If these resources don't provide accurate valuations of your property, you can always get formal appraisals. There are appraisers who are competent to value many types of property and specialists who appraise one type of property. People who buy and sell property, such as automobile or antique dealers, can also give appraisals.

The valuation of some new property, such as retirement benefits and businesses, poses special problems. These things have value, but there is no marketplace in which their value can be fixed. After all, you can't very well sell your pension to someone else. You may be able to sell a small business, but the market is often faulty and you won't get what it's really worth. Despite these problems, there are ways to assign value to new property so it can be divided in divorce cases.

Before you can value retirement benefits, you must know what kind of benefit it is. There are two basic kinds of plans providing retirement benefits:

Defined benefit plan. In a defined benefit plan, or pension plan, the employer promises to pay stipulated benefits at retirement or death. These benefits are paid according to formulas which are usually based on a combination of the employee's age, years of service and earnings.

What an employee with a defined benefit plan has is the employer's promise of benefits; there is no retirement account reserved for the employee. Instead, the employer's retirement contributions (typically only the employer contributes) are pooled in a common fund, and retirement benefits are drawn from the fund as needed.

Most large private- and public-sector employers have defined benefit plans, although some are now discontinuing them in favor of defined contribution plans, especially the popular 401(k) plan.

Other employers have adopted a new kind of defined benefit plan, called a cash balance plan, which resembles a 401(k) plan. In cash balance plans, employers make hypothetical contributions to employees' retirement "accounts," like in defined contribution plans. But in reality, these accounts are merely bookkeeping entries, and all retirement benefits are drawn from a common fund. Thus, a cash balance plan remains a defined benefit plan.

More Information

There are several free online real property valuation Web sites. The best of these are:

- Zillow.com

- RealEstateABC.com

- Listingbook.com

Stock quotes are available through most Web home pages and in the financial section of many newspapers.

The U.S. government savings bonds Web site, www.savingsbonds.gov, has a Savings Bond Calculator to figure the redemption value of E/EE and I bonds.

NADA has an online version of its bluebooks at www.nadaguides.com with values for automobiles (cars, trucks, vans, etc.), classic cars, motorcycles, boats, recreational vehicles and manufactured homes. The similar Kelley Blue Book can be accessed at www.kbb.com.

Schroeder's Antiques Price Guide, 29th ed., Paducah, KY: Collector Books, 2011, is the best general price guide for antiques.

2013 Davenport's Art Reference & Price Guide, Alison Becker, Phoenix: LTB Gordonsart, Inc., is a reliable price reference for fine art.

More Information

To find an appraiser, look in the yellow pages under "Appraisers."

Or contact one of the appraisal trade associations for a referral to a certified appraiser near you:

American Society of Appraisers at (800) 272-8258 or www.appraisers.org

International Society of Appraisers at (312) 981-6778 or www.isa-appraisers.org

Appraisers Association of America at (212) 889-5404 or www.appraisersassoc.org

Defined contribution plan.   In some ways, a defined contribution plan is the opposite of a defined benefit plan. With a defined contribution plan, the employer's contributions, instead of the retirement benefits, are fixed. Each employee has a separate retirement account earmarked for him/her, to which s/he may also contribute. The money in the employee's retirement account is invested (usually by the employer), and any investment income is added to the account. At retirement, benefits are paid from the account as the employee directs.

There are many types of defined contributions plans: 401(k), profit-sharing, ESOP and saving/thrift plans (provided by employers), and IRA, SEP and Keogh (HR-10) plans (individual plans). Typically, small businesses have defined contributions plans, although the giant TIAA-CREF (the Teachers Insurance and Annuity Account-College Retirement Equity Fund), which provides retirement benefits to public school teachers, is a defined contribution plan.

The value of a defined benefit plan lies in the benefits the plan will pay in the future. These future benefits can be reduced to a current lump-sum value, called present value. Figuring present value isn't easy, but an accountant or pension specialist can do it for you. To value a defined contribution plan, you simply take the current account balance. You can get this figure from a recent benefit statement or by requesting it from the retirement plan administrator.

Valuing a business is also difficult. If the business cannot be sold as a going concern, the book value of the business (tangible business assets minus business liabilities) may be used. But if the business is marketable, consider valuing the business by multiplying the average annual net earnings (before taxes) by a multiplier (1, 1½, 2, etc.) customary for that type of business. If you own a business jointly with others, you may have a buy-sell agreement with the co-owners fixing the value of your share, and you can use this value.

Dividing Property

All real property must be divided by separate property division provisions in the divorce judgment. Some personal property, including valuable things like motor vehicles and new property (retirement benefits, businesses, etc.) must also be divided individually. But you can divide most personal property, such as household goods, clothing, and personal items, by just splitting it up. "Property Division Provisions" in Appendix H has more information and sample provisions for all kinds of property divisions.

Does My Property Need Protection?

Divorce sometimes puts property at risk. Spouses may try to transfer property to others, before or during the divorce, to keep it out of the property division. If the divorce is bitter, spouses may take out their frustrations on the property.

A while ago, a Macomb County woman got back at her husband by destroying his collection of rare Frank Sinatra records (when Sinatra read about the incident he graciously offered to replace some of the discs). But that's nothing compared to a Seattle husband who, to spite his wife, took a bulldozer and demolished their $90,000 house!

Michigan courts have the power to prevent this kind of mischief. They can issue orders protecting property from transfer or destruction. Regrettably, this book doesn't have the instructions and forms to get these orders, so see a lawyer if you need one.

Debts can also jeopardize property and wealth during divorce. Financial stability often breaks down amid a divorce, as spouses are tempted to run up debts on joint accounts. Both spouses are liable for these joint debts regardless of which spouse incurred them. Thus, it's a good idea to close or at least freeze all joint accounts (credit card, charge accounts, etc.), if possible, immediately after separation.

You can close a joint account quickly if no debts remain in the account. If debts exist, you can pay these off or sometimes transfer them to individual accounts. Another option is to freeze the account, so no new debt is added, followed by payment later.

Do I Need to Change My Estate Plan?

Married couples often have estate plans mirroring each other. The husband's will may give all his property to the wife, and name her as personal representative, with her will doing the same. Or they may have living (*inter vivos*) trusts with each other as trustee and beneficiary. Their financial and health care powers of attorney may appoint the other spouse as agent. Spouses may also be the beneficiaries of life insurance and retirement benefits.

Even without an estate plan, spouses are entitled, by law, to many estate rights. These include the right to a share of a spouse's estate, dower (an estate that widows have in their husbands' real property), and other allowances from the spouse's estate.

As explained in "After Your Divorce" on page 145, a divorce terminates all these estate rights. But there is always a risk that one spouse may die or become incapacitated *during* the divorce, giving the other control of the property. If you're in good health, this risk is small and probably not worth worrying about. But if you're in poor health, you may want to do some quick estate planning during the divorce.

There are a few things you can do yourself without a lawyer. You can revise your will or living trust naming a new personal representative in the will or a new trustee/beneficiaries in the trust. If you've appointed your spouse as agent under a financial or health care power of attorney, you can make a new one with another agent. And unless you and your spouse have agreed otherwise, you can change the designation of your spouse as beneficiary of your life insurance and retirement benefits.

To do more, you're going to need legal help. In Michigan, you normally cannot totally disinherit your spouse by will, since spouses are guaranteed a minimum share of the estate. However, a lawyer can prepare a will for you reducing your spouse's share to that legal minimum. In exceptional cases, spouses can lose their estate rights by marital misconduct (bigamy, absence, desertion, neglect for one year or more). A lawyer can tell you whether you qualify for this exception, and how to disinherit your spouse if you do.

A lawyer can also advise you about releasing estate rights. You may have already done that in a prenuptial agreement. The lawyer can tell you whether the release was effective. It's also possible to release estate rights in a postnuptial agreement (signed after marriage), especially during a separation leading to divorce. A lawyer should prepare that kind of agreement. After any release of estate rights, you are free to benefit whomever you like in your will.

With a lawyer's help, you could also convert any joint tenancy property (also known as tenancy by the entirety property) into tenancy in common ownership. Unlike other forms of joint property, tenancy in common doesn't have rights of survivorship. So when a spouse-owner dies, the surviving spouse doesn't get everything. Instead, the deceased spouse's estate and the surviving spouse split the property. This division makes tenancy in common ideal for estranged spouses who want to keep their shares of joint property separate.

Do I Need "Preliminary Relief"?

In most lawsuits, you don't get any relief (the things you're asking for in your lawsuit) unless and until you win the case. Divorce is different. In divorce cases it's often possible to get some relief before the end of the divorce.

As mentioned in Part II of this chapter, courts may temporarily decide the issues of custody, parenting time, residence of children, child support and alimony. And as pointed out previously in this part, courts can also do some preliminary property division/protection during divorces. If a court grants an order for preliminary relief, the issue is not decided until the end of the case when the court makes a final decision.

Preliminary relief is important in contested cases, both for practical and tactical reasons. But this relief can be useful in uncontested cases as well. For example, a preliminary order can give one parent custody of the children and child support while the divorce is pending. Without a court order like this, both parents are entitled to share the children and the parental obligation to support the children cannot be legally enforced.

The trouble is, the legal procedures for getting preliminary relief are complicated. Before you seek the relief, decide whether it's really necessary.

Alternatives to Preliminary Relief

Preliminary relief is useful but it isn't required in divorce cases, and you can often get by without it. When you are self-sufficient, you may not need preliminary relief at all. Or if the defendant is unavailable, or impoverished and unable to provide any support, it may not be worth seeking.

If you believe preliminary relief is necessary, you may be able to improvise a substitute. You and the defendant can agree to have the equivalent of preliminary relief provided privately out of court. For example, you both might informally agree on custody, parenting time and payment of child support or alimony, without a court order, while your divorce is pending. In many ways, informal arrangements like this resemble what you might obtain in preliminary relief from the court, except that it won't be legally enforceable. *

Another option is to seek support before you file for divorce. As explained in "Separation" on page 41, you can obtain child support or alimony from a nonsupporting spouse under the family support laws Michigan and other states have. If you obtain a family support order, it will continue during the divorce and serve as a substitute for preliminary child support and/or alimony. But to get family support, you must ask for it *before* you file for divorce. Afterward, it's too late because the divorce law takes over and controls all requests for support.

> **More Information**
>
> On adjusting to life during and after divorce:
>
> *The New Creative Divorce*, Mel Krantzler, et al., Avon, MA: Adams Media Corp., 1998
>
> *The Good Divorce*, Constance Ahrons, New York: HarperCollins, 1994
>
> About being a single parent, contact a local chapter of **Parents Without Partners**. Its Web site, www.parentswithoutpartners.org, has a handy chapter finder.

If you meet income eligibility, you can also get support from the Family Independence Program (FIP). After FIP enrollment, county officials will typically seek family support from the noncustodial spouse, to get reimbursement for the FIP benefits. As with your own family support case, all this should be done *before* the divorce is filed. If you seek FIP payments after filing, then a preliminary order is necessary to get reimbursement.

If none of these substitutes works, and you believe you must have preliminary relief, see Appendix B, which has complete information, instructions and forms for seeking the interim kind of preliminary relief.

May I Socialize During the Divorce?

As couples split up, they often wonder whether they can start new social or sexual relationships. What you do during separation and divorce ought to be your own business. But regrettably, extramarital activity can be interpreted as marital fault, which could hurt you later.

In a contested divorce, marital fault from extramarital activity may influence custody, parenting time, property division and alimony. Marital fault shouldn't cause problems in uncontested cases since everything is agreeable. But the fault could be important later on, if custody or parenting time becomes contested in a post-divorce dispute.

---

*   Another problem with paying alimony informally out of court is that the payer won't be entitled to an income tax deduction for the payments, since they're not being paid in a divorce document.

As a result, use your common sense as you begin your single life. You don't have to live like a hermit. But as a parent, you should be discreet in your new social and sexual relationships. That will prevent any possible legal trouble now or later.

Can I Keep the Divorce Secret?

Although court files are public records, courts have the power to restrict access to the contents of files by sealing them. In fact, courts once routinely sealed divorce cases between wealthy or influential people.

Court rules govern court secrecy. One must file a motion to seal a file and convince the court that there is "good cause" for sealing.* Because of these rules, it's difficult to have divorce files sealed. If you want to try to get your file sealed, contact a lawyer for help.

Some local newspapers cover legal news and publish lists of divorces granted by the courts in their area. There is really no way to keep that information out of the papers, since the completion of a divorce is a matter of public record even if the divorce file itself has been sealed.

Will I Have Tax Problems from the Divorce?

At one time, divorce was a tax nightmare. Not only were the tax rules for divorce complex, divorce itself had many negative tax consequences. These rules were changed by the Tax Reform Act of 1984 (TRA). The TRA is a rare example of a tax law that actually made the law simpler and fairer.

The TRA redefined which divorce-related payments qualify as alimony (see "Alimony" on page 29 for more about these alimony tax rules). But the TRA didn't alter how alimony is taxed. It's still income for the recipient and a deduction (technically an adjustment to gross income) for the payer.

The TRA treats child support as it was under the old law. It's neither income to the recipient nor a deduction for the payer. However, the TRA scrapped the complicated old rules for claiming exemptions for dependent children. The TRA says that the custodial parent** is normally entitled to the dependency exemptions. The custodial parent may assign the exemptions to the noncustodial parent by filing an IRS form, Release of Claim to Exemption for Child of Divorced or Separated Parents (Form 8332). Or the divorce

---

*   A related problem is editing papers, which the defendant must receive, to keep selected personal information out of the hands of a defendant-spouse abuser. See "Keeping Personal Information away from a Spouse-Abuser" on page 66 for more about this issue.

**   For tax purposes, the custodial parent is the one with physical custody of the children. If parents have joint physical custody, the custodial parent is the one who has physical custody the most days during a year.

court can assign the dependency exemptions to the noncustodial parent (see "Assigning Dependency Exemptions" in Appendix H for more about dependency exemptions).

For many low-income custodial parents, there's a tax benefit more valuable than dependency exemptions: earned income tax credit (EIC). The EIC, which has a maximum value of $6,242 in 2015, not only provides a credit against income tax owed, it can also be converted into a cash payment if you don't owe any income tax.

The EIC was originally designed for custodial parents living with and taking care of children. Since 1994, non-custodians can also qualify for the EIC, but the credit is reduced for them. Either way, there are complicated rules for qualifying for the EIC, which are explained in the IRS's EIC publication. If you need help claiming the credit, look for a local nonprofit tax clinic or program. Michigan also has its own EIC which currently is 6% of the federal credit.

The most far-reaching change wrought by the TRA was to make all transfers of property between divorcing spouses nontaxable. Previously, spouses could gain or lose income from the property divisions of their divorces. Such gain or loss from a divorce is no longer possible under the new law, although income tax problems can still crop up later when a spouse sells property obtained in the divorce.

> ## More Information
>
> On taxes and divorce, obtain "Tax Information for Divorced or Separated Individuals" (Pub. 504).
>
> About the EIC, see "Earned Income Credit (EIC)" (Pub. 596).
>
> The booklets are available from any IRS office, by calling the agency at (800) 829-3676 or by accessing these at www.irs.gov/formspubs.

What If My Spouse Is Mentally Incompetent?

If your spouse has been declared mentally incompetent by a probate court, s/he must be specially represented in the divorce. After a declaration of mental incompetency, the probate court may appoint a conservator (a legal representative like a guardian) to manage the incompetent's affairs. A conservator has the authority to represent the incompetent in a divorce.

If you have been appointed as your spouse's conservator, you won't be able to represent him/her in the divorce because of the obvious conflict of interest. But you can ask the probate court for appointment of another person as conservator, and the new conservator could handle the divorce.

An alternative is to have a *guardian ad litem* (GAL) appointed for your mentally incompetent spouse. While a conservator has broad powers to manage affairs, a GAL's authority is limited to representing the incompetent in a single lawsuit. In a divorce, the court handling the divorce, not a probate court, can appoint a GAL for a spouse after the divorce is filed.

Whatever arrangements are made for your incompetent spouse, they should be completed before or soon after you file your divorce. Then you can serve the spouse's conservator or GAL with the divorce papers, and the divorce can proceed normally.

What If I Need to File for Bankruptcy?

Divorce and bankruptcy seem to go together because financial problems often cause divorce. According to one study, divorced people file for bankruptcy at three times the rate of the nondivorced population. Despite this link, divorce and bankruptcy aren't as compatible as they ought to be. Each procedure requires a separate case, filed in different courts (divorce in state court; bankruptcy in federal court), using different laws and rules.

Because of these problems, if you're considering both a divorce and a bankruptcy, seek legal advice. The lawyer can advise you about the relationship between divorce and bankruptcy, which type of bankruptcy to file (there are several), and whether to file singly or jointly (even separated spouses are permitted to file joint bankruptcies).

Don't wait to get legal help, because the timing of a divorce and bankruptcy can be important. In some cases, it's better to file the bankruptcy before completion of the divorce to protect exempt marital property. In other cases, the divorce should be finished before the bankruptcy is started so that some debts and obligations can be wiped out (a bankruptcy law protects most intra-family divorce obligations (child support, alimony and property division debts) from elimination; but some nonfamily divorce obligations are still dischargeable in bankruptcy). There are no firm rules about the sequence of cases; the timing will depend on the nature of your property and debts. Your lawyer should be able to explain what's best in your situation.

What If I Want to Dismiss the Divorce?

According to one estimate, 20-30% of all divorces are voluntarily withdrawn and dismissed. No one knows the exact reason for all these dismissals, but it's likely that most cases were dropped after the spouses reconciled.

There's no penalty for withdrawing your divorce after you start it. On the contrary, Michigan law encourages reconciliation and dismissal at every step of a divorce. In part, that's what the statutory waiting period is for. If you and your spouse decide to reconcile, see Appendix G for instructions and the form to dismiss your divorce.

What If My Spouse Abuses Me?

The physical abuse of one spouse by the other—usually, but not always, a wife at the hands of her husband—has been a constant problem with marriage and divorce. It's been estimated that spouse abuse is a problem in one out of three marriages. Sometimes this domestic violence becomes deadly. According to recent FBI figures, nearly a third of all female homicide victims are murdered by either their husbands or boyfriends.

For years, the legal system offered abused spouses little protection. It often seemed that family violence was a private matter into which the legal system wouldn't intervene. But that attitude has changed, and Michigan's spouse abuse laws have been toughened. Today it's possible to get personal protection orders (PPOs) preventing your spouse from:

- assaulting, attacking, beating, wounding or molesting you or someone else
- threatening to kill or physically injure you or someone else
- any act or conduct interfering with personal liberty or causing a reasonable apprehension of violence, such as stalking, harassment or unwanted contact
- interfering with you at work or school
- having access to your personal records or those of your children to get information about you
- purchasing or possessing a firearm
- entering property (so that your spouse can be ordered away from your home, even when it's the joint marital home)
- interfering with your removal of personal property or children from your spouse's property
- removing minor children from the person with legal custody, except as allowed by a court order

> ## More Information
>
> About spouse abuse, get:
>
> *Getting Free: You Can End Abuse and Take Back Your Life*, 4th ed., Ginny Nicarthy, Berkeley, CA: Seal Press, 2004
>
> Call the **National Domestic Violence Hotline** at (800) 799-7233 for information, support or referral to a spouse abuse shelter in your area.
>
> A list of abuse shelters in Michigan is also available at the Michigan Coalition to End Domestic & Sexual Violence's Web site at www.mcedsv.org, then to Members, to Our Members.

You don't have to wait until a divorce to get a PPO. They're available anytime there's domestic abuse, even before you file. After filing, you can get a PPO while the divorce is pending. It's also possible to get a permanent PPO injunction in your divorce judgment, which can remain in effect for any specified period of time.

When a spouse violates a PPO, s/he can be immediately arrested by the police, even if they didn't see the offense. Violation of a PPO is both a civil and criminal contempt of court, punishable by a maximum fine of $500 and 93 days in jail.

For all the protection it offers, Michigan's PPO law is complicated, making it difficult for nonlawyers to use. That's why it's best to have a lawyer when you're facing spouse abuse. If you have a low income, contact legal aid. The legal aid offices are very busy, but they usually give priority to spouse abuse cases. Or you can rely on a private lawyer for help. If you're determined to represent yourself, you can obtain PPO forms and instructions from the clerk of your circuit or family court. All Michigan circuit and family courts must make these materials available.

Whatever you do, keep in mind that a PPO cannot guarantee your safety. A court order is only a piece of paper; it won't stop someone bent on violence. If you believe your spouse is determined to harm you, take whatever precautions are necessary to protect yourself—with or without a PPO. This may even mean moving to a safe place. You may be able to find refuge with a friend or relative.

There are also special shelters for abused spouses (and their children). Michigan has around 50 shelters serving every part of the state.

Keeping Personal Information away from a Spouse-Abuser

Several divorce papers contain personal information about you, your children, employment and health care coverage. During the divorce, the defendant gets copies of these papers.

If there's a danger of spouse abuse from the defendant, and you're keeping a distance, you may not want to reveal your current address and employment to the defendant. In exceptional cases like this, you can receive permission to withhold personal information from the divorce papers, and provide it separately and confidentially to the court. Ask the friend of the court about withholding personal information this way.

Where Can I File If My Spouse or I Am Native American?

Did you know that Michigan has the largest Native American population in the Eastern United States? Michigan has 12 federally-recognized Indian tribes and 4 which are recognized by the state. These tribes keep tribal rolls listing all members of the tribe (persons not on these rolls aren't regarded as members).

The tribes often have their own reservations (these reservations plus satellite Indian communities are known as "Indian country") with separate tribal court systems which can grant divorces.

The jurisdiction rules for divorces involving at least one Native American spouse are still being worked out. It seems clear that when both spouses are Indian and living in Indian country, the tribal court has complete control of the divorce. If one or both Indian spouses are living in non-Indian country, a state court divorce is an option, but so is a tribal divorce because many tribal courts allow access based on tribal membership without strict regard to residence.

The far more difficult cases are when just one spouse is Native American and the other isn't. In these cases, jurisdiction depends on where the spouses are living (in or outside Indian country), which spouse (plaintiff or defendant) is Native American and what the tribal legal code says about jurisdiction. Another complication is division of tribal trust land, which state courts cannot do. If you're facing a complicated situation like this, you should talk to a lawyer who knows about Indian law.

Another concern is a federal law, the Indian Child Welfare Act, protecting the custody of Native American children. But this act doesn't normally apply to divorce, except when the custody of Indian children is assigned to nonparent third parties.

More Information

About divorce in tribal courts, contact:

Michigan Indian Legal Services
814 S. Garfield Ave.
Suite A
Traverse City, MI 49686
(231) 947-0122; (800) 968-6877
www.mils3.org

What If My Spouse or I Am an "Alien" (Noncitizen)?

If you or your spouse are aliens, your foreign nationality probably won't prevent you from getting a divorce in Michigan (see below about aliens and jurisdiction). But your alien status can have all kinds of hidden effects on the divorce, which are also explained below.

Can an Alien Get a Divorce in Michigan?

In the United States, divorce jurisdiction is based on residence. If you reside here you can get a divorce, regardless of your nationality. But in other countries, particularly civil law areas (basically the non-English speaking world), divorce jurisdiction is usually determined by nationality, not residence. In these countries, you must be a citizen to get a divorce. A few countries, such as the Philippines, don't bother with divorce jurisdiction at all because they refuse to permit divorce. If you're a citizen of one of those countries, a divorce you get in Michigan might not be recognized in your country. This won't be a problem if you have broken all ties with the country. But it could spell trouble if you intend to return to the country, or have children or property there. To find out how a Michigan divorce will be treated in your native country, check with your embassy or consulate.

> ## Glossary
>
> *Immigrant*—an alien who intends to settle in the country permanently.
>
> *Nonimmigrant*—an alien who is staying in the country temporarily.

Divorce by a Plaintiff-Alien

An alien living in Michigan can usually file for divorce here, and the divorce will go through. What an alien must consider is the impact the divorce will have on his/her residence rights. The impact is different for two types of aliens:

Immigrant. Aliens married to U.S. citizens typically apply for permanent residence here as spouses of citizens, becoming "lawful permanent residents." Aliens married two years or more quickly gain permanent residence. But aliens in shorter marriages usually get conditional residence, because of a suspicion that the marriage might be a sham.

A divorce during the two-year conditional residence period can be a problem for an immigrant. The divorce itself doesn't prove that the marriage is a sham (that's judged by the parties' intentions when they got married). But a divorce makes it more difficult to prove the marriage is real, especially without the help of an estranged spouse.

Nonimmigrant. A divorce can jeopardize the residence rights of a nonimmigrant, here temporarily, particularly if admission status depends solely on marriage. After the marriage is terminated by the divorce, this status is gone and the nonimmigrant may face deportation (there are some exceptions if there has been spouse/child abuse or in cases of extreme hardship).

Plaintiff-Citizen Filing Divorce against a Defendant-Alien

As a U.S. citizen filing for divorce, your citizenship is secure and won't be affected by the divorce. The divorce could have an impact on the defendant-alien's residence rights, as described above. Nevertheless, the divorce could also have an unforeseen effect on you.

Typically, U.S. citizens marrying aliens seek residence rights for them by filing an Affidavit of Support. The affidavit promises to support the alien-spouse or else reimburse the government for any public assistance the alien might receive until the alien: 1) becomes a U.S. citizen 2) establishes an earnings record in the U.S. This obligation to support, which is actually a contract, survives divorce. So if you divorce an alien, and the alien receives public assistance, you could be liable for reimbursement.

Do You Need Legal Help?

If your divorce looks too complicated for you to do yourself, you need legal help. How do you find a good lawyer? The best way is by recommendation from someone you trust. But if you can't find a lawyer by word of mouth, legal services and referrals are available from:

Legal aid. Those who meet federal poverty guidelines are eligible for legal aid from one of the legal aid organizations located throughout the state. The problem is, these programs are often so understaffed that they can help only a fraction of those eligible for their services. To find the legal aid office in your area, look under "Attorneys" or "Social Service Organizations" in the yellow pages or go to the State Bar of Michigan's Web site at www.michbar.org, then to For Public, then to Find Legal Assistance, then to Legal Aid Programs by County.

Legal clinics and services. Newspapers often carry advertisements for low-cost uncontested divorce services. Some of these services are offered by local attorneys doing business as clinics, while others may be branches of national legal service companies.

Lawyers. These days, lawyers aren't shy about advertising, and you can find their ads in newspapers and the yellow pages. County bar associations in several of the larger counties provide lawyer referral services. To obtain lawyer referrals in other counties, call the state bar referral service at (800) 968-0738.

On the other hand, you may have decided that your divorce isn't too complicated. If that's true, you're ready to move on to Chapter 2 and begin your divorce.

Chapter 2

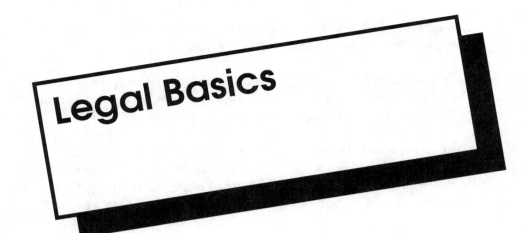

Legal Basics

For lawyers, an uncontested divorce isn't much more than a clerical task, which they usually assign to their secretaries. But nonlawyers are often stumped by the simplest things: How do I fill out the divorce papers? Where do I file them? When do I file them? How do I find the right court? This section deals with these legal basics and more, so you will be as well-prepared as any lawyer.

Court System

Before 1998, divorce cases were handled by the general circuit courts of Michigan. On Jan. 1, 1998, Michigan's court system was reorganized and new family courts (which are actually divisions of the circuit courts) went into operation. Michigan family courts deal with all kinds of family-related cases: divorce (including after-divorce matters), annulment, separate maintenance, family support, custody, parenting time, paternity, domestic violence, child abuse and neglect, juvenile delinquency, guardianship/conservatorship, adoption, emancipation of minors and name-change cases.

The philosophy of the family court system is to specialize in family law matters, unlike the general circuit courts which deal with all kinds of civil and criminal cases. Michigan family courts also have a "one-family, one-judge" policy, which brings all of a family's cases before the same judge, who is familiar with the family and its problems.

Family courts may be fairly new, but the court personnel haven't changed. The following people have responsibility for your divorce case:

Judge.   Your divorce is handled by a family court judge, who is either a circuit court or probate court judge on assignment to the family court. You cannot choose the judge for your case. Ordinarily, when you file, the clerk randomly assigns a judge to your case. But if you or members of your family have other family law cases pending in the court, the clerk will try to assign your divorce to the judge hearing the other case(s). With this assignment, the same judge will handle all the family's cases. If you dislike the judge, you cannot get another unless you can prove that the judge is actually biased or prejudiced against you.

Clerk   The family court clerk receives all your divorce papers and maintains a case file for them. Throughout this book, the family court clerk is simply called the clerk. In most counties, the county clerk is the clerk of the family court. But some counties have a special family court clerk, separate from the county clerk.

   To find out who does the family court clerking in your county, call the county clerk and ask for information. Or simply look up the county government listing in the telephone book, and see if there is a separate listing for a clerk of the family division of the circuit court.

Prosecuting attorney.   County prosecuting attorneys have the power to intervene in divorce cases to protect the interests of minor children and the "public good." Busy with criminal prosecutions, they seldom do that. Nevertheless, prosecuting attorneys (except in Kent, Macomb, Oakland and Wayne Counties) are entitled to notice of all divorces with minor children and must receive copies of the summons and divorce complaint.

Friend of the court.   When it became apparent that prosecuting attorneys weren't bothering with divorces, the office of the friend of the court was created to provide better supervision of divorces with minor children, and better supervision of divorces in which a spouse sought alimony.

   Friends of the court play a number of roles during divorce. They conduct investigations and make recommendations to the judge about the issues of custody, parenting time, child support, and alimony. They may also review and approve judgments and other orders before they are submitted to the judge. In contested cases, the friend of the court may act as a referee or mediator. The friend of the court was traditionally the collector, distributor and enforcer of child support and alimony. But many of these duties have now been transferred to the state disbursement unit.

   The friend of the court used to participate in every divorce case with minor children. But under a 2002 law, it's sometimes possible to "opt out" of the friend of the court system. After an opt-out (there are several kinds), the friend of the court won't manage the case, and the parties must assume this responsibility. For more about opting out, see Appendix C.

State disbursement unit. The SDU (sometimes abbreviated MiSDU), a state agency, is part of the Department of Health and Human Services' Office of Child Support. The SDU has taken over collection and distribution of support (child support and alimony) from the local county friends of the court. See "Centralization of Child Support Services" on page 26 for more about this transfer of duties.

Department of Health and Human Services. The DHHS is a state agency in charge of public assistance like the Family Independence Program (FIP), Medicaid and other benefits. The DHHS also assists in establishing and enforcing child support orders, particularly when the family is receiving public assistance.

Courtroom clerk. The courtroom clerk sits in the courtroom next to the judge while the court is in session. During a trial, the courtroom clerk is responsible for marking and receiving exhibits. In an uncontested divorce case, the courtroom clerk has a smaller role, but in some counties s/he may receive and file papers during the final hearing.

Assignment clerk. Several of the larger counties use special assignment clerks to schedule court hearings. In these counties, final hearings in uncontested divorce cases may be scheduled through assignment clerks.

Court reporter. The court reporter sits below the judge and records the court proceedings. In an uncontested divorce case, the court reporter makes a record of the final hearing, although it's unlikely that a transcript of the hearing will ever be needed.

Judge's secretary. Working in the judge's office, the judge's secretary may help in submitting papers to the judge for review.

Law clerk. Most judges have law clerks, who are often law students or new lawyers. Law clerks help judges with a number of tasks, including review of papers.

In many counties, these court personnel are conveniently located under one roof, usually in a courthouse or county building. But in other counties, whose court systems have outgrown their courthouses, court personnel may be scattered among several buildings. Before you begin your divorce, make sure you know where the court personnel are located.

The first person you want to find is the clerk, because you will begin your divorce in the clerk's office by filing the initial divorce papers there.

Papers

Many divorce-filers are surprised to find that courts won't do the divorce paperwork for you. Instead, it's your responsibility to prepare all the divorce papers. Don't try to do this all at once; prepare the papers as you need them, during each step of your divorce.

Preparing Papers

Whenever possible, type the divorce papers. But if you can't, it's permissible to print by hand in ink. Either way, make sure the papers are neat and legible.

The divorce papers you file must also be accurate and honest. Judges can penalize those who intentionally or even carelessly file false legal papers. Ordinarily, these penalties are payments of money to opponents hurt by the false papers.

But for some false papers the penalties are severe. When you sign an affidavit, you swear to the notary public that the contents are true. You do much the same when you sign papers with a verification declaration ("I declare that the statements above are true to the best of my information, knowledge, and belief."). According to Michigan law, it's a crime to knowingly file a false affidavit; the intentional falsification of a verified document is a contempt of court. Don't be alarmed by these penalties; just make sure that your papers are accurate and honest.

Among your divorce papers are several forms issued by the State Court Administrative Office (SCAO). These state forms include Michigan court forms and friend of the court forms, which are coded in the lower left corner by type (MC or FOC), number and date of release. Besides these state forms, a few counties, notably Wayne (number-coded), have local forms.

Added to the state forms are several Thunder Bay Press forms (code: TBP/number/date). The Thunder Bay Press forms include most of the important divorce papers, such as the complaint, default and judgment. The state used to publish these forms, but discontinued publication in 1989. The Thunder Bay Press forms have been created to replace them.

You may notice a difference in the type-size of the papers. In 2004, a court rule went into effect requiring that all court papers, except the state-issued (SCAO) forms, must be in 12-point type. Thus, the printing on all the TBP forms was increased to 12-point size. Also, when you fill in the papers, try to print or type in a larger size (no fine print) matching the printing on these forms.

The court rule also specifies that all court papers must be 8½ x 11." Previously, this was the maximum size, but papers could be a little smaller. Prior editions of this book were 8½ x 11," making the perforated forms .25" smaller after detachment from the book (perforation of the forms causes a .25" loss in the binding margin). Now, the book has been increased in overall width by .25" to make up this difference.

More Information

An affidavit is a legal paper stating facts that must be sworn to under oath before someone, such as a notary public, who can give oaths.

To obtain notary services, look in the yellow pages under "Notaries Public," or contact insurance agencies, banks or mailing/shipping stores, which often have notary services available.

Captions of Papers

Every form has a special purpose and each is prepared differently. Yet all the forms share similar captions which are filled in as follows:

STATE OF MICHIGAN Circuit Court - Family Division *OJIBWAY* **COUNTY**	JUDGMENT OF DIVORCE Page 1 of ___ pages	CASE NO. *09-00501-DM* *JUDGE TUBBS*
Plaintiff (appearing *in propria persona*):		**Defendant:**
DARLENE ANN LOVELACE *121 S. MAIN* *LAKE CITY, MI 48800* *772-0000*	v	*DUDLEY ERNEST LOVELACE* *900 S. MAPLE* *LAKE CITY, MI 48800* *773-3004*

STATE OF MICHIGAN Circuit Court - Family Division *OJIBWAY* **COUNTY**	JUDGMENT OF DIVORCE Page 2 of ___ pages	CASE NO. *09-00501-DM*
Plaintiff:		**Defendant:**
DARLENE ANN LOVELACE	v	*DUDLEY ERNEST LOVELACE*

As you can see, the papers have either a long or short caption. In a long caption, you must put the county where the divorce is filed in the upper left corner. The names, addresses and telephone numbers of you, as plaintiff, and your spouse, as defendant, go in the two large boxes.

Some state-issued forms have slightly different captions. In the upper left box, the MC forms may ask for the judicial circuit of your family court (in Michigan, the judicial circuits are numbered (1st (Hillsdale County), 2nd (Berrien County), 3rd (Wayne County), etc.). You can get the number of your local circuit court (of which the family court is a division) in a telephone book (look under the "County Government" listing in the blue (government) pages) or county directory which some counties publish or put online. Some MC or FOC forms may also ask for the court's or friend of the court's address and telephone number. This extra information is also available in the telephone book or county directory.

Incidentally, the italicized Latin phrase in the caption of many of the forms signals that this is a self-help divorce. *In propria persona* (sometimes abbreviated to *in pro per*) means "in your own person," indicating that you are doing the case yourself without a lawyer. Some of the state-issued forms, such as the Summons and Complaint (MC 01), have caption boxes for lawyer representatives. You can leave these boxes blank, or insert in them: "In Pro Per."

Your case number goes in the upper right corner. This number starts with a two-digit number for the year followed by several other numbers. It ends with a two-letter case-type code. All cases in Michigan have codes according to their type: A divorce with minor children bears a DM code and divorces without minor children have a DO code. Because a case number isn't assigned

To Obtain

Extra copies of Wayne County forms, call the Wayne County Friend of the Court's call center at (313) 224-5300.

The Wayne County circuit court system also has a Web site, www.3rdcc.org, from which you can view and/or download many forms.

You should have enough caption labels for all your papers. But if you run out, you can get more in the clerk's office in room 201 of the Coleman A. Young Municipal Center (CAYMC) (formerly the City-County Bldg.) at 2 Woodward Ave. in Detroit.

until filing, you won't have it for your initial divorce papers, so leave the case number spaces blank on them. But include your case number in the captions of all your subsequently filed court papers.

If you're in a larger county that has more than one family court judge, write the name of your judge below the case numbers on all the papers you file after the initial divorce papers. This will help direct the papers to the correct case file and judge.

With a short caption, you can omit much of the above information. All you need for a short caption is the court, case number and your and your spouse's names as plaintiff and defendant.

Oakland and Wayne Counties, which have the state's largest court systems, have a bar-coded caption-labeling system to prevent mishandling of court papers. When you file a divorce in these two counties, the clerk prints sheets of caption labels for both parties. Notice how the clerk takes several labels and affixes these to the captions of your initial divorce papers. As you file other papers, use labels from your sheet to label them in the same way. Save the other sheet of caption labels because you must have it served on the defendant later.

Copying Papers

As you prepare divorce papers, make some photocopies. Except for some of the initial papers, make three photocopies of each divorce paper. After copying, put "FOC" (an abbreviation for friend of the court) in the upper left corner of one photocopy of each paper. The friend of the court gets copies of all your papers through the clerk. By earmarking your papers with "FOC," you ensure that these copies are directed to the friend of the court. In all, you should have enough divorce papers and copies to distribute as follows:

- original - court (clerk)
- 1st copy - friend of the court
- 2nd copy - plaintiff
- 3rd copy - defendant

When you photocopy divorce papers, copy both sides of any two-sided forms because some papers have important information on the reverse. Most two-sided forms are tumble-printed, with their reverse sides upside down. This makes it possible to read the reverse sides while the papers are fastened to a file folder by simply lifting them up. When you photocopy these two-sided forms, you might not be able to run your copies through the photocopier again to make a tumble-printed form. If so, just make the paper into a two-page form and staple the pages together.

With all these papers and copies, it's easy to get disorganized. To keep track of everything, prepare a file for all your divorce papers. Not only will this file keep you organized during the divorce, it will give you a complete record of the case afterward.

Filing Papers

When you file your divorce, the clerk will open a file for your case. As you file papers, the clerk will ordinarily use the following procedure:

- keep the original for your case file
- take the copy marked "FOC" and forward it to the friend of the court
- return a copy for the plaintiff
- return a copy for the defendant

You can file papers with the clerk personally, by mail or sometimes even by facsimile (fax). Despite these options, it's usually best to file the initial divorce papers in person and the other papers this way whenever you can. By filing personally, you can pay any fees that are due and immediately get back copies of your papers for service on the other party.

For filing by mail, send your papers and any fees to the clerk along with a cover letter asking for filing and return of the copies you have enclosed. To get the copies back quickly, include a self-addressed envelope with postage.

Filing by fax isn't allowed when filing fees are due (unless you have paid in advance by depositing money with the clerk), because the clerk won't accept a filing without payment of the filing fee. Moreover, the clerk won't send or fax back copies of the papers you file, so there's no way to get copies. Thus, fax-filing should be used in emergency, when you have to file in a hurry to meet a filing deadline. So-called "e-filing," or transmitting papers to a court clerk by email through the Internet, is in its infancy in Michigan. E-filing is being tested in a few counties, but hasn't been adopted statewide yet.

> ## Glossary
>
> Return copies—that the clerk returns to you after filing original papers may be unstamped or stamped as "true copies." A true copy stamp is an informal way of saying that the copy is a duplicate of the original (a clerk can also provide official "certified copies," but there is a fee for certification).
>
> Try to get true copies of all papers you file, especially court orders (ex parte order and divorce judgment).

Fees

You must pay several fees to get a divorce (see "How Much Will My Divorce Cost?" on page 49 for a description of the fees). Except for the service fee, you pay these fees to the clerk. Clerks usually accept cash, personal checks and money orders as payment. After you pay, the clerk may give you a receipt, which you should keep as proof of payment.

The service fee is paid outside of court. As mentioned before, you can choose from among several methods of service: 1) acknowledgment 2) mail 3) delivery. You can usually obtain service by acknowledgment for free. When you use service by mail, you pay the post office for the mailing. If you use service

Courtroom Etiquette

During a court hearing, you should follow these rules of courtroom behavior:

- Dress neatly and be well-groomed.

- Turn off your cellphone while in the courtroom.

- Be on time.

- Be courteous to the judge and others.

- Wait until called on to speak.

- Don't interrupt while the judge or others are talking; you will get your chance to speak.

- After the judge makes a decision, don't persist in arguing your view.

by delivery, you pay the server, who is usually a sheriff or commercial process server. Ordinarily, the server bills you for the service fee after service when s/he returns the proof of service to you. But if you use service by delivery out of town or out of state, it's a good idea to prepay the service fee. When you send the service papers to the server, include a check or money order for $30 or so, and a note asking the server to refund/bill you for the difference between your prepayment and his service fee.

If you qualify, you can get an exemption from payment of the court fees. You are exempt from payment if you are receiving public assistance or have a low income. Appendix A has more about qualifying for a fee exemption, and instructions and the affidavit to apply for the exemption.

If you've received a fee exemption, you won't have to pay any court fees during your divorce (although you might have to pay them at the end of the divorce). If the clerk tries to charge you a fee during your divorce, refer the clerk to the fee exemption affidavit, which will be in your case file.

Time

During your divorce, you must deal with several important time periods and deadlines, including: 1) 180-day state residence requirement 2) 10-day county residence requirement 3) answering period (usually 21 or 28 days) 4) statutory waiting period (six months for divorces with minor children) 5) filing deadlines for various papers.

The court rules have detailed provisions to figure periods of time. For a time period of days, the period begins on the day after the day of an act (filing, service, establishment of residence, etc.); the day of the act itself isn't counted. The last day of the period is counted, unless it falls on a Saturday, Sunday or court holiday. In that case, the period extends to the next day that isn't a Saturday, Sunday or court holiday.

Example: You serve a defendant by mail on May 1. The 28-day answering period after service by mail begins on May 2 (the day after the day of service) and ends on May 29 (which in this example is not a Saturday, Sunday or court holiday). The defendant has until May 29 to answer.

Example: You serve a defendant by mail on May 1. The 28-day answering period after service by mail begins on May 2 (the day after the day of service) and ends on May 29. But this year May 29 is Memorial Day, a court holiday, so the answering period extends to May 30. The defendant must answer by May 30.

Like a time period of days, a time period of months begins on the day after the day of an act. The last day of the period is the same day of the month on which the period began. If there is no such day, the last day of the period is whatever the last day of that month is. As with time periods of days, a time period of months that ends on a Saturday, Sunday or court holiday extends to the next day that isn't a Saturday, Sunday or court holiday.

Example: You file your divorce complaint on May 1. The six-month statutory waiting period begins on May 2 (the day after the day of the complaint filing) and ends on November 2 (the same day of the month as the day on which the period began). Your final hearing could be scheduled anytime after November 2.

Example: You file your divorce complaint on May 30. The six-month statutory waiting period begins on May 31 (the day after the day of the complaint filing) and ends on November 30. The waiting period ends on November 30 because there is no Nov. 31. Your final hearing could be scheduled anytime after November 30.

To avoid time problems, you can simply estimate the time period and then add a little more time for safety. For example, if you figure that a time period ends sometime during the first week of a month, you could wait until the middle of the month to take action, avoiding any danger of acting too quickly.

Courthouse Appearances

During your divorce, you must appear once or possibly twice in court before the judge. You may also have to make an informal appearance or two at the courthouse, outside the courtroom.

Court Hearings

All divorce plaintiffs are expected to attend a final hearing, in court before the judge, at the end of the case. During the hearing, you must give some brief testimony to get a Judgment of Divorce (TBP 4). Less often, a court hearing may also be necessary if you seek preliminary relief, the defendant objects to the relief and the friend of the court's efforts to settle the dispute fail.

For either type of court hearing, make sure you know the location of the hearing beforehand. Court hearings normally take place in the courtroom of the judge assigned to your case, which is usually in the county courthouse or similar county building.

Go to the place of the court hearing on the scheduled day and time. Try to arrive around 30 minutes before the hearing, to take care of any last-minute business. By arriving early, you can also observe other hearings. Be prepared to spend most of the morning or afternoon at the hearing, since it may not start on time.

When your case is called by the courtroom clerk, step forward and identify yourself. Mention that you are representing yourself. Take a seat at one of the tables inside the bar (gate) of the courtroom, and get ready to begin your presentation.

Other Courthouse Appearances

You may also attend a case conference (in some counties) or referee hearing (if preliminary relief is sought and contested) outside of the courtroom. These are informal sessions held by court personnel without the judge. As with a formal court hearing, know where the meeting is held, be on time and observe normal courtroom etiquette.

Special Arrangements for a Courthouse Appearance

If you have a handicap (mobility, visual, speech or hearing impairment), court personnel can make special accommodations for your courthouse appearance. For non-English-speakers, the court can appoint an interpreter to translate the proceedings into your language.

Handicapper and Prisoner Accommodations

Tell court personnel about the handicap by preparing a Request for Reasonable Accommodations and Response (MC 70) (see the sample MC 70 at the end of this section). File or send the form to the clerk well ahead of the scheduled appearance. Court personnel will contact you before the appearance, and discuss the accommodation you need.

In exceptional cases, special accommodations aren't enough and you may be excused from the court appearance. If so, you can give information, such as testimony for a final hearing, in written or electronic form (by telephone, for example). Persons with severe handicaps may qualify for this exception. Prisoners are also frequently excused from court attendance, and can give written or electronic testimony (see "What If My Spouse or I Am Imprisoned?" on page 46 for more about this procedure).

Foreign Language Interpreters

The court can appoint a foreign language interpreter if you can't speak English well enough to understand the court proceedings. Use the Request and Order for Interpreter (MC 81) (a sample MC 81 appears at the end of this section). The judge may skip a hearing on this motion and simply sign the order.

You could file the MC 81 any time during the divorce. Whenever you file, send a copy of the motion to the defendant, even if s/he has defaulted, at his or her last known mailing address.

Incidentally, there are special foreign language Summons and Complaint (MC 01) forms available in Arabic, Chinese, Hmong, Korean, Russian and Spanish. You can get these from the clerk and use the special forms if your spouse speaks one of these languages, but isn't fluent in English.

Local Rules and Forms

For years, there were variations in divorce procedures among Michigan's 83 counties. In 1993, the state tried to standardize procedures by abolishing all local divorce rules and forms. But little by little, several counties, Wayne in particular, have been permitted to re-adopt local rules and forms.

Don't panic if you encounter some local practices that aren't described in this book. Ask the local authorities what the local practice is and adapt to it. Luckily, variations tend to be minor. They typically concern scheduling the final hearing or dealing with the friend of the court.

New Laws, Rules, Forms and Fees

These days, divorce laws, rules, forms and fees change regularly. Congress and the Michigan Legislature are constantly passing new divorce-related laws. Added to this are the thousands of decisions courts issue each year, some of which affect divorce. As a result of this activity, parts of this book may become outdated.

To Obtain

Laws, court rules and other legal information, visit a law library. Most county courthouses have law libraries which are open to the public. The divorce laws are in the MCLAs (Michigan Compiled Laws Annotated) and MCLS (Michigan Compiled Laws Service); the court rules are published in *Michigan Rules of Court - State* by Thomson Reuters (this volume also includes all the local court rules).

Online, you can access Michigan laws via www.michiganlegislature.org, using the search engine to search by section or by subject. The basic divorce laws are MCL 552.1 to 552.1803 and 722.21 to 722.31 (Child Custody Act of 1970).

For court rules, go to www.courts.mi.gov, select the Legal Community tab, then to the Court Rules quick link and choose: 1) under Michigan Court Rules, Chapter 3 Special Proceedings and Actions, for the divorce court rules of MCR 3.201 to 3.219 2) under Other Rules, Local Court Rules - Circuit Courts, for local court rules arranged by county.

Approved, SCAO

**REQUEST FOR REASONABLE
ACCOMMODATIONS AND RESPONSE**

Court name and address   OJIBWAY COUNTY CIRCUIT COURT - FAMILIY DIVISION
200 N. MAIN
LAKE CITY, MI 48800

Telephone number of ADA coordinator:

You should request accommodations as far as possible in advance of your court appearance or other court activity. To request accommodations, complete and return this form to the court at the above address. If you need help completing this form, contact the ADA coordinator at the above telephone number. To properly evaluate your request, the court may ask you for more information.

The ADA coordinator will respond to your request before the court appearance or other court activity. If your request is denied, you may request a review in accordance with the court's local administrative order. At your request, the court will provide you a copy of the local administrative order.

Today's date   8-10-2009

APPLICANT INFORMATION (to be kept confidential)

Applicant is	☐ Witness	☐ Juror	☐ Attorney	☒ Party	☐ Other (specify)

Case name and number (if applicable)

Name DARLENE A. LOVELACE	E-mail address

Address 121 S. MAIN			
City LAKE CITY	State MI	Zip 48800	Telephone no. 772-0000

1. What type of proceeding or court service, activity, or program are you attending (i.e., hearing, jury duty, mediation meeting, trial)?

   FINAL HEARING FOR DIVORCE

2. On what dates do you need accommodations?

   9-7-2009

3. For what impairment do you need accommodations (for a sign language interpreter, specify ASL, CDI, or CART)?

   PHYSICAL MOBILITY IMPARIMENT - HAVE A WHEELCHAIR

4. What type of accommodations do you need?

   ACCESSIBLE PHYSICAL LOCATION

RESPONSE TO REQUEST

☒ The request is **GRANTED**   ☐ from _____ to _____ , ☐ for an indefinite period,
   ☒ for the above matter or appearance,
      ☒ in whole as follows: (specify the accommodations)
         ASSISTANCE IN ENTERING COURTHOUSE FROM PARKING RAMP

      ☐ in part. As consented to by the applicant, alternative accommodations are as follows: (specify the accommodations)

☐ The request is **DENIED** because
    ☐ the applicant is not a qualified individual with a disability under the ADA.
    ☐ the request creates an undue financial or administrative burden on the court (as defined by the ADA).
    ☐ the request fundamentally alters the nature of the service, program, or activity (as defined by the ADA).
    ☐ the request (with alternative accommodations offered but rejected by the applicant.)
    The basis for this denial is: (Specify on separate sheet if needed. Include alternative accommodations offered but rejected by the applicant.)

The applicant was notified of the court's response   ☐ by phone   ☒ by mail   ☐ by e-mail   ☐ in person   on

8-12-2009   by   _Lester Tubbs_____ .
Date   Name

MC 70 (10/15) **REQUEST FOR REASONABLE ACCOMMODATIONS AND RESPONSE**   MCL 393.501 *et seq.*, 42 USC 12111 *et seq.*

Approved, SCAO

Original - Case file
Copy - Requester

REQUEST AND ORDER FOR INTERPRETER

CASE NO.

Print the name of the court. ___OJIBWAY COUNTY CIRCUIT COURT - FAMILY DIVISION___
Court

If you have a court case and need an interpreter, complete this Request using the English alphabet. Then, date and sign it, and mail or give it to the court where your case is to be heard. If the court appoints an interpreter for you, the court may order you to pay for interpretation costs if you can afford to pay.

Request for Interpreter

I need an interpreter who speaks: ___KOREAN___
Language

Print your full name. ___DARLENE A. LOVELACE___
Full name

Print your mailing address. ___121 S. MAIN, LAKE CITY, MI 48800___
Mailing address

Print your telephone number. ___772-0000___
Telephone no.

Are you a party in this case, a witness, or another interested person? Check one.

☒ I am a party.
☐ I am a witness.
☐ I am an interested person (Describe your interest in the space below.)

I ask the court to appoint an interpreter so that I can fully participate in this case.

___8-1-2009___
Date

___Darlene A. Lovelace___
Signature

Order Regarding Appointment of Interpreter

☒ 1. The request for an interpreter is granted.

☐ 2. The request for an interpreter is denied because: (Specify the reason[s] for denial.)

___8-2-2009___
Date

___Lester Tubbs___
Judge

Bar no.

Court Use Note: This completed and signed Request and Order must be placed in the case file. Bilingual versions of this form are available for informational use.

MC 81 (2/14) **REQUEST AND ORDER FOR INTERPRETER**

MCR 1.111(B), (F), (H)

Overview of Divorce Procedure

At first, divorce procedure may seem forbidding. But it's really not so mysterious when you break it down into steps and understand the purpose of each step.

Like any lawsuit, a divorce starts when the plaintiff files a paper known as a complaint. Despite its rather alarming name, a complaint is simply the document that starts a lawsuit. A divorce complaint contains facts about the parties and their marriage, and then asks for relief on the divorce issues. At filing, the clerk issues a summons in the case notifying the defendant and others that a divorce has been filed.

In some cases, the plaintiff wants preliminary relief, and files special papers for an order settling custody, parenting time, residence of children and child support while the divorce is pending. Preliminary relief is optional, and there are alternatives to the relief described in Part III of Chapter 1.

The complaint, summons, preliminary relief papers (if preliminary relief is sought) and several other papers make up the initial divorce papers.

Because the friend of the court and prosecuting attorney have interests in divorces with minor children, they must receive notice of the divorce by getting copies of the initial divorce papers. The defendant must also get notice. This is provided by serving the initial divorce papers on the defendant. There are three regular methods of service, plus a couple of alternate service methods for elusive or disappeared defendants.

After service, the defendant may respond to the plaintiff's complaint within an answering period. The defendant's response can be either by filing: 1) an answer to the complaint or 2) a motion objecting to the complaint. If the plaintiff has asked for preliminary relief, the defendant can object to this request, and then the issue is decided by a friend of the court referee or the judge.

In the vast majority of cases, defendants don't bother to respond, putting them in default. The plaintiff can then go to the clerk and have the defendant's default declared. With this declaration, the case is officially an uncontested divorce, or what lawyers sometimes call a *pro confesso* or "pro con" divorce case.

But if the defendant responds to the complaint within the answering period, the divorce is contested. In that case, the plaintiff should seek a lawyer to take over the case because it's difficult to handle a contested case without a lawyer.

Meanwhile, the six-month statutory waiting period is running. This waiting period gives the friend of the court a chance to investigate the case and make recommendations to the judge about several divorce issues. The friend of the court puts these recommendations in a report which the plaintiff must use in preparing the divorce judgment.

The Judgment of Divorce settles all the divorce issues once and for all, replacing any preliminary orders on the issues. The judgment is issued by the court at the end of the divorce, during a final hearing. The plaintiff must appear at the hearing and give testimony or "proofs" in support of the judgment. This sounds scary, but the final hearing is usually very brief and easy to get through. After the final hearing, the plaintiff files the divorce judgment making the divorce final.

Chapter 2 of this book organizes the divorce procedure into two parts: "Starting Your Divorce" (Part I) and "Finishing Your Divorce" (Part II). Part I has two steps: "Filing" and "Service." Part II includes three steps: "Default," "Waiting for Final Hearing" and "Final Hearing." The flowchart below summarizes these steps and the time to perform them.

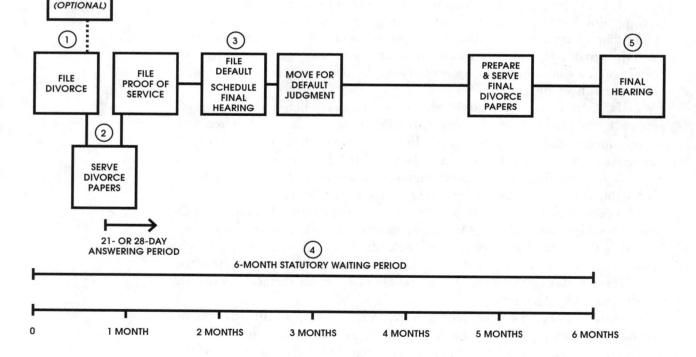

PART I: Starting Your Divorce

1 Filing

Preparing Your Initial Divorce Papers

You begin your divorce by preparing the initial divorce papers. These papers include the complaint, summons and several related papers. The divorce complaint describes the basic facts of your marriage. It also tells the court that your marriage has broken down by citing the no-fault grounds for divorce. Finally, the complaint asks the court to decide the divorce issues. The purpose of the summons is to notify the defendant that you have filed a divorce complaint, and that s/he may respond to it.

The complaint and summons are contained in a set of forms: the Summons and Complaint (MC 01) and Complaint for Divorce (TBP 1). The Summons and Complaint (MC 01) includes the summons in the case along with the first part of the complaint. The Complaint for Divorce (TBP 1) is a continuation of this form and contains the main body of the complaint.

Although the complaint and summons provide a good deal of information about your marriage, the friend of the court needs more personal and financial information. The friend of the court gets that extra information in the Verified Statement and Application for IV-D Services (FOC 23). This paper must be given to the clerk along with your initial divorce papers when you file for divorce. Unlike the other divorce papers, the clerk doesn't place the FOC 23 in your case file. Instead, the clerk forwards the statement to the friend of the court, without keeping a copy for the file.

Like all the other states, Michigan has adopted the Uniform Child Custody Jurisdiction and Enforcement Act (UCCJEA). Among other things, the act requires filing of the Uniform Child Custody Jurisdiction Enforcement Act Affidavit (MC 416) describing the past and present residences of your minor children. This information tells the court whether there is Michigan jurisdiction over the issues of custody, parenting time and residence of children when such jurisdiction is contested (see "Can I Get a Divorce in Michigan?" on page 43 for more about this).

Optional and Local Papers

Your initial divorce papers will include a few extra papers if you decide to seek preliminary relief (see "Do I Need 'Preliminary Relief'?" on page 60 for more about this option and Appendix B for complete information, instructions and forms for seeking the interim kind of preliminary relief). For interim relief, you will need an Ex Parte Order (TBP 5) and several companion forms to this order.

Symbols

- • regular paper
- ■ regular practice
- ★ optional paper or practice
- + local paper or practice

If you want a fee exemption, you must also prepare the Affidavit and Order, Suspension of Fees/Costs (MC 20) (see Appendix A for the form and instructions).

In every Wayne County divorce with minor children, you must file a Certificate on Behalf of Plaintiff Regarding Ex Parte Interim Support Order to say whether or not you are seeking interim relief. Also in Wayne County only, you can omit the Summons and Complaint (MC 01) from your initial divorce papers because the Wayne County Clerk will print out summonses for you when the case is filed.

The blank forms for the initial divorce papers and all other divorce papers are located in the forms section in the back of the book. Optional forms like the Ex Parte Order (TBP 5) and Waiver/Suspension of Fees and Costs (MC 20), and local forms like the Certificate on Behalf of Plaintiff Regarding Ex Parte Interim Support Order, for Wayne County divorces, are located in a special section. All the forms are perforated so you can easily tear them out of the book.

There are filled-in samples of the initial divorce papers at the end of this section; other sample forms appear at the end of the sections they relate to by subject matter. For general information about form preparation, see "Papers" on page 74.

Ordinarily, you must make three photocopies of your divorce papers. The clerk gets the original, leaving copies for the friend of the court, you and the defendant. But the initial divorce papers are distributed a little differently from the other divorce papers. The table below shows how many copies of the initial divorce papers you need:

- • Summons and Complaint   MC 01   5

- • Complaint for Divorce   TBP 1   4

- • Verified Statement and Application for IV-D Services   FOC 23   2

- Uniform Child Custody Jurisdiction Enforcement
  Act Affidavit   MC 416   3

★ interim relief papers, if relief is sought (see Appendix B)

★ Waiver/Suspension of Fees and Costs   MC 20   3

✦ Certificate on Behalf of Plaintiff Regarding Ex Parte
  Interim Support Order (in Wayne County only)   3

As explained in "Preparing Papers" on page 74, you must mark a copy of each paper with "FOC" in the upper left corner. This earmark reminds the clerk to forward the paper to the friend of the court.

Like the friend of the court, the prosecuting attorney (except in Kent, Macomb, Oakland and Wayne Counties) is also entitled to copies of the Summons and Complaint (MC 01) and Complaint for Divorce (TBP 1). Put "Pros. Atty." in the upper left corners of both papers to remind the clerk to forward them to the prosecuting attorney. Except for this pair of papers, the prosecuting attorney normally doesn't get any other papers during the divorce.

Filing Your Divorce

Start your divorce by filing it with the clerk (see "Court System" on page 71 for information about finding the clerk). To file, you must have all your initial divorce papers ready. And unless you receive a fee exemption, you must pay the filing fee (see "How Much Will My Divorce Cost?" on page 49 for the amount of the filing fee). In all, you should have the following items when you go to the clerk's office to file your divorce:

- Summons and Complaint   MC 01
  - original
  - 5 copies (one earmarked "FOC" and another "Pros. Atty.")

- Complaint for Divorce   TBP 1
  - original
  - 4 copies (one earmarked "FOC" and another "Pros. Atty.")

- Verified Statement and Application for IV-D Services   FOC 23
  - original

- Uniform Child Custody Jurisdiction Enforcement
  Act Affidavit   MC 416
  - original
  - 3 copies (one earmarked "FOC")

- money for the filing fee

★ interim relief papers, if relief is sought (see Appendix B)

★ Waiver/Suspension of Fees and Costs   MC 20
  • original
  • 3 copies (one earmarked "FOC")

✦ Certificate on Behalf of Plaintiff Regarding Ex Parte
  Interim Support Order (in Wayne County only)
  • original
  • 3 copies (one earmarked "FOC")

When you arrive at the clerk's office, tell the clerk that you want to file a divorce complaint. The clerk should then do the following to file your divorce:

■ Take the Summons and Complaint (MC 01) and the five copies and: 1) assign a judge to the case and stamp his/her name on these papers 2) enter a case number on them 3) complete the summons boxes in the middle of the papers. File the Summons and Complaint (MC 01), take the friend of the court's and prosecuting attorney's copies and return three copies to you.

■ File the Complaint for Divorce (TBP 1), take the friend of the court's and prosecuting attorney's copies, and return two copies to you.

■ Take the Verified Statement and Application for IV-D Services (FOC 23) for the friend of the court.

■ File the Uniform Child Custody Jurisdiction Enforcement Act Affidavit (MC 416), take the friend of the court's copy and return two copies to you.

■ Take the money for the filing fee.

★ File the Waiver/Suspension of Fees and Costs (MC 20), if used, to suspend the fees immediately; or submit the form to the judge for consideration. Take the friend of the court's copy and return two copies to you.

✦ In Wayne County only, file the Certificate on Behalf of Plaintiff Regarding Ex Parte Interim Support Order, take the friend of the court's copy and return two copies to you.

✦ In Oakland and Wayne Counties only, prepare caption labels, label the captions of the initial divorce papers and give you two sheets of caption labels.

If you are seeking interim relief, hold back the interim relief papers, such as the Ex Parte Order (TBP 5), from filing at this time. See Appendix B about when and how to present these to the judge, and if the relief is granted, how to file the papers.

Before You Leave the Clerk's Office

Before you leave the clerk's office, ask for two items not provided in this book: 1) two friend of the court pamphlets 2) a Record of Divorce or Annulment (DCH-0838). You will use these later in the divorce, but it's convenient to pick them up now during filing.

The friend of the court pamphlet describes the office of the friend of the court and its role in divorces. Keep one pamphlet for yourself. The other pamphlet must be served on the defendant along with the other service papers, as described in the next section.

The Record of Divorce or Annulment (DCH-0838) asks for personal and marital information. You complete and file the form at the end of the divorce, when you get the judgment. After filing, the clerk sends the DCH-0838 to the Michigan Department of Health and Human Services for addition to the state's vital records.

Are you seeking interim relief? If so, you might ask the clerk whether the county has a standard interim order form, and whether it's customary for the friend of the court to review interim orders before submission to the judge. In large counties, with many judges, you might also inquire whether the judge assigned to your case considers interim relief, or whether a specially designated judge considers these requests for all divorce cases.

> ## Obtain
>
> If the clerk doesn't have friend of the court pamphlets, you can get these from the friend of the court's office.
>
> Record of Divorce or Annulment (DCH-0838) forms are also available from:
>
> **Michigan Department of Health and Human Services**
> Vital Records Office
> 201 Townsend St.
> Capitol View Bldg. 3rd Floor
> Lansing, MI 48933
> (517) 335-8666

Getting Preliminary Relief

Before you leave the courthouse, it's a good time to ask for interim relief, if you have decided to seek it. You ask for an interim order directly from the judge, at the judge's office, using several papers filed shortly before and a few you held back. Appendix B has complete information, instructions and forms for seeking interim relief.

Approved, SCAO

Original - Court
1st copy - Defendant

2nd copy - Plaintiff
3rd copy - Return

STATE OF MICHIGAN
JUDICIAL DISTRICT
JUDICIAL CIRCUIT
COUNTY PROBATE

SUMMONS AND COMPLAINT

CASE NO.

Court address

Court telepho

Plaintiff's name(s), address(es), and telephone no(s).

v

Defendant's name(s), address(es), and telephone no(s).

FILL OUT CAPTION ON THIS AND ALL OTHER PAPERS AS SHOWN IN "PREPARING PAPERS"

Plaintiff's attorney, bar no., address, and telephone no.

SUMMONS　**NOTICE TO THE DEFENDANT**: In the name of the people of the State of Michigan you are notified
1. You are being sued.
2. **YOU HAVE 21 DAYS** after receiving this summons to **file a written answer with the court** and serve a copy on th
or take other lawful action with the court (28 days if you were served by mail or you were served outside this state).
3. If you do not answer or take other action within the time allowed, judgment may be entered against you for the r
in the complaint.

CLERK WILL COMPLETE SUMMONS BOXES

Issued	This summons expires	Court clerk
3-1-2009	5-31-2009	Martha Gee

*This summons is invalid unless served on or before its expiration date. This document must be sealed by the seal of the court.

COMPLAINT　*Instruction: The following is information that is required to be in the caption of every complaint and is to be completed
by the plaintiff. Actual allegations and the claim for relief must be stated on additional complaint pages and attached to this form.*

☐ This is a business case in which all or part of the action includes a business or commercial dispute under MCL 600.8035.

Family Division Cases
☒ There is no other pending or resolved action within the jurisdiction of the family division of circuit court involving the family or family
members of the parties.
☐ An action within the jurisdiction of the family division of the circuit court involving the family or family members of the parties has
been previously filed in _____ Court.
The action ☐ remains ☐ is no longer pending. The docket number and the judge assigned to the action are

Docket no.	Judge

DESCRIBE ANY PRIOR FAMILY CASES INVOLVING YOU OR YOUR FAMILY, SO DIVORCE CAN BE DIRECTED TO FAMILY COURT JUDGE HANDLING PRIOR CASES

General Civil Cases
☒ There is no other pending or resolved civil action arising out of the same transaction or occurrence as alleged i
☐ A civil action between these parties or other parties arising out of the transaction or occurrence alleged in the
been previously filed in _____
The action ☐ remains ☐ is no longer pending. The docket number and the judge assigned to the a

Docket no.	Judge

VENUE

Plaintiff(s) residence (include city, township, or village)	Defendant(s) residence (include city, township, or village)

(SEE CAPTIONS ABOVE)

Place where action arose or business conducted

Date	Signature of attorney/plaintiff
2-28-2009	Darlene A. Lovelace

If you require special accommodations to use the court because of a disability or if you require a foreign language interpreter to help
you fully participate in court proceedings, please contact the court immediately to make arrangements.

MC 01　(5/15)　**SUMMONS AND COMPLAINT**　MCR 2.102(B)(11), MCR 2.104, MCR 2.105, MCR 2.107, MCR 2.113(C)(2)(a), (b), MCR 3.206(A)

STATE OF MICHIGAN
Circuit Court - Family Division
COUNTY

COMPLAINT FOR DIVORCE

CASE NO.

INCLUDE FULL NAMES

Plaintiff: ☐ Husband ☒ Wife

DARLENE ANN LOVELACE

Defendant:

v

DUDLEY ERNEST LOVELACE

Plaintiff's name before this marriage:

DARLENE ANN ALBRIGHT

Defendant's name before this marriage:

SAME

1. Plaintiff's residence: at least
   ☒ 180 days in Michigan
   ☒ 10 days in this county
   and/or
   immediately before filing of this c[omplaint]

   Defendant's residence: at least
   ☒ 180 days in Michigan
   ☒ 10 days in this county
   immediately before filing of this compl[aint]

   SEE "CAN I GET A DIVORCE IN MICHIGAN?" FOR MORE ON RESIDENCE

   CHECK BOXES AS THEY APPLY

2. Date of marriage 9-1-2005 _____ Place of marriage LAKE CITY, MICHIGAN _____

3. The parties stopped living together as husband and wife on or about 1-15-2009 _____

4. There has been a breakdown of the marriage relationship to the extent that the objects of matrimony have been destroyed and there remains no reasonable likelihood that the marriage can be preserved.

5. Children of the parties or born during the marriage:

   a. Minor (under-18) children:

   DUANE WESLEY LOVELACE   6-1-2006
   DARRYL WENDELL LOVELACE   7-1-2007

   SEE "WHICH CHILDREN MUST BE INCLUDED IN MY DIVORCE?" FOR MORE ABOUT CHILDREN

   b. Adult children age 18-19½ entitled to support:

6. There ☐ is ☒ is no[t] *CHECK IF YOU HAVE ALREADY DIVIDED ALL PROPERTY* [w]ith prior continuing jurisdiction of minor children. The court with this jurisdi[ction] _____ case # _____

7. The wife ☒ is not p[regnant] and the estimated date of birth is _____

8. There ☒ is ☐ is no property to be divided; ☐ division of property is controlled by the parties' prenuptial agreement attached as exhibit 1.

TBP 1a (1/16) **COMPLAINT FOR DIVORCE, 1st extension page to MC 01**

IF YOU HAVE A PRENUPTIAL AGREEMENT, CHECK THIRD BOX IN PARAGRAPH 8, MAKE PHOTOCOPIES OF THE AGREEMENT, WRITE EXHIBIT 1 AT TOP OF EACH, AND ATTACH COPIES TO ORIGINAL TBP 1 AND ALL COPIES

STATE OF MICHIGAN Circuit Court - Family Division COUNTY	COMPLAINT FOR DIVORCE	CASE NO.

Plaintiff: _____ v **Defendant:** _____

☐ 9. I request an ex parte order for:

☐   a. custody   legal custody to: ☐ plaintiff ☐ defendant ☐ joint

                physical custody to: ☐ plaintiff ☐ defendant ☐ joint

☐   b. parenting time ☐ reasonable ☐ specific

       c. establishing residences of children

       d. support for children

☐ 10. I request an opt-out from the following friend of the court services: ☐ all friend of the court services ☐ all friend of the court services except collection and distribution of support through the SDU ☐ immediate income withholding only

11. I request a judgment of divorce, and:

       a. property   ☒ award to each party the property in his/her poss...

                ☒ divide

☒   b. change wife's last name to _ALBRIGHT_

☐   c. custody   legal custody to: ☒ plaintiff ☐ defendant ☐ joi...

                physical custody to: ☒ plaintiff ☐ defendant ☐ joi...

       d. parenting time: ☒ reasonable ☐ specific

       e. establish residences of children

       f. support for: ☒ children ☐ plaintiff ☐ defendant

       plaintiff/defendant earns_____ month_____and needs support

       plaintiff/defendant earns_____and can pay support

☐   g. other:

I declare that the information in my complaint is true to the best of my information, knowledge and belief.

Date_2-28-2009_   Plaintiff_Darlene A. Lovelace_

TBP 1b (1/16)   **COMPLAINT FOR DIVORCE, 2nd extension page to MC 01**

Callout notes:

IF YOU WANT TO SEEK INTERIM RELIEF, WHICH IS OPTIONAL, CHECK BOX AT PARAGRAPH 9 AND BOXES AT a AND b TO MATCH THE RELIEF YOU SEEK

YOU REQUEST NEW CASE OPT-OUTS HERE, SEE APPENDIX C ABOUT OPTING OUT

USE IF WIFE WANTS A NAME CHANGE

CHECK IF YOU HAVE ALREADY DIVIDED SOME OR ALL PROPERTY

CHECK BOX AND ADD INCOME INFORMATION IF YOU SEEK SPOUSAL SUPPORT (ALIMONY)

Approved, SCAO

Original - Friend of the court
1st copy - Plaintiff/Attorney
2nd copy - Defendant/Attorney

STATE OF MICHIGAN JUDICIAL CIRCUIT COUNTY	VERIFIED STATEMENT AND APPLICATION FOR IV-D SERVICES	CASE NO.

1. Mother's last name	First name	Middle name	2. Any other names by which mother is or has been known
LOVELACE	DARLENE	ANN	

3. Date of birth	4. Social security number	5. Driver's license number and state
5-1-1985	380-16-1010	L650 603 440 886 MICH

6. Mailing address and residence address (if different)
121 S. MAIN, LAKE CITY, MI 48800

7. E-mail address
dalovelace@mtran.com

8. Eye color	9. Hair color	10. Height	11. Weight	12. Race	13. Scars, tattoos, etc.
BLUE	BLONDE	5'6"	120	WHITE	

14. Home telephone no.	15. Work telephone no.	16. Maiden name	17. Occupation
772-0000	772-0011	ALBRIGHT	WAITRESS

18. Business/Employer's name and address	19. Gross weekly income
10,000 PANCAKES, 111 M-78, LAKE CITY, MI 48800	$250

20. Has mother applied for or does she receive public assistance? If yes, please specify kind.	21. DHS case number
☐ Yes ☒ No	

22. Father's last name	First name	Middle name	23. Any other names by which father is or has been known
LOVELACE	DUDLEY	ERNEST	

24. Date of birth	25. Social security number	26. Driver's license number and state
6-15-1984	379-10-5567	L649 601 402 201 MICH

27. Mailing address and residence address (if different)
900 S. MAPLE, LAKE CITY, MI 48800

28. E-mail address
delovelace@mtran.com

29. Eye color	30. Hair color	31. Height	32. Weight	33. Race	34. Scars, tattoos, etc.
BROWN	BLACK	6'	170	WHITE	

35. Home telephone no.	36. Work telephone no.	37. Occupation
773-3004	773-0011	SALESMAN

38. Business/Employer's name and address	39. Gross weekly income
WATERBED WORLD, 1000 SERVICE ROAD, LAKE CITY, MI 48800	$375

40. Has father applied for or does he receive public assistance? If yes, please specify kind.	41. DHS case number
☐ Yes ☒ No	

42. a. Name of Minor Child Involved in Case	b. Birth Date	c. Age	d. Soc. Sec. No.	e. Residential Address
DUANE WESLEY LOVELACE	6-1-2006	2	466-10-1001	121 S. MAIN, LAKE CITY, MI 48800
DARRYL WENDELL LOVELACE	7-1-2007	1	469-00-4411	" " "

43. a. Name of Other Minor Child of Either Party	b. Birth Date	c. Age	d. Residential Address

44. Health care coverage available for each minor child

a. Name of Minor Child	b. Name of Policy Holder	c. Name of Insurance Co./HMO	d. Policy/Certificate/Contract/Group No.
DUANE WESLEY LOVELACE	DUDLEY E. LOVELACE	LAKEVIEW HMO	2206-8978-24
DARRYL WENDELL LOVELACE	"	"	"

45. Names and addresses of person(s) other than parties, if any, who may have custody of child(ren) during pendency of this case

If any of the public assistance information above changes before your judgment is entered, you are required to give the friend of the court written notice of the change.
☒ I request support services under Title IV-D of the Social Security Act.

I declare that the statements above are true to the best of my information, knowledge, and belief.

2-28-2009
Date

Darlene A. Lovelace
Signature

FOC 23 (3/13) **VERIFIED STATEMENT AND APPLICATION FOR IV-D SERVICES**

MCR 3.206(B)

Original - Court
1st copy - FOC (if applicable)
2nd copy - Defendant/Respondent
3rd copy - Plaintiff/Petitioner

Approved, SCAO

STATE OF MICHIGAN JUDICIAL CIRCUIT PROBATE COURT COUNTY	UNIFORM CHILD CUSTODY JURISDICTION ENFORCEMENT ACT AFFIDAVIT	CASE NO.

Court telephone no.

Court address

CASE NAME: *LOVELACE V. LOVELACE*

1. The name and present address of each child (under 18) in this case is:

   DUANE WESLEY LOVELACE   *121 S. MAIN, LAKE CITY, MI 48800*

   DARRYL WENDELL LOVELACE   "   "

2. The addresses where the child(ren) has/have lived within the last 5 years are:

   SAME AS ABOVE

3. The name(s) and present address(es) of custodians with whom the child(ren) has/have lived within the last 5 y

   DARLENE A. LOVELACE   *121 S. MAIN, LAKE CITY, MI 48800*

   DUDLEY E. LOVELACE   *900 S. MAPLE,*   "

4. I do not know of, and have not participated (as a party, witness, or in any other capacity) in any other court proceeding (including divorce, separate maintenance, separation, neglect, abuse, dependency, gua termination of parental rights, and protection from domestic violence) concerning the custody or parenting time of in this state or any other state, **except:** Specify case name and number, court name and address, and date of child custody de

5. I do not know of any pending proceeding that could affect the current child custody proceeding, including a proceeding for enforcement or a proceeding relating to domestic violence, a protective order, termination of parental rights, or adoption, in this state or any other state, **except:** Specify case name and number, court name and address, and nature of the proceeding.

   That proceeding ☐ is continuing.   ☐ has been stayed by the court.
   ☐ Temporary action by this court is necessary to protect the child(ren) because the child(ren) has/have been subjected to or threatened with mistreatment or abuse or is/are otherwise neglected or dependent. Attach explanation.

6. I do not know of any person who is not already a party to this proceeding who has physical custody of, or who claims rights of legal or physical custody of, or parenting time with, the child(ren), **except:** State name(s) and address(es) of each person

7. The child(ren)'s "home state" is ___MICHIGAN___ . See back for

☐ 8. I state that a party's or child's health, safety, or liberty would be put at risk by the disclosure of this id

I have filled this form out completely, and I acknowledge a continuing duty to advise this court of any procee any other state that could affect the current child-custody proceeding.

Darlene A. Lovelace   *DARLENE A. LOVELACE*   *121 S. MAIN, LAKE CITY, MI*
Signature of affiant   Name of affiant (type or print)   Address of affiant

Subscribed and sworn to before me on _*2-28-2009*_ , _*OJIBWAY*_ County, Michigan.
                                       Date

My commission expires: _*1-1-2010*_   Signature: *Loretta Smiley*
                        Date

Notary public, State of Michigan, County of _*OJIBWAY*_   MCL 722.1206, MCL 722.1209

MC 416 (3/08) **UNIFORM CHILD CUSTODY JURISDICTION ENFORCEMENT ACT**

[Speech bubble:] IF YOU HAVE TO ANSWER EITHER OF THESE PARAGRAPHS, SEE "SPECIAL NOTICE TO A PRIOR COURT" IN APPENDIX E

[Speech bubble:] IF YOU HAVE TO ANSWER THIS PARAGRAPH, SEE "SPECIAL NOTICE TO A THIRD PARTY WITH CUSTODY" IN APPENDIX E

[Speech bubble:] NOTARY PUBLIC WILL COMPLETE THIS SECTION

STATE OF MICHIGAN THIRD JUDICIAL CIRCUIT WAYNE COUNTY | **CERTIFICATE ON BEHALF OF PLAINTIFF REGARDING EX PARTE INTERIM SUPPORT ORDER** | **CASE NO.**

PLAINTIFF'S NAME

REVIEW BOTH SIDES OF THIS FORM BEF

IF YOU ARE **NOT** PRESENTING AN EX PARTE ORDER, C
IF YOU ARE PRESENTING AN EX PARTE ORDER, COMPL
PLEASE PUT A LARGE 'X' ACROSS THE SIDE YOU AR

_X_ **I AM NOT PRESENTING AN EX PARTE INTERIM SUPP** TO THE
FOLLOWING REASON(S): (CHECK THE REASON(S) T

____ 1. A prior order for support of the minor child/children is i

Name of County _____ se Number _____

____ 2. The non-custodial party is not the parent of the c children named in the complaint and the complaint so states.

____ 3. The Court lacks personal jurisdiction over the endant because the whereabouts of the Defendant are unknown. Service will be by publication.

____ 4. The parties are presently residing together and the child/children are being adequately supported and there is no public assistance or application for public assistance pending.

_X_ 5. I am the custodial parent and the other party is providing appropriate support for the child/children and there is no public assistance or pending application for public assistance pending.

____ 6. The child/children are receiving Social Security Dependant Benefits as support.

____ 7. The non-custodial parent is unemployed, receives Public Assistance or Supplemental Security Income (SSI) and has no other source of income. A request for a Friend of the Court child support investigation has been made.

____ 8. The ability of the non-custodial parent to provide support for the minor child/children has not been determined. A motion for a temporary child support order has been filed.

____ 9. Other _____

I CERTIFY THAT THE ABOVE INFORMATION IS CORRECT TO THE BEST OF MY KNOWLEDGE.

DATE _2-28-2009_ _DARLENE LOVELACE_ | _Darlene Lovelace_ P _____
Attorney's or Party's Printed Name/Signature

Address _121 S. MAIN_ _____

City _LAKE CITY_ ____ State _MI_ ___ Zip Code _48800_ ___ Telephone _(517) 772-0000_

sign and serve the original of this certificate, the complaint (or counter-claim 600.659 custody affidavit upon the Court, the County Clerk, the Friend of ED STATEMENT - FRIEND OF THE COURT' MUST BE S OTHER PARTY. DO NOT GIVE THE COUNTY CLERK

t with a copy of the **PROOF OF SERVICE** setting forth th been served upon the other party.

[Speech bubble:] IF YOU'RE NOT SEEKING INTERIM RELIEF IN FORM OF EX PARTE ORDER, X-OUT FRONT SIDE OF FORM, CHECK FIRST LINE, AND LINES 1-9, AS THEY APPLY, EXPLAINING WHY YOU'RE SKIPPING INTERIM RELIEF.

[Speech bubble:] OR IF YOU ARE SEEKING AN EX PARTE ORDER FOR INTERIM RELIEF, X-OUT THE REVERSE OF FORM, CHECK LINE IN FIRST PARAGRAPH, DESCRIBE CUSTODY IN SECOND PARAGRAPH, CHECK LINES IN REMAINING PARAGRAPHS, AND FILL OUT BOTTOM.

[Speech bubble:] USE THIS FORM IN WAYNE COUNTY ONLY

2 Service

Your divorce affects more than just you, so others are entitled to know about it. In a divorce with minor children, the following persons must get notice of the divorce:

- friend of the court
- prosecuting attorney
- defendant

Whether you realize it or not, the friend of the court and prosecuting have already received notice when you earmarked copies of the initial divorce papers with "FOC" and "Pros. Atty." and filed them with the clerk. If you somehow neglected to do that, you should go back to the clerk's office and file the missing papers.

Serving the Defendant

Due process requires that the defendant receive notice of the divorce so s/he can respond to it. Notice to defendants is provided by serving copies of the initial divorce papers on them. You should begin service as soon as possible, within a few days after filing.

Although the purpose of service is notice, don't assume that you can skip it when the defendant already knows about the divorce. And don't try to serve the defendant by simply giving the divorce papers to him/her. No doubt your spouse would get informal notice of the divorce these ways. But the law requires that the defendant receive official notice of the divorce by service.

Official notice can only be accomplished by one of the service methods described below. With these methods, the court knows for sure that the defendant got notice of the divorce. For this reason, service is absolutely necessary. The service rules may seem artificial and even rather silly at times, but they must be followed carefully. If you omit service, or violate the service rules, there's a chance your whole divorce will be invalid.

There are three methods of serving defendants who are available to be served: 1) acknowledgment 2) mail 3) delivery. * Each method can be used anywhere in the state of Michigan. These service methods can also be used outside the state (including foreign countries), as long as there is Michigan jurisdiction over the nonresident defendant (see "Can I Get a Divorce in Michigan?" on page 43 for more about jurisdiction).

Despite service's wide reach, there are a few restrictions on serving papers. You, as a party to the case, are disqualified from serving the initial divorce papers yourself. Instead, you must have a neutral third party serve the papers for you. For service by delivery, a professional server, such as a sheriff or commercial process server, can serve for you. But when you choose service by acknowledgment or service by mail, you must enlist a helper (who can be any mentally competent adult), such as a friend, to help with service. The helper acts as a straw man through whose hands the divorce papers pass to the defendant.

Whichever service method you choose, you mustn't have the divorce papers served on a Sunday, an election day, or on the defendant while s/he is: 1) at, en route or returning from a court appearance 2) attending a religious worship service, going to or coming from the place of worship within 500 feet of the place. Michigan law provides immunity from service in all these situations.

Preparing for Service

The defendant must be served with papers listed below, which shall be referred to collectively as the "service papers:"

- Summons and Complaint   MC 01

- Complaint for Divorce   TBP 1

- Verified Statement and Application for IV-D Services   FOC 23

- Uniform Child Custody Jurisdiction Enforcement Act Affidavit   MC 416

- friend of the court pamphlet

★ interim relief papers, if relief has been obtained already (see Appendix B)

---

*   Since 2007, legal papers can also be served among parties to a lawsuit by email. However, the parties must first stipulate to this form of service and follow strict service rules. This makes email service unsuitable for service of the initial divorce papers and difficult for uncontested divorces where the defendant doesn't participate.

★ Waiver/Suspension of Fees and Costs   MC 20

✦ Certificate on Behalf of Plaintiff Regarding Ex Parte
   Interim Support Order (in Wayne County only)

✦ a sheet of caption labels (in Oakland and Wayne Counties only)

   After the defendant is served with these papers, service must be proved
in a proof of service. Each method of service (acknowledgment, mail, delivery)
is proved differently. But all are proved in the Proof of Service on the reverse of
your extra copy of the Summons and Complaint (MC 01). This paper will be
referred to as the "proof of service copy of the Summons and Complaint (MC
01)." After service, you file it with the clerk so that your case file shows that the
defendant was served.

Service by Acknowledgment

Service by acknowledgment is the simplest method of service. To use this
method, you need the cooperation of the defendant and the assistance of a
helper. If the defendant is in another county or state, you must find someone
there to act as your helper.
   Service is accomplished by having the helper hand the service papers
to the defendant. You may be present during the transfer, but the helper, not
you, must be the one who actually hands the service papers to the defendant.
The day of service is the day the defendant receives the service papers from the
helper.

Proving Service by Acknowledgment

Immediately after service, the helper should have the defendant date (with time
and day) and sign the Acknowledgment of Service, which is at the bottom of
the reverse of your proof of service copy of the Summons and Complaint (MC
01). Make three copies of this paper, earmark one "FOC" and save another for
filing later as your proof of service.

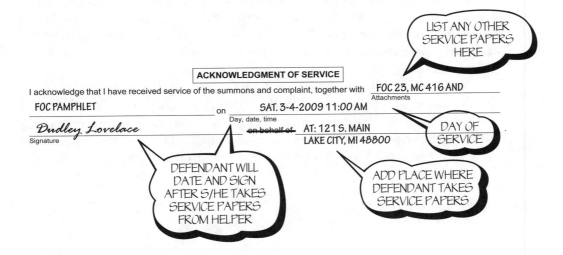

Service by Mail

Service by mail is a little more expensive than service by acknowledgment. But it's a very effective method of service because it goes anywhere U.S. mail is delivered—even overseas. The court rules permit service by mail through either registered or certified mail. Because certified mail is cheaper than registered mail, certified mail is the best choice.

More Information

Service by mail can be carried out by certified mail inside the United States, its territories and possessions, and to military APOs and FPOs.

For service by mail in foreign countries, ask the post office about recorded delivery, which is similar to domestic certified mail and offers restricted delivery and return receipt services. The Recorded Delivery Receipt (PS Form 8099) explains this type of delivery. Recorded delivery with full restricted delivery and return receipt services isn't available in all countries.

These days, return receipt service is available in two varieties: 1) by mail using the hardcopy Domestic Return Receipt (PS Form 3811) 2) electronically by fax or email notification. Despite these options, for now stick with the old receipt-by-mail system using the PS Form 3811 since courts are used to seeing this form as part of the proof of service by mail.

When you serve by mail, you need the assistance of a helper and the U.S. Postal Service. Your helper mails the service papers to the defendant and the postal service delivers these to him/her by certified mail.

To prove service, you need several special services available with certified mail: 1) restricted delivery 2) return receipt service. By restricting delivery, the service papers are delivered only to the defendant personally or someone s/he has designated in writing to receive mail. The return receipt provides proof of who received the papers, the date of delivery and the address of delivery only if this is different from the address on the envelope. This receipt becomes a key part of the proof of service.

Before you have the service papers mailed, prepare the mailing by placing your service papers in an envelope addressed to the defendant with your helper's name and address as the return address. In addition, you or your helper must prepare two certified mail forms: 1) Certified Mail Receipt (PS Form 3800) 2) Domestic Return Receipt (PS Form 3811), which are available at any post office.

On the PS Form 3800, fill in the defendant's name and address at the bottom of the form. For the PS Form 3811, write your helper's name and address on the front of the card, and on the reverse complete boxes #1-4. In section #2, transfer the article number from the PS Form 3800. In section #3, check the certified mail box, and ask for restricted delivery in #4.

After you complete the postal forms, peel off the plastic strips on the ends of the PS Form 3811 and attach the card to the envelope (there probably won't be room on the front of the envelope, so attach it to the reverse side). On the front of the envelope, to the left of the defendant's address and below your helper's return address, write "Restricted Delivery" and "Return Receipt Requested" on the envelope. By making these notations (the PS Form 3800 calls this "endorsement"), you will remind the letter carrier to restrict delivery and provide a receipt.

Have your helper take the envelope containing the service papers, with the Domestic Return Receipt (PS Form 3811) attached, the Certified Mail Receipt (PS Form 3800) and money to pay for the mailing to a post office window. The helper should ask the postal clerk to mail the envelope by certified mail with the special services you have checked on the PS Form 3811. The

clerk will prepare the certified mailing and return a postmarked Certified Mail Receipt (PS Form 3800) to your helper. Keep this receipt for your records.

Later, a letter carrier will deliver the mailing to the defendant, get his/her name (printed), signature and other delivery information on the reverse of the Domestic Return Receipt (PS Form 3811). Within a few days, your helper should get the PS Form 3811 back in the mail. You can then have your helper prove the service as described below. The day of service is the day the defendant receives the mailing from the letter carrier.

If your helper gets the whole envelope back, instead of the Domestic Return Receipt (PS Form 3811) alone, service by mail has failed. The defendant may have refused to accept the mailing, wasn't home or has moved without leaving a current forwarding order. Whatever the case, you will have to abandon service by mail because it only works when the defendant is ready and willing to take the certified mailing from the letter carrier. If service by mail fails, try service by delivery instead.

PROOF OF SERVICE	SUMMONS AND COMPLAINT Case No.

TO PROCESS SERVER: You are to serve the summons and complaint not later than 91 days from the date of filing or the date of expiration on the order for second summons. You must make and file your return with the court clerk. If you are unable to complete service you must return this original and all copies to the court clerk.

CERTIFICATE / AFFIDAVIT OF SERVICE / NONSERVICE

☐ **OFFICER CERTIFICATE**   **OR**   ☒ **AFFIDAVIT OF PROCESS SERVER**

I certify that I am a sheriff, deputy sheriff, bailiff, appointed court officer, or attorney for a party (MCR 2.104[A][2]), and that: (notarization not required)

Being first duly sworn... competent adult who is not... party, and that: (notariz...

(speech bubble: LIST ANY OTHER SERVICE PAPERS HERE)

☐ I served personally a copy of the summons and complaint,
☒ I served by registered or certified mail (copy of return receipt attached) a copy of the summons and complaint,
together with ___FOC 23, MC 416 AND FOC PAMPHLET___
List all documents served with the Summons and Complaint

_____ on the defendant(s):

Defendant's name	Complete address(es) of service	Day, date, time
DUDLEY E. LOVELACE	900 S. MAPLE, LAKE CITY, MI 48800	SAT. 3-4-2009

(speech bubble: GET DATE FROM PS FORM 3811)

(speech bubble: DAY OF SERVICE)

☐ I have personally attempted to serve the summons and complaint, together with any... following defendant(s) and have been unable to complete service.

Defendant's name	Complete address(es) of service	Day, date, time

I declare that the statements above are true to the best of my information, knowledge, and belief.

Ruth Darling
Signature
RUTH DARLING
Name (type or print)

Service fee	Miles traveled	Mileage fee	Total fee
$		$	$

Title

Subscribed and sworn to before me on ___3-7-2009___ , ___OJIBWAY___ County, Michigan.
Date

My commission expires: ___1-1-2010___   Signature: _Loretta Smiley_
Date   Deputy court clerk/Notary public

Notary public, State of Michigan, County of ___OJIBWAY___

Proving Service by Mail

After your helper gets the Domestic Return Receipt (PS Form 3811) back in the mail, have him/her prove service on the reverse of your proof of service copy of the Summons and Complaint (MC 01). Complete the information about the service by mail under the Affidavit of Process Server, and have the helper sign the form before a notary public. As proof of the defendant's receipt of the mailing, staple the Domestic Return Receipt (PS Form 3811) to the reverse of your proof of service copy of the Summons and Complaint (MC 01). Make three copies of this paper, earmark one "FOC" and save another for filing later as your proof of service.

Service by Delivery

You can also obtain service by having someone deliver the service papers to the defendant. Any mentally competent adult except you can do that. If the defendant is cooperative, you could have a helper perform service by delivery for you. But in that case it would be much easier to have the defendant simply acknowledge delivery of the service papers from your helper and get service by acknowledgment. Therefore, it's likely that you will use service by delivery for defendants who live out of town or state, or are otherwise hard to serve.

Service by delivery is usually carried out by a professional server, such as a sheriff or commercial process server. Whatever other service options you have, county sheriff departments will always serve papers for you. They often have a separate division or deputy in charge of service. In small towns or rural areas, the sheriff may be the only choice for service. Larger cities usually have commercial process servers as an alternative to the sheriff.

Both types of servers charge fees for service. By law, sheriffs charge a base service fee, currently $23, plus mileage billed at 1½ times the state civil service rate for travel during service (the travel distance is the shortest route between the court issuing the summons and the place of service times two (for going and returning)).

These fees can add up, but a sheriff's service fee can be suspended if you get a fee exemption (see Appendix A for details). Even if you have to pay, sheriffs' service fees are normally cheaper than those of commercial process servers, who often charge around $30-50 for service. On the other hand, commercial process servers may be more persistent in finding and serving defendants.

Whomever you choose, you can often reduce the service fees by having the defendant pick up the service papers at the server's office. This saves the server's mileage fee. It also spares the defendant the possible embarrassment of being served with legal papers at home or work. If the defendant is willing, tell the server that the defendant will pick up the papers, and then have the defendant call the server to arrange for pick-up.

More Information

To find sheriffs, look under the county government section for the sheriff department in a telephone directory. For commercial process servers, use a telephone directory for the defendant's area and search under "Process Servers" in the yellow pages.

Or you can find both kinds of process servers through process server trade associations, which provide referrals:

Michigan Court Officer, Deputy Sheriff & Process Servers Association (MCODSA) at (800) 992-4845 or www.mcodsa.com

National Association of Professional Process Servers (NAPPS) at (800) 477-8211 or www.napps.org

United States Process Servers Association (USPSA) at (314) 645-1735 or www.usprocessservers.com

To obtain service by delivery in your area, take the service papers along with your proof of service copy of the Summons and Complaint (MC 01) to the server and ask for service on the defendant. The server will serve the defendant at the address in the captions of your papers. If the defendant can be found at another place, tell the server about the other address.

When the defendant lives in another county or state, you must find a server nearby. After you find one, mail the service papers and your proof of service copy of the Summons and Complaint (MC 01) to the server. Enclose a note asking for service and return of a proof of service (see also "Fees" on page 77 about prepaying an out-of-town server's service fee).

When you're seeking service outside the state of Michigan, you should mention in your note that the server must prove service in the Affidavit of Process Server, on the reverse of the proof of service copy of the Summons and Complaint (MC 01). An out-of-state process server must use the affidavit, instead of the Officer Certificate, because only Michigan court officers (such as Michigan sheriffs and their deputies) may use the certificate. In addition, ask the process server to have the notary public affix a seal on the affidavit, since documents with out-of-state notarizations must be sealed.

If all goes as planned, the server will find the defendant and deliver the service papers to him/her. The day of service is the day the server delivers the service papers to the defendant.

Proving Service by Delivery

After service, the server will prove service on the reverse of the proof of service copy of the Summons and Complaint (MC 01) that you gave the server. For service by Michigan court officers, the proof of service will appear in the Officer Certificate; all other servers must use the Affidavit of Process Server.

After service is proved, the server will return your proof of service copy of the Summons and Complaint (MC 01) to you. Make three copies of this paper, earmark one "FOC" and save another for filing later as your proof of service.

Service Problems

In most cases, service by any of the three regular service methods goes smoothly. But certain service methods are best for particular defendants, such as prisoners and military servicemembers. And sometimes you may even have to use alternate service if a defendant is difficult to serve.

Serving Prisoners and Military Servicemembers

Service by mail seems to work best on incarcerated defendants. See "What If My Spouse or I Am Imprisoned?" on page 46 for tips on serving prisoners by mail. Service by mail is also the most effective way to serve military servicemembers, for reasons explained in "What If My Spouse or I Am in the Military?" on page 48.

SUMMONS AND COMPLAINT

PROOF OF SERVICE

TO PROCESS SERVER: You are to serve the summons and complaint not [...] filing or the date of expiration on the order for second summons. You must make and file your retu[...] able to complete service you must return this original and all copies to the court clerk.

(speech bubble) COMMERCIAL OR OUT-OF-STATE SERVERS MUST USE AFFIDAVIT

CERTIFICATE / AFFIDAVIT OF SERVICE

(speech bubble) LIST ANY OTHER SERVICE PAPERS HERE

☒ **OFFICER CERTIFICATE**	**OR**	☐ **AFFIDA[...] SERVER**
I certify that I am a sheriff, deputy sheriff, bailiff, appointed court officer, or attorney for a party (MCR 2.104[A][2]), and that: (notarization not required)		Being first duly sworn, I state that I am [...]ally competent adult who is not a party[...] and that: (notarization re[...]

☒ I served personally a copy of the summons and complaint,
☐ I served by registered or certified mail (copy of return receipt attached) a copy of the s[...]
together with ___ *FOC 23, MC 416 AND FOC PAMPHLET* ___
List all documents served with the Summons and Complaint

_____ — on the defendant(s):

Defendant's name	Complete address(es) of service	Day, date, time
DUDLEY E. LOVELACE	*200 N. MAIN, LAKE CITY, MI 48800*	*SAT. 3-4-2009* *11:00 AM*

(speech bubble) SERVER WILL COMPLETE THESE BOXES

(speech bubble) DAY OF SERVICE

☐ I have personally atte[...] [summon]s and complaint, together with any attachments, on the following defendant(s) and have been unabl[...]

Defendant's name	Complete address(es) of service	Day, date, time

I declare that the statements above are true to the best of my information, knowledge, and belief.

Service fee	Miles traveled	Mileage fee	Total fee
$ 21		$	$ 21

Chester Gunn
Signature
CHESTER GUNN
Name (type or print)
OJIBWAY COUNTY DEPUTY SHERIFF
Title

Subscribed and sworn to before me on _____ , _____ County, Michigan.
                                              Date

My commission expires: _____   Signature: _____
                            Date   Deputy court clerk/Notary public

Notary public, State of Michigan, County of _____

Alternate Service

The regular methods of service work only if the defendant is available for service. But if the defendant is elusive (avoiding service) or has disappeared, you must resort to some form of alternate service. Appendix D has complete instructions and forms for serving elusive or disappeared defendants.

If you're convinced you need alternate service, don't wait too long to seek it. The summons in the Summons and Complaint (MC 01) lasts for 91 days after it's issued (this expiration date should have been inserted by the clerk on the front of the summons). If you fail to complete service within that time, the summons will expire and the clerk will dismiss your case (see below for more about the danger of dismissal).

There is a way to ask the judge for a new summons before the old one expires, but it's a lot of bother. The better way is to use alternate service as soon as it becomes apparent that regular service methods aren't working.

Filing the Proof of Service

Whatever method of service you use, be sure to file the proof of service soon after service is completed. This is important because delay in filing the proof of service can result in dismissal of your divorce.

As mentioned above, a summons expires after 91 days. When there's no proof of service on file after 91 days, the clerk will assume that service has failed and begin dismissal of the case for "no progress." (The clerk should give advance warning of dismissal by sending you a Notice of Intent to Dismiss for No Progress (MC 26).) After dismissal for no progress, you can file a motion asking the judge to reinstate the case. But reinstatement isn't guaranteed, and the judge may deny the motion. In that case, you would have to refile your divorce and start over.

To avoid that trap, make sure that you file the proof of service quickly, well before the 91-day summons expiration period elapses. Take/send the proof of service, which is on the reverse of your proof of service copy of the Summons and Complaint (MC 01)*, plus three copies to the clerk. The clerk will file the original, take the friend of the court copy and return two copies to you.

Special Notice of Your Divorce

In the vast majority of divorces with minor children, the friend of the court, prosecuting attorney and defendant are the only ones entitled to notice of the divorce. But sometimes others may be entitled to special notice of the divorce. These include situations in which: 1) someone other than you or your spouse (a third party) has physical custody of your minor children 2) your minor child is subject to an ongoing case concerning the child's custody and/or parenting time. See Appendix E for more about these situations, and instructions and the form for giving special notice.

---

*   If alternate service was used, the proof of service is on the reverse of
either the MC 304 or MC 307.

1 Filing

Filed with the clerk during filing:

☐ Summons and Complaint   MC 01

☐ Complaint for Divorce   TBP 1

☐ Verified Statement and Application for IV-D Services   FOC 23

☐ Uniform Child Custody Jurisdiction Enforcement Act Affidavit   MC 416

☆ Waiver/Suspension of Fees and Costs   MC 20

✧ Certificate on Behalf of Plaintiff Regarding Ex Parte Interim
Support Order (in Wayne County only)

Requested from the clerk during filing (for use later):

☐ two friend of the court pamphlets

☐ Record of Divorce or Annulment   DCH-0838

✧ two sheets of caption labels (in Oakland and Wayne Counties only)

Filed with the clerk later, if interim relief has been obtained:

☆ Ex Parte Order   TBP 5

☆ Uniform Child Support Order   FOC 10/52

☆ Proof of Service of Order/Judgment Papers showing delivery
of the Domestic Relations Judgment Information form
(FOC 100) to the friend of the court   TBP 7

✧ Certificate of Conformity for Domestic Relations Order or
Judgment (in Wayne County only)   1225

**Filed with the clerk even later, if interim relief has been obtained, unless the
friend of the court does everything to start immediate income withholding:**

☆ Order Regarding Income Withholding   FOC 5

Symbols

☐ regular paper

☆ optional paper

✧ local paper

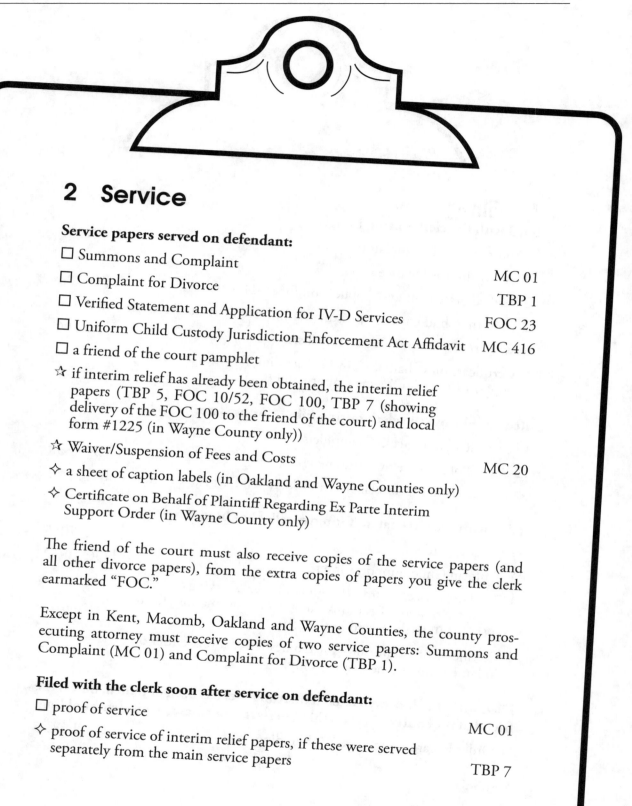

2   Service

Service papers served on defendant:

☐ Summons and Complaint

☐ Complaint for Divorce   MC 01

☐ Verified Statement and Application for IV-D Services   TBP 1

☐ Uniform Child Custody Jurisdiction Enforcement Act Affidavit   FOC 23

☐ a friend of the court pamphlet   MC 416

☆ if interim relief has already been obtained, the interim relief
papers (TBP 5, FOC 10/52, FOC 100, TBP 7 (showing
delivery of the FOC 100 to the friend of the court) and local
form #1225 (in Wayne County only))

☆ Waiver/Suspension of Fees and Costs

✧ a sheet of caption labels (in Oakland and Wayne Counties only)   MC 20

✧ Certificate on Behalf of Plaintiff Regarding Ex Parte Interim
Support Order (in Wayne County only)

The friend of the court must also receive copies of the service papers (and
all other divorce papers), from the extra copies of papers you give the clerk
earmarked "FOC."

Except in Kent, Macomb, Oakland and Wayne Counties, the county prosecuting attorney must receive copies of two service papers: Summons and
Complaint (MC 01) and Complaint for Divorce (TBP 1).

Filed with the clerk soon after service on defendant:

☐ proof of service

✧ proof of service of interim relief papers, if these were served
separately from the main service papers   MC 01

                                                                  TBP 7

PART II: Finishing Your Divorce

3 Default

You've filed the divorce and served notice of the case. After several weeks, you're ready for the final part of your divorce, which begins with the default.

A default is important because it means that the defendant isn't contesting the divorce. Until then, you're relying on the defendant's word that the divorce is agreeable. But with the default, your divorce becomes *officially* uncontested, making it impossible for the defendant to re-enter and contest the case without special permission from the court.

Although you may be anxious to get the default, you must wait and see if the defendant responds to your divorce complaint. S/he can respond by filing with the court and sending you either: 1) an Answer to your complaint 2) a motion objecting to the complaint. If the defendant does neither, you can go ahead and apply for a default from the clerk.

To avoid default, the defendant must respond in one of those two ways within the applicable answering period. All answering periods begin the day after the day of service (see "Time" on page 78 for more about computing time periods). The length of answering periods depends on the method of service. The chart on the next page depicts this.

Your copy of the proof of service, which you should have filed earlier, shows the day of service. Use that and the chart to figure the answering period in your case. If the defendant hasn't responded by the end of that answering period, you're ready to get the default.

Answering Periods

Method of service	Day of Service	Answering Period
Service by acknowledgment	Day defendant takes the service papers from helper.	21 days in Michigan or 28 days out of state
Service by mail	Day defendant takes the mailing of the service papers from letter carrier	28 days
Service by delivery	Day server delivers the service papers to defendant	21 days in Michigan or 28 days out of state
Alternate service:		
mailing	Day the service papers are sent	28 days
tacking	Day the service papers are tacked to door	28 days
household delivery	Day the service papers are delivered to person in defendant's household	28 days
publication	Day of final publication of advertisement	Set by judge in MC 307 (a minimum of 28 days after final publication date)
posting	Last day of posting period	Set by judge in MC 307 (a minimum of 28 days after last day of posting period)

Scheduling the Final Hearing

Although your divorce may only be a month or two old when you apply for the default, it's not too early to schedule the final hearing for your case. As required by law, you must appear in court at a final hearing to receive your divorce judgment. Final hearings in divorce cases are usually heard on special days, called motion days, which courts set aside each week or month. During these motion days, judges may hear many final hearings, often at 10- or 15-minute intervals. Nevertheless, judges' motion day schedules fill up quickly, so it's a good idea to schedule your final hearing at the time of the default. If you wait, you risk delaying the conclusion of your divorce.

As previously mentioned, Michigan imposes a six-month waiting period on divorce cases with minor children (see "How Long Will My Divorce Take?" on page 48 for more on statutory waiting periods). This means that at least six months must elapse between the day you filed your divorce (this date is stamped on your Summons and Complaint (MC 01)) and the day of your final hearing.

Although you may want to get your divorce over with sooner, you must observe the waiting period. So when you schedule your final hearing, set it for a day at least six months after the day you filed your divorce (see "Time" on page 78 for more about figuring time in months).

Courts use several methods to schedule final hearings in uncontested divorce cases. In many counties, you can schedule a final hearing orally. When you get the default, ask the clerk to schedule a final hearing sometime after the statutory waiting period has expired. The clerk will reserve a time for you on the judge's motion day schedule or calendar (make sure that you make a note of the time and date).

In other counties, you must file a written request for a final hearing. In Wayne County, for example, you must request a final hearing on a special request form known as a praecipe. Wayne County's praecipe is a yellow slip of paper called the At Issue Praecipe for Default Judgment in Domestic Relations Action (#1121), which is available from the clerk in room 201 of the Coleman A. Young Municipal Center (CAYMC) (formerly the City-County Bldg.) at 2 Woodward Ave. in Detroit. Several other counties also use praecipes or similar written forms. If your county is among them, ask the clerk for the particular form and use it as directed.

In some counties, such as Oakland, the clerk will schedule the final hearing for you. These counties typically have computerized case management systems that set final hearings automatically. After the hearing is set, a notice of the time and date will be sent to you.

As you can see, there is a great deal of variation when it comes to scheduling final hearings. In fact, there is probably more variation here than in any other part of divorce procedure. To find out the practice in your county, ask the clerk when you get the default.

After you schedule the final hearing, you must file a motion formally asking the court for a default judgment of divorce. The defendant must receive a copy of the motion which will include a notice of the place, date and time of the final hearing.

Getting the Default

When the defendant has failed to respond to your complaint within the applicable answering period, s/he has defaulted, allowing you to apply to the clerk for a default. The clerk declares or enters the default, but you must prepare the Default (TBP 2) form. You fill out the Request, Affidavit and (later after filing) Proof of Mailing sections. The middle Affidavit section must be signed by you before a notary public. During filing, the clerk will date and sign the Entry and Notice of Entry section of the TBP 2.

Default and the Military Relief Laws

More Information

With its enormous demands and responsibilities, active-duty military service isn't something you can easily keep secret. As a result, you should have personal knowledge (from observation of the defendant's activities and routines) about whether or not s/he is in the military.

But if the defendant is absent, disappeared or elusive, you may have to use the U.S. Department of Defense's Manpower Data Center (DMDC) to find out. The DMDC can tell you whether or not the defendant is in active-duty service in the U.S. military. You can contact the DMDC at:

Defense Manpower Data Center
Attn: Military Verification
1600 Wilson Blvd.
Suite 400
Arlington, VA 22209-2593
www.dmdc.osd.mil/appj/single_record.xhtml

You can request information from the DMDC about the defendant's (non)military status by mail or via the Internet. You need the defendant's full name and social security number and/or date/year of birth for a search. With either type of request, your goal is to receive a written DMDC "military status report" which you can attach to your Default (TBP 2) so the judge knows the defendant's (non)military status. There is no charge for a mail or Internet request.

A DMDC military status report should be: 1) *positive* indicating that the defendant is on active duty by giving his/her branch of service and date the active duty began 2) *negative* stating that it does not possess any information that the defendant is on active duty 3) *inconclusive* in rare cases when the data submitted was incomplete, faulty or resulted in multiple matches.

A Request for Military Status Report* form is included in this book for a request by mail. Fill in the form and mail it to the DMDC (enclose a self-addressed stamped envelope for the reply), and you should get a military status report back soon.

For an Internet request, go to the DMDC's Web site cited above. If you get a security warning, ignore it by clicking "continue to this website (not recommended)" (it won't hurt your computer). Select a single record request and fill in the data field. After a few seconds, you will get an on-screen military status report, which you must print so you have written evidence of the report.

*A related Military Locator Request form is used when you know the defendant is in U.S. military service and you want to find out where for service of the divorce papers or other reasons.

As you prepare the Default (TBP 2) you'll see some business in the Affidavit section about the defendant's possible service in the military. Why do you have to concern yourself with this issue when you get an uncontested divorce? It's necessary because of a pair of military relief laws (one federal and one state) that protect some defendant-servicemembers from hard-to-handle lawsuits, including divorces.

Appendix F has lots more about the military relief laws and their legal impact. In general, the laws provide lawsuit protection to *active-duty* servicemembers in the five branches (Army, Navy, Marine Corps, Air Force and Coast Guard) of the U.S. military and the two branches of the Michigan National Guard (Army National Guard and Air National Guard). See "Military Relief Laws" on page 227 for more about the scope of these laws.

Because of these military relief laws, in uncontested divorces you must determine whether or not the defendant is in active-duty military service (see the sidebox for advice about how to find this out). After you know (or don't know) the defendant's (non)military status, you can deal with the military relief laws during default as follows:

Defendant isn't in active-duty military service. You know for a fact (by personal knowledge or a negative military status report from the DMDC) that s/he isn't an active-duty servicemember. As a result, you can check the first indented box in paragraph #3a of the Default (TBP 2) to that effect. This will let the court know that the military relief laws don't apply to the defendant.

Defendant is in active-duty military service. In this scenario, you know (by personal knowledge or positive military status report from the DMDC) that s/he is in active-duty military service. You must check the second indented box in paragraph #3a of the Default (TBP 2). Before the divorce can go through, you must show how the military relief laws were satisfied (see "Satisfying the Military Relief Laws" on page 232 for more about ways to do this).

One easy way to satisfy these laws is to obtain a waiver of the laws' protections from the defendant.

You can get a waiver in the Appearance and Waiver of Military Relief Law Rights (TBP 6). In paragraph #3a of the Default (TBP 2), check the inside-the-paragraph box that defendant has appeared and waived all lawsuit relief rights, and attach the TBP 6 to the form. See "Waiver of Military Relief Law Rights by the Defendant" on page 232 for more about waiver.

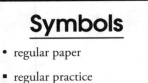

Symbols

- • regular paper
- ▪ regular practice
- ★ optional paper or practice
- ✦ local paper or practice

If the defendant didn't waive, you'll have to respond to the military relief the defendant has sought (stay issued, stay application denied, no response, etc.). Check the "other" box in paragraph #3a of the TBP 2 and say what happened in the blank line. For example, the defendant may have received a 90-day stay, which has now expired, allowing the divorce to go forward. "Satisfying the Military Relief Laws" on page 232 has more about stay applications and unresponsive defendants.

Defendant's (non)military status is unclear.   Sometimes, the defendant's (non)military status may be unclear. The defendant may be living far away, has disappeared or is elusive, so you don't know personally (hearsay (second-hand information) must be disregarded) whether s/he is in active-duty military service. Or maybe you know that the defendant is in the military, but aren't sure whether s/he is in active or inactive service (reservists frequently change status, especially during a call-up).

Try to clear up this uncertainty if you can. As explained in the sidebox, you should be able to use the DMDC to find out whether or not the defendant is in active-duty military service. You can then go forward under one of the scenarios described above.

But if for some reason your DMDC request results in an inconclusive military status report, check the box at #3b of the Default (TBP 2). The court will have to decide how to proceed when the defendant's military status is unknown. The SCRA (Servicemembers Civil Relief Act) provides several remedies in this situation, including requiring a bond from the plaintiff to protect the defendant's interests.

Applying for the Default from the Clerk

You can apply to the clerk for the default personally or by mail. Applying in person is best because you can also schedule the final hearing orally or by written request during the visit. Either way, when you apply for the default you should have:

- • Default   TBP 2
    - • original
    - • 3 copies (one earmarked "FOC")

- ★ special papers for dealing with a defendant-military servicemember, such as the Appearance and Waiver of Military Relief Law Rights (TBP 6) (see Appendix F)

- ✦ praecipe (if needed to schedule the final hearing)

While you're at the clerk office, it's often convenient to file the motion for a default judgment. You can do this if you are able to schedule a final hearing (orally or by praecipe) during your visit. Just in case, consider bringing the following motion materials with you when you file the default:

- Motion to Enter Default Judgment of Divorce (with caption-only completed)   TBP 3
    - original
    - 3 copies (one earmarked "FOC")

- $20 motion fee

At the clerk's office, say that you want to file a default. The clerk should do the following things:

- Take the Default (TBP 2) and the three copies and complete the Entry and Notice of Entry section of these papers. File the original Default (TBP 2), take the friend of the court's copy and return two copies to you.

★ File any special papers for dealing with a defendant-servicemember, take the friend of the court's copy and return two copies to you.

✦ After your oral or written request (by praecipe), schedule a final hearing for your case (unless you do it elsewhere or later).

If you can schedule a final hearing now, date, sign and complete paragraph #1 and the Notice of Hearing section in the Motion to Enter Default Judgment of Divorce (TBP 3) and copies at the clerk's office. The clerk will then:

- File the Motion to Enter Default Judgment of Divorce (TBP 3), take the friend of the court's copy and return two copies to you.

- Take the $20 motion fee.

As you fill out paragraph #1 of the Motion to Enter Default Judgment of Divorce (TBP 3), keep in mind what it says: You are seeking a divorce judgment granting the relief you asked for in paragraph #11 of your Complaint for Divorce (TBP 1). In fact, the relief you asked for in the complaint and the relief you plan to get in the judgment must match fairly closely so the defendant knows what the court is likely to order in the judgment. If they don't match up, you should check the box in paragraph #1 of the TBP 3 and describe the new or different relief in this paragraph. For example, you might not have asked for a name change in the complaint, but now want one. Or maybe you want to get out of the friend of the court system at the end of the divorce (open-case opt-out). These new or different items of relief should be described briefly on the blank line in paragraph #1.

After the Default

Despite the fact that the defendant is removed from the case when you get a default, s/he is entitled to notice about the default and default judgment. By getting this notice, the defendant can't complain later that s/he didn't know about the default or your request for a default judgment of divorce.

If you were able to file the Default (TBP 2) and Motion to Enter Default Judgment of Divorce (TBP 3) together, send copies of each to the defendant. If the defendant has disappeared, send the papers to his/her last known address.

Take the remaining copies of the forms and use these for proof of service. Fill out the Proof of Mailing sections showing when the papers were mailed to the defendant. Make two photocopies of these proof of service copies of the TBP 2 and 3 and earmark copies of each with "FOC." File/send to the clerk the original proof of service copies and friend of the court's copies, keeping one set for yourself.

You may not be able to schedule a final hearing when you file the default, and cannot file the motion for default judgment then. If so, send the Default (TBP 2) to the defendant and prove service as explained above. Later, after you get the final hearing date, complete and file with the clerk the Motion to Enter Default Judgment of Divorce (TBP 3), send a copy to the defendant and prove service, all as described above.

Typically, you will get the default and move for the default judgment two or three months into the divorce. The timing is mostly up to you, as long as it's after the answering period but not too late in the procedure.

STATE OF MICHIGAN Circuit Court - Family Division COUNTY	DEFAULT Request, Affidavit, Entry and Notice of Entry	CASE NO.

Plaintiff (appearing *in propria persona*):

v

Defendant:

INSERT DAY OF SERVICE

REQUEST

1. As shown by the pro____ __ file, defendant was served with a summons and complaint on ____3-4-2009____ , but did not respond to the complaint within 21 days (28 days if served by mail or out of state).

I request the clerk to enter the default of defendant for failure to plead or defend as provided by law.

Date___5-15-2009___   Plaintiff___*Darlene A. Lovelace*___

AFFIDAVIT

Plaintiff, being sworn, says:

2. Defendant is not a minor or an incompetent person.

3. Defendant's (non)military status:
    ☒ a. Based on ☒ my personal knowledge, ☐ attached military status report, defendant
       ☒ is not in active-duty military service
       ☐ is in active-duty military service, and ☐ has appeared and waived all lawsuit relief rights under the Servicemembers Civil Relief Act and/or MCL 32.517 (or similar military relief law from another state) in the attached appearance and waiver form.
       ☐ other:
    ☐ b. I am unable to determine whether or not defendant is in active-duty military service.

Date___5-15-2009___   Plaintiff___*Darlene A. Lovelace*___

Subscribed and sworn to before me on ___5-15-2009___ , ___OJIBWAY___ County, Michigan

My commission expires ___1-1-2010___   Signature___*Loretta Smiley*___

Notary public, State of Michigan, County of ___OJIBWAY___

PLAINTIFF MUST DATE AND SIGN AFFIDAVIT SECTION BEFORE A NOTARY PUBLIC

ENTRY AND NOTICE OF ENTRY

The default of defendant is entered for failure to plead or defend as provided by law.

Date ___5-16-2009___   County clerk ___*Martha Gee*___

TO DEFENDANT: Please take notice of this entry of default against you.

CLERK WILL DATE AND SIGN

PROOF OF MAILING

On the date below, I sent a copy of this Default to defendant by ordinary first-class mail at his/her address in the caption above, which is defendant's last known address.

I declare that the statement above is true to the best of my information, knowledge and belief.

Date___5-17-2009___   Plaintiff___*Darlene A. Lovelace*___

TBP 2 (1/16)   **DEFAULT, Request, Affidavit, Entry and Notice of Entry**

STATE OF MICHIGAN Circuit Court - Family Division COUNTY	MOTION TO ENTER DEFAULT JUDGMENT OF DIVORCE	CASE NO.

Plaintiff (appearing *in propria persona*):

Defendant:

v

1. After entry of defendant's default on ___5-16-2009___, I request the court to enter a default Judgment of Divorce granting the relief I requested in my Complaint for Divorce; ☐ and grant the following new/different relief _____

I declare that the statement above is true to the best of my information, knowledge and belief.

Date___5-16-2009___   Plaintiff___*Darlene A. Lovelace*___

INSERT FINAL HEARING INFORMATION HERE

NOTICE OF HEARING

A hearing on this motion will be held in the courtroom of the judge assigned to this case, located at (place) ___OJIBWAY COUNTY COURTHOUSE___ on (date) ___9-7-2009___ at (time) ___9:00 A.M.___

PROOF OF MAILING

On the date below, I sent a copy of this motion to defendant by ordinary first-class mail at his/her address in the caption above, which is defendant's last known address.

I declare that the statement above is true to the best of my information, knowledge and belief.

Date___5-16-2009___   Plaintiff___*Darlene A. Lovelace*___

TBP 3 (1/16)   **MOTION TO ENTER DEFAULT JUDGMENT OF DIVORCE**

Request for Military Status Report

TO:
Defense Manpower Data Center
Attn: Military Verification
1600 Wilson Blvd.
Suite 400
Arlington, VA 22209-2593

RE:
Case name _____LOVELACE v. LOVELACE_____
Case number___09-00501-DM_____
Full name of defendant_____DUDLEY ERNEST LOVELACE_____
Defendant's date of birth_____6-15-1984_____
Defendant's social security number____379-10-5567_____

    I am the plaintiff in the divorce case above seeking a default judgment of divorce against the defendant. I must know whether or not the defendant is currently in the active duty of the U.S. military service, to comply with the Servicemembers Civil Relief Act and/or Michigan Compiled Law 32.517 or a similar military relief law from another state.

    Please respond by providing a military status report on defendant as soon as possible. A self-addressed stamped envelope is enclosed for your response.

Date _3-15-2009_____

Signature _____Darlene A. Lovelace_____
Name _____DARLENE A. LOVELACE_____
Address _____121 S. MAIN_____
                 LAKE CITY, MI 48800_____
Telephone _(517) 772-0000_____

4 Waiting for Final Hearing

After filing, service and default, you must wait for your final hearing during the six-month statutory waiting period. You won't have to do much during the waiting period, but several important things can happen to you during the wait.

Friend of the Court Investigation

As mentioned in "Court System" on page 71, the friend of the court does several things during a divorce. One of the friend of the court's jobs is to investigate divorce cases and make recommendations about custody, parenting time, residence of children, child support and alimony. Judges may use these recommendations to decide divorce issues. The friend of the court's recommendations aren't binding on judges, but they're influential and often followed. Friend of the court investigations and recommendations are required in all contested divorce cases. In uncontested cases, they're optional. Nevertheless, many counties routinely use them in uncontested cases.

Ordinarily, the friend of the court will start the investigation. But in some counties, you must request it. If you haven't been contacted by the friend of the court within two or three months after filing your divorce, call and see if you must request an investigation.

The friend of the court is already familiar with your case because the clerk has given it copies of all your divorce papers. Even so, friends of the court need extra information for their investigations. To get more information, some friends of the court personally interview the parties. But since most don't have enough staff to hold interviews in every case, they often send questionnaires to the parties. Many use the Friend of the Court Case Questionnaire (FOC 39). This four-page questionnaire has questions about personal history, income, health care coverage and child care expenses. Your answers should give the friend of the court caseworker enough information to make recommendations about all the divorce issues.

After the investigation, the friend of the court prepares a recommendation on the divorce issues in a report. The report may be the Friend of the Court Support Recommendation (FOC 33) or it may be an informal letter on the friend of the court's letterhead. The friend of the court submits this report to the judge and sends copies to the parties.

Examine the friend of the court's report to see if it coincides with your and the defendant's position on the divorce issues. In most uncontested cases, the recommendations in the report should resemble your views on custody, parenting time, residence of children, child support and alimony. If they don't, you must be prepared to justify your position to the judge at the final hearing. If the difference between you and the friend of the court is small, you should be able to work out the difference. But if the difference is great, you might need a lawyer to get your views across.

Case Conference and Parenting Program

The friend of the court may not be the only one to intervene in your divorce during the waiting period. The clerk may send a notice asking you to attend a pretrial, scheduling or other conference about your case. These case conferences give the clerk a chance to find out more about the progress of cases. They also provide you with practical information about the court's final hearing and judgment procedures. Case conferences are designed for contested cases, but some counties also hold them for uncontested divorce cases.

If the clerk schedules a case conference for you, make sure you go because the court can dismiss your case if you don't attend. Case conferences are usually held in a conference room at the courthouse, not in a courtroom. The defendant probably won't show up, and this should add to the relaxed and informal atmosphere. Nevertheless, court personnel might use the conference to ask you about the case or have you complete a questionnaire about the progress of your case.

During this time, some counties may ask parents to attend programs or seminars designed to help families adjust to divorce. The SMILE (Start Making It Livable for Everyone) program is one of the most popular of these divorce-coping programs. Recently, there have been proposals to adopt these parenting programs statewide and make them mandatory in all divorces with children, but thus far these proposals have failed.

Prosecuting Attorney

Like the friend of the court, the prosecuting attorney knows about your divorce from the copies of the summons and complaint received during filing. Most prosecuting attorneys don't bother to intervene in divorces. But in some counties, the prosecuting attorney may file a paper, called an appearance, to show that s/he is aware of your divorce. In a few counties, the prosecuting attorney may also want to review your final divorce papers, particularly when the custodial parent is receiving FIP payments. Check with the friend of the court to see if this extra review is necessary in your county.

5 Final Hearing

The final hearing comes at the end of your divorce. This hearing is held in court before the judge assigned to your case. You must attend the hearing and give some brief testimony to get a Judgment of Divorce (TBP 4), which decides all the divorce issues. Your divorce becomes final immediately after the hearing, when the judgment is filed.

The final hearing requires careful preparation. You must prepare the final divorce papers several weeks in advance of the final hearing. Some of these papers must be given to the friend of the court and defendant before the hearing. Finally, you should plan the testimony required during your appearance at the final hearing. All these steps are explained below.

Preparing the Final Divorce Papers

About a month before the final hearing, prepare the final divorce papers. These include several judgment papers (Judgment of Divorce (TBP 4), uniform support order(s), maybe an Order Regarding Income Withholding (FOC 5), Domestic Relations Judgment Information form (FOC 100)) and a few other end-of-divorce papers.

Of these papers, the Judgment of Divorce (TBP 4) is by far the most important divorce paper. The judgment ends the marriage, awards custody, arranges parenting time, confirms children's residences, orders child support, divides property and deals with alimony. But the judgment doesn't stop there. The custody, parenting time, residence of children and child support provisions of the judgment continue until the youngest child becomes an adult. Hence, the Judgment of Divorce (TBP 4) may govern the lives of you, the defendant and your children far into the future.

The uniform support order(s) and Order Regarding Income Withholding (FOC 5) deal with support (child support and alimony), specifying the amount of support and taking care of other support-related issues. These topics used to be dealt with inside divorce judgments, but are now handled separately in these state-issued orders to achieve greater uniformity among support orders.

There are two kinds of uniform support orders: 1) Uniform Child Support Order (FOC 10/52) for child support 2) Uniform Spousal Support Order (FOC 10b) for alimony (spousal support). There are also alternate versions of both orders for cases that have totally or partially opted out of the friend of the court system: 1) Uniform Child Support Order, No Friend of Court Services (FOC 10a/52a) 2) Uniform Spousal Support Order, No Friend of Court Services (FOC 10c) (see Appendix C for more about using these alternate forms in opt-out cases).

Despite this choice of orders, in most divorces with minor children and friend of the court participation, the Uniform Child Support Order (FOC 10/52) is the only uniform support order that's used, so this is the one that will be cited. But keep in mind that other uniform support orders may be necessary when alimony is ordered or after a total or partial opt-out. Whichever uniform support orders are filed, the Judgment of Divorce (TBP 4b) refers to them in paragraph #17 and makes them part of the judgment.

The divorce judgment and child support order are orders of the court. Nevertheless, you must prepare these for the judge. Make four copies (one more than the usual three) of each paper and put these aside for the moment.

The Order Regarding Income Withholding (FOC 5) sets up automatic collection of support (child support and/or alimony) by immediate income withholding to the SDU, which, as explained in "Payment of Child Support" on page 24, is the normal way to pay support.

The Domestic Relations Judgment Information form (FOC 100) gives the friend of the court personal information about the parties and children. This information was once also included in divorce judgments, but is now kept separate in this form because of privacy concerns. Like the FOC 23, which also contains sensitive information, the FOC 100 goes to the friend of the court and parties, but isn't filed with the clerk (where it would become a public document).

You may have already filed a Domestic Relations Judgment Information form (FOC 100) at the beginning of the divorce if you got interim relief. If so, the one you prepare now can simply modify the previous form by showing any new information (the sample FOC 100 at the end of this section is a modification of a prior filing). On the other hand, if you skipped interim relief you must complete a full FOC 100 now, like the one on page 179.

Although the judgment papers are court orders, you must prepare them for the court. * The Judgment of Divorce (TBP 4) and Uniform Child Support Order (FOC 10/52) should reflect your and the defendant's informal agreement on the divorce issues. At the same time, the judgment should comply with the friend of the court's report on those issues. **

---

*   If income withholding is already in effect (from a pre-divorce family support case or an ex parte order issued during the divorce), you won't have to prepare another Order Regarding Income Withholding (FOC 5). In some counties, the friend of the court will prepare the FOC 5 for you; in others you must do this. Check with the friend of the court to find out the local policy.

**   See "Friend of the Court Investigation" on page 121 for what to do when the friend of the court's report conflicts with your views.

Besides the judgment papers described above, your final divorce papers include the Record of Divorce or Annulment (DCH-0838). You probably got this form from the clerk when you filed the divorce. If not, you can obtain it from the clerk any time. To prepare the Record of Divorce or Annulment (DCH-0838) for filing, answer questions #1-16 and #19-20.

In Wayne County only, you must prepare two extra papers: Certificate of Conformity for Domestic Relations Order or Judgment (1225) and Order Data Form-Support (FD/FOC 4002). The certification tells the judge that your divorce judgment and child support order satisfy all legal requirements and agree with the recommendations in the friend of the court's report. The data form paves the way for collection of support.

Approval of Final Divorce Papers by the Friend of the Court

Some counties want the friend of the court to review your final divorce papers to make sure everything is in order. If that's necessary in your county, submit the Judgment of Divorce (TBP 4), Uniform Child Support Order (FOC 10/52) and Order Regarding Income Withholding (FOC 5), if necessary, to the friend of the court a month before your final hearing. If the papers are satisfactory, the friend of the court will approve them orally or by signing the papers. If they're unsatisfactory, the friend of the court should suggest corrections (if you have to make corrections, make a new set of copies of the corrected papers).

In Wayne County, you don't need the friend of the court's approval if you can truthfully say in the Certificate of Conformity for Domestic Relations Order or Judgment (1225) that your judgment and child support order comply with the friend of the court's report. If they don't, you must get the Wayne County Friend of the Court's approval of those judgment papers.

Serving the Judgment Information Form on the Friend of the Court

The original Domestic Relations Judgment Information form (FOC 100) should be served on the friend of the court before the final hearing. If you're submitting your other judgment papers to the friend of the court for approval, include the FOC 100 also. If not, deliver or send the FOC 100 to the friend of the court separately.

Either way, after service prepare a Proof of Service of Order/Judgment Papers (TBP 7) proving service of the FOC 100 on the friend of the court. Proof of service on the friend of the court goes in paragraph #1 of the TBP 7. Save this paper to use during the next step.

Serving the Judgment Papers on the Defendant

You must send copies of the Judgement of Divorce (TBP 4) and Uniform Child Support Order (FOC 10/52) to the defendant at least 14 days before the final hearing. Prepare a mailing to send these papers to the defendant. Fill out paragraph #2b of the Proof of Service of Order/Judgment Papers (TBP 7) which you just used for the friend of the court. Send copies of the Judgment of Divorce (TBP 4), Uniform Child Support Order (FOC 10/52), Domestic

Relations Judgment Information form (FOC 100) and Proof of Service of Order/Judgment Papers (TBP 7) to the defendant at his/her last known address by the 14-day deadline.

Right after you mail these papers to the defendant, send/file the original Proof of Service of Order/Judgment Papers (TBP 7) to the clerk along with a copy of the form earmarked "FOC." This way, the proof of service will be in the court file by the final hearing so the judge can see it.

Preparing for Your Appearance at the Final Hearing

Before you appear in court for your final hearing, you may want to prepare the testimony for the hearing. Since you don't have a lawyer to question you during the hearing, you must give your testimony straight through, in a monologue. This is a little more difficult than testifying by answering questions. Therefore, you might find it helpful to plan your testimony beforehand.

One way you can do that is by using a script to organize your testimony. By preparing a testimony script, you should be able to memorize the bulk of your testimony. You can also take your testimony script with you to the final hearing and rely on it a bit if your memory fails while you're on the witness stand (using written materials to jog a witness' memory is called "refreshing the recollection" and is permitted by the rules of evidence).

Symbols

- regular paper
- regular practice
- ★ optional paper or practice
- ✦ local paper or practice

Luckily, the testimony you give during a final hearing is usually quite brief. In most cases, it's simply a repetition of the information contained in your divorce complaint, adding factual detail when necessary about the marital breakdown, custody, division of property, etc.

You give all the testimony for your hearing; you don't need any testimony from other witnesses, your children (most courts discourage attendance of children at divorce final hearings) or the defendant. The defendant will probably be absent; however, the defendant, even if defaulted, does have the right to attend the final hearing.

Having the defendant at the final hearing can be helpful to the judge. With the defendant present, the judge can ask him/her about special or complicated arrangements, such as:

- complicated property division, with the sale of a home or division of new property, such as retirement benefits, particularly after a marriage of long duration
- a lopsided property division with one spouse receiving the bulk of the property
- payment of alimony
- elaborate joint physical custody schedules
- change of the children's residence soon after the divorce
- opting out of the friend of the court system
- military issues, such as satisfaction of the military relief laws
- wife's name change

Before the Final Hearing

When you attend the final hearing, you must pay the $80 judgment fee (see "How Much Will My Divorce Cost?" on page 49 for more about this fee). It's also a good idea to bring your file with all your divorce papers to the final hearing. If you haven't kept a file, at least bring the following items:

- Judgment of Divorce   TBP 4
  - original
  - 3 copies (one earmarked "FOC")

- Uniform Child Support Order   FOC 10/52
  - original
  - 3 copies (one earmarked "FOC")

- Order Regarding Income Withholding   FOC 5
  - original
  - 3 copies (one earmarked "FOC")

- Proof of Service of Order/Judgment Papers   TBP 7
  - one copy (if you gave a FOC
    copy to the clerk earlier) or two
    copies (one earmarked "FOC,"
    if you still have the FOC copy to file)

- Record of Divorce or Annulment   DCH-0838

- $80 judgment fee

- testimony script

- ✛ Certificate of Conformity for Domestic Relations
    Order or Judgment (in Wayne County only)   1225
  - original
  - 3 copies (one earmarked "FOC")

- ✛ Order Data Form-Support (in Wayne County only)   FD/FOC 4002
  - original

Attending the Final Hearing

When you go to the courthouse for the final hearing, arrive early so you can take care of any final details. This is a good time to pay the judgment fee. Clerks often want you to check in with them to let them know that you are present and ready for the final hearing. In some counties, the clerk will give your case file to you to take to the courtroom. But in most counties the clerk will send the file to the courtroom ahead of time.

You should go to your judge's courtroom before the final hearing is scheduled to begin and wait in the visitor's section in back (see "Courthouse Appearances" on page 79 for more about how courts conduct hearings and how you should conduct yourself during a hearing in court). As your case is called, identify yourself, step forward and take a place at one of the tables. When the judge tells you to proceed, offer your judgment papers (Judgment of Divorce (TBP 4), Uniform Child Support Order (FOC 10/52) and Order Regarding Income Withholding (FOC 5)) to the judge, and say you're ready to give the testimony.

After you take the witness stand and are sworn in, give the testimony as you have planned it. If you omit something important, the judge may question you briefly to complete the testimony. When your testimony is finished, ask the judge to enter your divorce judgment as you've requested in the Motion to Enter Default Judgment of Divorce (TBP 3). If the judgment is satisfactory, the judge will sign the original Judgment of Divorce (TBP 4), Uniform Child Support Order (FOC 10/52), Order Regarding Income Withholding (FOC 5) and maybe some copies.

If the judge objects to your judgment papers, s/he should tell you what the problem is. It may be something you can fix on the spot. If not, ask the judge for an opportunity to correct the papers later. The court rules permit you to submit a corrected judgment to the judge within 14 days after the final hearing. If you get that chance, make any necessary modifications of your judgment papers and take these to the judge's office. S/he should sign the new papers there and you won't need another final hearing.

Filing the Final Divorce Papers

After the final hearing, file your final divorce papers with the clerk and pay the judgment fee (unless you paid the fee before the hearing). Filing the papers quickly is important because, according to paragraph #12 of the Judgment of Divorce (TBP 4a), your divorce only becomes final when you file the judgment. At that time, your marriage is ended and all the other provisions of the judgment take effect.

In a few counties, you can file your final divorce papers and pay fees with the courtroom clerk during the final hearing. But in most counties, you must return to the clerk's office, where the clerk will:

- File the Judgment of Divorce (TBP 4), take the friend of the court's copy and return two copies to you.

- File the Uniform Child Support Order (FOC 10/52), take the friend of the court's copy and return two copies to you.

- File the Order Regarding Income Withholding (FOC 5), take the friend of the court's copy and return two copies to you.

- You should have filed the original Proof of Service of Order/Judgment Papers (TBP 7) by mail before the final hearing and probably also sent a FOC copy to the clerk at that time. But if the friend of the court doesn't have a copy of the TBP 7 yet, the clerk will take the friend of the court's copy now.

- Take the Record of Divorce or Annulment (DCH-0838).

- Take the $80 judgment fee (unless you paid this fee before your final hearing began).

+ In Wayne County only, 1) file the Certificate of Conformity for Domestic Relations Order or Judgment (1225), take the friend of the court's copy and return two copies to you 2) take the Order Data Form-Support (FD/FOC 4002) for delivery to the Wayne County Friend of the Court along with the friend of the court's copy of the judgment.

Before you leave the clerk's office, you may want to obtain several *certified* copies of the Judgment of Divorce (TBP 4). These copies can be helpful in carrying out the judgment's property division or verifying a name change. See "After Your Divorce" on page 145 for more about these issues. Bring extra money for certified copies because the clerk charges $10 for issuing a certified copy plus $1 for each page of the document.

After the Final Hearing

Naturally, the defendant must know what the judgment papers, especially the Judgment of Divorce (TBP 4), say because these orders affect him/her. After the final hearing, the clerk should send the defendant a brief notice that a judgment was issued. However, the clerk doesn't send copies of the judgment papers themselves to the defendant along with this notice. That's your responsibility. You must serve the judgment papers on the defendant within seven days of the final hearing. To do that, send true copies of the Judgment of Divorce (TBP 4), Uniform Child Support Order (FOC 10/52) and Order Regarding Income Withholding (FOC 5) to the defendant by ordinary first-class mail at his/her last known mailing address.

After the mailing, prove service in the Proof of Service of Order/Judgment Papers (TBP 7). Make two copies of this form and earmark one "FOC." Then file/send the original and the friend of the court's copy to the clerk.

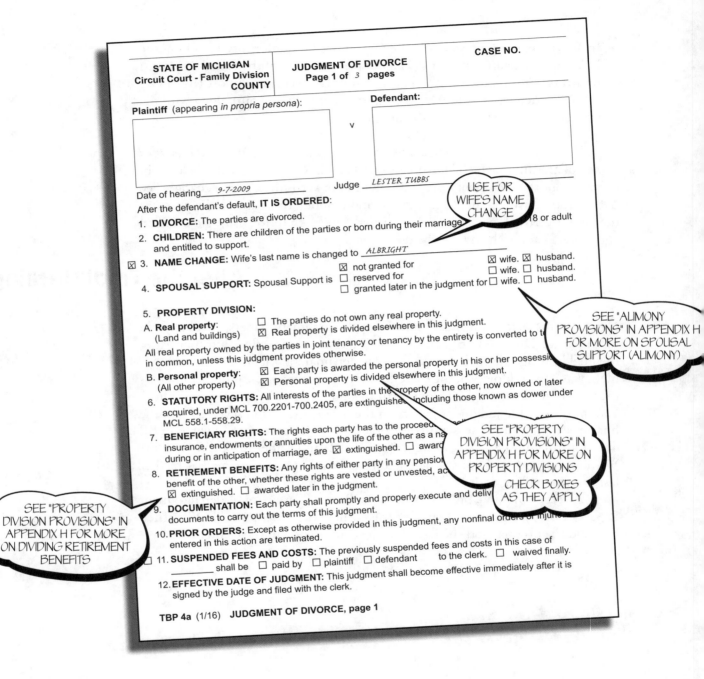

STATE OF MICHIGAN Circuit Court - Family Division COUNTY	JUDGMENT OF DIVORCE Page 1 of 3 pages	CASE NO.

Plaintiff (appearing *in propria persona*):

Defendant:

v

Date of hearing___9-7-2009___   Judge ___LESTER TUBBS___

USE FOR WIFE'S NAME CHANGE

After the defendant's default, **IT IS ORDERED**:

1. **DIVORCE:** The parties are divorced.

2. **CHILDREN:** There are children of the parties or born during their marriage [ ]18 or adult and entitled to support.

☒ 3. **NAME CHANGE:** Wife's last name is changed to ___ALBRIGHT___

4. **SPOUSAL SUPPORT:** Spousal Support is
   ☒ not granted for ☒ wife. ☒ husband.
   ☐ reserved for ☐ wife. ☒ husband.
   ☐ granted later in the judgment for ☐ wife. ☐ husband.

SEE "ALIMONY PROVISIONS" IN APPENDIX H FOR MORE ON SPOUSAL SUPPORT (ALIMONY)

5. **PROPERTY DIVISION:**

A. **Real property:**   ☐ The parties do not own any real property.
   (Land and buildings)   ☒ Real property is divided elsewhere in this judgment.
   ☒ Real property in joint tenancy or tenancy by the entirety is converted to t[...]

All real property owned by the parties in joint tenancy or tenancy by the entirety is converted to [...] in common, unless this judgment provides otherwise.

B. **Personal property:**   ☒ Each party is awarded the personal property in his or her possessi[...]
   (All other property)   ☒ Personal property is divided elsewhere in this judgment.

SEE "PROPERTY DIVISION PROVISIONS" IN APPENDIX H FOR MORE ON PROPERTY DIVISIONS

CHECK BOXES AS THEY APPLY

6. **STATUTORY RIGHTS:** All interests of the parties in the property of the other, now owned or later acquired, under MCL 700.2201-700.2405, are extinguishe[...] including those known as dower under MCL 558.1-558.29.

7. **BENEFICIARY RIGHTS:** The rights each party has to the procee[...] insurance, endowments or annuities upon the life of the other as a na[...] during or in anticipation of marriage, are ☒ extinguished. ☐ award[...]

8. **RETIREMENT BENEFITS:** Any rights of either party in any pensio[...] benefit of the other, whether these rights are vested or unvested, a[...] ☒ extinguished. ☐ awarded later in the judgment.

SEE "PROPERTY DIVISION PROVISIONS" IN APPENDIX H FOR MORE ON DIVIDING RETIREMENT BENEFITS

9. **DOCUMENTATION:** Each party shall promptly and properly execute and deliv[...] documents to carry out the terms of this judgment.

10. **PRIOR ORDERS:** Except as otherwise provided in this judgment, any nonfinal orders or inju[...] entered in this action are terminated.

☐ 11. **SUSPENDED FEES AND COSTS:** The previously suspended fees and costs in this case of _____ shall be ☐ paid by ☐ plaintiff ☐ defendant ___ to the clerk. ☐ waived finally.

12. **EFFECTIVE DATE OF JUDGMENT:** This judgment shall become effective immediately after it is signed by the judge and filed with the clerk.

TBP 4a (1/16)   **JUDGMENT OF DIVORCE, page 1**

STATE OF MICHIGAN
Circuit Court - Family Division
COUNTY

JUDGMENT OF DIVORCE
Page 2 of _3_ pages

CASE NO.

Plaintiff:

v

Defendant:

IT IS ALSO ORDERED:

13. **INALIENABLE RIGHTS OF CHILDREN:** The children have the right to the love and affection of both parents. The parties shall cooperate during child-rearing to promote the well-being of the children and maintain strong parent-child relationships. The parties must also cooperate in carrying out the child-related provisions of this judgment.

14. **CUSTODY:** Custody of the minor children is granted as follows:

PL = Plaintiff   DF = Defendant   JT = Joint   3rd = Third party, named here:

CHILD'S NAME	DATE OF BIRTH	LEGAL CUSTODY	PHYSICAL CUSTODY
DUANE WESLEY LOVELACE	6-1-2006	PL	PL
DARRYL WENDELL LOVE...	...7	PL	PL

(speech bubble) IF YOU WANT SPECIFIC PARENTING TIME, CHECK BOX AND SEE "PARENTING TIME PROVISIONS" IN APPENDIX H

(speech bubble) THIS IS SOLE CUSTODY; SEE "CUSTODY PROVISIONS" IN APPENDIX H FOR OTHER TYPES OF CUSTODY

15. **PARENTING TIME:** A... parent without physical custody shall have parenting time as follows:
☒ reasonable   ☐ specific (describe specific parenting time later in this judgment)

16. **RESIDENCE OF CHILDREN:**

a. **Local residences.** A parent whose custody of parenting time of a child is governed by this order shall not change the legal residence of the child except in compliance with section 11 of the ... Custody Act, MCL 722.31;   ☐   After an agreement of the parties according to the act, an _____, the residence of the following minor children:

Names_____

shall be changed from their current residence with   ☐ plaintiff   ☐ defendant

at_____

to_____

(speech bubble) YOU CAN CHANGE THE RESIDENCE OF CHILDREN HERE WITH THE AGREEMENT OF THE DEFENDANT

b. **State residence (domicile).** The minor children's residences (domicile) shall not be moved from the state of Michigan without the prior approval of the court.

c. **Notice of change of residence.** The person awarded custody shall promptly notify the friend of the court in writing when the minor is moved to another address.

17. **SUPPORT.** Child support and any spousal support is/are provided for in a uniform support order(s) which shall accompany and be incorporated into this judgment.
☐ (Instead of the paragraph above), ☐ child support ☐ spousal support is/are reserved until further order of this court, excusing filing of a uniform support order for that support now.

TBP 4b (1/16)   **JUDGMENT OF DIVORCE, page 2**

STATE OF MICHIGAN Circuit Court - Family Division COUNTY	JUDGMENT OF DIVORCE Final of 3 pages	CASE NO.

Plaintiff: v   **Defendant:**

IT IS ALSO ORDERED:

18.

19.

ETC.

> INCLUDE ADDITIONAL JUDGMENT PROVISIONS HERE AS NEEDED

> CHECK THESE BOXES TO CLOSE THE CASE

> JUDGE WILL DATE AND SIGN AT FINAL HEARING

...his judgment   ☒ resolves   ☐ does not resolve   the
...t pending claim in this case, and   ☒ closes   ☐ does
...t close   the case, except to the extent jurisdiction is
...etained by law.

Reviewed by FOC:

Date _9-7-2009_   Judge___*Lester Tubbs*___

TBP 4c (1/16)   **JUDGMENT OF DIVORCE, final page**

Approved, SCAO

Original - Court
1st copy - Plaintiff

2nd copy - Defendant
3rd copy - Friend of the court

STATE OF MICHIGAN	UNIFORM CHILD SUPPORT ORDER (PAGE 1)	CASE NO.
JUDICIAL CIRCUIT	☐ EX PARTE ☐ TEMPORARY	
COUNTY	☐ MODIFICATION ☒ FINAL	

Court address

Court telephone no.

Plaintiff's name, address, and telephone no.

v

Defendant's name, address, and telephone no.

Plaintiff's attorney name, bar no., address, and telephone no.

Defendant's attorney name, bar no., address, and telephone no.

Plaintiff's source of income name, address, and telephone no.

Defendant's source of income name, address, and telephone no.

[cloud callout: ADD SOURCES OF INCOME (EMPLOYERS) TO CAPTION]

This order is entered ☒ after hearing. ☐ after statutory review. ☐ on stipulation/consent of the parties.
☐ The friend of the court recommends child support be ordered as follows.
☐ If you disagree with this recommendation, you must file a written objection with _____
before **21 days** from the date this order is mailed. If you do not object, this proposed order will be presented to the court for entry. _____ on or
☐ Attached are the calculations pursuant to MCL 552.505(1)(h) and MCL 552.517b.

IT IS ORDERED, unless otherwise ordered in item 12 or 13:
1. **The children who are supported under this order and the payer and payee are:**   ☐ Standard provisions have been modified (see item 12 or 13):

Payer:	Payee:
DUDLEY E. LOVELACE	DARLENE A. LOVELACE

Children's names, birthdates, and annual overnights with payer:

Children's names	Date of birth	Overnights
DUANE W. LOVELACE	6-1-2006	48
DARRYL W. LOVELACE	7-1-2007	48

Effective ___9-7-2009___, the payer shall pay a monthly child support obligation for the children named above.

Children supported:	1 child	2 children	3 children	4 children	5 or more children
Base support: (includes support plus or minus premium adjustment for health-care insurance)					
Support:	$ 326	$ 349	$	$	$
Premium adjust.	$	$	$	$	$
Subtotal:	$ 326	$ 349	$	$	$
Ordinary medical:	$ 18	$ 36	$	$	$
Child care:	$	$	$	$	$
Other:	$	$	$	$	$
SS benefit credit:	$	$	$	$	$
Total:	$ 344	$ 385	$	$	$

☐ Support was reduced because payer's income was reduced.

[cloud callout: SEE "CHILD SUPPORT PROVISIONS" IN APPENDIX H FOR HOW TO FIGURE CHILD SUPPORT]

(Continued on page 2.)

FOC 10 / 52 (8/14) **UNIFORM CHILD SUPPORT ORDER, PAGE 1**

MCL 552.14, MCL 552.517, MCL 552.517b(3), MCR 3.211

Original - Court
1st copy - Plaintiff

2nd copy - Defendant
3rd copy - Friend of the court

Approved, SCAO

STATE OF MICHIGAN
JUDICIAL CIRCUIT
COUNTY

UNIFORM CHILD SUPPORT ORDER (PAGE 2)
☐ EX PARTE   ☐ TEMPORARY
☐ MODIFICATION   ☒ FINAL

CASE NO.

Court telephone no.

Court address

Plaintiff's name   v   Defendant's name

1. **Item 1** (continued).

   Uninsured Health-Care Expenses. All uninsured health-care expenses exceeding the annual ordinary medical amount will be paid ___39___ % by the plaintiff and ___61___ % by the defendant. Uninsured expenses exceeding the annual ordinary medical amount for the year they are incurred that are not paid within 28 days of a written payment request may be enforced by the friend of the court. The annual ordinary medical amount is ___$715___ .

   Obligation Ends. Except for child care, or as otherwise ordered, support obligations for each child end on the last day of the month the child turns age 18. The child-care obligation for each child ends August 31 following the child's 12th birthday. The parties must notify each other of changes in child-care expenses and must additionally notify the friend of the court if the changes end those expenses.
   ☐ **Post-majority Support:** The following children will be attending high school on a full-time basis after turning 18 years of age. Therefore, the support obligation for each specific child ends on the last day of the month as follows, except in no case may it extend beyond the time the child reaches 19 years and 6 months of age: (Specify name of child and date obligation ends.)

2. **Insurance.** For the benefit of the children, the ☐ plaintiff ☒ defendant shall maintain health-care coverage through an insurer (as defined in MCL 552.602) that includes payment for hospital, dental, optical, and other health-care expenses when that coverage is available at a reasonable cost, including coverage available as a benefit of employment or under an individual policy
   ☐ up to a maximum of $ _____ for plaintiff.   ☐ up to a maximum of $ _____ for defendant.
   ☐ not to exceed 5% of the plaintiff's/defendant's gross income.

   Michigan Child ... **ation.** ... deviation and the requi...
   Formula. The attached ... addendum (FOC 10d) pro...

☐ 13. **Other:** (Attach separate sheets as needed.)

_____   Date   _____   Date
Plaintiff (if consent/stipulation)   Defendant (if consent/stipulation)

_____   Date   _____   Date
Plaintiff's attorney   Defendant's attorney

Prepared by: ___DARLENE A. LOVELACE___
               Name (type or print)

___9-7-2009___   *Lester Tubb*
Date   Judge   Bar no.

CERTIFICATE OF MAILING

I certify that on this date I served a copy of this order on the parties or their attorneys by first-class mail addressed to their last-known addresses as defined in MCR 3.203. ☐ I certify that I also served the Deviation Addendum (FOC 10d) with this order.

_____   _____
Date   Signature

COURT USE ONLY

FOC 10 / 52 (8/14) **UNIFORM CHILD SUPPORT ORDER, PAGE 3**   MCL 552.14, MCL 552.517, MCL 552.517b(3), MCR 3.211

Approved, SCAO

Original - Friend of the court
Copies - All parties

STATE OF MICHIGAN JUDICIAL CIRCUIT COUNTY	DOMESTIC RELATIONS JUDGMENT INFORMATION, PAGE 1	CASE NO.

☐ TEMPORARY   ☒ FINAL

USE NOTE: Complete this form and file it with the friend of the court (**do not file this form with the office of the clerk of the court**) when the first temporary custody, parenting-time, or support order is entered and when submitting any final proposed judgment awarding custody, parenting time, or support. Mail a copy to each party and file proof of mailing with the court (may use form MC 302, Proof of Mailing).

The information previously provided   ☒ is changed   ☐ is unchanged. (Complete only the fields that have changed.)

_9-5-2009_
Date

Darlene A. Lovelace
Signature

Plaintiff Information

Name
Address
Social security number	Telephone number 214-5502
E-mail address
Employer name, address, telephone number, and FEIN (if known)
Driver's license number and state
Occupational license number(s), type(s), issuing state(s), and date(s)

Defendant Information

Name
Address
Social security number	Telephone number
E-mail address
Employer name, address, telephone number, and FEIN (if known)
Driver's license number and state
Occupational license number(s), type(s), issuing state(s), and date(s)

CUSTODY PROVISIONS   sole, plaintiff = P   sole, defendant = D   joint = J   other = O _____
(must identify)

Child's name	Social security number	Date of birth	Physical custody P, D, J, O	Child's primary residence address	Legal custody P, D, J, O

SUPPORT PROVISIONS

☒ Support provisions are stated in the Uniform Support Order.
Medical Support provisions are stated on page 2 of this form.

FOC 100 (3/14) **DOMESTIC RELATIONS JUDGMENT INFORMATION, PAGE 1**

MCR 3.211(F)

Approved, SCAO

STATE OF MICHIGAN
JUDICIAL CIRCUIT
COUNTY

MEDICAL SUPPORT PROVISIONS
name of each child in this

Plaintiff's Insurance Coverage

Provider name and address

Defendant's Insurance

Provider name and

FOC 100 (3/14) **DOMESTIC RELATIONS JUDGMENT INFORMATION, PAGE 2**

MCR 3.211(F)

STATE OF MICHIGAN Circuit Court - Family Division COUNTY	PROOF OF SERVICE OF ORDER/JUDGMENT PAPERS	CASE NO.

Plaintiff (appearing *in propria persona*):

v

Defendant:

I served the following papers in this case as described below:

1. On __8-12-2009__, I ☒ delivered ☐ sent by first-class mail to the friend of the court at its official address, these papers:
   ☒ Original Domestic Relations Judgment Information form for ☐ Ex Parte Order
   ☒ Judgment of Divorce

   ☐ Other:

2. On __8-15-2009__, I sent to defendant by first-class mail at his/her address in the caption above, which is defendant's last known mailing address, copies of these papers:

a. Interim relief papers:
   ☐ Domestic Relations Judgment Information form
   ☐ Ex Parte Order
   ☐ Uniform Child Support Order
   ☐ Other:

b. Judgment papers:
   ☒ Domestic Relations Judgment Information form
   ☒ Judgment of Divorce: ☒ Proposed ☐ Final
   ☒ Uniform support order(s): ☒ Uniform Child Support Order ☐ Uniform Spousal Support Order
   ☐ Order Regarding Income Withholding
   ☐ Other:

I declare that the statements above are true to the best of my information, knowledge and belief.

Date __8-15-2009__   Plaintiff __Darlene A. Lovelace__

TBP 7 (1/16)   PROOF OF SERVICE OF ORDER/JUDGMENT PAPERS

Approved, SCAO	Original - Court 1st copy - Friend of the court	2nd copy - Plaintiff 3rd copy - Defendant Additional copies to all sources of income

STATE OF MICHIGAN JUDICIAL CIRCUIT COUNTY	ORDER REGARDING INCOME WITHHOLDING	CASE NO.

Court address

Court telephone no.

Plaintiff's name, address, and telephone no.

v

Defendant's name, address, and telephone no.

THE COURT FINDS:

1. The requirements for implementation or adjustment of income withholding
   ☒ have
   ☐ have not
   been met.

☐ 2. The proposed administrative adjustment of income withholding
   ☐ will
   ☐ will not
   produce an unjust or inappropriate result.

IT IS ORDERED:

3. Income withholding is
   ☐ discontinued.
   ☐ effective.
   ☐ effective in an amount pursuant to the Michigan Child Support Formula to pay current support and arrears.
   ☐ effective as follows:

_9-7-2009_
Date

Lester Tubbs
Judge   Bar no.

CERTIFICATE OF MAILING

I certify that on this date I served a copy of this order on the parties and sources of income by first-class mail addressed to their last-known addresses as defined in MCR 3.203.

Date

Signature

FOC 5 (3/08) **ORDER REGARDING INCOME WITHHOLDING**

MCL 552.601 *et seq.*

Testimony

1) My name is [full name], my address is [address], and I am the plaintiff in this case.

2) I was married to the defendant on ___SEPT. 1, 2005___ at ___LAKE CITY, MICHIGAN___ by a person authorized to
   Date and place of marriage
   perform marriages.

3) Before the marriage my/[my wife's] name was ___DARLENE ANN ALBRIGHT___.
   Wife's former name

4) I filed my complaint for divorce on ___MARCH 1, 2009___. Before I filed the complaint, I had resided in Michigan since .
   Filing date
   ___1990___ and in this county since ___1990___.
   State residence   County residence

5) As I said in my complaint, there has been a breakdown in our marriage relationship to the extent the objects of matrimony
   have been destroyed because ___WE COULD NEVER GET ALONG TOGETHER___ and there remains no reasonable
   Brief facts to support grounds
   likelihood that our marriage can be preserved because ___WE ARE TOTALLY INCOMPATIBLE___.
   Brief facts to support grounds

6) The defendant and I have ___2___ minor children ___DUANE WESLEY LOVELACE, 3; ETC.___.
   Names and ages of minor children
   I/[my wife] am not now pregnant.

7) The friend of the court has recommended that I should have ___SOLE___ custody of the children with
   Custody
   ___REASONABLE___ parenting time to the defendant. S/he and I have agreed that this arrangement is satisfactory.
   Parenting time

8) The friend of the court has also recommended that I receive ___$385___ monthly in child support and I believe that
   Child support
   this should be sufficient.

9) I am working at ___A RESTAURANT AS A WAITRESS___ and am able to support myself. As a result, no
   Source of support
   alimony is being ordered.

10) We own some ___CLOTHING AND HOUSEHOLD GOODS___ that we have split between us. We have also agreed that the
    General description of personal property
    defendant is to give me ___A 2004 DODGE INTREPID___ and I will pay off the debt on it.
    Specific items of personal property transferred in judgment

11) We also own ___A HOUSE IN LAKE CITY___ worth around ___$75___
    Description of any real property
    We have agreed to ___SELL IT, PAY OFF THE MORTGAGE AND SPLIT THE REST.___
    Manner of division

    USE WHEN APPLICABLE

12) I would like my former name of ___ALBRIGHT___ back.
    Wife's name change

13) My court fees were suspended when I filed this divorce. Since then, ___I AM STILL GETTING FIP PAYMENTS AND MY HUSBAND IS UNEMPLOYED.___
    Current financial condition

14) Does the court have any questions?

STATE OF MICHIGAN THIRD JUDICIAL COURT WAYNE COUNTY	CERTIFICATE OF CONFORMITY FOR DOMESTIC RELATIONS ORDER OR JUDGMENT	CASE NO.

Penobscot Bldg. 645 Griswold Ave. Detroit, MI 48226

313-224-5372

PLAINTIFF'S NAME	v	DEFENDANT'S NAME

I certify the attached Order of Judgment as presented for entry to be in full conformity with the requirements set forth by statute, INCLUDING A PROVISION FOR IMMEDIATE INCOME WITHHOLDING (WHICH SHALL BE IMPLEMENTED BY THE FRIEND OF THE COURT). THE PAYER'S SOCIAL SECURITY NUMBER AND THE NAME AND ADDRESS OF HIS/HER SOURCE OF INCOME, IF KNOWN, UNLESS OTHERWISE ORDERED BY THE COURT, and with Michigan Court Rules 3.201 and following and if applicable, includes all provisions of the Friend of the Court recommendation or is in conformity with the decision of

_____ rendered on the _____ day of

_____, 20_____.

9-5-2009
_____
Date

Darlene A. Lovelace

Instructions: Please sign and present this certificate to the Court Clerk when the Order or Judgment is presented for entry. If an ex parte interim order is being presented to the Judge, please complete the "Certificate on behalf of Plaintiff regarding Ex Parte Interim Support Order" and follow Local Court Rule 3.206.

USE THIS FORM IN WAYNE COUNTY ONLY

#1225 (11/04) CERTIFICATE OF CONFORMITY FOR DOMESTIC RELATIONS ORDER OR JUDGEMENT

PAGE 1 OF 2

ORDER DETAILS

FOR P

(PLACE L

STATE OF MICHIGAN
COUNTY OF WAYNE
THIRD JUDICIAL CIRCUIT COURT
FAMILY DIVISION

ORDER DATA FORM-SUPPORT
Re: SUBMISSION FOR LOADING
ATTACHED SUPPORT ORDER INTO
MiCSES ON FOC COMPUTER SYSTEM

THE ORDER WAS ENTERED ON:
_9-7-2009_
(DATE ON ORDER STAMPED BY JUDGE'S CLERK)

CAS

JUDGE

> USE THIS FORM IN
> WAYNE COUNTY ONLY.
>
> SEE THE BLANK FORM
> WHICH HAS A TWO-
> PAGE PREFACE WITH
> MORE INSTRUCTIONS

*INDICES REQUIRED INFORMATION

CHECK ONLY THE BOXES WHICH APPLY TO PROVISIONS IN THE SUBMITTED ORDER

* PLAINTIFF NAME:
DARLENE ANN LOVELACE

* DEFENDANT NAME:
DUDLEY ERNEST LOVELACE

*THIS ORDER IS:
☐ EX PARTE (PROOF OF SERVICE REQUIRED) ☐ TEMPORARY ☒ JUDGMENT ☐ MODIFICATION
*WERE CHILD SUPPORT GUIDELINES FOLLOWED? ☒ YES ☐ NO

*THE CHILD SUPPORT PAYER IS ☐ PLAINTIFF ☒ DEFENDANT ☐ NOT APPLICABLE.
☐ PAY DIRECT, NOT THROUGH FOC.

☐ CHILD SUPPORT. COMMENCEMENT DATE IS _9-7-2009_

* 5 CHILDREN PER WEEK	* 4 CHILDREN PER WEEK	* 3 CHILDREN PER WEEK	* 2 CHILDREN PER WEEK	* 1 CHILD PER WEEK
CHILD SUPPORT AMOUNT	CHILD SUPPORT AMOUNT	CHILD SUPPORT AMOUNT	CHILD SUPPORT AMOUNT	CHILD SUPPORT AMOUNT
$	$	$	$ 385/MONTH	$ 344/MONTH

☒ INCOME WITHHOLDING: ☒ PROCESS AT GUIDELINE AMOUNT ☐ PROCESS AT $ _____ PER WEEK
☒ CHILD SUPPORT ARREARAGE:
  ☒ PRESERVED ☐ CANCELED AS OF DATE: _____ ☐ SET AT $ _____ AS OF DATE: _____
☐ CHILD CARE EXPENSES: $ _____ PER WEEK, COMMENCEMENT DATE IS _____ ;
  END DATE IS ☐ GUIDELINE DATE **OR** ☐ DATE: _____
☐ CHILD CARE ARREARAGE:
  ☐ PRESERVED ☐ CANCELED AS OF DATE: _____ ☐ SET AT $ _____ AS OF DATE: _____
☐ ARREARAGE ADJUSTMENT:
  ☐ DIRECT CREDIT IN AMOUNT OF $ _____ ☐ ADD ADDITIONAL OBLIGATION IN AMOUNT OF $ _____
☒ MEDICAL INSURANCE IN ORDER.
☒ CHILD SUPPORT PAYER RESPONSIBLE FOR _61_ % OF UNINSURED MEDICAL EXPENSES.
☐ PARENTING TIME ABATEMENT: ____ % PARENTING TIME CREDIT AFTER ___ CONSECUTIVE OVERNIGHTS.
☒ PARENTING TIME ORDERED: (CHECK ONE):
  ☒ REASONABLE ☐ SPECIFIC ☐ SUPERVISED ☐ RESERVED ☐ REFER TO FAMILY COUNSELING/OTHER

*THE SPOUSAL SUPPORT PAYER IS ☐ PLAINTIFF ☐ DEFENDANT ☒ NOT APPLICABLE.
☐ SPOUSAL SUPPORT: ☐ $ _____ PER WEEK, COMMENCEMENT DATE: _____
  ☐ PERMANENT ☐ END DATE _____ ☐ PAY DIRECT, NOT THROUGH FOC
☐ SPOUSAL SUPPORT ARREARAGE:
  ☐ PRESERVED ☐ CANCELED AS OF DATE: _____ ☐ SET AT $ _____ AS OF DATE: _____

☐ ORDER REFERS MATTERS TO DIVORCE INVESTIGATION/MODIFICATION FOR FURTHER INVESTIGATION.

I CERTIFY THAT THE ABOVE INFORMATION IS TRUE TO THE BEST OF MY KNOWLEDGE,
INFORMATION AND BELIEF, AND IS IN FULL CONFORMITY WITH THE REQUIREMENTS SET FORTH
BY STATUTE AND COURT RULE AND THE DECISION OF THE COURT. (NOTE: FOC WILL NOT READ
THE ORDER WHEN ENTERING IT ON MiCSES.)

_9-5-2009_   _Darlene A. Lovelace_
DATE: SIGNATURE OF ~~ATTORNEY~~ _PLAINTIFF_   BAR NO.
PLEASE PRINT:

ATTORNEY NAME
121 S. MAIN
ADDRESS
LAKE CITY, MI 48800   _772-0000_
CITY/STATE/ZIP   TELEPHONE NO.

FD/FOC 4002 (11/06/02) ORDER DATA FORM-SUPPORT

American LegalNet, Inc.
www.USCourtForms.com

(ACE LABEL HERE)

CASE #:

RK)   JUDGE

I THE SUBMITTED ORDER
Y DEFENDANT NAME:
EST LOVELACE

* SOCIAL SECURITY NUMBER(S)
_466-10-1001_
_469-00-4411_

AINTIFF ☒ **DEFENDANT**
HOME TELEPHONE NO:
_773-3004_
BERS: FIA/TANF NO.:

NOW ACTIVE: ☐ YES ☐ NO
EMPLOYER FED I.D. NO.:
_38-0017760_

NTIFF ☐ **DEFENDANT**
HOME TELEPHONE NO:
_772-0000_
RS: FIA/TANF NO.:

NOW ACTIVE: ☐ YES ☐ NO
EMPLOYER FED I.D. NO.:
_38-1111707_

LEDGE, INFORMATION
TH BY STATUTE AND
HE ORDER WHEN

BAR NO.

American LegalNet, Inc.
www.USCourtForms.com

STATE OF MICHIGAN Circuit Court - Family Division COUNTY	PROOF OF SERVICE OF ORDER/JUDGMENT PAPERS	CASE NO.

Plaintiff (appearing *in propria persona*):

Defendant:

v

I served the following papers in this case as described below:

1. On_____, I ☐ delivered   ☐ sent by first-class mail   to the friend of the court at its official address, these papers:
   ☐ Original Domestic Relations Judgment Information form for   ☐ Ex Parte Order
   ☐ Other: ☐ Judgment of Divorce

2. On _9-8-2009_____, I sent to defendant by first-class mail at his/her address in the caption above, which is defendant's last known mailing address, copies of these papers:

a. Interim relief papers:
   ☐ Domestic Relations Judgment Information form
   ☐ Ex Parte Order
   ☐ Uniform Child Support Order
   ☐ Other:

b. Judgment papers:
   ☐ Domestic Relations Judgment Information form
   ☒ Judgment of Divorce: ☐ Proposed   ☒ Final
   ☒ Uniform support order(s):   ☒ Uniform Child Support Order   ☐ Uniform Spousal Support Order
   ☒ Order Regarding Income Withholding
   ☐ Other:

I declare that the statements above are true to the best of my information, knowledge and belief.

Date_ _9-8-2009_____   Plaintiff___ _Darlene A. Lovelace_____

TBP 7 (1/16)   **PROOF OF SERVICE OF ORDER/JUDGMENT PAPERS**

Symbols
☐ regular paper
☆ optional paper
◇ local paper

3   Default

Filed with the clerk around the time the default is received:

☐ Default   TBP 2

☆ Appearance and Waiver of Military Relief Law Rights, if defendant is in active-duty military service and is willing to waive military relief law rights   TBP 6

◇ praecipe or other written request for a final hearing   TBP 3

☐ Motion to Enter Default Judgment of Divorce

Filed with the clerk after the default:

☐ copies of the Default and Motion to Enter Default Judgment of Divorce with proof of service on defendant   TBP 2 & 3

4   Waiting for Final Hearing

It's possible a friend of the court questionnaire, case conference form or other case management documents may be filed during this period.

5   Final Hearing

Served on the friend of the court:

☐ Domestic Relations Judgment Information form   FOC 100

Served on defendant at least 14 days before the final hearing:

☐ (Proposed) Judgment of Divorce   TBP 4

☐ Uniform Child Support Order   FOC 10/52

☐ Domestic Relations Judgment Information form   FOC 100

☐ Proof of Service of Order / Judgment Papers showing service of FOC 100 on FOC and all these papers on defendant; proof filed with the clerk before the final hearing   TBP 7

Filed with the clerk after the final hearing:

☐ Judgment of Divorce   TBP 4

☐ Uniform Child Support Order   FOC 10/52

☐ Order Regarding Income Withholding   FOC 5

☐ Record of Divorce or Annulment   DCH-0838

◇ Certificate of Conformity for Domestic Relations Order or Judgment (in Wayne County only)   1225

◇ Order Data Form-Support (in Wayne County only)   FD/FOC 4002

Filed with the clerk after service of the judgment papers on defendant:

☐ Proof of Service of Order/Judgment Papers   TBP 7

After Your Divorce

Although your divorce is over, there's still some work to do. The Judgment of Divorce (TBP 4) takes legal effect at filing, but you must carry out several judgment provisions. What's more, the end of your marriage may require changes in your will, powers of attorney, insurance, retirement benefits, etc.

Transferring Property

The Judgment of Divorce (TBP 4) divided your property, but it's your responsibility to transfer ownership of the property.

Ownership of real property must be transferred by deed. For transfers between ex-spouses, a simple form of deed called a quit claim deed is customarily used. Lawyers or real estate brokers can prepare these for a small fee.

If your ex-spouse is uncooperative or unavailable for transfer, you can sometimes use the divorce judgment to transfer ownership of real property yourself. To use the judgment this way, it must describe the property in detail (see "Property Division Provisions" in Appendix H for more about describing property using legal descriptions or identification numbers). You must also have an official certified copy of the judgment for the transfer. These are available from the clerk for a small fee.

You can transfer Michigan real property by recording a certified copy of the divorce judgment with the register of deeds for the county where the property is located. This transfer method isn't available for out-of-state real property.

To Obtain

A certified copy of your divorce judgment, go to the clerk of the court that granted your divorce.

There is a $10 fee for issuing a certified copy, plus $1 for each page of the document.

As mentioned in "Will I Have Tax Problems from the Divorce?" on page 62, real property transfers between ex-spouses aren't subject to income taxation. Nevertheless, the transferee (party receiving ownership) must report the transfer in IRS Form 1099-S and file the form with the IRS and give a copy to the transferor.

Within 45 days of a divorce property transfer, the transferee should also file a Property Transfer Affidavit (L-4260) with the local city or township tax assessor. Check the box near the bottom indicating that it is a "transfer creating or ending a joint ownership if at least one person is an original owner of the property (or his/her spouse), and the assessor cannot adjust the taxable value of the property.

Personal property without titles (clothing, household goods, etc.) can be transferred by simply changing possession of the items. But both possession and title must be transferred for personal property with titles (stocks, bonds, motor vehicles, etc.). Stocks and bonds can be transferred through the designated transfer agent (usually a bank but sometimes the issuing company itself).

Transfer titles to motor vehicles through a secretary of state office by applying for a new title after the current owner has signed off on the back of the old certificate of title.

If the owner refuses to cooperate, you can use a certified copy of the divorce judgment for transfer of title. When you apply for a new title, submit a certified copy of the judgment, and you won't need your ex's signature on the old certificate of title.

Debts

You may have already closed or frozen joint accounts (see "Does My Property Need Protection?" on page 58 for more about handling joint accounts during divorce). If you haven't, do this at once. Otherwise, your ex can add new joint debt after the divorce for which you may be liable.

Health Care Coverage

With the high cost of health care these days, health care coverage is a necessity. Your children need this coverage, and maybe you need coverage for yourself.

Coverage for Children

Divorce judgments typically require one or both parents to continue (or obtain) health care plans covering the children, if available at a reasonable cost. Even with coverage, there are bound to be small (ordinary) or large (extraordinary) uninsured expenses created by deductibles, co-payments or other gaps in coverage.

"Health Care" on page 259 explains how to handle health care coverage and has suggestions if no coverage is available. This section also explains absorbing ordinary and extraordinary health care expenses of children.

If you choose COBRA-coverage through your ex-spouse's employer, as described on page 261, contact his/her employee benefits office within 60 days after your divorce judgment is granted. Wait longer and you can lose the right to obtain health care through the COBRA law.

Coverage for Spouse

Some of the health care plans and programs, such as MIChild and Healthy Kids, are designed for children and don't apply to adults. But others do. Parents of children receiving Medicaid through the Healthy Kids program can qualify for Medicaid themselves. Ex-spouses are also eligible for COBRA-coverage and individual policies. These options are described on page 261.

Estate Planning

Several judgment paragraphs extinguish rights and claims you and your ex-spouse have against each other's property (unless you choose to preserve these in the judgment). For example, paragraphs #7 and #8 of the Judgment of Divorce (TBP 4a) extinguish life insurance and retirement benefits, and paragraph #6 cuts off will and estate rights.

Michigan has a will, inheritance, and probate law called the Estates and Protected Individuals Code (EPIC). The EPIC says that divorce revokes all property transfers to and appointments of (as agent, beneficiary, trustee, personal representative, etc.) an ex-spouse and his/her relatives, such as your stepchildren, in all sorts of estate planning devices including:

- life insurance
- all kinds of retirement plans
- power of attorney
- trust
- will
- miscellaneous (such as payable-on-death (POD) bank accounts)

Despite this helpful provision in the EPIC, it's still necessary to follow up after divorce and review or revise many estate planning documents.

It's particularly important to contact your insurance agent and/or retirement plan administrator and revoke any designations of your spouse as beneficiary. Because of a peculiarity in the law, neither the judgment's nor EPIC's revocations are always effective, making individual revocation necessary. As you make the revocations, it's a good time to designate new beneficiaries.

The EPIC revokes appointments of an ex-spouse (or relatives) as agent under two popular kinds of powers of attorney: 1) durable power of attorney (DPA) for financial affairs 2) patient advocate designation (PAD) for health care decision-making, often including the power to terminate life-sustaining treatment.

With both kinds of powers of attorney, revocation of your ex as agent often means promotion of successor agents to first-choice status (frequently, spouses designate each other as first-choice agents, with successors named as back-ups). Nevertheless, it's a good idea to make new powers of attorney with new sets of first-choice and successor agents after divorce.

Trusts are another popular estate planning devices which come in two varieties: 1) living, or *inter vivos*, trust 2) testamentary trust in a will. The EPIC says that divorce revokes an ex-spouse (and relatives) as beneficiary of a trust and as trustee. Even so, it's still smart to amend the trust and remove your ex from the trust.

Both your divorce judgment and the EPIC revoke rights that your ex (and relatives) have in your will, including: 1) will gifts and other property transfers 2) appointments as personal representative, trustee (of a testamentary trust) or other roles.

But besides these selected will provisions, divorce doesn't touch other parts of a will. The will, minus the provisions benefiting an ex-spouse (or relatives), remains in force. Nevertheless, you should carefully review your will after divorce. The removal of your ex from the will may have upset your scheme of property distribution and appointments. After review, you may decide that your will needs revision or even replacement.

You should also remove your ex as beneficiary of pay-on-death (POD) bank accounts, brokerage accounts and bonds. If you hold a safe deposit box jointly with your ex, you should terminate this arrangement. As with other estate planning devices, the EPIC terminates spousal rights in these things, but it's still advisable to do this in fact.

Name Change

If you changed your name during the divorce, you must report the name change to the following agencies and offices, so documents issued by them can be revised:
- Michigan Secretary of State (driver's license and voter registration)
- Social Security Administration (social security card)
- passport acceptance agency (U.S. Post Office, county clerk, etc.) (passport)
- financial institutions (bank accounts, credit cards, etc.)
- insurance companies (life, disability and health insurance policies and documents)
- heath care providers (health care files and documents at doctor, dentist, etc.)
- utilities (accounts with utilities, telephone companies, cable television, etc.)
- employer (employee benefits documents)
- schools and alumni associations (school records, alumni directories, etc.)
- airlines (frequent flier programs)

Typically, you must visit many of these offices and agencies in person to change your name; it's difficult to make the change over the telephone or Internet. Many of these agencies and offices also require evidence of your name change. For proof, bring certified copies of the Judgment of Divorce (TBP 4).

You must also give a special notice of your name change to the Michigan Department of Health and Human Services. This notice allows the department to add the TBP 4 with the name change to your birth records. When you get copies of the TBP 4, ask the clerk for an Application to Record Court-Ordered Legal Name Change to a Michigan Birth Record (DCH-0850). File the form according to the instructions in the form.

Credit Problems

Today, in our consumer economy, credit is more important than ever. As always, lenders look at credit reports (tracking a person's borrowing and payment habits) when making lending decisions. But more and more, automobile and homeowner insurance companies are using credit histories to determine insurability and premiums, and mortgage companies base interest rates on creditworthiness.

After divorce, many women suddenly discover that they can't get credit because they have no credit history. A woman may lose credit if her credit was reported in her previous married name. Even women who don't change their names may suffer a loss of credit if they obtained credit through their husbands' credit reports.

The solution to these credit woes is building a credit history in your own name. If you had credit under your former married name, you can add this information to your credit file. Joint accounts with your husband may have been reported in your husband's name only (all joint accounts opened after June 1, 1977, are supposed to be reported in both spouses' names). If so, you can sometimes persuade credit reporting agencies to add these credit references to your file.

In addition, you can apply for new credit from banks, retailers and other creditors to build a credit history. A federal law, the Equal Credit Opportunity Act (ECOA), bars creditors from canceling old credit accounts you had during marriage if you still meet their lending standards (you may have to submit new information to prove your creditworthiness). The ECOA also guarantees creditworthy persons access to credit regardless of sex or marital status, and outlaws various discriminatory credit practices.

As you build a credit history, make sure you pay your bills on time, because this factor has the biggest impact on credit. It's also smart to have a good mix of credit, with both revolving (credit cards, charge accounts) and installment (mortgages, loans) debt.

More Information

Credit agencies receive credit information from lenders and merchants, compile this information into credit reports and sell these to lenders and others. To check on your credit status, get copies of your credit reports from the three main credit reporting agencies:

Equifax: P.O. Box 740241, Atlanta, GA 30374, (888) 202-4025 or www.equifax.com

Experian: (888) 397-3742 or www.experian.com

TransUnion: P.O. Box 1000, Chester, PA 19022, (800) 888-4213 or www.transunion.com

Each report is around $10, but consumers are entitled to one free report per year from each company under the new Fair and Accurate Credit Transactions Act. You can request the free reports from:

Annual Credit Report Request Service
P.O. Box 105281
Atlanta, GA 30348
www.annualcreditreport.com

This is the official free credit report service. Watch out for look-alike or sound-alike for-profit companies that charge fees for the available-for-free credit reports.

Enforcing or Modifying the Divorce Judgment

Divorced people face all kinds of after-divorce problems, some as small as deciding who buys shoes for the children, others as important as changing the custody or residence of children. Big or small, all these problems really amount to just two things: *enforcement* of the judgment or *modification* of the judgment.

Enforcement

By far the most important documents from your divorce are the Judgment of Divorce (TBP 4) and the Uniform Child Support Order (FOC 10/52), which goes with the judgment. Examining these documents, you'll see that they contain a number of provisions or orders, arranged by subject: end of marriage (the actual divorce), custody, parenting time, residence of children, child support, alimony, property division, etc. All these orders must be observed and obeyed by the parties.

If all goes well, you and your ex cooperate and carry out the judgment of divorce without much fuss. But if your ex disobeys any judgment order, you must enforce the order against your ex, usually with the help of the court that granted the divorce.

Grounds for Enforcement

It's simple: Violation of a divorce judgment provides grounds for enforcement. The various orders inside the judgment tell the ex-spouses to do various things: take care of the children (custody order), spend time with them at specified intervals (parenting time order), maintain a residence for the children (residence-of-children order), pay child support (child support order), etc. If one of the parties disobeys any of these orders, the other party has grounds for enforcing the judgment.

Methods of Enforcement

You can sometimes enforce a divorce judgment yourself, without going to court. For example, a well-crafted judgment should authorize you to carry out the property division by recording the judgment with the register of deeds to transfer ownership of property.

You will need the help of the court system for most kinds of enforcement. Your first stop is always the friend of the court. By law, the friend of the court is supposed to enforce all custody, parenting time, residence-of-children, child support and alimony orders. If your ex is violating any of these orders, notify the friend of the court, in writing, and it may take care of the problem for you.

These days, the friend of the court possesses a number of powerful enforcement remedies. It can enforce custody or parenting time orders by threatening the violator with a contempt of court. The friend of the court can collect child support or alimony by withholding money from the payer's income, threaten contempt or revocation of driver's, occupational or sporting/recreational licenses, reporting the nonpayment to consumer reporting agencies, such as credit bureaus, or adding surcharges to the debt. State agencies teamed with the friend of the court have other even more powerful remedies, such as seizure of state and/or federal income tax refunds.

If the friend of the court won't intervene, you will have to seek enforcement yourself. Most of the friend of the court's enforcement remedies aren't available to you. But you can collect support by a contempt-of-court proceeding or normal debt collection methods, such as execution (seizure) against property or garnishment of money. It's also possible to enforce custody or parenting time orders through state, federal or international kidnapping laws, and child support and alimony orders by invoking state or federal criminal nonsupport laws.

Modification

A divorce judgment remains in effect until the youngest child of the divorced parties reaches the age of 18. Thus, if you have young children when you divorce, your divorce judgment may govern your lives for many years to come. During that time, the circumstances of you, your ex and children can change, requiring modification of the divorce judgment. Fortunately, divorce courts keep control of divorce cases and can modify their judgments during the post-judgment period.

Of the seven important issues in a divorce, two—end of marriage and property division—are closed by a divorce and normally cannot be modified later. There is an exception to this rule when the divorce judgment is legally defective (because of fraud, duress, serious legal irregularity, etc.). In that case, the end-of-marriage or property division issues can be reopened. The orders for the other five issues are modifiable by the divorce court, with proper grounds for modification.

Grounds for Modification

The customary grounds for modifying custody, parenting time, residence-of-children, child support and alimony orders have been a post-divorce-judgment change of circumstances. The person seeking modification must show a change of circumstances of the ex-spouses and/or children since divorce to obtain modification.

Recently, some Michigan courts and laws have shifted away from change-of-circumstances grounds a bit and now require "proper cause," "good cause" or "reasonable cause" for a post-divorce modification.

Despite the different wording, the two modification grounds overlap quite a bit. The change-of-circumstances grounds are usually the bare facts for modification, while proper cause grounds are the same set of facts and a legal rule supporting modification.

> *Example:* A father receives a cut in pay and moves for a decrease in child support, alleging the pay-cut as a change in circumstances. Proper cause for the decrease would be the reduced ability of the father to pay child support after the pay-cut (as explained in "Child Support" on page 22, the ability of parents to pay child support from their income is part of the legal basis for child support).

Both grounds are based on the same facts: the loss of pay. But the change of circumstances is just the fact of the pay-cut, while proper cause is the pay-cut and application of the legal rule of ability of the father to pay the support.

Methods of Modification

A modification must be court-ordered to be binding legally. An informal modification where you and your ex informally agree to a change, outside of court, works while you abide by the agreement. But when there's a violation, courts will refuse to enforce your agreement, making an informal modification practically worthless.

Sometimes, you don't have to do anything for a modification, since the friend of the court does everything for you. The friend of the court is supposed to review child support periodically. It may decide that the amount ordered in your judgment needs adjustment and ask for an increase or decrease.

If you and your ex agree on the modification, you can stipulate to a modification order, without appearing in court. The court, which has the final say on all modifications, could reject your proposed modification, but will usually approve it.

No agreement? Then you must file a motion for modification. The court may refer the matter to the friend of the court for mediation or refereeing, and the issue may be settled there. If not, the motion must be heard by the judge during a court hearing. The judge decides the motion and signs an order either accepting or rejecting the proposed modification.

Updating Your Personal Information

When your case is still in the friend of the court system, you have an obligation to notify the friend of the court, in writing, of any changes in your personal information within 21 days of a change. Paragraph #6 of the Uniform Child Support Order (FOC 10/52) imposes this obligation and cites the kind of information (address, employment, health care coverage, etc.) that must be kept up to date. This obligation lasts while child support is owed in your case.

To make a change, use the Change in Personal Information (FOC 108). Insert your new information in the form and file it with friend of the court.

The duty to keep your personal information up to date may be affected by an opt-out from the friend of the court system. After a limited opt-out, you must still give the friend of the court updates because the friend of the court still has responsibility for your case (see paragraph #3 of the Agreement Suspending Immediate Income Withholding (FOC 63) and Order Suspending Immediate Income Withholding (FOC 64) about this duty to notify after a limited opt-out).

With a total or partial opt-out, you must still give notice, in writing, of changes in your personal information within 21 days of a change. But the notice goes to your ex, not the friend of the court, which has been removed from the case. Paragraph #5 of the Uniform Child Support Order, No Friend of Court Services (FOC 10a/52a) imposes this obligation and says which information must be updated. There's no form for this notice. Just make sure it's in writing and keep a copy for your records.

Original - Friend of the court
Copy - Filing party

Approved, SCAO

STATE OF MICHIGAN JUDICIAL CIRCUIT COUNTY	CHANGE IN PERSONAL INFORMATION	CASE NO.
		Telephone no.

Friend of the court address

Please type or print information. Complete only those sections that apply. You can only file changes for yourself or those minor children of whom you have physical custody. Use another form when making changes for more than one person. **You must sign this form and send it to the friend of the court.**

☒ for party and minor child(ren)   ☐ for party only

1. New Address and/or Telephone Number ☐ for minor child _____ no longer living with custodial parent
Name

Street address 401 LAKE			Area code and telephone number
City LAKE CITY	State MI	Zip 48800	

I understand that by filing this change of address, it will be used to automatically update address information on any other child-support cases I have in Michigan. This change is effective for (check all that apply)

☒ all addresses you have listed for me.
☐ residence address only (where I live).
☐ an address that is confidential by court order and which remains confidential with this change.
☐ the single mailing address to which all notices and papers will be served.

2. Alternate Address
The court has entered an order making my address confidential under Michigan Court Rule 3.203(F). The following is an alternate address for the court, the friend of the court office, and the other party to use in serving me with notice and other court papers. I will retrieve all my mail regarding this case from this alternate address.

Street address	City	State	Zip

3. Name Change (Attach order changing name or certificate of marriage.)

New name

4. New Employer   ☐ Employer information is confidential by court order.

Employer name	Street address		
City	State	Zip	Area code and telephone number

5. New Driver's License

Issuing state	License number	Expiration date

6. New Occupational License

Issuing state	Type of occupation	License number	Expiration date

7. New Social Security Number   ☐ for you   ☐ for minor child _____
Name

Social security number

8. Health Care Insurance Provider

Provider name	Provider address and telephone number	Group number	Policy number

9. Other Information: (To be provided as ordered by the court.) (Attach separate sheet.)

Signature of party filing the change	Name of party filing the change (type or print)
Darlene A. Lovelace	DARLENE A. LOVELACE
Date of filing 10-31-2010	Social security number 380-16-1010	E-mail address

FOC 108 (3/13) **CHANGE IN PERSONAL INFORMATION**

Appendices

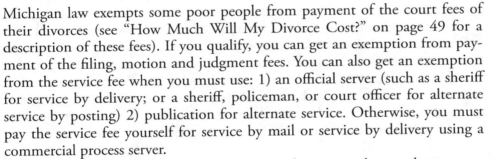

Appendix A: Fee Exemption

Michigan law exempts some poor people from payment of the court fees of their divorces (see "How Much Will My Divorce Cost?" on page 49 for a description of these fees). If you qualify, you can get an exemption from payment of the filing, motion and judgment fees. You can also get an exemption from the service fee when you must use: 1) an official server (such as a sheriff for service by delivery; or a sheriff, policeman, or court officer for alternate service by posting) 2) publication for alternate service. Otherwise, you must pay the service fee yourself for service by mail or service by delivery using a commercial process server.

Who can qualify for a fee exemption? The court rules say that persons receiving "any form of public assistance" are automatically entitled to a fee exemption. According to instructions on the reverse of the exemption form (MC 20), public assistance includes any help from the Michigan Department of Health and Human Services (DHHS), including Medicaid (a joint state-federal program), and federal Supplemental Security Income (SSI). Public assistance doesn't include veterans or unemployment benefits.

In addition, the court rules say that indigent persons may qualify for fee exemptions. Indigent is just another word for poor. In Michigan, judges determine indigency on a case-by-case basis after they have reviewed applicants' financial information (income and assets versus obligations).

The fee exemption rules apply to all types of lawsuits, but there is a special rule for divorce cases. Although you and your spouse may be separated and financially independent, you're still treated as a family unit for fee exemption purposes. If you cannot pay the fees, but your spouse can, s/he may be ordered to pay them for you. If neither of you can pay the fees, because of: 1) receipt of public assistance 2) indigency, both of you are exempt from payment.

Obtaining a Fee Exemption

Obtaining a fee exemption is a two-step procedure: 1) initial suspension of fees when a divorce is filed 2) final waiver (or payment) of the fees at the end of the divorce. To get fees suspended initially, prepare the Affidavit section of the Waiver/Suspension of Fees and Costs (MC 20), and submit it to the clerk when you file your initial divorce papers.

A fee exemption request itself is a kind of motion for which a motion fee would normally be paid. However, the court rules say that no motion fee is due for fee exemption requests.

The clerk gives automatic fee exemptions to plaintiffs receiving public assistance. If you claim indigency, the clerk will pass the Waiver/Suspension of Fees and Costs (MC 20) onto the judge for review (the MC 20 should provide enough facts for the judge, but s/he could hold a hearing on the issue when the claim of indigency is in doubt). If the judge agrees that you're indigent, s/he will order a fee suspension at the bottom of the Waiver/Suspension of Fees and Costs (MC 20). A denial of your application would be indicated in the same place.

If your application is successful, you won't have to pay any fees during your divorce. However, the court will review your fee exemption at the end of the divorce. At that time, it will take another look at your financial condition and make a final decision about the fees.

During your testimony at the final hearing, you must mention that your fees were suspended at the beginning of the divorce. The judge will then re-examine your financial condition and either: 1) order you or your spouse to pay the fees 2) give you and your spouse a final waiver from payment of the fees. The same standards apply then as before; those on public assistance get an automatic exemption, while those claiming indigency must cite facts to prove it. To prove indigency, you should give extra testimony about your present financial condition.

Whatever the judge decides, you can provide for payment of the suspended fees (by you or the defendant) or a final fee waiver in paragraph #11 of the Judgment of Divorce (TBP 4a). Insert the amount of the suspended fees and check the correct box.

Original - Court	3rd copy - Friend of the court
1st copy - Applicant	(when applicable)
2nd copy - Other party	PROBATE JIS CODE: OSF

Approved, SCAO

STATE OF MICHIGAN	**WAIVER/SUSPENSION OF FEES AND COSTS**	**CASE NO.**
JUDICIAL DISTRICT	**(AFFIDAVIT AND ORDER)**	
JUDICIAL CIRCUIT		
COUNTY PROBATE		Court telephone no.

Court address

Plaintiff's/Petitioner's name	v	Defendant's/Respondent's name
Plaintiff's/Petitioner's attorney and bar no.		Defendant's/Respondent's attorney and bar no.

☐ Probate   In the matter of _____

NOTE: Requests for waiver/suspension of transcript costs or mediation fees must be made separately by motion.

AFFIDAVIT

1. I ask the court to waive/suspend fees and costs for the following reason: (check either a or b)
   ☒ a. I am currently receiving public assistance: My DHS case number is _VI33609213_ .
   (MCR 2.002[C] requires the court to suspend payment of fees and costs.)
   OR
   ☒ b. I am unable to pay fees and costs because of indigency, based on the following facts:
   My average gross income is about $ _250_ every ☒ week.   ☐ two weeks.   ☐ month.
   ☐ I am receiving unemployment benefits.
   ☐ I am not employed.
   ☒ I have a vehicle: Year: _2004_ Make: _DODGE_ Model: _INTREPID_ Amount Owed: $ _900_
   The total amount in all my bank accounts is: $ _1000_
   Write down any other assets and how much they are worth. If you need more space, attach a separate sheet.

   I pay $ _250_ in rent/mortgage every month. I pay $ _100_ in utilities (water, electricity, gas) every
   month. I pay $_____ for court-ordered child support. I pay $_____ for court-ordered _____
   Write down any other obligations and how much you pay. If you need more space, attach a separate sheet.   specify

   CHILD CARE OF $100 MONTHLY

2. The number of people living in my household is _3_
3. ☐ I am signing this affidavit for a person who ☐ is a minor. ☐ has the following disability _____

Darlene A. Lovelace   _DARLENE A. LOVELACE_
Applicant signature   Name (type or print)

____ribed and sworn to before me on _2-28-2009_ , _OJIBWAY_ County, Michigan.
                                    Date
____mission expires: _1-1-2010_ Signature: _Loretta Smiley_
                        Date   Deputy clerk/Register/Notary public
___ublic, State of Michigan, County of _OJIBWAY_

ORDER

IT IS ORDERED:
☒ 1. The applicant has shown by ex parte affidavit that he/she is
   ☒ a. receiving public assistance, and payment of fees and costs are waived/suspended pursuant to MCR 2.002(D).
   ☐ b. indigent and payment of fees and costs are waived/suspended pursuant to MCR 2.002(D).
   The applicant is required to notify the court if the reason for waiving/suspending the fees and costs no lon___
☐ 2. The application is denied.

_3-1-2009_   _Lester Jubbs_
Date   Judge

NOTE: This order must be served on the other party at the time the pleading ___ served.

MC 20 (4/14) WAIVER/SUSPENSION ___ AND COSTS ___ FFIDAVIT AND ORDER)   MCR 2.002

COMPLETE 1a. IF ___ ARE RECEIVING ___LIC ASSISTANCE

COMPLETE 1b. INSTEAD IF YOU ARE CLAIMING INDIGENCY. PRISONERS CLAIMING INDIGENCY SHOULD CHECK BOX 1b., SKIP REST OF THE SECTION, AND ATTACH CERTIFIED COPY OF THEIR INSTITUTIONAL ACCOUNT FOR PRIOR YEAR

JUDGE WILL SUSPEND FEES OR DENY FEE SUSPENSION BELOW

IF YOU MUST USE AN OFFICIAL SERVER, OR MUST GET ALTERNATE SERVICE BY PUBLICATION, EXPLAIN THAT ON A SHEET ATTACHED TO THIS FORM

JUDGE WILL DATE AND SIGN

Appendix B: Preliminary Relief

As explained in "Do I Need 'Preliminary Relief'?" on page 60, you can ask for preliminary relief deciding custody, parenting time, residence of children, child support and alimony, while the divorce is pending. If the request succeeds, the order granting preliminary relief settles these issues until final decision in the Judgment of Divorce (TBP 4).

Courts provide preliminary relief in two forms: 1) quick interim relief, without prior notice to the defendant, followed by an interim order 2) temporary relief, after input from both parties, issued in a temporary order.

Plaintiffs typically seek interim relief right after they file for divorce. The judge considers the request informally, and either denies interim relief or grants it by signing a so-called ex parte order. The defendant must receive a copy of this order, and afterward has a chance to object to the order. If the defendant doesn't object, the ex parte order goes into effect, and governs custody, parenting time, residence of children and child support, until the end of the divorce.

To object, the defendant must file a written objection to the ex parte order within 14 days. After an objection, the friend of the court must intervene and try to settle the dispute. If this effort fails, a hearing must be held before the judge, with both sides in court, to decide interim relief.

Temporary relief begins and ends as a two-sided procedure. The plaintiff starts by filing a motion asking for temporary relief. The friend of the court usually intervenes to investigate, referee or mediate the request. If this fails, the

> ## Glossary
>
> *Ex parte order*–(pronounced "X-par-tay") is an order granting interim relief. The "ex parte" phrase means "from a part," denoting that the order is obtained by the plaintiff alone, without input from the defendant.
>
> *Temporary order*–is an order granting temporary relief after a hearing with both sides present.

motion goes to the judge, who decides the issue during a court hearing with both sides present.

By the time requests for interim and temporary relief reach the judge, there is hardly any difference between them. As a result, the relief the judge grants at a court hearing on interim relief is in the form of a temporary order. A temporary order is also issued after a hearing on a request for temporary relief.

Interim vs. Temporary Relief

In many ways, interim and temporary relief are similar, and actually merge during a court hearing on disputed relief. Which type of relief is the better choice?

To be sure, there are a few differences in what can be obtained from each type of relief. You can get custody, parenting time, residence of children and child support, but never alimony, with interim relief; temporary relief can decide all five issues. In addition, interim relief may only confirm the status quo, not change it. For example, if your husband has moved out and left you with control of the children, an ex parte order can give you sole or joint custody. Reversing the scenario, the husband cannot move out, file for divorce and get an ex parte order transferring custody of the children to him, since this would upset the custody status quo. A temporary order, by contrast, can either confirm or change the status quo existing at the beginning of the divorce.

On the other hand, interim relief is usually much easier to obtain. A plaintiff can receive the relief directly from the judge, without a hearing, and then the burden is on the defendant to oppose it. With temporary relief, you must file a motion and schedule and attend a hearing on the motion. In fact, you may have to do this twice, if the motion is first refereed by the friend of the court and then heard by the judge in court later.

All in all, from a plaintiff's point of view, it usually makes more sense to start with interim relief, and hope the defendant doesn't object (many defendants don't). If an objection is filed, the plaintiff must deal with the friend of the court and attend a court hearing later. But both of these steps are also necessary for temporary relief, so a plaintiff isn't much worse off by having tried interim relief first.

Preparing a Request for Interim Relief

If you want to seek interim relief, it's easy to make the request right after you file for divorce. So while you're preparing your initial divorce papers, as described in "Filing" on page 87, you will have to make some special preparations for interim relief.

You must first request interim relief in your Complaint for Divorce (TBP 1b), by checking boxes a and/or b, in paragraph #9, for the type of relief you want. The facts to support this request are embedded in the complaint and other initial divorce papers; normally you don't have to add more information in affidavits or other supporting documents, as was once necessary.

Counties handle interim relief orders in different ways. Some counties have a standard ex parte order form, whose use is encouraged or even required. In other counties, it's your responsibility to prepare an ex parte order before submitting it to the judge.

If you must do an interim order yourself, use the Ex Parte Order (TBP 5). For guidance, see the sample order at the end of this appendix. The bulk of the TBP 5 is what lawyers call "boilerplate," or standard provisions required by law. But key paragraphs #1, #2 and #3 deal with custody, parenting time and residence of children; child support is handled separately in its own order, the Uniform Child Support Order (FOC 10/52), which is incorporated into the TBP 5.

In paragraph #1 of the Ex Parte Order (TBP 5), you can assign custody of minor children. There are several custody options, including sole, joint, split and mixed custody (see "Custody" on page 9 and "Custody Provisions" on page 251 for more about custody choices and how to provide for these in the custody box in paragraph #1). As you choose custody, remember that an ex parte order may only confirm existing custody, not reassign it.

For simplicity, paragraph #2 provides for reasonable parenting time only. This choice avoids devising a complicated specific parenting time schedule for a fairly brief time until the end of the divorce.

Similarly, paragraph #3 confirms the dual local residences of the children established at divorce-filing. If you want to move early in the divorce, consider moving before you file since residence isn't normally fixed until filing (see "Residence of Children" on page 17 for more about residence of children).

Except in special cases, child support is determined by the Michigan child support formula (see "Child Support Provisions" on page 257 in Appendix H for more about child support, including the health care component of support). As explained in the appendix, figuring child support has gotten complicated, so your best bet is to have the friend of the court do this for you when you have that office review your interim relief papers (see "Friend of the Court Review" on page 165 for more about this review). Leave paragraphs #1 and 2 in the Uniform Child Support Order (FOC 10/52) blank for now and then fill these in after the friend of the court gives you the numbers.

One difficulty with preliminary child support during divorce is the problem of cohabitation. Parties seldom live together after a divorce, but sometimes stay together temporarily while a divorce is pending. The Michigan child support formula has difficulty coping with cohabitation because the formula assumes that the parties have divided into separate households. When parents are living together with the children, this assumption is invalid and the formula doesn't really fit.

Despite this problem, cohabitation periods during divorce tend to be brief, and can usually be worked around. For example, you might live with the defendant after filing for divorce while s/he looks for another place to live. If you get an ex parte order for child support during the period of cohabitation, you can reserve child support in paragraph #4 of the Ex Parte Order (TBP 5b) (see "Reserving Child Support" on page 263 for more about reservation of child support). Then, when the defendant moves out, you can go back to the judge and modify the ex parte order by adding child support. The friend of the court can help with the modification, using the Order Modifying Ex Parte Order (FOC 62).

Along with the Ex Parte Order (TBP 5) itself, you must prepare a Uniform Child Support Order (FOC 10/52) to provide for child support. And you'll need a Domestic Relations Judgment Information form (FOC 100) also (this is an information form for the friend of the court describing the parties and children; make two copies only of the form because, like the FOC 23, the friend of the court gets the original FOC 100 and the form isn't filed with the clerk).

In every Wayne County divorce with minor children, you must file a Certificate on Behalf of Plaintiff Regarding Ex Parte Interim Support Order. The sample certificate on page 97 is for a case without interim relief, with an explanation of why the relief isn't being sought on the reverse of the form. But when you are requesting interim relief, describe this relief on the front side, as suggested in the sample form.

Wayne County plaintiffs must also complete a Certificate of Conformity for Domestic Relations Order or Judgment (1225), saying that the ex parte order satisfies court requirements (this form would be identical to the sample one on page 141). The certificate must be submitted to the judge with the Ex Parte Order (TBP 5), and then filed with the clerk and served on the defendant with the TBP 5.

And finally, Wayne County requires an Order Data Form-Support (FD/FOC 4002) for support processing. There is a sample of this form on page 142, for the divorce judgment. You also must prepare one for an Ex Parte Order (TBP 5), and send or deliver it to the Wayne County Friend of the Court. The instructions with the form explain this procedure.

Paragraph #3 of the Uniform Child Support Order (FOC 10/52) provides for payment of child support by immediate income withholding. But because of a legal peculiarity, this provision doesn't go into effect until later. See "After You Get Interim Relief" on page 178 for more about setting up immediate income withholding through an Order Regarding Income Withholding (FOC 5), after an ex parte order takes effect.

After you prepare an Ex Parte Order (TBP 5) and the companion forms (Uniform Child Support Order (FOC 10/52) and Domestic Relations Judgment Information form (FOC 100) and any extra forms for Wayne County only), make three copies of each (exception: two copies only of the FOC 100) and mark one copy of each as the friend of the court's copy. See "Papers" on page 74 for more about preparing forms like these.

Getting an Interim Order

You can seek interim relief right after you file for divorce, or return to the courthouse and ask for the relief later. It's usually convenient to ask for the relief immediately after filing—you're at the courthouse anyway—so that's the procedure described below.

To seek interim relief right away, bring the various interim relief papers described above as you file for divorce. But hold these papers back from filing then. The judge must approve your request for interim relief before you file the interim order; if the request is denied, the order is withdrawn and never filed.

After the divorce is filed, you may want to ask the clerk about interim relief procedures before you leave. See "Before You Leave the Clerk's Office" on page 91 about which information you need to know. Remember: The clerk can only give general information about divorce procedures and cannot give specific legal advice.

Friend of the Court Review

Some counties want the friend of the court to review the interim relief papers before submission to the judge. Even when this review isn't required, it's still a good idea, and necessary, to get child support figures from the friend of the court so you can complete the Uniform Child Support Order (FOC 10/52).

When you go to the friend of the court's office, take copies of the initial divorce papers you have filed and the unfiled interim relief papers with you. A staff member there may be able to review the papers while you wait and provide child support figures to you. If your interim relief papers are satisfactory, the staff member may sign the TBP 5b, showing approval. Or the staff member may suggest modification of the papers, which you might be able to do on the spot. Afterward, the friend of the court will return all the papers to you.

Serving the Judgment Information Form on the Friend of the Court

The original Domestic Relations Judgment Information form (FOC 100) must be served on the friend of the court before the judge can grant interim relief. Now's a good time to do that. After delivery, complete the Proof of Service of Order/Judgment Papers (TBP 7) showing service on the friend of the court. See if you can make three copies of the TBP 7 on a photocopier at the courthouse. Add the TBP 7 to your interim relief papers so the judge will know that the friend of the court got the FOC 100. Later, you will file the TBP 7 with the clerk and provide copies to the friend of the court and defendant.

Requesting Interim Relief from the Judge

In most counties, you must seek interim relief from the judge assigned to your case at filing. In a few large counties, there may be a specially designated judge who reviews interim relief requests from all divorce cases.

Whoever handles your request, go to that judge's office. Judges consider requests for interim relief informally, in their offices. For the request, the judge must review the unfiled interim relief papers and copies of your already-filed initial divorce papers. If you're trying to opt out of the friend of the court system, this is also a good time to submit your opt-out papers to the judge (see

Appendix C for more about opt-out papers and procedures). The judge may have quick access to your case file with the filed papers or you can leave your own copies with the judge temporarily.

Ask the judge's secretary or law clerk to have the judge review your interim relief request and find out when you can return for a decision on the request. If you're lucky, the judge may be able to review your papers while you wait or within a short time later.

On return, ask the judge's secretary or law clerk about the judge's decision. If the request was denied, the judge will note the denial on the case file-copy of your Complaint for Divorce (TBP 1). If the problem was small, you might be able to correct the papers then or later and resubmit these to the judge. But after a complete denial of relief, you must withdraw the interim relief papers. If you want to seek preliminary relief again, you must file a motion for temporary relief.

If the judge grants interim relief as submitted, s/he will sign the Ex Parte Order (TBP 5) and companion Uniform Child Support Order (FOC 10/52) and maybe some copies. Return to the clerk's office and file the interim relief papers (omitting the for-the-friend of the court-only FOC 100). The clerk will take the original papers and friend of the court's copies, returning two copies of each form to you, which you should keep for your records and for service on the defendant.

Serving the Interim Relief Papers on the Defendant

For service, just include copies of the interim relief papers (TBP 5, FOC 10/52, TBP 7 (showing service of the FOC 100 on the friend of the court) and the FOC 100 itself) among the service papers served on the defendant (see "Service" on page 99 for more about service and proving service). After service, when you prove service on the reverse of the Summons and Complaint (MC 01), list the interim relief papers as additional service papers.

If interim relief was delayed, and you already have had the service papers served, you can serve the interim relief papers separately. Send copies of the interim relief papers cited above to the defendant by ordinary first-class mail. Afterward, make a photocopy of the Proof of Service of Order/Judgment Papers (TBP 7) (this will give you an extra to use now; you'll need two more copies of this form at the end of the divorce). Prove service on this form, make two copies and file the original and friend of the court's copy with the clerk.

Whichever service method you choose, don't delay service or making and filing a proof of service. The ex parte order is enforceable only after service, and the friend of the court needs a proof of service of the order to start income withholding.

The Defendant's Response to the Ex Parte Order

After receiving an ex parte order, the defendant has a choice: do nothing and let the order go into effect or object to the order. Each choice has important

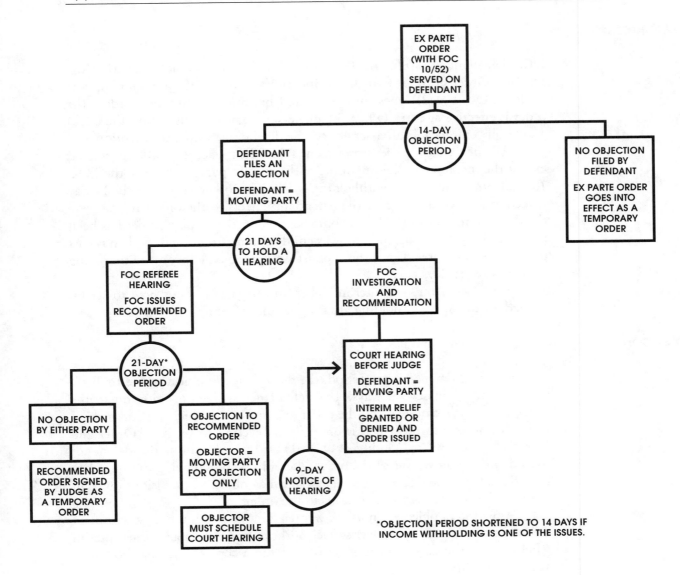

EX PARTE ORDER (WITH FOC 10/52) SERVED ON DEFENDANT

14-DAY OBJECTION PERIOD

DEFENDANT FILES AN OBJECTION

DEFENDANT = MOVING PARTY

NO OBJECTION FILED BY DEFENDANT

EX PARTE ORDER GOES INTO EFFECT AS A TEMPORARY ORDER

21 DAYS TO HOLD A HEARING

FOC REFEREE HEARING

FOC ISSUES RECOMMENDED ORDER

FOC INVESTIGATION AND RECOMMENDATION

21-DAY* OBJECTION PERIOD

COURT HEARING BEFORE JUDGE

DEFENDANT = MOVING PARTY

INTERIM RELIEF GRANTED OR DENIED AND ORDER ISSUED

NO OBJECTION BY EITHER PARTY

OBJECTION TO RECOMMENDED ORDER

OBJECTOR = MOVING PARTY FOR OBJECTION ONLY

9-DAY NOTICE OF HEARING

RECOMMENDED ORDER SIGNED BY JUDGE AS A TEMPORARY ORDER

OBJECTOR MUST SCHEDULE COURT HEARING

*OBJECTION PERIOD SHORTENED TO 14 DAYS IF INCOME WITHHOLDING IS ONE OF THE ISSUES.

consequences for what happens next in the case. These are depicted in the chart above and described in the following sections.

The defendant has 14 days to object after receiving service of the ex parte order. If the order was added to the service papers, service is made when the service papers are served on the defendant by acknowledgment, mail or delivery, as described in "Service" on page 99. If the order was served separately by mail as described above, service is complete when sent (not received). See "Time" on page 78 for more about figuring time periods like the 14-day objection deadline.

No Objection

If the defendant doesn't file an objection within the 14-day objection period, the Ex Parte Order (TBP 5) (which also incorporates the Uniform Child Support Order (FOC 10/52)) goes into effect and becomes a temporary order. The order is effective at entry (when the judge-signed order is filed with the clerk) and legally enforceable after service on the defendant, with one exception.

All the ex parte order's provisions take effect when the order is entered except the income withholding order authorized in paragraph #3 of the FOC 10/52. Immediate income withholding is delayed another week after the 14-day objection period (or longer if the defendant objects to the order; in that case the delay continues until after a court hearing on the ex parte order has been held). As a result, the defendant owes child support from the day when the ex parte order was entered, but the support isn't payable by income withholding until at least 21 days later.

See "After You Get Interim Relief" on page 178 about how to set up immediate income withholding after it goes into effect.

Objection

During the 14-day objection period, the defendant can object to the Ex Parte Order (TBP 5) in several ways. The defendant can file an objection to the order, move to rescind (cancel) the order or combine an objection and motion to rescind in one form, which is often the Objection to Ex Parte Order and Motion to Rescind or Modify (FOC 61). In the objection, the defendant should cite the provisions of the order s/he objects to, removing the agreed-to provisions from the dispute. The defendant may object to provisions outright or object by suggesting modifications in the order.

Any kind of objection must be written and filed with the clerk within 14 days after the defendant receives service of the ex parte order and other interim relief papers. The defendant must also send you a copy of the objection at or around that time.

After the defendant's objection, the friend of the court must schedule a hearing on the disputed order. The hearing must take place 21 days after the defendant's objection. The matter could be set for a court hearing directly before the judge. But often the friend of the court will schedule a hearing before one of its referees, in an effort to settle the dispute. The notice of hearing sent by the friend of the court will say which kind of hearing (referee or court) has been scheduled.

Friend of the Court

As explained in "Court System" on page 71, the friend of the court plays several roles during divorce, including investigation and refereeing. In a dispute over interim relief, the friend of the court may do either an investigation (summed up in a report and recommendation to the judge) or refereeing, but probably not both.

Investigation

Before the case is heard in court, the friend of the court may investigate your request for interim relief and make a report and recommendation to the judge. During an investigation, the friend of the court investigator may contact the parties, their children and others to gather facts about the dispute. Or if you want input, you can request an interview during the investigation.

The investigator summarizes the facts in a report which also contains a recommendation to the judge about deciding the request. The investigator's report is sent to the parties and put in the case file for the benefit of the judge. The judge may consider the report and recommendation, but isn't bound by either. The report cannot be submitted as evidence later at a court hearing (it usually contains lots of hearsay), unless both parties agree to admission of the report.

Refereeing

Refereeing is a more direct way to settle contested interim relief. The friend of the court, as referee, assumes a semi-judicial role, hears the request in a simulated court hearing and then issues a recommended decision. Either party can reject the recommendation, sending the case onto the judge.

Any kind of request for interim relief can be refereed. The parties can agree to refereeing, one party can ask for it or the judge can order it. But typically, family court judges in a county decide which kinds of issues are suitable for refereeing, and all these requests are routinely refereed. Some counties use refereeing selectively, while other counties, such as Wayne, require refereeing for every dispute over interim relief.

In many ways, a referee hearing resembles a court hearing. Each side can have a lawyer, testimony may be taken, the rules of evidence apply and the proceedings are recorded. The difference is informality. A referee hearing is typically held in a conference room at the friend of the court's office or a similar casual setting, instead of a courtroom.

During a referee hearing, the defendant presents his/her case against interim relief. Then, it's your turn to support the relief. Both sides may offer limited evidence, usually their own testimony (seldom from other witnesses), or documents like paycheck stubs or W-2 forms.

Afterward, the friend of the court referee must make findings in the case, and must read these into the record of the hearing or put them in a written report. The referee must also issue a recommended order deciding the interim relief request. The parties may be satisfied with the recommendation, and then the recommended order will be signed by the judge as a temporary order.

Either party can object to the friend of the court's recommended order because of a perceived factual or legal error in the recommendation. An objector who objects merely to harass or delay can be assessed costs by the court. The instructions below explain how to object.

Objecting to the Friend of the Court's Recommendation

You have 21 days to object to a referee's recommended order. This objection period begins when you receive the recommended order and the deadline is satisfied by filing an objection with the clerk (see "Time" on page 78 for more about figuring time periods of days).

Fill out the objection form

Use the Objection to Referee's Recommended Order (FOC 68) for your objection. Fill out the objection as shown in the sample form at the end of this appendix. Incidentally, the objector becomes the moving party for the purposes of the objection only.

Schedule a court hearing

After an objection to a referee's recommended order, the dispute moves onto a court hearing before a judge. It's up to the objector to schedule this hearing.

Contact the clerk or friend of the court office to find out who schedules court hearings in the county. Typically, court hearings are arranged by the (court) clerk or a special assignment clerk, with a simple request.

But in some counties, you must file a written request for a hearing in a special request form known as a praecipe. In Wayne County, for example, you ask for a hearing by filing a Request for Hearing on a Motion (Praecipe) Order/Judgment (FD/FOC 4021). Ask the Wayne County Clerk for a copy of this form as part of a larger Miscellaneous Motion Packet (FD/FOC 4037), which includes instructions and related material.

Before scheduling the court hearing, the objector should estimate how much time the court will need to hear the matter. The type of court hearing—whether it's evidentiary or nonevidentiary—dictates the amount of time necessary for the hearing (see "Court Hearing" below for an explanation of the difference and which issues require each type of hearing).

A nonevidentiary hearing normally takes 15-30 minutes. Short hearings like this are often scheduled on the motion days that judges hold each week. An evidentiary hearing requires a bigger chunk of time, since it takes more time to receive evidence. You should be able to obtain a bigger block of time on the judge's motion day or during a non-motion day.

In scheduling a court hearing, the objector must set it far enough in advance to give the opponent enough notice, so s/he can prepare for the hearing. For an objection served by mail, nine days' notice is necessary. Thus, there must be at least a nine-day interval between service of the objection by mail (which is complete upon mailing) and the court hearing. See "Time" on page 78 for information about figuring time periods of days.

After the objector gets the information about the date, time and place of the hearing, s/he must insert this information in the Notice of Hearing section of the Objection to Referee's Recommended Order (FOC 68), and make three copies of the form.

File the objection

The objector must take the Objection to Referee's Recommended Order (FOC 68) and copies to the clerk. The clerk will file the original objection, keep a copy for the friend of the court and return two copies to the objector.

Serve the objection

The objector must serve the objection on the other party by sending a copy to him/her by ordinary first-class mail. Afterward, the objector must prove service in the Certificate of Mailing at the bottom of the FOC 68. The objector should make an extra copy of the FOC 68, fill out the certificate and make two copies of this form. The objector must send the filled-in form and a friend of the court's copy to the clerk, and also keep a copy.

Court Hearing

If the friend of the court's investigation or refereeing didn't settle the matter, your request for interim relief will be decided by the judge during a court hearing. The judge considers the disputed interim relief anew or "de novo" as the FOC 68 says. Previously, courts would start from scratch at de novo hearings, as if the refereeing never happened. Today, courts can use material from the referee hearing, but the parties can supplement this with new or additional evidence.

There are two kinds of court hearings: 1) nonevidentiary hearing where little or no evidence is introduced and the parties merely make legal arguments to the judge 2) evidentiary hearing where evidence, such as testimony, is presented. Which type of court hearing do you need? The test is whether you and the defendant agree on the facts surrounding the interim relief request. If these facts aren't in dispute, a nonevidentiary hearing will do; disputed facts spell the need for a full evidentiary hearing.

There are four possible issues at stake in an interim order: custody, parenting time, residence of children and child support. Parenting time is unlikely to be disputed because the reasonable parenting time the ex parte order provides for is noncontroversial. The children's residence is also a nonissue because the ex parte order merely confirms the established residences.

Custody, on the other hand, almost always involves factual issues, and will probably require an evidentiary hearing. Disputes over child support usually concern the amount of the child support or the method of payment. With either issue, the facts are often known or easily proved, calling for either a very limited evidentiary hearing or a nonevidentiary one.

Preparing for a Court Hearing

Regardless of which issues are at stake, you must plan all parts of your case carefully. Your legal arguments must be well-organized, with convincing evidence to support them.

Securing evidence is by far the most important part of prehearing preparation. If you want testimony from witnesses, you must have them attend the hearing. Any documents or other things you want to introduce at the hearing must also be obtained beforehand.

Sometimes, witnesses volunteer to testify and important documents are readily available. But other times, you must obtain this evidence by subpoena.

Subpoenas

For an evidentiary court hearing, you may need the testimony of witnesses and/or portable items (documents, photographs, etc.) which witnesses have in their control. If they won't provide these to you voluntarily, you may have to get them by subpoena.

Who Can Be Subpoenaed?

Not everyone can be subpoenaed. Michigan's court rules say that subpoenas may only be issued to people who are present inside the state of Michigan; out-of-state individuals are immune from Michigan subpoenas.

Subpoena Costs

Courts issue subpoenas without charge. But to encourage attendance, a subpoenaed witness is entitled to a daily court attendance fee of the greater of: 1) $12 (for a full day) or $6 (for a half-day), or 2) the witness' daily lost wages or salary up to a maximum of $15 per day (unless unemployed, most witnesses will qualify for an attendance fee of $15 per day). The witness must also receive mileage at the state government rate for unclassified employees for travel to and from the courthouse for each day at court.

In most cases, these court attendance fees (daily attendance fee and mileage fee) must be offered to the witness, in the form of cash, money order or cashier's check, when the subpoena is served on the subpoenaed witness. There may also be costs for serving subpoenas, which are described in "Serving Subpoenas" below.

Time for Subpoena

You must obtain subpoenas in advance of a court hearing and have them served before the hearing. The extra time gives the subpoenaed witness the chance to make arrangements to attend court and/or obtain requested items. According to the court rules, subpoenaed witnesses are entitled to a minimum of two days' notice. As a result, make sure your subpoenas are served on the witnesses at least two days before the hearing. See "Time" on page 78 for help with figuring time periods of days.

Obtaining a Subpoena

Lawyers, who are officers of the court, can issue their own subpoenas. As a nonlawyer, you will have to get your subpoenas from the clerk.

Some clerks have automated systems for issuing subpoenas, and will make them for you at their office. But in most counties, you must prepare a Subpoena (MC 11) and then submit it to the clerk for issuing.

Complete the Subpoena (MC 11) as shown in the sample at the end of this section. Make four copies. Go to the clerk and have the clerk issue the subpoena by signing and sealing the original and all copies.

Set aside one copy of the Subpoena (MC 11) for proof of service. After service, you must have proof that the Subpoena (MC 11) was served on the witness. You prove service on the reverse of the extra copy of the MC 11, which will be referred to as the proof of service copy of the Subpoena (MC 11).

Serving Subpoenas

There are three ways to serve subpoenas: acknowledgment, mail and delivery. Service by acknowledgment is easiest and cheapest, followed by mail and then delivery.

Service by Acknowledgment

Service by acknowledgment is by far the simplest method of service. There are actually two ways to acknowledge service: personally and by mail. Both are easy to use.

Personal Acknowledgment

For personal acknowledgment, you simply hand the Subpoena (MC 11) and the court attendance fees to the witness. If the witness is in another Michigan county, you can arrange to have someone give the MC 11 and fees to the witness there. Service by personal acknowledgment is complete when the witness receives the Subpoena (MC 11) from you or your helper.

Proving Service by Personal Acknowledgment

Immediately after service, you or your helper should have the witness date (with both time and day) and sign the Acknowledgment of Service, which is at the bottom of the reverse of your proof of service copy of the Subpoena (MC 11). Afterward, make three copies of this paper, earmark one "FOC" and save for filing later as your proof of service.

Acknowledgment by Mail

A subpoenaed witness can also acknowledge service through the mail. You simply send the Subpoena (MC 11), your proof of service copy of the MC 11 and the court attendance fees to the witness by ordinary first-class mail. Service by acknowledgment by mail is complete when the subpoenaed witness receives the mailing.

Proving Service by Acknowledgment by Mail

Right after service, the witness should date (with both time and day) and sign the Acknowledgment of Service, which is at the bottom of the reverse of your proof of service copy of the Subpoena (MC 11). The witness must then give or mail the proof of service copy of the MC 11 to you. Afterward, make three copies of this paper, earmark one "FOC" and save one for filing later as your proof of service.

Service by Mail

Service by mail is a little more expensive than service by acknowledgment. But it's a very effective method of service because it goes anywhere U.S. mail is delivered. The court rules permit service by mail through either registered or certified mail. Use certified mail because it's cheaper than registered mail.

Cheaper (and easier) yet is service by acknowledgment by mail, since you can obtain acknowledgment by ordinary mail. Thus, you will probably want to use the acknowledgment method for witnesses who are friendly and willing to acknowledge service by mail. Service by mail, on the other hand, is better suited for witnesses you don't know or whom you suspect are uncooperative.

Serving a subpoena by mail is much like serving the service papers by mail. So see "Service by Mail" on page 102 for complete instructions for service by mail and proving service. Just substitute the MC 11 for any reference to the MC 01 in that section.

Service by Delivery

You can also serve a Subpoena (MC 11) by delivering it to the witness. You or any mentally competent adult can deliver a MC 11.

If the witness is friendly and cooperative, consider service by personal acknowledgment instead of service by delivery. Therefore, it's likely that you will serve by delivery when the witness is unfriendly, lives faraway or is otherwise difficult to serve. Moreover, service by delivery will probably be carried out by a professional process server, such as a commercial process server or a sheriff.

The procedure for serving a subpoena or the service papers by delivery is about the same. So see "Service by Delivery" on page 105 for instructions for service by delivery and proving service. Just substitute the MC 11 for any reference to the MC 01 in that section.

Witness in Court

If the witness obeys the subpoena, s/he will appear at the court hearing and give the testimony or produce the things you seek. But if the witness doesn't show up, you can ask for adjournment of the hearing. The court should grant your request for more time. The court can also force the uncooperative witness to appear for the next hearing by threatening to hold him/her in contempt of court.

Making Your Case in Court

At the court hearing, the defendant is the moving party because s/he made interim relief the issue by objecting to the relief. This is true even if you were the objector-moving party against the referee's recommended order. If so, you re-assume the role of non-moving party at the court hearing.

During the court hearing, the judge will listen to both sides: the defendant's objection to the interim relief and your reasons for it. Your case for the relief is really made up of two things: the facts (evidence) and legal rules (law) supporting relief.

Custody

Custody is decided according to the best interests of the children and the two custody presumptions (custodial and parental), when these presumptions apply to the case.

The best interests of the children are determined by the 12 or 13 factors in the child custody act of 1970 (see "Custody" on page 9 for a complete list). During the hearing, the judge must make factual findings on *all* the best interest factors. Consequently, both parties must deal with each factor as they present evidence and make legal arguments. Some factors may not apply to the case, yet even these must be considered and rejected.

The custody presumptions may not be factors in the case. If the parents have been living together with the children just before the divorce, there probably hasn't been enough time for establishment of a custodial environment. But if one parent has been absent during that period, it may apply and be important.

The parental presumption isn't likely to be an issue because it's usually parents who battle for custody during a divorce. But third parties sometimes intervene in ongoing custody disputes, such as divorces, and seek custody. If this happens, the parental presumption is important in defending against the third party's custody claim.

When a presumption applies, "clear and convincing" evidence must be introduced to overcome the presumption. For example, in a custody dispute between a noncustodial parent and a custodial parent invoking the custodial presumption, the noncustodian might show physical abuse of the children by the custodian. This kind of evidence would probably qualify as clear and convincing evidence that the best interests of the children are for transferring custody from one parent to the other.

Since a custody hearing is likely to be evidentiary, with important issues at stake, you must make careful preparations for the hearing. Sometimes, it may even be necessary to subpoena witnesses, such as teachers, counselors, social workers or neighbors. See "Preparing for a Court Hearing" above for more information about prehearing preparations.

Glossary

Clear and convincing evidence–is strong evidence that makes something highly probable.

Or you could look at it this way: On an imaginary evidence scale, clear and convincing evidence falls somewhere between a preponderance of evidence (factual assertions are "more likely than not") standard used in ordinary civil cases, but less than the beyond-a-reasonable-doubt test in criminal cases.

Child Support

When child support is contested, the issues usually boil down to two things: 1) amount of child support (not only the base support amount, but also adjustments or add-ons for health care, child care and educational expenses) 2) method of payment.

As explained in "Child Support" on page 22, the amount of child support is determined by the incomes of both parents and the needs of the children. These factors are embodied in the Michigan child support formula which sets child support in most cases. In exceptional cases, departure from the formula is allowed.

There are frequently disputes over the amount of income a parent receives, but this issue can be resolved with documentary evidence like paycheck stubs, W-2 forms and income tax returns. Health care, child care and educational expenses can be proved with medical bills, child care provider statements, etc. After the facts are established, the Michigan child support formula provides detailed rules about which parent should pay and how much.

As for the method of payment, immediate income withholding is the normal way of paying child support. You can avoid immediate income withholding by opting out of the friend of the court system. Appendix C explains the various opt-out options.

Court Hearing Itself

See "Courthouse Appearances" on page 79 for information about appearing in court, including finding the courtroom, arrival there and how to conduct yourself during the hearing.

When your case is called by the courtroom clerk, step forward and identify yourself. Mention that you are representing yourself. Take a seat at one of the tables inside the bar (the gate) of the court, and get ready to present your case.

The format of the hearing hinges on whether the defendant shows up for the hearing. If s/he is absent, the hearing should be brief, with you winning by default. A full hearing with arguments from both sides is necessary when the defendant appears at the hearing. Expect to have the defendant at the hearing. Then you'll be prepared if s/he attends and relieved if s/he doesn't.

The Defendant Doesn't Attend the Hearing

The defendant, as the moving party, must appear to argue against your request for interim relief. Thus, the defendant's absence should result in dismissal of the defendant's objection and confirmation of the ex parte order as a temporary order granting relief.

The Defendant Attends the Hearing

Things won't be so easy when your ex is present at the hearing. Facing opposition, you must present your case forcefully to counter the defendant's objections to your interim relief.

The judge will probably start the hearing with some informal questioning of both parties. For a nonevidentiary hearing, the judge will go right to the legal arguments, since evidence isn't necessary. Each side gets to present their legal arguments for or against interim relief, with the defendant arguing first as the moving party. After the first round of arguments, the judge may ask each side for rebuttal arguments, responding to what has already been said. After arguments, the judge decides whether to sustain defendant's objection to the ex parte order.

At an evidentiary hearing, evidence precedes legal argument. The judge will ask the defendant, as the moving party, to go first. S/he must take the witness stand, be sworn and give testimony. The defendant may also introduce documents during the testimony or call other witnesses, who may also have documents. You and the judge may ask questions during the defendant's testimony or that given by the witnesses.

Then the reverse happens: You give testimony and the defendant and the judge can question you. Witnesses or documentary evidence you present are also subject to questioning and examination.

After all the evidence is received, the judge gives both parties the opportunity to present their legal arguments. The judge may then ask for another round of arguments, in rebuttal, allowing each party one last word.

When the arguments are finished, the judge decides the objection. The judge may rule immediately "from the bench," or take the case "under submission" and rule later, perhaps in writing. The judge will probably rule right away on simple issues, like child support, after a nonevidentiary hearing; more complicated issues, like custody, presented in a full evidentiary hearing, may require more time for decision.

After the judge rules, the decision must be put into a court order. Since the defendant is the moving party, it's his/her responsibility to prepare the order granting or denying your request for interim relief.

An order denying interim relief might be very brief, just a one-paragraph order rejecting relief. If relief is granted completely, the Ex Parte Order (TBP 5) can simply be confirmed as a temporary order. But if the judge's decision was mixed, with relief granted in part and denied in part, the defendant must prepare a proposed order following the judge's decision.

You have the right to review any proposed order the defendant makes and can agree to it, if you believe the order follows the judge's decision. If not, you can object to the proposed order, and the correct wording of the order (but not the legal issues in the order) must be decided during another court hearing. The friend of the court distributes a form for objecting, Objection to Proposed Order (FOC 78), which comes with an instruction booklet.

After You Get Interim Relief

If your request for interim relief is ultimately successful (from the defendant's failure to object to the ex parte order initially or after a referee or court hearing), you must put the ex parte/temporary order into effect. The main concern is starting immediate income withholding for collection of child support.

In most counties, the friend of the court sets up income withholding after receiving copies of the ex parte/temporary order and proof of service of the order. The friend of the court will get an Order Regarding Income Withholding (FOC 5) from the judge and issue an income withholding notice to the payer's source of income (an employer usually). After this, income withholding may begin.

But in some counties, you must start this process by preparing and submitting an Order Regarding Income Withholding (FOC 5) to the judge for signing, and provide copies to the defendant and friend of the court. The FOC 5 for collection of support from an ex parte/temporary order would be identical to the sample one on page 139.

Modification or Termination of the Order

An ex parte/temporary order remains in force until the end of the divorce. But during this time, either party can file a motion to modify the order. The motion must be decided at a referee or court hearing, and may be granted for "good cause." Or the parties can agree to a modification, which the friend of the court and judge must review and approve.

Ordinarily, an ex parte order/temporary order terminates at the end of the divorce, when the divorce judgment decides all issues. However, it's permissible to carry over a provision from a preliminary order into the judgment and sometimes it makes sense to do so. For example, unpaid child support due from a preliminary order must be preserved or else it's canceled. Paragraph #11 of the Uniform Child Support Order (FOC 10/52), which handles support for ex parte orders and judgments, preserves such unpaid child support. To preserve other things, you must add extra provisions in the Judgment of Divorce (TBP 4c).

Approved, SCAO

| STATE OF MICHIGAN JUDICIAL CIRCUIT COUNTY | DOMESTIC RELATIONS JUDGMENT INFORMATION, PAGE 1 ☒ TEMPORARY   ☐ FINAL | Original - Friend of the court Copies - All parties CASE NO. |

USE NOTE: Complete this form and file it with the friend of the court (**do not file this form with the office of the clerk of the court**) when the first temporary custody, parenting-time, or support order is entered and when submitting any final proposed judgment awarding custody, parenting time, or support. Mail a copy to each party and file proof of mailing with the court (may use form MC 302, Proof of Mailing).

The information previously provided   ☐ is changed   ☐ is unchanged. (Complete only the fields that have changed.)

2-28-2009
Date

Darlene A. Lovelace
Signature

Plaintiff Information

Name
DARLENE ANN LOVELACE

Address
121 S. MAIN
LAKE CITY, MI 48800

| Social security number | Telephone number |
| 380-16-1010 | 772-0000 |

E-mail address
dalovelace@mtran.com

Employer name, address, telephone number, and FEIN (if known)
10,000 PANCAKES
111 M-78
LAKE CITY, MI 48800
772-0011 FEIN: 38-1111707

Driver's license number and state
L650 603 440 886 MICH.

Occupational license number(s), type(s), issuing state(s), and date(s)

Defendant Information

Name
DUDLEY ERNEST LOVELACE

Address
900 S. MAPLE
LAKE CITY, MI 48800

| Social security number | Telephone number |
| 379-10-5567 | 773-3004 |

E-mail address
delovelace@mtran.com

Employer name, address, telephone number, and FEIN (if known)
WATERBED WORLD
1000 SERVICE RD.
LAKE CITY, MI 48800
773-0011 FEIN: 38-0017760

Driver's license number and state
L649 601 402 701 MICH

Occupational license number(s), type(s), issuing state(s), and date(s)

CUSTODY PROVISIONS   sole, plaintiff = P   sole, defendant = D   joint = J   other = O _____ (must identify)

Child's name	Social security number	Date of birth	Physical custody P, D, J, O	Child's primary residence address	Legal custody P, D, J, O
DUANE WESLEY LOVELACE	446-10-1001	6-1-2006	P	121 S. MAIN, LAKE CITY, MI 48800	P
DARRYL WENDELL LOVELACE	469-00-4411	7-1-2007	P	" "	P

SUPPORT PROVISIONS

☒ Support provisions are stated in the Uniform Support Order. Medical Support provisions are stated on page 2 of this form.

FOC 100 (3/14) **DOMESTIC RELATIONS JUDGMENT INFORMATION, PAGE 1**   MCR 3.211(F)

Approved, SCAO

STATE OF MICHIGAN
JUDICIAL CIRCUIT
COUNTY

MEDICAL SUPPORT PROVISIONS
name of each child in this case

Plaintiff's Insurance Coverage
Provider name and address

Defendant's Insurance
Provider name and address

LAKEVIEW HMO

FOC 100 (3/14)

STATE OF MICHIGAN Circuit Court - Family Division COUNTY	PROOF OF SERVICE OF ORDER/JUDGMENT PAPERS	CASE NO.

Plaintiff (appearing *in propria persona*):

                                   Defendant:

                             v

I served the following papers in this case as described below:

1. On _3-1-2009_____, I ☒ delivered   ☐ sent by first-class mail   to the friend of the court at its official address, these papers:
   ☒ Original Domestic Relations Judgment Information form for   ☒ Ex Parte Order
   ☐ Other: ☐ Judgment of Divorce

2. On_____, I sent to defendant by first-class mail at his/her address in the caption above, which is defendant's last known mailing address, copies of these papers:
a. Interim relief papers:
   ☐ Domestic Relations Judgment Information form
   ☐ Ex Parte Order
   ☐ Uniform Child Support Order
   ☐ Other:
b. Judgment papers:
   ☐ Domestic Relations Judgment Information form
   ☐ Judgment of Divorce: ☐ Proposed   ☐ Final
   ☐ Uniform support order(s):   ☐ Uniform Child Support Order   ☐ Uniform Spousal Support Order
   ☐ Order Regarding Income Withholding
   ☐ Other:

I declare that the statements above are true to the best of my information, knowledge and belief.

Date_ _3-1-2009_____

                              Plaintiff_ _Darlene A. Lovelace_____

TBP 7 (1/16)   **PROOF OF SERVICE OF ORDER/JUDGMENT PAPERS**

STATE OF MICHIGAN Circuit Court - Family Division COUNTY	EX PARTE ORDER for Custody, Parenting Time, Residence of Children and Support	CASE NO.

Plaintiff (appearing *in propria persona*):

v

Defendant:

Date of order___3-1-2009___   Judge ___LESTER TUBBS___

While this case is pending, **IT IS ORDERED**:

1. **CUSTODY:** Custody of the minor children is granted as follows:

PL = Plaintiff   DF = Defendant   JT = Joint   3rd = Third party, named here:

CHILD'S NAME	DATE OF BIRTH	LEGAL CUSTODY	PHYSICAL CUSTODY
DUANE WESLEY LOVELACE	6-1-2006	PL	PL
DARRYL WENDELL LOVELACE	7-1-2007	PL	PL

2. **PARENTING TIME:** Any parent without physical custody shall have reasonable parenting time.

3. **RESIDENCE OF CHILDREN:**

   a. **Local residences.** A parent whose custody of parenting time of a child is governed by this order shall not change the legal residence of the child except in compliance with section 11 of the Child Custody Act, MCL 722.31.

   b. **State residence (domicile).** The minor children's residences (domicile) shall not be moved from the state of Michigan without the prior approval of the court.

   c. **Notice of change of residence.** The person awarded custody shall promptly notify the friend of the court in writing when the minor is moved to another address.

TBP 5a (1/16)   **EX PARTE ORDER, page 1**

STATE OF MICHIGAN Circuit Court - Family Division COUNTY	EX PARTE ORDER for Custody, Parenting Time, Residence of Children and Support	CASE NO.

Plaintiff:

v

Defendant:

IT IS ALSO ORDERED:

4. **CHILD SUPPORT:** Child support is provided for in a uniform support order which shall accompany and be incorporated into this order.
   ☐ (Instead of the paragraph above), child support is reserved until further order of this court, excusing filing of a uniform support order now.

5. **EFFECTIVENESS AND ENFORCEABILITY:** This order is effective when entered with the clerk and enforceable after service on defendant.

6. **OTHER:**

TO THE DEFENDANT:

> **NOTICE**

7. You may file a written objection to this order or a motion to modify or rescind this order. You must file the written objection or motion with the clerk of the court within 14 days after you were served with this order. You must serve a true copy of the objection or motion on the friend of the court and the party who obtained the order.

8. If you file a written objection, the friend of the court must try to resolve the dispute. If the friend of the court cannot resolve the dispute and if you wish to bring the matter before the court without the assistance of counsel, the friend of the court must provide you with form pleadings and writ... instructions and must schedule a hearing with the court.

9. The ex parte order will automatically become a temporary order if you do not file a... or motion to modify or rescind the ex parte order and a request for a hearing. Eve... is filed, the ex parte order will remain in effect and must be obeyed unless change... order.

Reviewed by FOC:

Date_____3-1-2009_____   Judge_____*Lester Tubbs*_____

JUDGE WILL DATE AND SIGN IF S/HE APPROVES THE ORDER

TBP 5b (1/16)   **EX PARTE ORDER, page 2**

Approved, SCAO

Original - Court
1st copy - Plaintiff

2nd copy - Defendant
3rd copy - Friend of the court

STATE OF MICHIGAN JUDICIAL CIRCUIT COUNTY	UNIFORM CHILD SUPPORT ORDER (PAGE 1) ☒ EX PARTE ☐ TEMPORARY ☐ MODIFICATION ☐ FINAL	CASE NO.

Court address

Court telephone no.

Plaintiff's name, address, and telephone no.		Defendant's name, address, and telephone no.

v

Plaintiff's attorney name, bar no., address, and telephone no.

Defendant's attorney name, bar no., address, and telephone no.

Plaintiff's source of income name, address, and telephone no.

Defendant's source of income name, address, and telephone no.

This order is entered ☒ after hearing. ☐ after statutory review. ☐ on stipulation/consent of the parties.
☐ The friend of the court recommends child support be ordered as follows.
☐ If you disagree with this recommendation, you must file a written objection with _____
before **21 days** from the date this order is mailed. If you do not object, this proposed order will be presented to the court for entry. ___ on or
☐ Attached are the calculations pursuant to MCL 552.505(1)(h) and MCL 552.517b.

IT IS ORDERED, unless otherwise ordered in item 12 or 13:
1. **The children who are supported under this order and the payer and payee are:** ☐ Standard provisions have been modified (see item 12 or 13):

Payer: DUDLEY E. LOVELACE   Payee: DARLENE A. LOVELACE

Children's names, birthdates, and annual overnights with payer:

Children's names	Date of birth	Overnights
DUANE W. LOVELACE	6-1-2006	48
DARRYL W. LOVELACE	7-1-2007	48

Effective 3-1-2009 , the payer shall pay a monthly child support obligation for the children named above.

Children supported:	1 child	2 children	3 children	4 children	5 or more children
Base support: (includes support plus or minus premium adjustment for health-care insurance)					
Support:	$ 326	$ 349	$	$	$
Premium adjust.	$	$	$	$	$
Subtotal:	$ 326	$ 349	$	$	$
Ordinary medical:	$ 18	$ 36	$	$	$
Child care:	$	$	$	$	$
Other:	$	$	$	$	$
SS benefit credit:	$	$	$	$	$
Total:	$ 344	$ 385	$	$	$

☐ Support was reduced because payer's income was reduced.

(Continued on page 2.)
FOC 10 / 52 (8/14) **UNIFORM CHILD SUPPORT ORDER, PAGE 1**   MCL 552.14, MCL 552.517, MCL 552.517b(3), MCR 3.211

Approved, SCAO

Original - Court 1st copy - Plaintiff	2nd copy - Defendant 3rd copy - Friend of the court

STATE OF MICHIGAN
JUDICIAL CIRCUIT
COUNTY

UNIFORM CHILD SUPPORT ORDER (PAGE 2)
☒ **EX PARTE**   ☐ **TEMPORARY**
☐ **MODIFICATION**   ☐ **FINAL**

CASE NO.

Court telephone no.

Court address

Plaintiff's name   v   Defendant's name

1. **Item 1** (continued).

   Uninsured Health-Care Expenses. All uninsured health-care expenses exceeding the annual ordinary medical amount will be paid _39_ % by the plaintiff and _61_ % by the defendant. Uninsured expenses exceeding the annual ordinary medical amount for the year they are incurred that are not paid within 28 days of a written payment request may be enforced by the friend of the court. The annual ordinary medical amount is _$715_ .

   Obligation Ends. Except for child care, or as otherwise ordered, support obligations for each child end on the last day of the month the child turns age 18. The child-care obligation for each child ends August 31 following the child's 12th birthday. The parties must notify each other of changes in child-care expenses and must additionally notify the friend of the court if the changes end those expenses.

   ☐ **Post-majority Support:** The following children will be attending high school on a full-time basis after turning 18 years of age. Therefore, the support obligation for each specific child ends on the last day of the month as follows, except in no case may it extend beyond the time the child reaches 19 years and 6 months of age: (Specify name of child and date obligation ends.)

   _____

   _____

2. **Insurance.** For the benefit of the children, the ☐ plaintiff ☒ defendant shall maintain health-care coverage through an insurer (as defined in MCL 552.602) that includes payment for hospital, dental, optical, and other health-care expenses when the ~~coverage~~ is available at a reasonable ~~cost~~ including coverage available as a ~~benefit of~~ employment or under an ~~...~~

~~...~~ **Orders.** Th~~...~~ any prior support or~~...~~ ~~...~~ served and paid at~~...~~
   order. Past-due amoun~~...~~ the arrearage guideline in the Michigan Child Support Formula.

☐ 12. **Michigan Child Support Formula Deviation.** The support provisions ordered do not follow the Michigan Child Support Formula. The attached deviation addendum (FOC 10d) provides the basis for deviation and the required findings by the court.

☐ 13. **Other:** (Attach separate sheets as needed.)

	Date		Date
Plaintiff (if consent/stipulation)		Defendant (if consent/stipulation)	
	Date		Date
Plaintiff's attorney		Defendant's attorney	

Prepared by: _DARLENE A. LOVELACE_
Name (type or print)

Lester Tubbs _____   Bar no.
Judge

_3-1-2009_
Date

CERTIFICATE OF MAILING

I certify that on this date I served a copy of this order on the parties or their attorneys by first-class mail addressed to their last-known addresses as defined in MCR 3.203.   ☐ I certify that I also served the Deviation Addendum (FOC 10d) with this order.

_____   _____
Date   Signature

COURT USE ONLY

FOC 10 / 52 (8/14) **UNIFORM CHILD SUPPORT ORDER, PAGE 3**   MCL 552.14, MCL 552.517, MCL 552.517b(3), MCR 3.211

Approved, SCAO

Original - Court
1st copy - Moving party
2nd copy - Objecting party

3rd copy - Friend of the court
4th copy - Proof of service
5th copy - Proof of service

CASE NO.

**STATE OF MICHIGAN
JUDICIAL CIRCUIT
COUNTY**

**OBJECTION TO
REFEREE'S RECOMMENDED ORDER**

Court telephone no.

Court address

Plaintiff's name, address, and telephone no.   ☒ moving party

Defendant's name, address, and telephone no.   ☐ moving party

v

PARTY WHO OBJECTS TO ORDER IS MOVING PARTY HERE

Third party's name, address, and telephone no.   ☐ moving party

I object to the entry of the referee's recommended order dated _____3-30-2009_____ and request a de novo review by the court. My objection is based on the following reason(s):

IN DECIDING CUSTODY, REFEREE DIDN'T CONSIDER ALL THE BEST INTEREST FACTORS. THE REFEREE OMITTED THE DOMESTIC VIOLENCE FACTOR, ALTHOUGH THERE WAS EVIDENCE OF SUCH ABUSE BY DEFENDANT.

SAY WHY YOU BELIEVE REFEREE ERRED IN ITS DECISION

_____4-15-2009_____
Date

Darlene A. Lovelace
Moving party's signature
DARLENE A. LOVELACE
Name (type or print)

NOTICE OF HEARING

A hearing will be held on this objection before _____LESTER TUBBS_____
Judge

on _____5-15-2009_____ at _____9:00 AM_____ at _____OJIBWAY COUNTY COURTHOUSE_____ .
Date   Time   Location

If you require special accommodations to use the court because of a disability, or if you require a foreign language interpreter to help you fully participate in court proceedings, please contact the court immediately to make arrangements. When contacting the court, provide your case number(s).

CERTIFICATE OF MAILING

I certify that on this date I served a copy of this objection and notice of hearing on the parties or their attorneys by first-class mail addressed to their last-known addresses as defined in MCR 3.203.

_____4-15-2009_____
Date

Darlene A. Lovelace
Signature of objecting party

MCR 3.215(E)

FOC 68 (5/10) **OBJECTION TO REFEREE'S RECOMMENDED ORDER**

Approved, SCAO

Original - Return
1st copy - Witness
2nd copy - File
3rd copy - Extra

STATE OF MICHIGAN
JUDICIAL DISTRICT
JUDICIAL CIRCUIT
COUNTY   PROBATE

SUBPOENA
Order to Appear and/or Produce

CASE NO.

Court address

Court telephone no.

Police Report No. (if applicable):

Plaintiff(s)/Petitioner(s)

☐ People of the State of Michigan
☒ *DARLENE A. LOVELACE*

☒ Civil   ☐ Criminal

☐ Probate   In the matter of

v

Defendant(s)/Respondent(s)

DUDLEY E. LOVELACE

Charge

In the Name of the People of the State of Michigan. TO: *JOHN QUICK, LAKESIDE FAMILY*
COUNSELING CENTER, 100 S. FRONT, LAKE CITY, MI 48800

If you require special accommodations to use the court because of disabilities, please contact the court immediately to make arrangements.

YOU ARE ORDERED TO:

☒ 1. Appear personally at the time and place stated below: You may be required to appear from time to time and day to day until excused.

☒ The court address above   ☐ Other:

| Day   *TUESDAY* | Date   *5-15-2009* | Time   *9:00 AM* |

☒ 2. Testify at trial / examination / hearing.

☒ 3. Produce/permit inspection or copying of the following items: *ALL DOCUMENTS, RECORDS AND FILES*
REGARDING PSYCHOLOGICAL TESTING AND/OR EVALUATION OF
DUANE W. LOVELACE AND DARRYL W. LOVELACE.

☐ 4. Testify as to your assets, and bring with you the items listed in line 3 above.

☐ 5. Testify at deposition.

☐ 6. Abide by the attached prohibition against transferring or disposing of property. (MCL 600.6104(2), 600.6116, or 600.6119.)

☐ 7. Other:

☒ 8. Person requesting subpoena
DARLENE A. LOVELACE   Telephone no.   *772-0000*
Address   *121 S. MAIN*
City   *LAKE CITY*   State   *MI*   Zip   *48800*

NOTE: If requesting a debtor's examination under MCL 600.6110, or an injunction under item 6. this subpoena must be issued by a judge. For a debtor examination, the affidavit of debtor examination on the other side of this form must also be completed. Debtor's assets can also be discovered through MCR 2.305 without the need for an affidavit of debtor examination or issuance of this subpoena by a judge.

FAILURE TO OBEY THE COMMANDS OF THE SUBPOENA OR TO APPEAR AT THE STATED TIME AND PLACE MAY SUBJECT YOU TO PENALTY FOR CONTEMPT OF COURT.

5-1-2009
Date   *Martha Gee*
Judge/Clerk/Attorney   Bar no.

Court use only
☐ Served   ☐ Not served

MC 11 (3/15) **SUBPOENA, Order to Appear and/or Produce**

MCL 600.1455, 600.1701, 600.6110, 600.6119, MCR 2.506

> CHECK BOX #2 TO OBTAIN WITNESS' TESTIMONY AND/OR BOX #3 TO OBTAIN DOCUMENTS OR OTHER THINGS THE WITNESS HAS

SUBPOENA

Case No.

PROOF OF SERVICE

...VER: You must make and file your return with the court clerk. If you are unable to complete service, you must ... and all copies to the court clerk.

CERTIFICATE / AFFIDAVIT OF SERVICE / NONSERVICE

☐ **OFFICER CERTIFICATE**   OR   ☐ **AFFIDAVIT OF PROCESS SERVER**

I certify that I am a sheriff, deputy sheriff, bailiff, appointed court officer, or attorney for a party [MCR 2.104(A)(2)], and that: (notarization not required)

Being first duly sworn, I state that I am a legally competent adult who is not a party or an officer of a corporate party, and that: (notarization required)

☐ I served a copy of the subpoena, together with _____ (including any required fees) by
Attachment

☐ personal service   ☐ registered or certified mail (copy of return receipt attached)   on:

Name(s)	Complete address(es) of service	Day, date, time

☐ I have personally attempted to serve the subpoena and required fees, if any, together with _____
Attachment
on the following person(s) and have been unable to complete service.

Name(s)	Complete address(es) of service	Day, date, time

Service fee $	Miles traveled	Fee $	TOTAL FEE $	Signature
Incorrect address fee $	Miles traveled	Fee $		Name (type or print)

Title _____ County, Michigan.

Subscribed and sworn to before me on _____ Date

My commission expires: _____ Date   Signature: _____ Deputy court clerk/Notary public

Notary public, State of Michigan, County of _____

ACKNOWLEDGMENT OF SERVICE

I acknowledge that I have received service of the subpoena and required fees, if any, together with _____
Attachment

on *MONDAY, 5-5-2009, 9:00 AM*
Day, date, time

~~on behalf of~~   *AT: 100 S. FRONT*
LAKE CITY, MI 48800

John Quick
Signature

AFFIDAVIT FOR JUDGMENT DEBTOR EXAMINATION

I request that the court issue a subpoena that orders the party named on this form to be examined under oath before a judge concerning the money or property of:
for the following reasons:

Signature _____ County, Michigan.

Subscribed and sworn to before me on _____ Date

My commission expires: _____ Date   Signature: _____ Deputy court clerk/Notary public

Notary public, State of Michigan, County of _____

MCR 2.105

USE OFFICER CERTIFICATE OR AFFIDAVIT OF PROCESS SERVER TO PROVE SERVICE BY DELIVERY OR SERVICE BY MAIL

THIS IS A PROOF OF SERVICE BY ACKNOWLEDGMENT

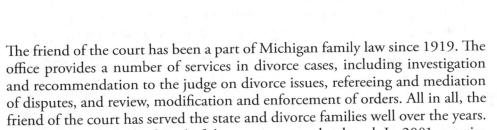

Appendix C: Opting Out of the Friend of the Court System

The friend of the court has been a part of Michigan family law since 1919. The office provides a number of services in divorce cases, including investigation and recommendation to the judge on divorce issues, refereeing and mediation of disputes, and review, modification and enforcement of orders. All in all, the friend of the court has served the state and divorce families well over the years.

But cracks in the friend of the court system developed. In 2001, a major *Detroit News* investigation found that many county friends of the court were struggling with a backlog of cases and provided poor service. The next year, Michigan lawmakers tried to improve the system, passing a package of laws reforming friend of the court operations.

In the biggest break from the past, a law allows divorce parties to *opt out* of the friend of the court system. Lawmakers had found that more than half of divorce cases go smoothly, with parents meeting all obligations. They decided to remove some of these cases from the system, letting the friend of the court concentrate on problem cases.

In fact, the opt-out law, which is explained below, is a good deal more complicated than that. There are several types of opt-outs. And there are many restrictions on opting out, and automatic triggers for bringing cases back under friend of the court control.

Is it worth considering an opt-out? Supporters of the opt-out law say that friend of the court intervention in a divorce isn't necessary if the spouses are cooperative. Opponents of the law argue that threat of friend of the court enforcement makes parents more agreeable, and without this leverage there will be more disputes during divorce and judgment violations afterward.

It's true, some divorces are totally amicable and don't need the friend of the court. But for others, the friend of the court plays the honest broker when divorce-related disputes arise. The office performs an important bookkeeping function, keeping track of support payments (support and parenting time are the source of most divorce judgment violations). The friend of the court also has special powers to order and enforce health care coverage which can be lost by opting out.

Maybe the best approach is to stay within the friend of the court system for a while, at the beginning of the divorce, and see if you like it. If you don't, you can then see about opting out. Or if you decide to opt out, consider either a partial or limited opt-out, instead of a total one.

Types of Opt-Outs

The opt-out law allows several kinds of opt-outs from the friend of the court system:

- *total* opt-out from all friend of the court services
- *partial* opt-out from all friend of the court services except collection and distribution of support through the state disbursement unit (SDU) (with or without immediate income withholding as the method of payment)
- *limited* opt-out from immediate income withholding only, but receipt of all other friend of the court services

Total Opt-Out

In some cases, you can opt out of the friend of the court system completely, giving up all friend of the court services in your divorce. Afterward, you are responsible for all future management of your case, including payment of support (you lose SDU-payment of support with a total opt-out). You must have the consent of the defendant to get (and keep) a total opt-out. And the judge must review and approve your opt-out request, which must be granted if the case is eligible for opting out (see below).

The timing of an opt-out is important. You can get a total opt-out at the beginning of a divorce (new case) or later while the case is pending (open case). The procedures for new- and open-case opt-outs are a little different, and these are described below.

Total Opt-Out in a New Case

You can opt out of a new-filed case, so the friend of the court never enters the case and never opens a file for the case. Not every case is eligible for this kind of opt-out. The opt-out law bars opting out of a new case when:

- a party is eligible for DHHS services (also known as title IV-D services) because of past or current receipt of public assistance
- a party is applying for DHHS services
- a party requests friend of the court services
- there is evidence of 1) domestic violence, or 2) uneven bargaining position between the parties; and evidence that a party is opting out against the best interests of that party or the children
- the parties have not signed and filed a FOC 101, showing consent to the opt-out

If your case is eligible for opting out, you must request an opt-out at the start of your divorce, when you file. As you prepare your initial divorce papers (see "Filing" on page 87 for more about preparing these papers), make additions to two of these papers:

- In the Complaint for Divorce (TBP 1b), check the outdented box for paragraph #10 to show you want to opt out, and then check the first box inside that paragraph to opt out of "all friend of the court services" (total opt-out).
- In the Uniform Child Support Order, No Friend of Court Services (FOC 10a/52a) (the special opt-out version of the FOC 10/52 which provides child support for an Ex Parte Order (TBP 5)), add a provision at paragraph #9 like this:

Child support shall be paid directly to the payee without immediate income withholding.

You must also prepare two extra papers (with copies), which will be referred to as the "opt-out papers:"

• Advice of Rights Regarding Use of Friend of the Court Services	FOC 101	2
• Order Exempting Case from Friend of the Court Services	FOC 102	2

The FOC 101 warns you which services you lose by opting out. You and the defendant must receive separate copies of the FOC 101, and both of you must date and sign the original form, which will be filed with court. This tells the court that both parties consent to the opt-out.

The FOC 102 is the actual opt-out order. You select a total opt-out by leaving the boxes at paragraph #13a and b unchecked. The sample form shows you how to make the correct choice. Afterward, paperclip the signed FOC 101 to the FOC 102.

After you file your divorce, you must bring the opt-out request to the judge right away. By acting quickly, you can keep the friend of the court out of the case before it opens a file. A good time for opting out is when you seek interim relief, if you are asking for this form of preliminary relief (see Appendix

B for more about interim relief). When you apply to the judge for the relief, just add your (unfiled) opt-out papers to the (unfiled) interim relief papers. This procedure is described in "Requesting Interim Relief from the Judge" on page 165.

Not everyone seeks interim relief. If you're not, you must apply to the judge separately for an opt-out. Again, see "Requesting Interim Relief from the Judge" on page 165, and use the same procedure to request an opt-out from the judge in his/her office.

If the judge approves an opt-out, file the opt-out papers with the clerk (the friend of the court won't get copies since it has dropped out of the case), and serve another set of copies on the defendant with the service papers (see "Service" on page 99 for more about service). After receiving a denial (because of a lack of consent from the defendant, ineligibility of the case for opting out or some other irregularity), you must withdraw your opt-out papers and the judge will note the denial on the Complaint for Divorce (TBP 1) or in the case file.

After an opt-out, the friend of the court won't participate in your case. As a result, disregard all references in Chapter 2 to the friend of the court's receiving papers, investigating, recommending, refereeing, mediating or reviewing orders. Despite the opt-out, don't be surprised if the friend of the court reappears in your case. Some judges will have the friend of the court step back into a case, even after a total opt-out, for limited purposes, such as refereeing.

As the divorce continues, you may change your mind and want the friend of the court back in your case. All you have to do is submit a simple written request to the friend of the court; no motion is necessary. You can use the Request to Reopen Friend of the Court Case (FOC 104) for this purpose. The friend of the court will also intervene on its own when: 1) either party requests friend of the court services 2) a party applies for public assistance.

At the end of the divorce, you must decide whether you want the friend of the court in or out of your case during the after-divorce (called the post-judgment) period. During this time, which can last for years (until the youngest child turns 18), the friend of the court provides services for modification and enforcement of the divorce judgment (the FOC 101 has a good summary of these post-judgment duties).

If you still want the friend of the court out of the case, you must say so in your judgment papers. Ordinarily, the opt-out order would expire according to paragraph #10 of the Judgment of Divorce (TBP 4a), as a nonfinal order. But you can extend the total opt-out order in the blank space at paragraph #9 of the Uniform Child Support Order, No Friend of Court Services (FOC 10a/52a), which handles judgment support, as follows:

> The previously-ordered opt-out of this case from all friend of the court services shall remain in effect. Child support shall be paid directly to the payee without immediate income withholding.

Omit the Order Regarding Income Withholding (FOC 5) from your final divorce papers because this is unnecessary. Also, explain the opt-out to the judge during your testimony at the final hearing.

If you want the friend of the court back in your case post-judgment, you could file a Request to Reopen Friend of the Court Case (FOC 104) before the hearing. Or you could let paragraph #10 of the Judgment of Divorce (TBP 4a) terminate the prior total opt-out as a nonfinal order. This will reinstate friend of the court services and the normal method of support payment specified by the Uniform Child Support Order (FOC 10/52) (use this instead of the FOC 10a/52a, which is the opt-out version of the order): payment by immediate income withholding to the SDU. With this payment method back in place, you will also need the Order Regarding Income Withholding (FOC 5).

There's yet another choice: You want to change your opt-out, switching from a total opt-out to a partial or limited one. For a partial opt-out, see "Partial Opt-Out" for general information and "Partial Opt-Out in an Open Case" below about the steps for opting out at the end of a divorce. Likewise, see "Limited Opt-Out" and "Limited Opt-Out in an Open Case" below about limited opt-outs.

To switch opt-outs, let the prior opt-out expire as a nonfinal order as explained above. Then provide for the different type of opt-out (partial or limited) as described in the relevant open-case section below.

Total Opt-Out in an Open Case

The friend of the court may have participated in your case while it was pending. But now you want to opt out totally from the friend of the court system for the after-divorce (called the post-judgment) period. It's possible to have the friend of the court withdraw from the case and close its file that way with the consent of the defendant and approval of the court, which must be granted if the case is eligible for opting out.

Not every open divorce case is eligible for total opt out. Like a new case, there are several open-case restrictions which are similar to but not the same as the ones for a new case:

- a party objects to opting out
- a party is eligible to receive DHHS services (also known as title IV-D services) because the party receives public assistance
- a party is eligible to receive DHHS services because the party received public assistance and an arrearage is owed to the state
- a support arrearage or custody or parenting time order violation has occurred in the last 12 months
- either party has reopened a friend of the court case during the last 12 months
- there is evidence of 1) domestic violence, or 2) uneven bargaining position between the parties; and evidence that a party is opting out against the best interests of that party or the children
- the parties have not signed and filed a FOC 101, showing consent to the opt-out

If you want to opt out late in your case, the final hearing, when the divorce judgment is granted, is a convenient time. Otherwise, you must file a separate motion and schedule a hearing on your request. Before the final hearing, prepare two extra "opt-out papers:"

- Advice of Rights Regarding Use of Friend of the
  Court Services   FOC 101   2

- Order Exempting Case from Friend of the Court
  Services   FOC 102   2

The FOC 101 warns you which services you lose by opting out. You and the defendant must receive separate copies of the FOC 101, and both of you must date and sign the original form which will be filed with the court. This tells the court that both parties consent to the opt-out.

The FOC 102 is the actual opt-out order. You select a total opt-out by leaving the boxes at paragraph #13a and b unchecked. The sample form shows you how to make the correct choice. Afterward, paperclip the signed FOC 101 to the FOC 102.

> ## More Information
>
> When you're also providing for alimony in your divorce judgment and want a total or partial opt-out for alimony too, you must use the Uniform Spousal Support Order, No Friend of Court Services (FOC 10c) instead of the Uniform Spousal Support Order (FOC 10b) (a FOC 10c is included in the forms section of this book).
>
> The alternate support payment paragraph (citing spousal support, not child support) would go in the blank space below paragraph #8 of the FOC 10c.

You must also prepare your judgment papers to go along with a total opt-out. You will use the Uniform Child Support Order, No Friend of Court Services (FOC 10a/52a), which is the special opt-out version of the FOC 10/52 dealing with judgment child support issues. At paragraph #9 of the FOC 10a/52a, add a support payment provision like this:

Child support shall be paid directly to the payee without immediate income withholding.

Omit the Order Regarding Income Withholding (FOC 5) from your final divorce papers because this is unnecessary.

During the final hearing, include the FOC 101 and 102 among your final divorce papers (see "Final Hearing" on page 125 for more about preparing, filing and sending the final divorce papers to the defendant after the divorce). In your testimony, say that you want to opt out. It's also helpful to have the defendant on hand to confirm the opt-out; but the defendant's signing the FOC 101 is sufficient to show consent.

If the judge denies your opt-out request, replace the Uniform Child Support Order, No Friend of Court Services (FOC 10a/52a) with the Uniform Child Support Order (FOC 10/52) as your uniform child support order. This substitution will make support payable by immediate income withholding to the SDU. You will also need the FOC 5.

After opting out, the friend of the court won't help with any judgment modification or enforcement during the post-judgment period. But if you want the friend of the court back in your case, just file the Request to Reopen Friend of the Court Case (FOC 104). The friend of the court will also re-enter the case automatically if: 1) either party requests friend of the court services 2) a party applies for public assistance.

Partial Opt-Out

Ordinarily, when you opt-out totally from the friend of the court system you give up all friend of the court services, including payment of support (child support and/or alimony) through the SDU. See "Court System" on page 71 for more about SDU operations. SDU-payment is an efficient means of collecting and distributing support, and not everyone opting out wants to lose this.

Luckily, the opt-out law allows partial opt-outs: You give up all friend of the court services except payment of support to the SDU. If you choose this option, you also have two subchoices: 1) SDU-payment by immediate income withholding 2) SDU-payment without immediate income withholding and payment from the payer directly to the SDU.

A partial opt-out is a lot like a total opt-out (they're really just different choices in the Order Exempting Case from Friend of the Court Services (FOC 102)), and they share similar procedures. And as with a total opt-out, the steps for opting out of new cases (before the friend of the court's entry into the case) are a little different from open-case opt-outs (after the friend of the court has entered the case).

More Information

Ordinarily, the friend of the court helps set up payment of support to the SDU. If you opt out, the friend of the court won't do this and you have to contact the SDU yourself.

To make payment arrangements, call the SDU at (800) 817-0805 or go to www.misdu.com, then to Register, to Individual Registration.

The SDU will help you set up (or continue) immediate income withholding, if you chose that option, or issue a payment coupon book to the payer if you've selected direct payment to the SDU.

Partial Opt-Out in a New Case

The procedures (form preparation, submission of papers to the judge, etc.) for a partial opt-out in a new case are almost identical to those in a new-case total opt-out. And the same five restrictions apply (eligibility for DHHS services, application for DHHS services, etc.). For information about these procedures and restrictions, see "Total Opt-Out in a New Case" on page 190.

Where a total and partial opt-out diverge is in the paperwork. When you prepare the FOC 102, pay special attention to paragraph #13 (untouched in a total opt-out). This is where a partial opt-out occurs. Having opted out of the friend of the court system, you, in essence, opt back in for SDU-payment.

After you bring the SDU back, you have a further choice: Do you want the SDU to collect the support by immediate income withholding or by direct payment from the payer? By checking #13a of the FOC 102, you get SDU-payment by immediate income withholding. You have to set this up (or continue it), the friend of the court (which is out of the case) won't do this for you. With choice #13b, you get SDU-help without immediate income withholding. Instead, the payer must pay the support directly to the SDU. You must make arrangements for this method of payment.

Your interim relief papers must mirror the choices you made. In the Uniform Child Support Order, No Friend of Court Services (FOC 10a/52a), which deals with interim support in partial opt-out cases, add a support payment provision at paragraph #9 like this:

> Child support shall be paid through the SDU by [immediate income withholding/direct payment from the payer.]

If you skip the immediate income withholding option, omit the Order Regarding income Withholding (FOC 5) from your interim relief papers.

After an opt-out, the friend of the court won't participate in your case. As a result, disregard all references in Chapter 2 to the friend of the court's receiving copies of papers, investigating, recommending, refereeing, mediating or reviewing orders. The only friend of the court involvement will be the SDU. Despite the opt-out, don't be surprised if the friend of the court reappears in your case. Some judges will have the friend of the court step back in a case, even after a partial opt-out, for limited purposes, such as refereeing.

As the divorce continues, you may change your mind and want the friend of the court back in your case. Or you may want a total or limited opt-out for the post-divorce period. See "Total Opt-Out in an Open Case" on page 193 about reopening a friend of the court case or switching the opt-out at the end of the divorce.

Partial Opt-Out in an Open Case

Partially opting out from an open case resembles an open-case total opt-out. And the same seven restrictions (objection, eligibility for DHHS services, etc.) apply. See "Total Opt-Out in an Open Case" on page 193 for more about these procedures and restrictions.

There is a difference in the paperwork. When you prepare the Order Exempting Case from Friend of the Court Services (FOC 102), pay close attention to paragraph #13 (unused in a total opt-out). This is where a partial opt-out occurs. Having opted out of the friend of the court system, you, in essence, opt back in for SDU-payment.

After you opt back for SDU-collection, you have a choice: Do you want the SDU to collect the support by immediate income withholding or by direct payment from the payer? By checking #13a of the FOC 102, you get SDU-payment by immediate income withholding. You have to set up the withholding yourself (or continue it), the friend of the court won't do this for you. With choice #13b, you elect payment from the payer to the SDU, without immediate income withholding.

Your judgment papers must also follow the choices you have made. In the Uniform Child Support Order, No Friend of Court Services (FOC 10a/52a), which controls judgment child support in partial opt-out cases, add a support payment provision at paragraph #9 like this:

> Child support shall be paid through the SDU by [immediate income withholding/direct payment from the payer.]

If you skip the immediate income withholding option, omit the Order Regarding Income Withholding (FOC 5) from your final divorce papers.

Limited Opt-Out

You may be happy with the friend of the court's services for custody, parenting time and support; all you want is a different method of support (child support and/or alimony) payment. The law allows you to opt out of immediate income withholding only, which is the normal means of paying support, and choose another payment method. Other payment options include: 1) payment to the SDU directly 2) direct payment to the support payee/recipient.

After a limited opt-out, you will have access to the usual friend of the court services. You may or may not have SDU-collection and -distribution of support. But either way, the friend of the court will monitor payments and enforce support obligations, including health care.

There are two ways to avoid immediate income withholding through a limited opt-out: 1) with the consent of the defendant 2) for "good cause," without the consent of the defendant. Either kind requires court approval.

As with total and partial opt-outs, there are some restrictions, although fewer ones, on limited opt-outs. You can't opt out for good cause if: 1) support is already past due 2) it's in the best interests of the children to have immediate income withholding.

Limited Opt-Out in a New Case

You can get a limited opt out at the beginning of your divorce, if * and when you seek interim relief. That way, none of the interim child support will be paid by income withholding, and you can choose another method of payment.

As you prepare your initial divorce papers (see "Filing" on page 87 for more about preparing these papers), make additions to two of these papers:

- In the Complaint for Divorce (TBP 1b), check the outdented box in paragraph #10 to show you want to opt out, and then the third box inside that paragraph to opt out of "immediate income withholding only" (limited opt-out).
- In the Uniform Child Support Order (FOC 10/52) (which provides for child support for an Ex Parte Order (TBP 5)), add a provision at paragraph #13 like this:

> Notwithstanding other provisions of this order, child support shall
> be paid without immediate income withholding by the payer [to
> the SDU/directly to the payee].

---

*   If you aren't seeking interim relief, there's no court-ordered support and
     no need for a limited opt-out at this point.

You must also prepare one or two extra papers, which will be referred to in this section as the "opt-out papers." To opt out with the agreement of the defendant, you need both forms; opt-outs for cause use the order only:

- Agreement Suspending Immediate Income Withholding   FOC 63   3

- Order Suspending Immediate Income Withholding   FOC 64   3

In an agreed-to opt-out, both you and the defendant must sign the FOC 63. Indicate the alternate method of payment you want in paragraph #2. The FOC 64 is used in both agreed-to and for-cause opt-outs. See the sample forms at the end of this appendix for help with both forms.

For convenience, you can seek the opt-out when you ask for interim relief (see Appendix B for more about this form of preliminary relief). When you apply to the judge for interim relief, just add your (unfiled) opt-out papers to the (unfiled) interim relief papers. This procedure is described in "Requesting Interim Relief from the Judge" on page 165.

If the judge approves an opt-out, file the opt-out paper(s) and friend of the court copies with the clerk, and serve another set of copies on the defendant with the service papers (see "Service" on page 99 for more about service). After a denial, you must withdraw your opt-out papers and the judge will note the denial on the Complaint for Divorce (TBP 1) or in the case file. With a denial, any interim child support will be paid by immediate income withholding.

After a limited opt-out, the friend of the court will participate in your case, as in other divorces. The only difference is that interim child support won't be paid by immediate income withholding. The friend of the court should help you set up the other method of payment.

During the divorce, the friend of the court will take steps to reinstate immediate income withholding if past-due support equals or exceeds one month of support. The payer can also agree to resume immediate income withholding or the payee can ask for this, although this takes a separate motion and hearing.

At the end of the divorce, you must decide how you want support paid during the after-divorce period. Do you want to continue the limited opt-out, do you want payment by immediate income withholding or do you want another type of opt-out?

To continue without immediate income withholding, you must extend the FOC 64, which would normally expire as a nonfinal order. At paragraph #13 of the Uniform Child Support Order (FOC 10/52), the order handling judgment support in limited opt-out cases, add a provision extending the limited opt-out like this:

> The previously-ordered suspension of immediate income withholding shall remain in effect. And notwithstanding other provisions of this order, child support shall be paid without immediate income withholding by the payer [to the SDU/directly to the payee].

Also, omit the Order Regarding Income Withholding (FOC 5) from your final divorce papers.

If you want to reinstate immediate income withholding, you can let paragraph #10 of the Judgment of Divorce (TBP 4a) terminate the prior opt-out as a nonfinal order (these expire unless specifically preserved). With this, the FOC 10/52 will reimpose the normal method of support payment: immediate income withholding to the SDU. Add back the FOC 5 also.

There's another possibility: You want to change your opt-out, switching from a limited opt-out to a total or partial one. For a total opt-out, see "Total Opt-Out" for general information and "Total Opt-Out in an Open Case" above about the steps for opting out at the end of a divorce. Likewise, see "Partial Opt-Out" and "Partial Opt-Out in an Open Case" above about partial opt-outs.

Limited Opt-Out in an Open Case

You may have had interim support paid by immediate income withholding or skipped interim relief completely. But now, at the end of the divorce, you want a limited opt-out of immediate income withholding for the post-divorce period.

The final hearing is a good time to ask for an opt-out because you're going before the judge anyway. Prior to the final hearing, prepare one or two extra "opt-out papers." To opt out with the agreement of the defendant, you need both forms; opt-outs for cause use the order only:

- Agreement Suspending Immediate Income Withholding   FOC 63   3

- Order Suspending Immediate Income Withholding   FOC 64   3

You must obtain the consent of the defendant for an agreed-to opt-out. At a minimum, the defendant must sign the FOC 63. It's also helpful if the defendant can attend the final hearing and confirm that s/he agrees to payment without immediate income withholding. But the defendant's signing the FOC 63 should be sufficient to show consent.

You must also prepare your judgment papers to go along with a limited opt-out. You do this in the Uniform Child Support Order (FOC 10/52), which controls judgment support in limited opt-out cases. At paragraph #13 of the FOC 10/52, add a support payment provision like this:

Notwithstanding other provisions of this order, child support shall be paid without immediate income withholding by the payer [to the SDU/directly to the payee].

Also, omit the Order Regarding Income Withholding (FOC 5) since this goes with immediate income withholding.

More Information

When you want a limited opt-out for alimony also, insert a support payment paragraph like the one appearing to the left (naturally, referring to spousal support, not child support) in the blank space below paragraph #10 of the Uniform Spousal Support Order (FOC 10b), which is the alimony order in limited opt-out cases.

During the final hearing, include the FOC 63 and/or 64 among your final divorce papers (see "Final Hearing" on page 125 for more about preparing, filing and sending final divorce papers to the defendant). In your testimony, say that you want to avoid immediate income withholding and describe your alternate method of payment.

If the judge denies your opt-out request, just strike the support payment provision you added at paragraph #13 of the Uniform Child Support Order (FOC 10/52). The denial will make support payable by immediate income withholding to the SDU. You will also need the FOC 5.

If the judge approves your opt-out request, the support will be paid without immediate income withholding. The friend of the court will take steps to reinstate income withholding if past-due support equals or exceeds one month of support. The payer can also agree to resume immediate income withholding or the payee can ask for this, although this takes a separate motion and hearing.

Approved, SCAO

STATE OF MICHIGAN
JUDICIAL CIRCUIT
COUNTY
Friend of the court address

1. **Right to Refuse Friend of the**

   a. You have the right to refuse F
      services, you must file with th
      a signed copy of this advice o
      this advice of rights and it de
      1) Under MCL 552.505a, r
      2) There is no evidence of
      3) The court finds that dec

   b. If you already have a friend
      parties agree and have sig
      1) Neither of you receive
      2) There is no evidence
      3) The court finds that d
      4) No money is due the
      5) No arrearage or viol
      6) Neither of you has re

2. **Friend of the Court Servi**

   a. **Accounting Services**
      Friends of the court mu
      1) friend of the court ac
      and 3) annual stateme
   b. **Support Enforcement**
      The friend of the court
      child-support enforcen
      • paying support out
      • asking the court to
      • having unpaid sup
      • reporting support
      • collecting support
      If you choose not to r
      of the court is no lor
      changing income
   c. **Medical Support E**
      The friend of the co
      the amounts that a
      authorized to instru
   d. **Support Review**
      Once every three
      amount. After con
      that it recommend
      be modified.
   e. **Custody and Pa**
      For disputes abd
      and provide rep
   f. **Mediation Serv**
      Friend of the co
      parenting-time
   g. **Custody and P**
      For friend of th
      it is violated. C

FOC 101 (3/13) AD

Approved, SCAO

STATE OF MICHIGAN **JUDICIAL CIRCUIT** **COUNTY** Friend of the court address	**ADVICE OF RIGHTS REGARDING** **USE OF FRIEND OF THE COURT SERVICES** **(PAGE 2)**	Original - Court (to be filed with motion) 1st copy - Plaintiff 2nd copy - Defendant **CASE NO.**

Telephone no.

2. **Friend of the Court Services** (you will not receive these services if you choose not to use the friend of the court)
   (continued from page 1)
   g. **Custody and Parenting-Time Enforcement Services** (continued from page 1)
      • asking the court to order the noncooperating party to come to court to explain the failure to obey the parenting-time order.
      • suspending the licenses of individuals who deny parenting time.
      • awarding makeup parenting time.
      • joint meetings to resolve complaints.

3. **Michigan State Disbursement Unit and IV-D Services**

   a. **Michigan State Disbursement Unit (MiSDU)**
      If you choose not to receive friend of the court services, you may continue to make and receive child support payments through MiSDU. MiSDU will keep track of the amount paid and sent out. However, MiSDU cannot provide you with all the accounting functions the friend of the court provides. All payments made through MiSDU must be distributed according to the amounts due as required by federal law. When a payer has more than one case, federal law determines how a payment is divided among the cases. **Even if you choose not to receive friend of the court services, payments through MiSDU must be divided among all a payer's cases and distributed in the same manner as payments on friend of the court cases. You cannot discontinue friend of the court services if you want to use MiSDU unless you first provide to MiSDU all the information that MiSDU needs to set up an account.**

   b. **Your Rights Under Title IV-D of the Social Security Act**
      Title IV-D of the Social Security Act provides federal government resources to collect child support and it allows certain funding to be used for parenting-time and custody services. In Michigan, critical Title IV-D services are delivered by the friend of the court. **If you choose not to receive friend of the court services, you cannot receive most Title IV-D services.**

4. **Public Assistance**

   Receipt of public assistance means receipt of any of the following benefits: cash assistance, medical assistance, food assistance, foster care, and/or child care.

ACKNOWLEDGMENT REGARDING SERVICES

Check below only if you do not want to receive friend of the court services. Then date, print name, and sign.

I have read this advice of rights and I understand the friend of the court services I am entitled to receive.

☒ I acknowledge that by signing below **I am choosing not to receive** any friend of the court services. I understand that before this choice can take effect, a motion requesting this choice and the other party's agreement must be filed with the court for approval. I also understand that the court may deny this choice if certain conditions are not met as stated in this advice of rights.

DARLENE A. LOVELACE
Name (type or print)

Darlene A. Lovelace   2-28-2009
Signature   Date

DUDLEY E. LOVELACE
Name (type or print)

Dudley E. Lovelace   2~28~2009
Signature   Date

If you did not check the above box, you are choosing to receive friend of the court services. **For the most effective friend of the court services**, you can request Title IV-D services by dating and signing below.

I request Title IV-D services through the friend of the court office.

Date   Signature

FOC 101 (3/13) **ADVICE OF RIGHTS REGARDING USE OF FRIEND OF THE COURT SERVICES, PAGE 2**

Back Form (partially visible)

Approved, SCAO

STATE OF MICHIGAN
JUDICIAL CIRCUIT
COUNTY

Court address

Plaintiff's name, address, and telephone no.

Attorney:

Date of hearing: _3-1-2009_

THE COURT FINDS:

1. There is no evidence of domestic v...

2. Granting the parties the relief they...

3. The parties have filed executed...

4. Neither party receives public ass...

5. No money is due the governmen...

6. No arrearage or custody or par...

7. Neither party has reopened a f...

☒ 8. The parties do not want Title...
should be checked unless excep...

IT IS ORDERED:

9. Subject to the provisions of...

☒ 10. This case is not a Title...

11. The friend of the court sha...
time, or support in this cas...

12. The parties are responsib...

FOC 102 (3/15) ORDER EXEMPTING CASE FROM FRIEND OF THE COURT SERV...

Front Form (PAGE 2)

Approved, SCAO

	Original - Court	
	1st copy - Plaintiff	2nd copy - Defendant
		3rd copy - Friend of the court

STATE OF MICHIGAN
JUDICIAL CIRCUIT
COUNTY

ORDER EXEMPTING CASE FROM FRIEND OF THE COURT SERVICES (PAGE 2)

CASE NO.

Court address

Telephone no.

Plaintiff's name   v   Defendant's name

13. Except as indicated below, there is no income withholding in this case, support will be paid directly by the payer to the payee, and the friend of the court shall terminate any existing income withholding. Should this case become a friend of the court case, the payer must keep the friend of the court advised of the name and address of the payer's source of income and any health-care coverage that is available to the payer as a benefit of employment or that the payer maintains, including the name of the insurance company, health-care organization, or health maintenance organization; the policy, certificate, or contract number; and the names and birth dates of the persons for whose benefit the payer maintains the coverage.

☐ a. Child support shall be paid through the Michigan State Disbursement Unit (MiSDU) by income withholding to the extent allowed by statutes and court rules; however, the friend of the court is not responsible for income withholding. The friend of the court shall notify the employer that it is no longer involved in the case and that any further information concerning income withholding will be provided by the parties.

☐ b. Child support shall be paid through MiSDU by the payer.

14. If child support payments are to be made through MiSDU by income withholding or otherwise, the friend of the court shall not close the friend of the court case until MiSDU notifies the friend of the court that it has been provided with the information necessary to process the child-support payments. There will be no accounting for support that is paid through MiSDU.

15. The friend of the court shall open a friend of the court case if a party applies for or receives public assistance, a child is placed in foster care, or either party submits to the friend of the court a written request to reopen the friend... this case becomes a friend of the court case for any reason, the following provisions shall apply...

a. The parties must cooperate fully with the friend of the court in establishing the case as...

b. The parties must provide copies of all orders in their case to the friend of the court.

c. The parties must supply any documents that a party to a friend of the court case is... done so.

d. The friend of the court is not responsible for determining any support arrearage th... MiSDU.

e. Support is payable through MiSDU effective the date the case becomes a frie...

f. The friend of the court may prepare and submit, ex parte, a uniform support order... of a Michigan support order as long as the order does not contradict the existin...

g. At the request of the friend of the court, the parties shall complete a Verified Statemen...

_3-1-2009_
Date

Lester Tubbs
Judge

CERTIFICATE OF MAILING

I certify that on this date I served a copy of this order on the parties or their attorneys by first-class mail addressed to their last-known addresses as defined in MCR 3.203.

Date

Signature

FOC 102 (3/15) **ORDER EXEMPTING CASE FROM FRIEND OF THE COURT SERVICES, PAGE 2**

> THIS ORDER IS FOR A TOTAL OPT-OUT.
>
> CHECK THE BOX AT # 13a FOR A PARTIAL OPT-OUT WITH SDU-PAYMENT BY IMMEDIATE INCOME WITHHOLDING; CHECK THE BOX AT # 13b FOR A PARTIAL OPT-OUT WITH SDU-PAYMENT BUT WITHOUT IMMEDIATE INCOME WITHHOLDING

Original - Court
1st copy - Friend of the court

2nd copy - Plaintiff
3rd copy - Defendant

Approved, SCAO

STATE OF MICHIGAN
JUDICIAL CIRCUIT
COUNTY

REQUEST TO REOPEN
FRIEND OF THE COURT CASE

CASE NO.

Telephone no.

Court address

Plaintiff's name, address, and telephone no.

v

Defendant's name, address, and telephone no.

Attorney:

Attorney:

1. On ___3-1-2009___ an order was entered exempting this case from friend of the court services.
   Date

I REQUEST that the friend of the court case be reopened upon filing of this request with the friend of the court office. Attached is a completed Verified Statement (form FOC 23).

☒ I request support services under Title IV-D of the Social Security Act.

___7-1-2009___
Date

Darlene A. Lovelace
Signature

CERTIFICATE OF MAILING

I certify that on this date I served a copy of this request on the friend of the court and on the parties or their attorneys by first-class mail addressed to their last-known addresses as defined in MCR 3.203.

___7-1-2009___
Date

Darlene A. Lovelace
Signature

MCL 552.505, MCL 552.505a

FOC 104 (3/09) **REQUEST TO REOPEN FRIEND OF THE COURT CASE**

Approved, SCAO

STATE OF MICHIGAN **JUDICIAL CIRCUIT** **COUNTY**	**AGREEMENT SUSPENDING** **IMMEDIATE INCOME WITHHOLDING**	**CASE NO.**

Original - Court
2nd copy - Friend of the court
3rd copy - Plaintiff
4th copy - Defendant

Court address

Court telephone no.

Plaintiff's name, address, and telephone no.

v

Defendant's name, address, and telephone no.

NOTE: MCL 552.604(3) requires that all new and modified support orders after December 31, 1990, include a provision for immediate income withholding and that income withholding take effect immediately unless the parties enter into a written agreement that the income withholding order shall not take effect immediately.

We understand that by law an order of income withholding in a support order shall take effect immediately. Ho[...] agree to the following.

1. The order of income withholding shall not take effect immediately.

2. An alternative payment arrangement shall be made as follows:

DEFENDANT SHALL PAY THE SUPPORT DIRECTLY TO THE SDU.

DESCRIBE OTHER METHOD OF PAYMENT

3. Both the payer and the recipient of support will notify the friend of the court, in writing, within 21 days of any change in
   a. the names, addresses, and telephone numbers of their current sources of income;
   b. any health-care coverage that is available to them as a benefit of employment or that is maintained by them; the names of the insurance companies, health-care organizations, or health-maintenance organizations; the policy, certificate, or contract numbers; and the names and birth dates of the persons for whose benefit they maintain health-care coverage under the policies, certificates, or contracts; and
   c. their current residences, mailing addresses, and telephone numbers.

4. We further understand that proceedings to implement income withholding shall commence if the payer of support falls one month behind in his/her support payments.

5. We recognize that the court may order withholding of income to take effect immediately for cause or at the request of the payer.

9-5-2009
Date

Darlene A. Lovelace
Plaintiff's signature

9-5-2009
Date

Dudley E. Lovelace
Defendant's signature

FOC 63 (3/08) **AGREEMENT SUSPENDING IMMEDIATE INCOME WITHHOLDING**

MCL 552.604

Original - Court
1st copy - Friend of the court
2nd copy - Plaintiff
3rd copy - Defendant

Approved, SCAO

| STATE OF MICHIGAN | ORDER SUSPENDING | CASE NO. |
| JUDICIAL CIRCUIT COUNTY | IMMEDIATE INCOME WITHHOLDING | |

Court telephone no.

Court address

Plaintiff's name, address, and telephone no.

v

Defendant's name, address, and telephone no.

CHECK THIS BOX FOR A LIMITED OPT-OUT FOR "GOOD CAUSE" WITHOUT THE CONSENT OF THE DEFENDANT

1. Date of hearing: _9-7-2009_____   Judge: _LESTER TUBBS_____   Bar no.

2. THE COURT FINDS:

☒ a. There is good cause for the order of income withholding not to take effect immediately as follows.
   1) It is in the best interest of the child for immediate income withholding not to take effect for the following reasons:

   DEFENDANT IS A SALESMAN WORKING ON COMMISSION

   WITH AN IRREGULAR INCOME, SO IMMEDIATE INCOME

   WITHHOLDING IS NOT PRACTICAL.

   2) Proof of timely payment of previously-ordered support has been provided.

☐ b. The parties have entered into a written agreement that has been reviewed and entered in the record as follows.
   1) The order of income withholding shall not take effect immediately.
   2) An alternative payment arrangement has been agreed upon and is attached.

OR CHECK THIS BOX FOR AN AGREED-TO LIMITED OPT-OUT WITH THE CONSENT OF THE DEFENDANT

3. Both the payer and the recipient of support [...] the friend of the court, in writing, within 21 days of any change in [...] income;
   a. the names, addresses, and tel[...] or that is maintained by them, the names of the
   b. any health-care coverage that [...] nizations; the policy, certificate, or contract
      insurance companies, he[...] maintain health-care coverage under the
      numbers; and the names an[...]
      policies, certificates, or contra[...]
   c. their current residence, mail[...]

IT IS ORDERED:

4. Income withholding shall not take effect im[...]tely.
5. Income withholding shall take effect if the fixed amount of arrearage is reached, as specified in law.

___9-7-2009_____   _Lester Tubbs_____
Date   Judge

FOC 64 (3/08) ORDER SUSPENDING IMMEDIATE INCOME WITHHOLDING   MCL 552.511, MCL 552.604, MCL 552.607

Appendix D: Alternate Service

The regular service methods of service by acknowledgment, mail and delivery are very effective when defendants are available for service. But if the defendant is hiding from service (an elusive defendant), or has disappeared entirely (a disappeared defendant), you must use another method of service.

Luckily, the court rules authorize alternate service on elusive and disappeared defendants. By using alternate service, your divorce can go ahead normally, just as if you had served the defendant by one of the regular service methods.

Forms of Alternate Service

Alternate service can take several forms including: 1) mailing 2) tacking (attaching papers to a door) 3) household delivery (delivering papers to an adult in the defendant's household) 4) publication (with or without an accompanying registered mailing) 5) posting (with or without an accompanying registered mailing) 6) any combination of #1-5 7) something completely different (by itself or in combination with any of #1-5).

The judge picks from among these options to devise a method of alternate service for the defendant. The method is designed to give the defendant actual notice of the divorce. But if the alternate service doesn't give actual notice, that's all right. Elusive and disappeared defendants are legally entitled to whatever notice alternate service provides, even if this means no actual notice.

When the defendant is elusive, the judge will probably order either mailing, tacking, household delivery or a combination of these. But these things won't work on disappeared defendants whose whereabouts are unknown. For them, judges normally order publication or posting. With either method, judges can order registered mailing of the service papers to the defendant's last known address. If that address appears to be outdated, the judge can skip the mailing and order publication or posting alone.

Whatever form alternate service takes, keep in mind that you cannot perform it yourself because you're disqualified from serving as a party to the divorce. Like regular service, you must have a server—a helper or professional server—to carry out alternate service. You can apply for and help with the alternate service, but the helper or server must serve the service papers for you (see "Preparing for Service" on page 100 for which papers make up your service papers).

Alternate Service for an Elusive Defendant

With an elusive defendant, you know his/her home and/or business address. Before you apply for alternate service, you must try service by delivery on the defendant at those or other places. For service by delivery, use the procedure described in "Service by Delivery" on page 105. Since the service will probably be difficult, use a professional server, such as a sheriff or commercial process server. Tell the server to attempt delivery not once but three or four times.

You must also ask the server to describe each attempt in the Verification of Process Server section of the Motion and Verification for Alternate Service (MC 303), which you should give to the server along with the service papers. The server's description of each delivery attempt must include specific information about the date, place and result of the attempt, as shown in the sample form at the end of this appendix.

If the server succeeds in serving the defendant during those attempts, you have obtained service on the defendant by delivery, and don't need alternate service. But if service by delivery fails, the server will return the service papers to you and you can apply for alternate service.

Make sure that the server has completed the Verification of Process Server section in the Motion and Verification for Alternate Service (MC 303), and then pay the server for the attempted service. You must complete the top portion of the Motion and Verification for Alternate Service (MC 303), above the verification section. Because you are trying to serve an elusive defendant, complete paragraph #2a of the motion showing that you know the defendant's current home and/or business address. You should also complete the caption and paragraph #1 of the Order Regarding Alternate Service (MC 304), and return to the clerk with:

- Motion and Verification for Alternate Service   MC 303
    - original
    - two copies (one earmarked "FOC")

- Order Regarding Alternate Service   MC 304
  - original

- $20 motion fee

File the Motion and Verification for Alternate Service (MC 303) and the friend of the court's copy with the clerk. After filing, go to your judge's office and submit a copy of the Motion and Verification for Alternate Service (MC 303) and the original Order Regarding Alternate Service (MC 304) to the judge's secretary. The judge will review your motion in his/her office (although probably not while you wait), so a court hearing on the motion won't be necessary. If the judge grants your motion for alternate service, get the papers back from the judge's office, make four photocopies of the Order Regarding Alternate Service (MC 304) and earmark one "FOC." Return to the clerk and file the original and the friend of the court's copy.

Examine the Order Regarding Alternate Service (MC 304) to see which method of alternate service the judge has designed for the defendant. It will probably be either mailing, tacking, household delivery or a combination of these. (If the judge has ordered several things, prepare multiple sets of the service papers and the Order Regarding Alternate Service (MC 304) because you will need separate sets of these papers for each form of alternate service ordered.) However, the judge could order another method of alternate service, which would be described in paragraph #2d. If the judge orders publication or posting, see the sections on these below.

Mailing

For this type of mailing, ordinary first-class mailing is permissible. Have your helper or server mail the service papers and a copy of the Order Regarding Alternate Service (MC 304) to the person named by the judge in paragraph #2a of the order. The recipient might be the defendant personally or a friend or relative of the defendant. The day of service is the day the mailing is sent, not received. After the mailing is sent, have the helper or server complete paragraph #1 in the Proof of Service section on the reverse of one of your copies of the Order Regarding Alternate Service (MC 304).

Tacking

When tacking has been ordered, have your helper or server take the service papers and a copy of the Order Regarding Alternate Service (MC 304) to the address indicated at paragraph #2b of the order, and attach them to the front door at this address. The day of service is the day the papers are tacked to the door. After tacking, the helper or server must complete paragraph #2 in the Proof of Service section on the reverse of the copy of the Order Regarding Alternate Service (MC 304) that you're using to prove service.

Household Delivery

To use this service method, your helper or server takes the service papers and a copy of the Order Regarding Alternate Service (MC 304) to the defendant's house and delivers them to any adult living there. The helper or server must also tell that person to give the papers to the defendant. The day of service is the day the papers are delivered to the person in defendant's household. After delivery, the helper or server must prove service on the reverse of your proof of service copy of the Order Regarding Alternate Service (MC 304). In this case, proof of the household delivery is made in paragraph #3 in the Proof of Service section of that paper.

Proof of Service by Mailing, Tacking or Household Delivery

After service by mailing, tacking or household delivery has been proved on the reverse of a copy of the Order Regarding Alternate Service (MC 304), make three copies of this paper, earmark one "FOC" and save another for filing later as your proof of service.

Alternate Service for a Disappeared Defendant

If you don't know the current home or business address of the defendant, you might be able to convince the court that the defendant has disappeared and obtain alternate service by publication or posting. But before you ask for that, you must prove the defendant's disappearance by searching for his/her current home and business addresses.

Your search will be shaped by the information you have about the defendant. If you don't know much, start with one of the general sources of information listed below, moving to specific sources as you find out more.

¶ *Telephone directories.* If you know the city where the defendant lives, look in the telephone book for that city. Many libraries keep large collections of telephone books. You can also get the same information by calling 411 for directory assistance (there is a fee for this service). For free directory assistance, go to a telephone directory Web site like www.switchboard.com, www.anywho.com or www.whitepages.com.

¶ *City/suburban directories* Libraries frequently have these "reverse" directories, such as Polk's and Bresser's, which cross-index names, addresses and telephone numbers in various ways (Polk: names, addresses and telephone numbers; Bresser: addresses and telephone numbers). So for example, if you have someone's telephone number, Polk's will give you that person's name and street address. Polk's is also online at www.citydirectory.com.

¶ *Internet.* The Internet has revolutionized searching for people. Some of the best ways are:

- *Search engines.* Look for items about the defendant on search engines like Google, Bing, Ask or multiple compiler engines like Dogpile. If s/he has a common name, put the name inside quotation marks or you'll get too much unsorted information. Also, try variations in the first name. Search via several search engines because they have different data.
- *Social media.* Check Facebook, Twitter, MySpace, LinkedIn or other social media sites.
- *People search sites.* There are specialized people search sites like ZabaSearch.com or Intelius.com offering free or fee-based search packages.

> ## Obtain
>
> *Find Anyone Fast*, 3rd ed., Richard Johnson and Debra Knox, Spartanburg, SC: MIE Publishing, 2001
>
> This book is loaded with helpful information about finding people, including a list of all 50 state vital records offices, prison locator services and DMV offices. Regrettably, it's a little out of date and needs updating.

¶ *News database.* The defendant may have been in the news recently. Check the Web site of the newspaper(s) in the defendant's area. Nexis (also available through Lexis) compiles a lot of this material. Nexis is expensive to subscribe to, but some libraries offer free access. Factiva is another service with similar data.

¶ *Motor vehicle records.* Like most states, Michigan provides information about licensed drivers and vehicle registration/ownership (title). This information isn't given out as freely as it used to be (you once could get it over the telephone). Now you have to submit an application and have a good reason to receive the information.

In Michigan, driver's license and motor vehicle registration/ownership information is available from the Secretary of State's record lookup service. Call (517) 322-1624 and ask for a record request form. Information is also available at www.michigan.gov/sos, then to Other Business Services, to Driver and Vehicle Record Request, to Requesting a Driving or Vehicle Record, to Requesting Another Person's Record. You can download a record request form from this site. In sec. 4D of the request form, say that you are making the request in connection with a civil proceeding. The fee is $8.00 for each record lookup.

In other states, these record lookup requests are typically handled by department of motor vehicles (DMV) offices. The Johnson and Knox book lists the offices nationwide. Or go to www.dmv-department-of-motor-vehicles.com for links to every state DMV.

¶ *Voter registration.* If the defendant is registered to vote, you can obtain address information from the voting registrar, which is the city or township clerk in Michigan.

¶ *Real property records.* The defendant may have been involved in a real property transaction as a seller, buyer, mortgagor (mortgage-borrower), etc. You can get this information from:

- *County register of deeds.* At the register of deeds office there are indexes listing sellers or mortgagors (grantors) and buyers (grantees) of property. Some counties have put this information online; try the Web site of the county where you think the defendant's real property is located.

- Several private Internet companies provide real property information nationwide:
  Public Records Online at www.netronline.com/public_records.htm
  Search Systems at www.searchsystems.net

  Note: Most searches are free, but some require payment; not all counties have put their property records online.

¶ *Association memberships.* If you know or believe the defendant is engaged in a trade or profession or belongs to a trade, professional or social organization, contact the organization for information.

- *Association directories.* These directories list associations which may have directories of members:
  Directories in Print, 36th ed., Detroit: Gale, 2014
  Encyclopedia of Associations, Detroit: Gale; available in international, national, and state and local editions
  National Trade and Professional Associations Directory of the United States, Bethesda, MD: Columbia Books, 2015.

- *State licensing bureau.* In Michigan, many trades and professions are regulated by the Bureau of Professional Licensing. You can find out if someone is licensed to practice a trade or profession in the state by calling the bureau's licensing verification unit at (517) 373-8068 or go to www.michigan.gov/bpl, then to Online Services, to Verify an Occupational License, Registration or Permit.

¶ *School directories.* If the defendant is a student or faculty member at a school, get the school directory.

  Has the defendant graduated from a school? Schools, especially colleges and universities, keep extensive data on their alumni. Contact the school directly for information or try www.alumni.net. Classmates.com and Reunion.com provide alumni information about their millions of registered members.

¶ *Contact friends, relatives, etc.* Contact the defendant's friends, relatives, former neighbors, landlords and employers to see if they know where s/he is now.

¶ *Parent locator.* Michigan and the federal government have parent locator services which have special access to public records to find missing parents. Contact the friend of the court or the DHHS to use these services. You may have to pay a small fee for these services unless you're receiving FIP payments.

¶ *Postal search.* The U.S. Postal Service has discontinued the release of change-of-address information. But you can sometimes get the equivalent by:

1) Sending a first-class letter to the defendant's last known address. On the envelope, put your return address and just below that write: "Do not forward—Address correction requested"

2) If the defendant has an active change-of-address card on file (they last for one year), the letter will come back to you with the defendant's new address.

The defendant may have special characteristics or circumstances which will influence the search.

¶ *Military servicemember.* If the defendant is an active-duty servicemember, reservist or veteran, there are special ways to search for the defendant. See "Divorcing a Defendant-Servicemember" on page 230 for more about locating active-duty servicemembers. The Johnson and Knox book on locating military personnel cited in that section also has tips on locating reservists and veterans.

¶ *Prisoner.* Do you know or suspect the defendant is an inmate in a state or federal prison? If you do, see "What If My Spouse or I Am Imprisoned?" on page 46 for more about finding prisoners through state or federal prison locator services.

¶ *Overseas resident.* The U.S. Department of State has visa information about expatriates, but normally can't release the information without a privacy waiver from the expat. You can call the state department's Overseas Citizens Services office at (888) 407-4747 and see what information about the defendant is available.

If you know the foreign country where the defendant is residing, call the American Citizen Service section of the U.S. embassy or consulate in that country and see if it can help (they sometimes have public domain telephone books or directories for finding people). Or you can try to locate the defendant yourself using Infobel.com, an international telephone directory.

¶ *Professional search.* If you can afford it, hire a private investigator to find the defendant. They have access to special databases which are very effective. The cost is around $30-200 to do a basic search of five databases. For a PI in your area, look in the yellow pages or ask for a referral from one of these trade groups:

Michigan Council of Professional Investigators
(517) 482-0706
www.mcpihome.com

National Association of Investigative Specialists
(512) 719-3595
www.pimall.com/nais

During your search for the defendant, keep a written record of what and when you did something. For example, if you contact relatives or friends of the defendant, record the date, person with whom you spoke and what s/he said. Keep any written evidence of your attempts to find the defendant, such as return-to-sender letters to him/her or correspondence with others about the defendant's disappearance. All this information is valuable because you will use it later when you apply for alternate service.

If you find the defendant's home and/or business address during your search, attempt service on him/her using one of the regular service methods.* But if you cannot locate the defendant, the failure will show that the defendant has disappeared, allowing you to apply for alternate service by publication or posting.

Complete the top portion of the Motion and Verification for Alternate Service (MC 303) above the Verification of Process Server section, which you can leave blank. Since you're trying to serve a disappeared defendant, complete paragraph #2b of the motion saying that you don't know the defendant's current home and business addresses.

After you complete the Motion and Verification for Alternate Service (MC 303), attach any written materials (undelivered letters, correspondence with the defendant's friends and relatives, etc.) showing that you failed to discover the defendant's whereabouts. Then complete the caption and first two lines of the Order for Service by Publication/Posting and Notice of Action (MC 307). After you prepare these papers, return to the clerk with:

- Motion and Verification for Alternate Service   MC 303
  - original
  - two copies (one earmarked "FOC")

- Order for Service by Publication/Posting and Notice
  of Action   MC 307
  - original

- $20 motion fee

File the Motion and Verification for Alternate Service (MC 303) and the friend of the court's copy with the clerk. After filing, go to your judge's office and submit a copy of the Motion and Verification for Alternate Service (MC 303) and the original Order for Service by Publication/Posting and Notice of Action (MC 307) to the judge's secretary. The judge will review your motion in his/her office (although probably not while you wait), so a court hearing on

---

*   If you discover the defendant's current home or business address, but
     fail to have him/her served there, see above on serving an elusive defen-
     dant.

the motion won't be necessary. If the judge grants your motion for alternate service, get the papers back from the judge's office, make three photocopies of the Order for Service by Publication/Posting and Notice of Action (MC 307) and earmark one "FOC." Return to the clerk and file the original and the friend of the court's copy.

Examine the Order for Service by Publication/Posting and Notice of Action (MC 307) to see which method of alternate service the judge has devised for the defendant. It's probably either publication (paragraph #2) or posting (paragraph #3), and possibly a registered mailing (paragraph #4). If registered mailing has been ordered, make an extra photocopy of the Order for Service by Publication/Posting and Notice of Action (MC 307).

Publication

If the judge has ordered publication as the alternate service in your case, you must publish a legal advertisement in a newspaper. Maybe you have seen fine-print legal advertisements in your local newspaper. This is the kind of ad you must have published.

The court rules say that the legal advertisement must be published in a newspaper in the county where the defendant resides when you know the defendant's residence. If you don't know where the defendant is residing, the court rules permit advertisement in the county where the case is filed. Since your defendant has disappeared, you can advertise in the county where you filed for divorce, which is probably your county.

See which newspaper the judge has chosen as the publisher of your advertisement in paragraph #2 of the Order for Service by Publication/Posting and Notice of Action (MC 307). Take/send a copy of the MC 307 to that newspaper and ask it to prepare a legal advertisement for you. The newspaper will create an advertisement using the caption and paragraph #1 of the Order for Service by Publication/Posting and Notice of Action (MC 307). It will publish the advertisement as instructed in paragraph #2 of the order. Ordinarily, publication must be once a week for three consecutive weeks.

Once the advertisement has been published the required number of times, the newspaper will bill you for the cost of publication. After you pay the bill, the newspaper will complete the Affidavit of Publishing on the reverse of the copy of the Order for Service by Publication/Posting and Notice of Action (MC 307) that you gave it and return this paper to you.

If the defendant's last known address is out of date, the judge will probably omit registered mailing of the service papers to the defendant. But if the defendant's last known address is fairly recent, mailing may be required.

If the judge has ordered registered mailing, have a helper mail the service papers and a copy of the Order for Service by Publication/Posting and Notice

---

More Information

The cost of a legal advertisement depends on the size of the ad and frequency of publication. Since you really only need to publish the caption and paragraph #1 of the Order for Service by Publication/Posting and Notice of Action (MC 307), your advertisement should not be very large. The newspaper may want to print the entire order, but that is unnecessary and will cost you more.

Your advertisement will probably be published three times. In that case, there is a minimum charge of $59 (adjusted annually for inflation), but the cost will probably be slightly more, perhaps $60–$100.

of Action (MC 307) to the defendant at his/her last known address. This mailing must be by registered (not certified) mail, return receipt requested. The mailing must be sent sometime before the date of the last publication of the legal advertisement.

Afterward, have your helper complete the Affidavit of Mailing on the reverse of a copy of the Order for Service by Publication/Posting and Notice of Action (MC 307), and attach both the Receipt for Registered Mail (PS Form 3806) and the Domestic Return Receipt (PS Form 3811), signed or unsigned by the defendant, to it. Your helper can use the Affidavit of Mailing on the same copy of the Order for Service by Publication/Posting and Notice of Action (MC 307) that the newspaper used to prove publication, or you can use another copy. Either way, make three copies of the reverse of the order(s), mark "FOC" on one copy and save another for filing later as your proof of service.

Posting

Judges seem to prefer publication as the method of alternate service for disappeared defendants, and posting is seldom ordered. But if posting was ordered in your Order for Service by Publication/Posting and Notice of Action (MC 307), look at paragraph #3 to see who was designated as the poster. That person might be a sheriff, policeman or court official, such as a bailiff. Take four copies of the Order for Service by Publication/Posting and Notice of Action (MC 307) to the person designated as the poster and request posting of the order.

The poster will post the order in the courthouse and the two other public places the court has specified in paragraph #3. Ordinarily, the order will remain posted for three consecutive weeks. After the posting period expires, the poster will bill you for posting services and prove the posting in the Affidavit of Posting on the reverse of the extra copy of the Order for Service by Publication/Posting and Notice of Action (MC 307).

Like alternate service by publication, alternate service by posting can be with or without registered mailing of the service papers to the defendant. If the judge has ordered registered mailing in paragraph #4 of the Order for Service by Publication/Posting and Notice of Action (MC 307), have your helper mail the service papers and a copy of the MC 307 to the defendant at his/her last known address. This mailing should be made by registered (not certified) mail, return receipt requested. The mailing must be sent sometime before the last week of the posting.

Afterward, have your helper complete the Affidavit of Mailing on the reverse of a copy of the Order for Service by Publication/Posting and Notice of Action (MC 307), and attach both the Receipt for Registered Mail (PS Form 3806) and the Domestic Return Receipt (PS Form 3811), signed or unsigned by the defendant, to it. Your helper can complete the Affidavit of Mailing on the same copy of the Order for Service by Publication/Posting and Notice of Action (MC 307) that the poster used to prove posting, or you can use another copy. Either way, make three copies of the reverse of the order(s), mark "FOC" on one copy and save another for filing later as your proof of service.

Original - Court
1st copy - Serving party
2nd copy - Extra

Approved, SCAO

STATE OF MICHIGAN	MOTION AND VERIFICATION	CASE NO.
JUDICIAL DISTRICT	FOR ALTERNATE SERVICE	
JUDICIAL CIRCUIT		
COUNTY PROBATE		Court telephone no.

Court address

Plaintiff name(s), address(es), and telephone no(s).

v

Defendant name(s), address(es), and telephone no(s).

In the matter of _____ DUDLEY E. LOVELACE _____ cannot reasonably be made

1. Service of process upon _____ as otherwise provided in MCR 2.105, as shown in the following verification of process server.

2. Defendant's last known home and business addresses are:

___900 S. MAPLE_____ *LAKE CITY*_____ *MI*_____ *48800*____
Home address   City   "   State   "   "   Zip

___1000 SERVICE RD._____ City_____ State_____ Zip
Business address

a. I believe the ☒ home   address shown above is current.
                 ☒ business

b. I do not know the defendant's current ☒ home   address. I have made the following efforts to ascertain the current
                                          ☒ business

address: *3-4-2009 SEARCHED TELEPHONE AND CITY DIRECTORIES / 3-7-2009 REQUESTED*
ADDRESS CORRECTION FROM USPS / 3-7-2009 DID RECORD LOOKUP AT MICHIGAN
SECRETARY OF STATE / 3-7-2009 WROTE TO MABEL LOVELACE (MOTHER) (SEE
ATTACHED LETTER); ALL WITHOUT RESULTS.

3. I request the court order service by alternate means.

I declare that the statements above are true to the best of my information, knowledge, and belief.

___3-15-2009_____   *Darlene A. Lovelace*_____
Date   Plaintiff/Plaintiff's attorney signature
                                           DARLENE A. LOVELACE _____ Bar no.
                                           Name (type or print)

Address

City, state, zip   Telephone no.

VERIFICATION OF PROCESS SERVER

1. I have tried to serve process on this defendant as described: State date, place, and what occurred on each occasion.

3-4-2009 TRIED TO SERVE DEFENDANT AT 900 S. MAPLE, LAKE CITY, MI, BUT A WOMAN THERE TOLD ME
DEFENDANT WAS NOT AT HOME WHEN IT APPEARED HE WAS.
3-5-2009 " TRIED TO SERVE DEFENDANT AT 1000 SERVICE RD., LAKE CITY, MI, BUT HIS EMPLOYER PREVENTED SERVICE.
3-7-2009 TRIED TO SERVE DEFENDANT AT 1000 SERVICE RD., LAKE CITY, MI, BUT HE SPED AWAY IN HIS CAR.
3-8-2009 TRIED TO SERVE DEFENDANT AT 1000 SERVICE RD., LAKE CITY, MI, BUT HE SPED AWAY IN HIS CAR.

I declare that the statements above are true to the best of my information, knowledge, and belief.

___3-14-2009_____   *Chester Gunn*_____
Date   Signature
                                           CHESTER GUNN _____
                                           Process server (type or print)

MC 303 (3/11) MOTION AND VERIFICATION FOR ALTERNATE SERVICE   MCR 2.105

COMPLETE 2b. INSTEAD FOR A DISAPPEARED DEFENDANT

COMPLETE 2a. FOR AN ELUSIVE DEFENDANT

SERVER MUST COMPLETE VERIFICATION OF PROCESS SERVER FOR ATTEMPTED SERVICE ON AN ELUSIVE DEFENDANT

Approved, SCAO

Original - Court
1st copy - Defendant
2nd copy - Plaintiff
3rd copy - Return

STATE OF MICHIGAN		
JUDICIAL DISTRICT	ORDER REGARDING	CASE NO.
JUDICIAL CIRCUIT	ALTERNATE SERVICE	
COUNTY PROBATE		

Court address

Court telephone no.

Plaintiff name(s), address(es), and telephone no(s).

v

Defendant name(s), address(es), and telephone no(s).

Plaintiff's attorney, bar no., address, and telephone no.

THE COURT FINDS:

☒ 1. Service of process upon the defendant, _____DUDLEY E. LOVELACE_____,

cannot reasonably be made as provided in   ☒ MCR 2.105   ☐ MCR 2.107(B)(1)(b)   and service of process
may be made in a manner that is reasonably calculated to give the defendant actual notice of the proceedings and an opportunity
to be heard.

IT IS ORDERED:

☒ 2. Service of the   ☒ summons and complaint   ☒ other: _FOC23, MC416 AND FOC PAMPHLET_

and a copy of this order shall be made by the following method(s).

☒ a. First-class mail to _900 S. MAPLE, LAKE CITY, MI_

☒ b. Tacking or firmly affixing to the door at _____"_____

☒ c. Delivering at _____"_____

to a member of the defendant's household who is of suitable age and discretion to receive process, with instructions to
deliver it promptly to the defendant.

☐ d. Other:_____

For each method used, proof of service must be filed promptly with the court.

☐ 3. The motion for alternate service is denied.

_3-17-2009_
Date

Lester Tubbs
Judge   Bar no.

MC 304 (9/09) **ORDER REGARDING ALTERNATE SERVICE**   MCR 2.103, MCR 2.105

LIST ANY OTHER SERVICE PAPERS HERE

JUDGE WILL CHOOSE ONE OR MORE OF THESE METHODS

A MICHIGAN COURT OFFICER CARRYING OUT SERVICE WILL USE THE OFFICER CERTIFICATE

PROOF OF SERVICE	ORDER REGARDING ALTERNATE SERVICE Case No.

PROCESS SERVER: You must serve the copies of the order regarding alternate service and file proof of service with the court. If you are unable to complete service, you must return this original and all copies to the court clerk.

CERTIFICATE / AFFIDAVIT OF SERVICE / NONSERVICE

☐ **OFFICER CERTIFICATE**
I certify that I am a sheriff, deputy sheriff, bailiff, appointed court officer, or attorney for a party (MCR 2.104[A][2]), and that: (notarization not required)

OR

☒ **AFFIDAVIT OF PROCESS SERVER**
Being first duly sworn, I state that I am a legally competent adult who is not a party or an officer of a corporate party, and that: (notarization required)

DAY OF SERVICE

I served a copy of the   ☒ summons and complaint   ☒ other: *FOC23, MC416, AND FOC PAMPHLET*

and a copy of the order for alternate service upon *DUDLEY E. LOVELACE* _____ by

☒ 1. First-class mail to *900 S. MAPLE, LAKE CITY, MI* _____, on Date *WED. 3-18-2009* .

☒ 2. Tacking or firmly affixing to the door at _____ " _____, on Date *WED. 3-18-2009* .

☒ 3. Delivering at _____ ...e and discretion to receive process, with ins...ctions to deliver _____, on Date *FRI. 3-20-2009* .

to a member of the de...

it promptly to the defen... _____, on Date _____

HELPER/SERVER MUST PROVE EVERY SERVICE METHOD ORDERED AND USED

IF SEVERAL SERVICE METHODS WERE USED ON DIFFERENT DAYS, USE LAST DAY AS DAY OF SERVICE (3-20-09 IN THIS CASE)

☐ 4. Other: _____ specify

I declare that the statements abo... ...mation, knowledge, and belief.

Service fee $	Miles traveled Fee $		TOTAL FEE $
Incorrect address fee $	Miles traveled Fee $		

Ruth Darling
Signature
RUTH DARLING
Name (type or print) _____
_____
Title

Subscribed and sworn to before me on *3-21-2009* , *OJIBWAY* _____ County, Michigan.
                                    Date

My commission expires: *1-1-2010* _____ Signature: *Loretta Smiley* _____
                          Date   Deputy court clerk/Notary public

Notary public, State of Michigan, County of *OJIBWAY* _____

Approved, SCAO

Original - Court
1st copy - Defendant
2nd copy - Moving party
3rd copy - Return

STATE OF MICHIGAN JUDICIAL DISTRICT JUDICIAL CIRCUIT COUNTY PROBATE	ORDER FOR SERVICE BY PUBLICATION/POSTING AND NOTICE OF ACTION	CASE NO.

Court address

Court telephone no.

Plaintiff name(s), address(es), and telephone no(s).

v

Defendant name(s), address(es), and telephone no(s).

Plaintiff's attorney, bar no., address, and telephone no.

TO: DUDLEY E. LOVELACE

IT IS ORDERED:

1. You are being sued in this court by the plaintiff to   OBTAIN A JUDGMENT OF DIVORCE

_____ . You must file your answer or take other action
permitted by law in this court at the court address above on or before   6-1-2009
Date
so, a default judgment may be entered against you for the relief demanded in the complaint filed in this case.   . If you fail to do

(callout: COMPLETE THIS LINE)

(callout: JUDGE WILL COMPLETE REST OF ORDER)

2. A copy of this order shall be published once each week in   OJIBWAY NEWS
[X] three consecutive weeks,   Name of publication
for [ ] _____ , and proof of publication shall be filed in this court.

(callout: JUDGE WILL CHOOSE EITHER PUBLICATION OR POSTING)

3.   CHESTER GUNN
Name
_____ shall post a copy of this order in the courthouse, and
at   100 S. MAIN, LAKE CITY, MI
Location
at   201 W. LAKE, LAKE CITY, MI   and
Location
[X] three continuous weeks,
for [ ] _____ , and shall file proof of posting in this court.

4. A copy of this order shall be sent to   DUDLEY E. LOVELACE
Name
by registered mail, return receipt requested, before the [X] date of the last publication,   at the last-known address
[X] last week of posting,
____ed with this court.   and the affidavit of mailing shall be

(callout: MAILING MAY OR MAY NOT BE ORDERED TO GO ALONG WITH PUBLICATION OR POSTING)

3-17-2009
Date

Lester Tubbs
Judge   Bar no.

MC 307 (9/09) ORDER FOR SERVICE BY PUBLICATION/POSTING AND NOTICE OF ACTION   MCR 2.106, MCR 5.101(C)

AFFIDAVIT OF PUBLISHING

Name of ☒ publisher ☐ agent of publisher
ELTON BEAN
Name of newspaper | County where published
OJIBWAY NEWS | OJIBWAY

Attach copy of publication here

This newspaper is a qualified newspaper. The order for service was published in this newpaper at least once each week for three consecutive weeks on the following dates.

3-25-2009, 4-1-2009, 4-8-2009

Elton Bean
4-15-2009 | Affiant signature
Date

Subscribed and sworn to before me on 4-15-2009 , OJIBWAY County, MI
Date

My commission expires: 1-1-2010 Signature: _Loretta Smiley_
Date | Court clerk/Notary public

Notary public, State of Michigan, County of OJIBWAY

AFFIDAVIT OF POSTING

OJIBWAY COUNTY courthouse and the
I have posted this order in a conspicuous place in the _____

following places as ordered by this court: 100 S. MAIN AND 201 W. LAKE, LAKE CITY, MI

It has been posted for ☒ three continuous weeks ☐ _____ continuous weeks as ordered by this court.

Chester Gunn
4-15-2009 | Affiant signature
Date

Subscribed and sworn to before me on 4-15-2009 , OJIBWAY County, Michigan.
Date

My commission expires: 1-1-2010 Signature: _Loretta Smiley_
Date | Court clerk/Notary public

Notary public, State of Michigan, County of OJIBWAY

AFFIDAVIT OF MAILING

Attach mailing receipt and return receipt here.

As ordered, on 3-18-2009 I mailed a copy of the summons and complaint
Date

and this order to DUDLEY E. LOVELACE
Name

at 900 S. MAPLE, LAKE CITY, MI
Address

The mailing receipt and return receipt are attached at right.

Ruth Darling
3-18-2009 | Affiant signature
Date

Subscribed and sworn to before me on 3-18-2009 , OJIBWAY County, Michigan.
Date

sion expires: 1-1-2010 Signature: _Loretta Smiley_
Date | Court clerk/Notary public

State of Michigan, County of OJIBWAY

NEWSPAPER WILL ATTACH A COPY OF THE ADVERTISEMENT

NEWSPAPER WILL COMPLETE

POSTER WILL COMPLETE

ATTACH BOTH PS FORM 3806 AND PS FORM 3811

HELPER/SERVER WHO PERFORMED REGISTERED MAILING MUST COMPLETE

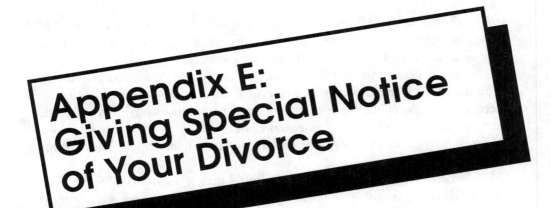

Appendix E: Giving Special Notice of Your Divorce

In most divorce cases with minor children, only the friend of the court, prosecuting attorney and defendant are entitled to notice of the divorce. However, you must give special notice of your divorce in two special situations: 1) when someone other than you or the defendant (a non-parent third party) has physical custody of your minor children 2) when a minor child of yours is subject to a continuing prior custody and/or parenting time case in Michigan.*

Special Notice to a Third Party with Custody

Sometimes parents informally give physical custody of their minor children to family or friends. In other cases, parents may lose physical custody of their minor children by court order during independent third-party custody, paternity, juvenile delinquency, protective (abuse/neglect or dependency), guardianship, mental commitment or adoption cases.** If any of these things has happened to you, so that a third party has physical custody of your children

---

*   When your minor child(ren) is involved in a continuing prior custody and/or parenting time case in a court outside of Michigan, there could be a lack of Michigan jurisdiction for the custody and parenting time issues of your divorce (see the footnote in "Can I Get a Divorce in Michigan?" on page 43 for more about this possibility).

**   If one of these cases has resulted in full termination of your parental rights, the children may no longer be yours (see "Which Children Must Be Included in My Divorce?" on page 51). On the other hand, it's possible to lose custody of children without losing full parental rights.

(this fact should have been noted in paragraph #6 of your Uniform Child Custody Jurisdiction Enforcement Act Affidavit (MC 416)), the third-party custodian is entitled to special notice of your divorce.

The purpose of the notice is to let the third party know that a divorce has been filed which might result in a return of custody to you or the defendant. Recent court decisions have curtailed third-party custody rights, so a third party must have a very strong case to prevail in a custody dispute with parents. As a result, the third party's odds of gaining custody are small, but they must be notified anyway.

When special notice is due, you should give it during the "Service" step of your divorce. To give this notice, prepare an extra set of service papers and have them served on the third party by service by mail or delivery, as described in "Service" on page 99. Have that service proved on the reverse of an extra copy of the Summons and Complaint (MC 01), and file it and a friend of the court's copy with the clerk.

Dealing with a Third Party in a Divorce

After you serve notice on a third-party custodian, s/he could respond by filing an appearance, motion or other paper in the case. The filing may be a formality, with the third party agreeing to the custody relief you are seeking in your complaint (transfer of custody back to the parent-parties or continuation of the third-party custody). Or the third party may dispute custody, turning your divorce into a contested case (not by the defendant, but by the third party).

Either way, a third party who is involved or intervenes in a divorce should be treated as an extra party to the case. You should provide copies of all papers in the case to the third party (a few papers have special caption boxes for third parties; for the papers that don't, try to squeeze the third party's name and address into the defendant's caption box) and show this on your proofs of service of these papers.

One more thing: If the third party received custody of your children during a prior court proceeding, you might also have to give special notice to the court and court officials, as described below.

Special Notice to a Prior Court

The divorce court will almost always determine the issues of custody, parenting time and residence of children in divorce cases with minor children. When another court has already decided these issues in a prior case, the divorce court's decision could possibly upset the prior court's decision. The divorce court is permitted to make a new custody, parenting time and residence order—it isn't bound by the prior court's decision—but special notice of the divorce must sometimes be given to the prior court letting it know that its order is being replaced.

You don't need to give special notice to a prior court in every case. Notice is due only when the prior court is: 1) a Michigan court, which 2) made a custody, parenting time and/or residence of children order about minor children 3) in a case that is "continuing." Examples of these cases include independent third-party custody or parenting time, paternity, juvenile delinquency, protective (abuse/neglect or dependency), guardianship, mental commitment or adoption cases. Your affirmative response to paragraph #4 or #5 of the Uniform Child Custody Jurisdiction Enforcement Act Affidavit (MC 416) is a tip-off that a prior court has made the kind of order triggering special notice.

Nevertheless, the prior court is only entitled to notice if the case is continuing; if the prior case is over, no notice is due. For example, let's assume that while you were living in another Michigan county your 14-year-old child committed a crime and was returned to you for two-year home probation after a juvenile delinquency proceeding in family court. In this instance, the family court and several officials must get special notice of your divorce during the two-year probationary period since the case is continuing. But after expiration of the two-year probation, the family court in the other county wouldn't be due notice because the juvenile delinquency case is no longer continuing.

When you're in doubt about the status of a prior case involving your minor children, call the court and ask. If you're still confused, send the special notice anyway since it's usually better to give an unnecessary notice than fail to give one that's required.

If you must give special notice of your divorce to a prior court, do it in the middle of your divorce, after you schedule your final hearing. Don't wait too long because the notice must be sent *at least 21 days before the final hearing*.

To give the special notice, prepare the Notice to Prior Court of Proceedings Affecting Minor(s) (MC 28), and make four photocopies. Send copies of the notice to the: 1) clerk or register of the prior court 2) the friend of the court, juvenile officer and/or prosecuting attorney involved in the prior case.

Afterward, file the Notice to Prior Court of Proceedings Affecting Minor(s) (MC 28) and the friend of the court copy with the clerk of the court where your divorce is filed. In addition, if the prior court gave physical custody of the children to someone other than you or the defendant, you might also have to give special notice to that third-party custodian, as described above.

At the end of the divorce, the clerk is supposed to send the prior court a copy of the Judgment of Divorce (TBP 4). You may want to check with the clerk to make sure the judgment is sent.

Original - Originating court
Copies as needed
JIS CODE: NPC

Approved, SCAO

STATE OF MICHIGAN
JUDICIAL CIRCUIT
PROBATE COURT
COUNTY

NOTICE TO PRIOR COURT OF PROCEEDINGS AFFECTING MINOR(S)

CASE NO.

Court telephone no.

Court address

Name(s) of parent(s)/guardian(s)/plaintiff/defendant
DARLENE A. LOVELACE
DUDELEY E. LOVELACE

Name(s), alias(es), and date(s) of birth of minor(s)
DUANE WESLEY LOVELACE   6-1-2006

87-1024 -DL
Case no. of other court

TO: County of ___*SUPERIOR CIRCUIT COURT - FAMILY DIVISION*___
☒ Court clerk or Register
☐ Friend of the court
☒ Prosecuting attorney
☒ Juvenile officer

NOTICE:

1. ☒ a. A complaint/petition/motion was filed with this court t...   ...subject to the continuing

jurisdiction of your court. A hearing on the complaint...

9-7-2009
Date
9:00 A.M.
Time
COURTROOM OF JUDGE TUBBS
Location

(INSERT DATE, TIME AND PLACE OF THE FINAL HEARING)

☐ b. The attached order was entered on ___ Date

2. The actions of the court in this matter may supersede part or all of the order(s) previously entered by your court as the best interests of the minor(s) require.

CERTIFICATE OF SERVICE

I certify that on this date I served a copy of this notice on the prior court by ☒ first-class mail. ☐ personal delivery.

Darlene A. Lovelace
Signature

6-15-2009
Date

Note: If item 1a is checked, this notice must be mailed at least 21 days before the hearing.

Do not write below this line - For court use only

MCL 712A.2(b)(2), MCL 712A.3a, MCR 3.205, MCR 3.927, MCR 5.112

MC 28 (9/08) **NOTICE TO PRIOR COURT OF PROCEEDINGS AFFECTING MINOR(S)**

Appendix F: Divorce and the Military

Divorce by or against a spouse in active-duty military service creates several special problems. Right away, there can be practical problems with locating and serving papers on the servicemember who may be stationed at a distant military base. The military has its own retirement plan and health care system which are unlike civilian ones and often difficult to navigate. The military also has special benefits, like PX and commissary, that can be divided during divorce.

Military Relief Laws

By far the biggest problem posed by a divorce against a military spouse are the military relief laws protecting active-duty servicemembers. There are actually two laws: the federal Servicemembers Civil Relief Act (SCRA) and a similar Michigan relief law.

Federal Servicemembers Civil Relief Act (SCRA)

The SCRA, which has the widest scope, covers servicemembers in the active duty of the U.S. military (see the sidebox for which personnel are covered by the SCRA). The act offers several forms of relief to servicemembers protecting them from some kinds of debts, taxes, installment contracts, lawsuits, etc. The

More Information

(1) The SCRA covers all five service branches of the U.S. military:

- **Army**
- **Navy**
- **Marine Corps**
- **Air Force**
- **Coast Guard**

The act also covers commissioned officers in the Public Health Service and National Oceanic and Atmospheric Administration.

The SCRA protects servicemembers on *active duty* in the U.S. military. The U.S. military is made up of two components:

Active component. Members of regular units (Regular Army, Regular Navy, etc.).

Reserve component. Servicemembers activated from the two segments of the military reserve:

- *Reserves.* Each service branch has its own reserve unit (Army Reserve (Army), Naval Reserve (Navy), etc.), which is always under federal command.

- *National Guard.* State Army National Guard (attached to the Army) and Air National Guard (attached to the Air Force) units, including Michigan's army and air units. National Guard units fall under state control, unless they have been called to federal active duty by the president. After 30 consecutive days of federal service, guardmembers are protected by the SCRA.

The SCRA protects servicemembers lawfully away from active duty, such as during a period of leave or hospitalization. The act also covers military inductees after receiving induction orders. The act doesn't apply to civilians working for the military.

(2) Michigan's military relief law covers members in Michigan's two National Guard units:

- **Army National Guard**
- **Air National Guard**

This law protects guardmembers on active duty for more than seven days after activation by the governor: 1) to support civilian authority (such as during a riot, flood, etc.) 2) for a war or emergency of the state or nation.

The protections of the Michigan law extend beyond the period of active duty for some things, but not for lawsuit relief which is the focus here.

Note: Other states have similar military relief laws protecting their National Guardmembers, which could be an issue if a party is on active duty in an out-of-state unit.

intent of the SCRA is to protect servicemembers from these obligations so they can focus on their military duties.

It's the lawsuit relief protections of the SCRA that have an impact on divorce. In essence, these protections shield defendant-servicemembers from hard-to-handle lawsuits, including divorces. There are two main lawsuit relief remedies:

Stay.   During a lawsuit, a servicemember can ask for a stay or freezing of the case (see "Satisfying the Military Relief Laws" on page 232 for more about two kinds of stays and the grounds for issuing them). The court can grant a stay for 90 days or more, effectively stopping the case for this period. Typically, a stay will last only until the servicemember can get leave so s/he can deal with the lawsuit.

Reopening a default judgment.   If a servicemember doesn't participate in the lawsuit, and a default judgment is ultimately issued, s/he can ask for reopening of the case. The request must be made no later than 90 days after the servicemember leaves military service. Reopening isn't guaranteed; the member must have a good defense and show that military service impaired his/her ability to take part in the case.

The SCRA's lawsuit relief remedies are really designed for different situations. But sometimes a servicemember can use both remedies; other times using one means loss of the other. The SCRA also allows a servicemember to waive (give up) these relief protections. The chart on the opposite page explains how these remedies fit together.

During peacetime, the SCRA's lawsuit relief protections seldom totally bar a divorce against a servicemember. At a minimum, the act requires a little extra paperwork and the divorce can go through as smoothly as one against a civilian. At most, the divorce will be frozen until the servicemember can respond, either by obtaining leave or by separation from the service.

In a war, the SCRA's stay remedy may be extended. For example, during the Persian Gulf War in 1990-91, stays were expanded effectively freezing all lawsuits against active-duty servicemembers until after the war. This kind of total-but-temporary freeze could be used again in a future war or crisis.

SCRA Lawsuit Relief Rights

	Right to request stay	**Right to request reopening of default judgment**
Defendant appears and signs a waiver of SCRA rights	No	No
Defendant asks court for a stay	Yes	No
Defendant doesn't respond in case:		
open case	Court must appoint a lawyer for servicemember who can ask for a stay or other relief	Yes
closed case	(2) Yes, if case is reopened	(1) Yes, then may ask for a stay

Michigan's Military Relief Laws

Many people don't know it, but Michigan has a military relief law similar to the SCRA. The state law covers Michigan National Guardmembers on active duty (see the sidebox for the scope of coverage). Like the federal law, Michigan's law offers protection from some debt collection, foreclosures, utility shutoffs and lawsuits.

Unlike the SCRA, Michigan's relief law offers absolute protection from lawsuits without regard to hardship for the servicemember. After a seven-day activation of guardmembers, Michigan's law effectively freezes lawsuits against them until termination of their active-duty service for the state.

Besides Michigan's primary military relief law, in 2005 the state adopted a related law protecting the custody rights of active-duty military servicemembers. The law freezes the custody of children of servicemember-parents at the date of the parent's activation, except in certain emergency situations. After the servicemember returns from active-duty service, the absence cannot be counted against him/her during a custody determination. The following year, the state passed a similar law permitting the reduction of child support obligations (called a "military service adjustment") of reservists or guardmembers called to active duty for more than 30 days.

Divorce by a Plaintiff-Servicemember

Before filing, a plaintiff-servicemember must decide where to file. Choosing the correct state is known as jurisdiction (see "Can I Get a Divorce in Michigan?" on page 43 about jurisdiction), while choice of county inside Michigan is called venue (venue rules are covered in "Can I File the Divorce in My County?" on page 45). Both jurisdiction and venue are based on residence or one's permanent home.

Special residence rules apply to military servicemembers. Ordinarily, servicemembers keep their pre-enlistment state and county residence. So if you were a Michigan resident before enlistment, you're still a resident of Michigan and your home county regardless of where you are stationed now. You may then file either in your old home county or the Michigan county where the defendant is residing now.

It is possible for servicemembers to change residence and adopt a new residence where they are stationed. Changing residence takes more than simply filing a military State of Legal Residence Certificate; it requires a combination of things in the new state (registration to vote, ownership or rental of real property, payment of taxes, etc.), showing an intent to regard the new state as a permanent home. If you have lost your Michigan residence that way, you can still file for divorce here, but only in the Michigan county where the defendant lives.

> ## More Information
>
> About military retirement benefits, health care coverage and other benefits (such as PX and commissary) available to a divorced nonmilitary spouse, contact:
>
> **Ex-Partners of Servicemembers for Equality (Ex-Pose)**
> P.O. Box 11191
> Alexandria, VA 22312
> (703) 941-5844
> www.ex-pose.org
>
> About division of military retirement pay from a servicemember's point of view, get:
>
> *Divorce and the Military II: A Comprehensive Guide for Service Members, Spouses, and Attorneys*, 2nd ed., Marsha L. Thole and Frank W. Ault, Redlands, CA: The American Retirees Association, 2001

Wherever you file, you can file by mail and have the divorce papers served by any of the service methods. Later on, other papers can be filed by mail and the divorce conducted from afar.

Divorcing a Defendant-Servicemember

Before you begin the divorce, choose the correct state (this choice is known as jurisdiction and is covered in "Can I Get a Divorce in Michigan?" on page 43) and county (choice of county is known as venue; see "Can I File the Divorce in My County?" on page 45 for venue rules) for filing. Both jurisdiction and venue are based on residence or one's permanent home.

There are special residence rules for servicemembers which can affect jurisdiction and venue. Ordinarily, servicemembers keep their pre-enlistment state and county residence, no matter how far away they are stationed now. So if the defendant resided in Michigan with you during your marriage just before entry into the service, there should be full Michigan jurisdiction. For convenience, you will probably file in the Michigan county where you live.

Before you can have the divorce papers served, you must know where the defendant is stationed. If you've lost touch, there are ways to find military personnel through a military locator service. The sidebox explains how to contact a base locator (when you know where the defendant is stationed) or a service branch locator (when you lack specific information).

The best way to serve a military spouse is by mail, since the U.S. Postal Service delivers mail (including certified mail necessary for service) to military bases all over the world. Military mail overseas can be a little slow, so allow extra time for service outside the country. See "Service" on page 99 for more about serving by mail and by the other service methods.

If a defendant is stationed at a stateside military installation and refuses to accept mailed service, contact the sheriff or a commercial process server in the county and arrange for service by delivery. Military personnel living off base can be served at home without a problem. But except for the Air Force, most service branches don't allow process servers to enter military bases and serve servicemembers there directly. Instead, the defendant-servicemember's commanding officer sets up a time and place for service, if the member agrees to accept the papers; if s/he refuses service, the commanding officer notifies the server of the refusal. Sheriffs and commercial process servers in areas with military bases should be familiar with these service procedures.

Oddly, service can be easier at a military base in a foreign country. Overseas, commanding officers can help carry out service, but are discouraged from acting as actual process servers. As a compromise, you can contact the defendant's unit commander and suggest service by acknowledgment (see "Service by Acknowledgment" on page 101 for instructions). The commander can hand the service papers to the defendant and ask for acknowledgment of service. If the defendant refuses service, the commanding officer cannot force service and will notify you of the refusal.

More Information

It can be difficult to find the address of active-duty servicemembers. But there are several resources that can help. For good general information, get:

How to Locate Anyone Who Is or Has Been in the Military: Armed Forces Locator Guide, 8th ed., Richard Johnson and Debra Knox, Spartanburg, SC: MIE Publishing, 1999.

If you know where the defendant is stationed, call the base locator (often just the telephone information operator at the base). The Johnson and Knox book has a list of base locator telephone numbers for all military installations in the U.S. and worldwide. Or you can get the same information from Military OneSource at (800) 342-9647 or www.militaryonesource.mil, then to View a Directory of Military Installations. Besides finding the defendant, the base locator can also provide information about contacting the defendant's commanding officer for carrying out service.

You should know the defendant's service branch, either from personal knowledge or a military status report from the Defense Manpower Data Center (DMDC) (a DMDC report confirming the defendant's active-duty service should also show the defendant's service branch, but no actual location information).

To make a military locator request, you need the defendant's full name and date of birth or social security number; other information like rank, service number and last duty assignment/last known military address is helpful. The locators charge fees for requests, but these are usually waived for close family member-requesters.

The five military locators generally take requests by mail only (none has interactive Internet access). Recently, the Coast Guard began taking locator requests by telephone or email. For convenience, a Military Locator Request form, addressed to all five locators, is included in this book. Send your request to the correct military locator with a stamped self-addressed envelope and expect a response within two-four weeks.

One problem with all the military locators is that they typically won't release current military addresses or duty assignments of troops overseas, aboard ships or in a war zone, for security reasons. You may be able to get around this problem if you know the defendant's overseas base or ship. The Johnson and Knox book cited above has lists of all overseas military installations and Navy and Coast Guard ships and home ports. The book has suggestions about improvising addresses to servicemembers overseas or at sea using APO (Army Post Office serving Europe and the Middle East) and FPO (Fleet Post Office for the Pacific and Far East) addresses.

You might get lucky and contact the defendant that way. If not, you will have to use a form of alternate service (see Appendix D for more about alternate service). Be sure to attach the (failed) locator response to your motion for alternate service. The alternate service may involve service on the defendant's relatives who probably have his/her military address.

Satisfying the Military Relief Laws

After service, you must come to grips with the military relief laws. If the defendant-servicemember is protected by Michigan's military relief law, or if the SCRA has put a temporary ban on all lawsuits, you can only proceed with a waiver from the defendant (see below about getting a waiver).

But typically, the defendant will be protected by the SCRA's lawsuit relief remedies (stay and default judgment reopening). As explained before, these are flexible remedies which often allow divorces to go through. Here are several typical scenarios in which the SCRA is satisfied allowing completion of the divorce.

Waiver of Military Relief Law Rights by the Defendant

As with other legal rights, a defendant-servicemember can voluntarily waive (give up) the lawsuit relief rights provided by the military relief laws. The waiver cuts off these rights, allowing the divorce to go through normally. Waiver is the only way to satisfy Michigan's military relief law and the SCRA when it has imposed a temporary wartime freeze on lawsuits. But even if the SCRA applies in its normal peacetime form, waiver always makes it easier for the divorce to proceed.

If the defendant is willing to waive, send the Appearance and Waiver of Military Relief Law Rights (TBP 6) to the defendant and have him/her sign the form. After you get the TBP 6 back, attach the form to the Default (TBP 2) as described in "Default and the Military Relief Laws" on page 114.

The Defendant Applies for a SCRA Stay

After receiving the divorce papers, the defendant may contact the court and apply for a stay under the SCRA. The application can be quite informal—just a letter or other communication—but must include:

- information from the servicemember showing: 1) how military duties materially affect the servicemember's ability to appear 2) a date when the servicemember can appear
- information from the servicemember's commanding officer confirming that: 1) military duties prevent the servicemember from appearing, and 2) military leave is not currently available

During a stay application, the primary issue is whether the servicemember's military service has a material effect on his/her ability to appear in the case. Courts have defined material effect in terms of two main factors:

Geographical distance. This is probably the most important factor. If the defendant-servicemember is at sea or stationed overseas, a good argument can be made that military service is hampering the defendant in the case. On the other hand, leave can cancel distance, since the servicemember can often use the leave to return home and participate in the case. Thus, the availability of leave is often the pivotal issue for a stay request. It's also important for determining the length of the stay, if one is issued.

Financial hardship.   Courts want to know if military service has caused a financial hardship for the servicemember, which has impaired the ability to appear. Military service often means a loss of income and extra financial obligations. On the other hand, some large employers make up the difference in pay and offer extra benefits to activated employees, resulting in no net loss of income. Under- or unemployed servicemembers may actually see an increase in income from military service.

A servicemember's Leave and Earnings Statement (LES) can answer both issues. The LES, which the military provides twice a month, shows a servicemember's accrued leave and details his/her military pay (base pay, allowances and allotments). If the defendant hasn't submitted a recent LES with the stay application, s/he should be required to submit one to the judge reviewing the application.

When the defendant's stay application shows the four things enumerated in the list above, the court must grant the defendant's application. The SCRA says that a stay must be a minimum of 90 days, but can be longer. The court can also add even more time in an additional stay.

But typically, the stay will last only until the defendant has time to deal with the divorce. This could be until the next period of leave or when the defendant leaves the service, when discharge is imminent. You can wait until the stay expires and then resume the divorce where you left off.

If the stay is long, the clerk may try to dismiss the case for no progress. You can prevent dismissal by pointing out the stay to the clerk, and explain that this is the reason for delay in the case.

Whether a stay is granted or denied, the fact that the defendant applied for the stay is important. The stay request is regarded as the defendant's chief SCRA remedy and results in loss of the right to request reopening of any default judgment of divorce entered later.

As a result, when you the file the Default (TBP 2), describe the defendant's stay application on the blank line in paragraph #3a. Bring this to the judge's attention also during your testimony at the final hearing.

The Defendant Doesn't Respond

It's more difficult dealing with a defendant-servicemember who doesn't respond. The fact is, the defendant may have very good reasons for not responding, such as absence aboard a ship or service in combat. The SCRA recognizes these difficulties and has special protections for unresponsive defendants.

When a defendant doesn't respond, the SCRA says that the court must appoint a lawyer for the defendant. The appointed lawyer and the defendant don't have the usual lawyer-client relationship because the servicemember may not have ever spoken to the appointed lawyer or even know that s/he exists.

Nevertheless, the appointed lawyer may ask for a stay for the defendant, which the court must grant for a minimum of 90 days if:

- the defendant has a defense to the divorce that can't be presented without the defendant; or
- the appointed lawyer has been unable to contact the defendant or determine if a good defense exists

Ordinarily, a stay application is significant because it results in loss of the right to request reopening a default judgment later. But this rule doesn't necessarily apply to an appointed lawyer's stay application because of the peculiar relationship between the appointed lawyer and the servicemember described above. As a result, the servicemember doesn't lose his/her right to request reopening a default judgment after the stay application.

If the divorce goes forward to a default judgment, the defendant can request reopening the judgment. The defendant can make the request anytime while in military service and even within 90 days after leaving the service. Reopening of the case isn't automatic. The defendant must show both a material effect from military service and a good defense to get back in the case.

If the case is reopened, the defendant may be able to participate right away. But if the defendant is still serving in the military, or just recently discharged, s/he can apply for a stay, to get extra time to defend. The application would be treated like a prejudgment stay request, as described in "The Defendant Applies for a SCRA Stay" on page 232.

Naturally, you'll want to describe this activity on the blank line in paragraph #3a of the Default (TBP 2). The judge should be familiar with this, but mention it at the final hearing.

STATE OF MICHIGAN Circuit Court - Family Division COUNTY	APPEARANCE AND WAIVER OF MILITARY RELIEF LAW RIGHTS	CASE NO.

Plaintiff (appearing *in propria persona*):

v

Defendant:

Defendant says:

1. I am in the active duty of the following unit of the U.S. military:

   333RD MILITARY POLICE COMPANY, MICHIGAN ARMY NATIONAL GUARD

2. I am currently stationed at:

   FORT LEONARD WOOD
   WAYNESVILLE, MO

3. I previously received copies of the summons and complaint for divorce and any other initial divorce papers in this case.

4. I make a general appearance and waive all lawsuit relief rights, including the right to request a stay or adjournment of proceedings, provided to me in this case by the Servicemembers Civil Relief Act (50 USC App. 501 et seq.) and/or Michigan's military relief law (MCL 32.517) (or similar military relief law from another state).

Date___4-1-2009___

Defendant___*Dudley E. Lovelace*___

TBP 6 (1/16)   **APPEARANCE AND WAIVER OF MILITARY RELIEF LAW RIGHTS**

Military Locator Request

TO:

Army
Army World Wide Locator Service
Enlisted Records and Evaluation Center
8899 East 56th Street
Indianapolis, IN 46249-5301

Air Force
Air Force Manpower and Personnel Center
ATTN: Air Force Locator / MSIMDL
550 C Street West, Suite 50
Randolph Air Force Base, TX 78150-4752

Navy
Bureau of Naval Personnel
PERS-312E
5720 Integrity Drive
Millington, TN 38055-3120

Coast Guard
Commander
Coast Guard Personnel Command
4200 Wilson Blvd., Suite 1100 (CGPC-adm-3)
Arlington, VA 20598-7200

Marine Corps
Commandant of The Marine Corps
Headquarters, U.S. Marine Corps (MMSB10)
2008 Elliott Road, Suite 201
Quantico, VA 22134-5030

RE:

Case name _____ LOVELACE V. LOVELACE _____

Case number _____ 09-00501-DM _____

Full name of defendant _____ DUDLEY ERNEST LOVELACE _____

Defendant's date of birth _____ 6-15-1984 _____

Defendant's social security number _____ 379-10-5567 _____

Defendant's rank and service number (if known) _____ — _____

Defendant's last duty assignment (if known) _____ — _____

Defendant's last military address (if known) _____ — _____

I am the plaintiff in the case above seeking a divorce against the defendant. I request information about the defendant's *current* rank, service number, unit of assignment and military address. I need this information for service of the divorce papers, to satisfy the military relief laws and other reasons related to this divorce case. A self-addressed stamped envelope is enclosed for your response.

As the defendant's spouse, I ask for waiver of the locator request fee.

Date _____ 3-6-2009 _____

Signature _____ Darlene A. Lovelace _____

Name _____ DARLENE A. LOVELACE _____

Address _____ 121 S. MAIN _____

_____ LAKE CITY, MI 48800 _____

Telephone _____ (517) 772-0000 _____

Appendix G: Dismissing Your Divorce

If you and your spouse reconcile during the divorce, you may be anxious to dismiss the divorce immediately. But this may not always be wise. It takes a lot of work to file a divorce, so why jeopardize all your effort with a hasty dismissal? Wait a while and see if the reconciliation lasts. If it does, go ahead and dismiss your divorce as described below. But if your reconciliation fails, pick up the divorce where you left off and finish it.

At one time, it was possible to let a divorce remain in court for months or even years while the parties attempted reconciliation. These days, courts are under pressure to move cases along quickly, so they won't tolerate very much delay. Nevertheless, you probably could let your divorce sit for a few months. Just make sure that your proof of service is on file with the clerk or else the clerk may dismiss the case for no progress after the 91-day summons expiration period (see "Filing the Proof of Service" on page 108 for more about this danger).

After you decide that your reconciliation is going to last, go ahead and dismiss your divorce. To dismiss your uncontested divorce, fill out the Notice of Dismissal by Plaintiff section of the Dismissal (MC 09). Choose dismissal "without prejudice" because this makes it easier to file another divorce later should your marriage break down again. After you prepare the Dismissal (MC 09), file it and the friend of the court's copy with the clerk. You should also send a copy to the defendant.

Incidentally, if your fees were suspended at the beginning of the divorce, you must deal with the fees again before you file the Dismissal (MC 09). At that time, the court can order a final fee exemption or require payment of the fees (see Appendix A for more about the fee exemption procedure).

Approved, SCAO

		Original - Court 1st copy - Applicant Other copies - All appearing parties

STATE OF MICHIGAN
JUDICIAL DISTRICT
JUDICIAL CIRCUIT
COUNTY PROBATE

DISMISSAL

CASE NO.

Court address

Court telephone no.

Plaintiff's name(s) and address(es)

v

Defendant's name(s) and address(es)

Plaintiff's attorney, bar no., address, and telephone no.

Defendant's attorney, bar no., address, and telephone no.

☒ **NOTICE OF DISMISSAL BY PLAINTIFF**

1. Plaintiff/Attorney for plaintiff files this notice of dismissal of this case ☐ with
   ☒ all defendants.   ☒ without   prejudice as to:
   ☐ the following defendant(s): _____

2. I certify, under penalty of contempt, that:
   a. This notice is the first dismissal filed by the plaintiff based upon or including the same claim against the defendant.
   b. All costs of filing and service have been paid.
   c. **No answer or motion has been served upon the plaintiff by the defendant** as of the date of this notice.
   d. A copy of this notice has been provided to the appearing defendant/attorney by ☒ mail ☐ personal service.

_7-1-2009_ _____   *Darlene A. Lovelace* _____
Date   Plaintiff/Attorney signature

☐ **STIPULATION TO DISMISS**

I stipulate to the dismissal of this case ☐ with
☐ all parties.   ☐ without   prejudice as to:
☐ the following parties: _____

Date _____   _____
                                                        Plaintiff/Attorney signature

Date _____   _____
                                                        Defendant/Attorney signature

☐ **ORDER TO DISMISS**

IT IS ORDERED this case is dismissed ☐ with
                                          ☐ without   prejudice. Conditions, if any: _____

_____

_____

☐ This order resolves the last pending claim and closes the case.

Date _____

MC 09   (4/14)   **DISMISSAL**   Judge _____

                                                                Bar no.

                                                                MCR 2.504

Appendix H: Additional Judgment Provisions

The first two pages of the Judgment of Divorce (TBP 4a and b) and the companion Uniform Child Support Order (FOC 10/52) contain standard judgment provisions that should take care of most divorce cases with minor children. But in special cases, these standard provisions might not be enough.

Luckily, the judgment form is open-ended and expandable allowing you to add extra judgment provisions. When your divorce includes alimony, add the Uniform Spousal Support Order (FOC 10b) to provide for the payment of alimony. Insert other kinds of extra provisions (specific parenting time, specific joint physical custody schedule, property division, etc.) in the blank space on the Judgment of Divorce (TBP 4c). If you need even more room, use the Judgment of Divorce (TBP 4x). Among your judgment papers, sandwich the TBP 4x between the TBP 4b and 4c as a third page of the judgment, with the TBP 4c becoming the fourth page. If you need even more space, make photocopies of the TBP 4x and add several of these expansion pages. As you expand the judgment this way, remember to number the judgment pages consecutively in the captions of the forms.

The sections below deal with special situations in which you might need additional judgment provisions. Sample judgment provisions are also included which you can use or adapt to your case.

Property Division Provisions

Before you can provide for a property division in your judgment, you must do a complete inventory and valuation of your property (see "Can I Get a Fair Property Division?" on page 53 for more about inventorying and valuing property). You and the defendant should also agree to an overall division of your property. If you have a prenuptial agreement dealing with divorce, this document will normally control the division. Otherwise, you must decide the shares each of you is to receive. Are you going to divide your property equally, 55-45, 60-40, etc.? After you do all those things, you're ready to begin the actual division of property.

Dividing Real Property

All real property must be divided specifically in your divorce judgment. This rule applies both to real property owned by spouses jointly (joint real property) and real property that a spouse owns alone (solely-owned real property). The provisions below divide joint and solely-owned real property in three ways: 1) trade-off 2) buy-out (by one spouse from the other) 3) sale (to third parties). There are several other ways to divide real property, but these are far too complicated to do by yourself.

If you and your spouse don't own any real property, check the first box in paragraph #5A of the Judgment of Divorce (TBP 4a). If you are property-owners, check the second box and then divide the property in the Judgment of Divorce (TBP 4c).

As you divide real property, include the street address and legal description. Adding the legal description is important because this permits you to use the judgment as a substitute deed if one spouse refuses to sign a deed for the property (see "Transferring Property" on page 145 for more about using a judgment to transfer property this way). You can find the legal description in a deed, land contract, mortgage, abstract of title or title insurance policy for the property.

More Information

The court rules specify a judgment style which you must follow in adding provisions to your judgment:

- There must be only one subject or topic per judgment provision.

- All provisions must be numbered consecutively.

- All provisions must have a descriptive introductory heading, which is normally in bold on printed forms. However, you can underline introductory headings as a substitute for bold-face type.

Joint Real Property

If you do nothing with joint real property in your divorce judgment, the property automatically converts to tenancy in common ownership. This might be acceptable for a while. As tenants in common, you and the defendant would each get an equal share of the property. If either of you were to die, your share would pass to your heirs/will beneficiaries, not your ex-spouse, because tenancy in common property doesn't have rights of survivorship.

But in the long run, tenancy in common ownership isn't practical for divorced persons. A tenancy in common is really like a partnership. Both tenants in common have an equal right to possess and use the property, and each has a duty to maintain it. This kind of close-knit arrangement is seldom suitable for ex-spouses.

Consequently, you should divide your joint real property in another way. The provisions below suggest several division options, some of which you may be able to handle yourself.

Trade-Off

If enough property is available, one spouse can trade his/her share of the joint property for an equivalent amount of other property. For example, let's say that spouses jointly own a house worth $50,000 and have $50,000 of miscellaneous property. If the spouses agree to an equal property division, the defendant could trade his/her one-half share of the house for the plaintiff's half-interest in the miscellaneous property. After giving all the miscellaneous property to the defendant elsewhere in the property division, the spouses might use a provision like the one below to give the jointly-owned house to the plaintiff:

18. <u>Real Property.</u>   Plaintiff is awarded the property located at 121 S. Main, Lake City, Michigan, and described below, free of any claims of defendant:
Lot 2 of Assessor's Plat, Lake City, Ojibway County, Michigan
Plaintiff shall be responsible for any indebtedness against the property and hold defendant harmless from liability for this debt.

Buy-Out

Instead of a trade-off, one spouse could purchase the other's share of the joint real property. The provision below provides for a buy-out of the defendant's share by the plaintiff for cash:

18. <u>Real Property.</u>   Plaintiff shall be awarded the property located at 121 S. Main, Lake City, Michigan, and described below, free of any claims of defendant, upon the payment of $25,000 to defendant:
Lot 2 of Assessor's Plat, Lake City, Ojibway County, Michigan
Plaintiff shall be responsible for any indebtedness against the property and hold defendant harmless from liability for this debt.

This provision lets the plaintiff buy out the defendant with a single cash payment. If the buyer-spouse can't afford to pay cash, s/he could make installment payments. But to provide for that type of buy-out, one must know about installment sales, how to secure them and their tax consequences. All these things are quite complicated, so seek legal help if you want to provide for a buy-out on an installment basis.

Sale

The sale of joint property to third parties is another way to handle joint property. You can arrange for an immediate sale at the time of your divorce or delay the sale until later. Either way, the sale provision will usually convert the joint property into a tenancy in common until the sale. Then, the provision will typically require: 1) pay-off of any mortgage or land contract against the property 2) payment of all selling costs (broker's commission, closing costs, etc.) 3) division of any remaining proceeds. A good sale provision should also say who shall possess and maintain the property before the sale. All these things are included in the immediate sale provision below:

18.   Real Property.   The property located at 121 S. Main, Lake City, Michigan, and described below, shall be owned by plaintiff and defendant as tenants in common:
Lot 2 of Assessor's Plat, Lake City, Ojibway County, Michigan
This property shall be sold as soon as possible at a price and terms the parties shall agree upon. After the property is sold, the proceeds of the sale shall be applied first to satisfy any indebtedness against the property, then against all the costs of sale (including any broker's commission and closing costs). Any remainder shall be divided [equally] between the parties.
Until the closing of the sale, plaintiff shall have sole possession of the property. Plaintiff shall be responsible for any mortgage or land contract payments, taxes, insurance and other expenses of maintaining the property during this time until the day of closing.

An immediate sale is simple and provides for a clean break between the spouses. There may also be sound tax reasons for selling real property around the time of a divorce, especially when the property is the former marital home. However, an immediate sale may displace a parent and children living at the home.

A delayed sale can solve that problem. It can permit the in-home parent to live in the former marital home for a while, yet will eventually allow the other parent to receive his/her share of the property when the delayed sale occurs. The trouble is, a delayed sale is difficult to provide for in a judgment. The events triggering the delayed sale (remarriage of the in-home parent, maturity of children, etc.) must be anticipated and carefully described in the provision. The other parent may want interest on his/her share of the property, and have it protected by a mortgage or other security. Finally, the income tax consequences from a delayed sale can be unfavorable. For all these reasons, if you want a delayed sale, go to a lawyer for help.

Solely-Owned Real Property

If you fail to deal with solely-owned real property in your judgment, the owner-spouse retains ownership of the property free of any claim or interest of the other spouse (in part, that's what paragraph #6 of the Judgment of Divorce (TBP 4a) is about). But you shouldn't leave it at that. Even if you want the owner-spouse to keep his/her solely-owned property (presumably because of a trade-off or buy-out), you should say so in your judgment. When you want another disposition of the property, such as a sale to a third party, you must provide for that as well.

Trade-Off

In this case, the nonowner is trading off his/her hypothetical share in the owner-spouse's solely-owned real property for equivalent property elsewhere in the property division. The owner-spouse keeps ownership of the property:

18.   <u>Real Property.</u>   Plaintiff is awarded the property located at 121 S. Main, Lake City, Michigan, and described below, free of any claims of defendant:
Lot 2 of Assessor's Plat, Lake City, Ojibway County, Michigan
Plaintiff shall be responsible for any indebtedness against the property and hold defendant harmless from liability for this debt.

Buy-Out

The owner-spouse buys out the nonowner's "share" in his/her solely-owned real property for cash:[*]

18.   <u>Real Property.</u>   Plaintiff shall be awarded the property located at 121 S. Main, Lake City, Michigan, and described below, free of any claims of defendant, upon the payment of $25,000 to defendant:
Lot 2 of Assessor's Plat, Lake City, Ojibway County, Michigan
Plaintiff shall be responsible for any indebtedness against the property and hold defendant harmless from liability for this debt.

Sale

In this scenario, the solely-owned property must be sold as soon as possible to a third party followed by a division of the proceeds:[**]

18.   <u>Real Property.</u>   The property located at 121 S. Main, Lake City, Michigan, and described below, shall be owned by plaintiff and defendant as tenants in common:
Lot 2 of Assessor's Plat, Lake City, Ojibway County, Michigan
This property shall be sold as soon as possible at a price and terms the parties shall agree upon. After the property is sold, the proceeds of the sale shall be applied first to satisfy any indebtedness against the property, then against all the costs of sale (including any broker's commission and closing costs). Any remainder shall be divided [equally] between the parties.
Until the closing of the sale, plaintiff shall have sole possession of the property. Plaintiff shall be responsible for any mortgage or land contract payments, taxes, insurance and other expenses of maintaining the property during that time until the day of closing.

---

[*]   As an alternative, you can provide for an installment sale. But as explained above, that's probably too difficult for you to arrange yourself.

[**]   Instead of an immediate sale, you could choose a delayed sale. Yet, as mentioned above, you will probably need legal help to provide for that arrangement.

Dividing Personal Property

You may have already divided the bulk of your personal property, such as clothing, household goods, bank accounts and motor vehicles, during or even before your divorce. Courts usually permit informal divisions of personal property because they know that you cannot wait until the end of your divorce to divide essential items. If you have already divided some or all of your personal property that way, confirm the division by checking the first box in paragraph #5B of the Judgment of Divorce (TBP 4a).

On the other hand, you should specifically mention personal property that hasn't yet been transferred to the intended recipient at the time of your final hearing. This avoids confusion about ownership later. For example, if you and the defendant have agreed that the defendant must give you an automobile, a dinette set and a $1,000 bank account, you should say so in your judgment. Check the second box in paragraph #5B of the Judgment of Divorce (TBP 4a), and include this provision in the Judgment of Divorce (TBP 4c):

18.   Personal Property.   Plaintiff is awarded the following personal property free of any claims of defendant:

2004 Dodge Intrepid automobile VIN VL29C4B266259

Five-piece (table and four chairs) Contemporary dinette set

Ojibway State Bank savings account #XXXXXXXXX-021, with a current balance of $1,000

Plaintiff shall be responsible for any indebtedness against this property and hold defendant harmless from liability for this debt.

You can adapt this provision to divide almost any type of personal property. But use it only for the distribution of important items of personal property. Don't clutter up your judgment by mentioning every piece of furniture or article of clothing.

Whenever you use such a provision, include a complete description of the property since this aids transfer of the item later (see "After Your Divorce" on page 145 for more information about transferring property). Describe the property fully and mention any identification numbers (account numbers for financial accounts, vehicle identification numbers (VINs) for automobiles, hull numbers for boats, etc.). You may want to disguise the full account numbers of financial accounts or credit cards because divorce judgments are public documents and this sensitive information could fall into the wrong hands. In the example above, the account number is partially disguised (as is often done on credit card receipts), with just a few digits showing.

Dividing Retirement Benefits, Businesses and Other New Property

A divorce property division isn't complete without considering so-called new property (retirement benefits, businesses, etc.). The problem is, new property is often difficult to divide. Unlike a house or an automobile, you can't put retirement benefits on the market, sell them and divide the proceeds (most retirement plans prohibit this kind of sale or transfer even if you could find a buyer).

A business can also be hard to liquidate. Some one-person businesses depend on the skill of their owner-operators and may be impossible to sell as going concerns. And even when a small business can be sold, it must often be sold a piece because few people will buy a share of a small business.
Despite these problems, the law has devised ways to divide new property, often without actually distributing it.

Dividing Retirement Benefits

Michigan courts have approved two methods for dividing retirement benefits:
1) trade-off 2) division of payments.

In a trade-off, the nonemployee-spouse trades his/her interest in the retirement benefits for a like share of other property. As an example, let's assume that a couple owns an automobile worth $10,000 and the husband has retirement benefits with a present value of $10,000. If the spouses agree to an equal property division, the wife might trade her one-half interest in the retirement benefits for the husband's half-interest in the automobile. Thus, the retirement benefits stay with the husband, but the wife gets the automobile. By this means, the retirement benefits have been divided, but without actually distributing them.

The other method of division—division of payments—results in the actual distribution of the retirement benefits to both spouses. With this method, the retirement benefits are divided fractionally between the spouses as payments are made. For example, if the husband is receiving monthly payments, and the parties want an equal division of property, they could assign one-half of the payments to each spouse monthly.

Each of these methods has pluses and minuses. Trade-off is nice because it gives the nonemployee-spouse value immediately, without waiting for the retirement plan to mature (pay benefits). But it requires an estimation of the present value of the benefits, which is complicated (see "Can I Get a Fair Property

Division?" on page 53 for more about the valuation of retirement plans). Trade-off also places the risk that the employee-spouse will never collect the benefits (because of premature death, early retirement, discharge, bankruptcy of the employer, etc.) on the employee-spouse alone. If the employee-spouse never gets benefits, s/he has traded off other property for nothing. And finally, a trade-off may not be possible if the value of the retirement benefits is great and there is no other property that can be traded for them.

It's simpler to just divide the retirement benefits. Unlike a trade-off, you normally won't have to estimate the total value of the benefits, since your dividing the payments, not the total benefits package. This avoids making a difficult present value calculation. Dividing payments also spreads the risks associated with the retirement benefits to both spouses. If the retirement plan fails, both spouses share the loss; if benefits increase in the future, each spouse shares in the gain.

But unless the retirement plan is mature (paying benefits), dividing payments often won't give the nonemployee-spouse any property immediately after the divorce. What's more, a division-of-payments order is difficult to provide for in a divorce judgment. You must use precise language or it won't be legally effective. For this reason, if you want to divide retirement benefits during divorce yourself, you will have to use the trade-off method. To do that, simply check the first box in paragraph #8 of your Judgment of Divorce (TBP 4a), and then give or get equivalent property elsewhere in the property division. If you want to use the division-of-payments method, see a lawyer.

Individual retirement arrangements (IRAs), which are individual retirement plans, can be divided in several ways, including: 1) transfer from the owner-spouse to the other spouse 2) trade-off 3) withdrawal and division of the proceeds.

To transfer an IRA, describe the account and provide for transfer in a judgment provision, like the bank account example on page 244. This kind of divorce-related transfer isn't considered a withdrawal, so no tax or early withdrawal penalty is imposed. But tax and an early withdrawal penalty may be due if the new owner of the account withdraws money from it prematurely. If you want to trade off an IRA for other property, make sure that you have checked the first box in paragraph #8 of your Judgment of Divorce (TBP 4a), and give the nonowner-spouse equivalent property elsewhere in the judgment. You can also withdraw the money in an IRA and divide it. But if the IRA-owner is younger than 59½, that's a premature withdrawal and a penalty will be imposed.

Keogh (HR-10) plans are another type of individual retirement plan. Like IRAs, these plans can be transferred, traded or withdrawn and divided. But transferring or withdrawing Keoghs can have bad tax consequences, leaving trade-off as the best method of division in most cases.

Dividing Businesses and Other New Property

Business interests can be transferred between spouses or liquidated and divided. In many cases, trade-off is the best method of division. To trade off a business, create a judgment provision like the one below, assigning the business to the business-owner, and then give the nonbusiness-owner equivalent property elsewhere in the property division.

18. <u>Personal Property</u>.   Defendant is awarded all the assets, including inventory, supplies, fixtures, equipment, accounts and goodwill, in the House of Waterbeds, Lake City, Michigan, free of any claims of plaintiff. Defendant shall hold plaintiff harmless from any liability in connection with this business.

Division of Debts

As you end your marriage, who is responsible for debts you leave behind? If you do nothing, the following general rules govern liability for individual debts (debts incurred by a spouse alone) and joint debts (debts taken on by spouses together):

Individual debt.   The spouse who incurred the debt (debtor-spouse) remains liable for it after the divorce. The nondebtor-spouse generally won't be liable for the debt unless s/he gave the debtor-spouse authority, as agent, to incur debts on the nondebtor-spouse's behalf. The agent's authority can be express, implied or even given after the fact, by ratification of what the debtor-spouse did.

Joint debt.   Because both spouses incurred joint debts, each remains liable for these after divorce.

By dividing debts in your divorce judgment, you can modify this liability to an extent. A debt provision can shift the liability for an individual debt from the debtor-spouse to the other spouse. Or the provision could have one spouse assume total liability for a joint debt.

Not all debts may be reassigned that way. Educational and personal loans are better left with those incurring them, since they have a bigger incentive to pay them. Likewise, debts secured by property (mortgages, land contracts and other liens) are customarily transferred to the recipients of the secured property. (For this reason, all the sample property division provisions in this appendix transfer secured debts together with the property securing them.) On the other hand, general unsecured debts, such as credit card or charge account debts, are good choices for division.

Whatever you decide, any debt provision you insert in your judgment must describe the debt and say who is responsible for paying it, as in the following provision:

18. <u>Debts.</u>   Defendant is responsible for, and must hold plaintiff harmless from, the following debts:

Lake City Department Store charge account #XXXXXX45 with a current balance of $540

Mastercredit account #XXXXX XXXXX XXXXX 6529 with a current balance of $1,233.33

Debt Division and Creditors' Rights

Although you and the defendant can rearrange debts in your judgment, your arrangements won't affect the rights of the creditors holding the debts. Your creditors will have the same rights after your divorce as they had before.*

> ## Glossary
>
> *Indemnity*–legal claim making someone else answerable for your obligation to a third person.

Example: A couple got a joint car loan from a bank (creditor). In their divorce, the wife received ownership of the car and the car loan was assigned to her by a debt provision in the divorce judgment. She falls behind on the car payments. The bank could sue the husband because the debt division didn't affect his liability to the bank.

If a debt division doesn't change creditors' rights, why go to the trouble of dividing debts in your divorce judgment? The advantage to debt division is that it provides a legal claim, known as indemnity, against the spouse assuming the debt. The indemnity can then be used as a defense or as a direct claim.

Example: A couple gets a joint car loan from a bank (creditor). In their divorce, the wife gets the car and agrees to pay the loan off in a debt division provision. After she falls behind in car payments, the bank sues both spouses. The husband could cite the indemnity from the debt division and shift liability to the wife. Had the bank sued the husband alone, he could add the wife to the case and raise the indemnity against her this way.

Alimony Provisions

Every divorce judgment must deal with alimony** and settle the issue for both spouses by: 1) waiver (giving up alimony totally and irrevocably) 2) reservation (leaving the issue open so you can ask for alimony later, with no guarantee that it will be granted then) 3) grant of alimony (resulting in an order for alimony).

When you're dealing with alimony in your judgment, make sure that you settle it for both parties in one of the three ways described above. If you fail

---

*   A creditor can agree to release a spouse from liability for a joint debt. In that case, the released spouse would no longer be liable to the creditor for the debt. Nevertheless, most creditors won't consent to such releases because they prefer to have two debtors rather than one.

**   In the judgment, alimony is called by its real name: spousal support.

to settle alimony for a party, the failure automatically reserves alimony for the neglected party.

Waiver of Alimony

When you want to waive alimony for you and/or the defendant, indicate in paragraph #4 of your Judgment of Divorce (TBP 4a) that alimony is "not granted for" that particular party. Frequently, both parties mutually waive alimony, so no alimony is ordered.

Reservation of Alimony

If you want to leave the issue of alimony open for a party, check the box in paragraph #4 of the TBP 4a that alimony is "reserved for" that party. You should also mention the reservation in paragraph #17 of the TBP 4b, especially if you're also reserving child support (see "Reserving Child Support" on page 263 for more information and instructions).

   You cannot reserve alimony merely because you find the issue of alimony bothersome and don't want to deal with it now. To reserve alimony, you must have a good reason for the reservation, such as: 1) there is only limited jurisdiction in the case (see "Can I Get a Divorce in Michigan?" on page 43 about why limited jurisdiction isn't enough for alimony) 2) the payer is elusive or has disappeared and you cannot determine his/her ability to pay alimony 3) the would-be recipient of the alimony is making a personal or career change and isn't sure of his/her financial needs now. When alimony is reserved for a party, s/he can come back to court after the divorce and ask for alimony. At that time, the court will decide whether it should be paid.

Grant of Alimony

If you and the defendant have agreed on some type of alimony, check the box in paragraph #4 of the TBP 4a that says alimony is "granted later in the judgment for" the recipient (payee). You must then provide for alimony fully in a Uniform Spousal Support Order (FOC 10b), which will accompany your divorce judgment along with a Uniform Child Support Order (FOC 10/52) (a sample FOC 10b appears at the end of this appendix). In Wayne County only, you must also fill in the spousal support section on the first page of the Order Data Form-Support (FD/FOC 4002).

   The Uniform Spousal Support Order (FOC 10b) allows for payment of either short- or long-term alimony. The provisions excerpted from the FOC 10b below show both kinds. The provisions make the alimony subject to several conditions. You can omit any of these or add others. But keep in mind that the death-of-the-payee condition is necessary to qualify the payments as alimony for federal tax purposes. Without that condition, the payments may not be deductible by the payer.

Short-Term Alimony

After stating the payer and payee, amount and effective date of the alimony in paragraph #1 of the FOC 10b, you can add conditions to end the alimony in paragraph #3. The addition of an end-date makes this short-term alimony (two-year in this example).

3. This order continues until the death of the payee or until the earliest of the following events:
- [X] Date: _9-7-2011_   [ ] $_____ is paid.
- [X] Remarriage of the payee.   [X] Death of the payer.
- [X] Other (specify all other events): _COHABITATION BY THE PAYEE WITH A MEMBER OF THE OPPOSITE SEX_
OR MODIFICATION BY THE COURT

Long-Term Alimony

After describing the alimony in paragraph #1 of the FOC 10b, you can add conditions to end the alimony in paragraph #3. By leaving out an end-date and having the alimony open-ended, you make the alimony long term.

3. This order continues until the death of the payee or until the earliest of the following events:
- [ ] Date: _____   [ ] $_____ is paid.
- [X] Remarriage of the payee.   [X] Death of the payer.
- [X] Other (specify all other events): _COHABITATION BY THE PAYEE WITH A MEMBER OF THE OPPOSITE SEX_
OR MODIFICATION BY THE COURT

Choosing an Alimony Payment Method

When you provide for alimony, you must also arrange for a method of payment. As with the other kind of support, child support, the normal way of paying alimony is by immediate income withholding through the friend of the court system to the SDU. With this method, the alimony payer's source of income (usually an employer) deducts the alimony from the payer's wages or salary and sends the money to the SDU, which forwards it to the alimony recipient. The friend of the court monitors payment, so it can enforce the obligation.

If you want payment of alimony by immediate income withholding to the SDU, you don't have to do anything extra because the Uniform Spousal Support Order (FOC 10b) is set up for this payment method.

Or you could choose another method of paying alimony. You could skip immediate income withholding and provide for payment to the SDU or directly to the payee. You can choose these other payment options by opting out (either totally, partially or in a limited way) from the friend of the court system. Appendix C has complete information about this, with special forms and alternate method-of-alimony-payment provisions.

Incidentally, the methods for paying alimony and child support don't have to match, and you can mix methods. For example, you can have child support paid by immediate income withholding to the SDU and then bypass income withholding and have alimony paid directly to the payee.

Custody Provisions

Parents have a number of custody choices: sole custody, several forms of joint custody, split custody, mixed custody and third-party custody.

The sample judgment on page 133 contains sole custody provisions for the children. The custody provisions below depict two types of joint custody; joint legal custody for Duane and joint physical custody for Darryl:

14. **CUSTODY:** Custody of the minor children is granted as follows:

PL = Plaintiff   DF = Defendant   JT = Joint   3rd = Third party, named here:

CHILD'S NAME	DATE OF BIRTH	LEGAL CUSTODY	PHYSICAL CUSTODY
DUANE WELSEY LOVELACE	6-1-2006	JT	PL
DARRYL WENDELL LOVELACE	7-1-2007	JT	JT

Joint Physical Custody

Whenever you choose joint physical custody, you must decide whether to provide for a specific physical custody schedule or leave it open and flexible. It's permissible to leave joint physical custody open, allowing you and the defendant to exchange custody as you go and at your convenience. If you want this arrangement, you needn't do any more than choose the joint physical custody option, as shown above.

But joint physical custody is difficult to manage. If you anticipate problems, you should specify in advance how you and the defendant will share physical custody. To provide for joint physical custody with a specific custody schedule, choose joint physical custody in paragraph #14 of the Judgment of Divorce (TBP 4b), as described above. Then add a specific joint physical custody provision in the Judgment of Divorce (TBP 4c). The provisions below are examples of split-time, block-time, and bird's nest joint physical custody provisions which you can adapt to your situation.

Split-Time Custody

More Information

About devising complicated joint physical custody or parenting time schedules, subscribe to the schedule planning program offered by OurFamilyWizard.com.

18. <u>Joint Physical Custody.</u> The parties shall have joint physical custody of their minor children as follows: Plaintiff shall have physical custody during weekdays from 8:30 a.m. Monday until 6:00 p.m. Friday. Defendant shall have physical custody during weekends from 6:00 p.m. Friday until 8:30 a.m. Monday.

You can arrange for split-time custody in many ways. The sample provision above provides for weekday/weekend split-time custody, but you could substitute another schedule listed below, or any other schedule:

- day/day
- 3½ days/3½ days
- 3 days/4 days
- weekdays/weekend
- one week/one week
- two weeks/two weeks
- one week/three weeks
- month/month
- two months/two months
- etc.

Block-Time Custody: school year/summer vacation

18. <u>Joint Physical Custody.</u> The parties shall have joint physical custody of their minor children as follows: Plaintiff shall have physical custody from [seven] days before the first day of school in the fall until [seven] days after the last day of school in the spring. Defendant shall have physical custody of the children during the remaining summer school vacation period.

"Bird's Nest" Custody

18. <u>Joint Physical Custody.</u> The parties shall have joint physical custody of their minor children as follows: The parties will alternate residence in the family home [monthly]. Each party shall exercise physical custody while residing with the children at the family home.

When you select joint physical custody, don't forget about parenting time. Some types of joint physical custody, such as frequent split-time or bird's nest custody, might not require any or much parenting time (except perhaps during holidays). But parenting time may be necessary for infrequent split-time or block-time custody. In that case, you should include a parenting time provision in your judgment as described below.

Split Custody

You can split sole, joint legal or even joint physical custody of children. Split sole or joint legal custody by assigning physical custody to different parents (legal custody stays with each custodial parent in split sole custody; it's shared with split joint legal custody). The custody provision below depicts split sole custody:

14. **CUSTODY:** Custody of the minor children is granted as follows:

PL = Plaintiff   DF = Defendant   JT = Joint   3rd = Third party, named here:

CHILD'S NAME	DATE OF BIRTH	LEGAL CUSTODY	PHYSICAL CUSTODY
DUANE WELSEY LOVELACE	6-1-2006	PL	PL
DARRYL WENDELL LOVELACE	7-1-2007	DF	DF

It's possible to split joint physical custody by putting the children on different custody schedules, so they don't move in sync between the parents. The custody provisions below specify split block-time joint physical custody:

14. **CUSTODY:** Custody of the minor children is granted as follows:

PL = Plaintiff   DF = Defendant   JT = Joint   3rd = Third party, named here:

CHILD'S NAME	DATE OF BIRTH	LEGAL CUSTODY	PHYSICAL CUSTODY
DUANE WELSEY LOVELACE	6-1-2006	JT	JT
DARRYL WENDELL LOVELACE	7-1-2007	JT	JT

18. Split Joint Physical Custody. The parties shall have custody of their minor children as follows:

(a) Plaintiff shall have physical custody of Duane Wesley Lovelace from [seven] days before the first day of school in the fall until [seven] days after the last day of school in the spring. Defendant shall have physical custody of Duane Wesley Lovelace during the remaining summer school vacation period.

(b) Defendant shall have physical custody of Darryl Wendell Lovelace from [seven] days before the first day of school in the fall until [seven] days after the last day of school in the spring. Plaintiff shall have physical custody of Darryl Wendell Lovelace during the remaining summer school vacation period.

Mixed Custody

You can mix custody by choosing different types of custody for the children within a family. The custody provision below mixes sole custody and joint physical custody:

14. **CUSTODY:** Custody of the minor children is granted as follows:

PL = Plaintiff   DF = Defendant   JT = Joint   3rd = Third party, named here:

CHILD'S NAME	DATE OF BIRTH	LEGAL CUSTODY	PHYSICAL CUSTODY
DUANE WELSEY LOVELACE	6-1-2006	PL	PL
DARRYL WENDELL LOVELACE	7-1-2007	JT	JT

[A specific joint physical custody provision for Darryl is optional here.]

Third-Party Custody

To assign custody to a nonparent "third party," name the nonparent in the space near the third party notation. Then, insert 3rd in the legal and physical custody columns as you would PL, DF or JT.

Parenting Time Provisions

If you want the flexible type of parenting time known as reasonable parenting time, check the "reasonable" box in paragraph #15 of the Judgment of Divorce (TBP 4b), as in the sample judgment on page 133. By selecting that option, you and the defendant can arrange parenting time as you like.

To fix parenting time according to a specific schedule, check the "specific" box in paragraph #15 of the Judgment of Divorce (TBP 4b). Then add a specific parenting time provision in the TBP 4c or 4x later in the judgment. In this provision, you can specify the time, terms, and conditions of the parenting time. Naturally, the provision must suit you and your children, but you should be able to adapt one of the following examples to your situation:

18.   <u>Specific Parenting Time.</u>   Defendant shall have parenting time during:

(a) alternate weekends from 6:00 p.m. Friday until 6:00 p.m. Sunday. If a state holiday falls on a Monday following a weekend visitation, the visitation shall extend to 6:00 p.m. on that Monday holiday

(b) in even-numbered years, from 6:00 p.m. on the last day before Christmas school vacation until noon on Christmas Day

(c) in odd-numbered years, from noon on Christmas Day until 6:00 p.m. on the day before school resumes

(d) in odd-numbered years, from 6:00 p.m. on the Wednesday before Thanksgiving Day until 6:00 p.m. on the following Sunday

(e) Easter Sunday in even-numbered years

(f) in even-numbered years, from 6:00 p.m. on the last day before spring school vacation until 6:00 p.m. on the day before school resumes

(g) in even-numbered years, the children's birthdays

(h) [Two] weeks during the children's summer school vacation, beginning not less than 30 days after written notice to plaintiff and ending at least seven days before school resumes.

(i) other times as the parties may agree upon

At the beginning of any period of parenting time, plaintiff shall have the children ready at the time specified and defendant shall return them promptly at the end of the parenting time. Plaintiff shall be responsible for transporting the children to begin parenting time and defendant shall be responsible for returning them from parenting time.

This parenting time provision is suitable for parents who live close to each other after their divorce. For parents living far apart, parenting time on alternating weekends and split holidays is impractical. In these cases, parents should choose infrequent parenting time, where the noncustodial parent has extended periods of parenting time instead of more frequent access. The provision below is designed for parents who live a considerable distance from each other, requiring airplane travel for the parenting time:

18.   <u>Specific Parenting Time.</u>   Defendant shall have parenting time during:

(a) in even-numbered years, Christmas school vacation

(b) in odd-numbered years, Thanksgiving school vacation

(c) in odd-numbered years, spring school vacation

(d) [Four] weeks during the children's summer school vacation, beginning not less than 30 days after written notice to plaintiff and ending at least seven days before school resumes.

(e) other times as the parties may agree upon

At the beginning of any period of parenting time, plaintiff shall have the children ready at the time specified and defendant shall return them promptly at the end of the parenting time. [The parties shall share equally] the cost of transporting the children to and from the parenting time.

Change of Children's Residence Provisions

As explained in "Residence of Children" on page 17, at divorce-filing local residences of minor children are established with each parent. The divorce also has the effect of fixing residence in the state of Michigan.

It's possible that the children's local residences have changed during the divorce. Many intrastate moves are permissible without court review, under one of the exclusions and exceptions allowed by Michigan's residence law. Out-of-state moves during this period seldom happen.

Wherever the actual residences of the children are at the end of the divorce, paragraph #16 reaffirms the residences of the children established at divorce-filing. These residences become a reference point for judging some future moves, as explained in "Residence of Children" on page 17.

This might become an issue right away because parents sometimes want to move around the end of the divorce or soon afterward. The moveaway may be covered by an exclusion or exception, so no court review is necessary (only some intrastate moves require court review; most interstate moves require at least formal court approval). But if none of the exclusions or exceptions applies, the defendant must consent and the court must approve the move.

After defaulting, the defendant is out of the case so it's difficult for him/her to give consent for the moveaway. The best way is for the defendant to appear at the final hearing and give oral consent. See "Preparing for the Final Hearing" on page 128 for more about having the defendant attend the final hearing.

In reviewing an agreed-to moveaway, courts are concerned about the impact of the move on the stay-behind parents' custody and parenting time. You can avoid this problem by shaping your joint custody and parenting time to fit the proposed move. So, you might choose both with less frequent exchanges of the children. And if long-distance travel is necessary, you should specify how and who pays. By looking ahead this way, the court should be satisfied that the move won't upset the custody and parenting time arrangements in your judgment.

You also need to authorize the moveaway in paragraph #16 of the Judgment of Divorce (TBP 4b). Check the box inside paragraph #16a that there has been an agreement about change of residence. Include the effective date of the move, the names of the children moving, which parent is relocating and their current and new residences.

After the move takes place, you must notify the friend of the court of the new address of you and the children, as required by paragraph #16c of the Judgment of Divorce (TBP 4b) and paragraph #6 of the Uniform Child Support Order (FOC 10/52). You can use the Change in Personal Information (FOC 108) for the notice.

Child Support Provisions

When you provide for child support in your divorce judgment, two main issues are at stake: the amount of child support (including its components of base support and adjustments, additions for health care, child care or educational expenses) and the method of payment.

Amount of Child Support

As mentioned in "Child Support" on page 22, the amount of child support is normally set by the Michigan child support formula. At one time, it was quite easy to use the formula to figure child support: You determined each parent's income and used charts or schedules in the formula manual to arrive at a support amount payable from the noncustodial parent to the custodial parent.

Over the last 20 years, the Michigan child support formula has gotten more and more complicated. Adjustments were added to the formula to deal with new issues, particularly in the area of children's health care which assumed new importance as medical costs rose.

The formula was also designed for an era when sole custody was the norm and few parents shared caretaking of their children. But as parents began to share these duties more, through frequent parenting time or joint physical custody, the formula didn't work very well. It didn't give the noncustodial payer-parent a break on child support when caring for the children or recognize that the custodial parent had fewer expenses when the children were away.

In 2008, the state revised the child support formula by, among other things, adding a "parental time offset" to each child support calculation, which recognized the new reality of shared caretaking by parents even after divorce and attempted to compensate for this fact.

All this tinkering has made the formula fairer, but at a high price of complexity. The 2013 formula manual has 32 pages of explanatory text bristling with mathematical formulas, tables and charts. As a result, today it's difficult to calculate child support yourself.

The best option is to let the friend of the court do the computation. The friend of the court should give you child support figures when it makes a recommendation on the issue. You can simply plug these into your child support order.

Michigan Child Support Formula

Even when the friend of the court figures child support for your case, it's still helpful to understand where the numbers come from. The section below will guide you through the various steps for figuring child support and show where the numbers go in paragraph #1 of the Uniform Child Support Order (FOC 10/52):

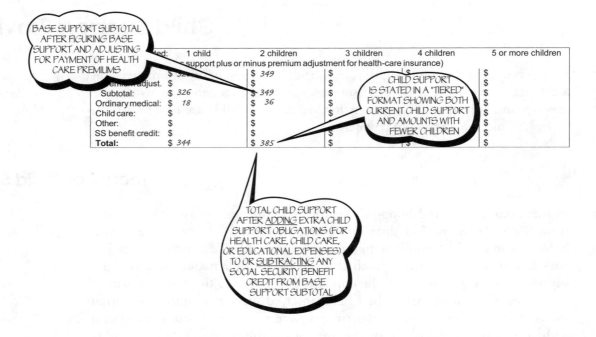

As you can see from the sample paragraph above, the total child support amount for each child is made up of several components using the following procedure.

1) *Determine the net incomes of the parents.* The first step in figuring child support is determining the gross and net incomes of both parents. Gross income includes wages, salary, commissions and most other types of gain. Pages 6-10 of the Michigan Child Support Formula Manual explain the concept of income and several exclusions from income, such as gifts, inheritances and many public benefits (FIP payments, food stamps, SSI, etc.). Pages 11-12 of the manual describes the various deductions from gross income (income taxes, FICA/Medicare taxes, etc.) which, after subtraction, leave net income.

　　Special rules apply to low-income parents (currently, parents whose monthly incomes don't exceed $851), who generally get a break so they aren't discouraged from working. To prevent abuse of the low-income break, courts are allowed to "impute" (assign) income to parents, according to their earning potential, who are avoiding work to get more child support or avoid paying it. The manual explains these special low-income rules on pages 9-10 and 13.

2) *Calculate the base support obligations of both parents.* On page 15, the manual has an equation (general care equation) to calculate the base support obligations of both parents. Or these figures can be derived from the child support schedules in the supplement to the manual. Either way, a parent's base support obligation is fixed by their percentage share of total net family income.

3) *Apply parental time offset to base support obligations.* The manual, on page 16, has another equation (parental time offset equation) that takes into account the cost and savings from shared caretaking (from parenting time and/or joint physical custody). Both parents' base support obligations are

plugged into the equation, along with the number of overnights the children spend with each parent annually (this division of overnights must also be inserted into the child support box). The equation produces a base support amount owed by one parent (usually the nonprimary caretaker (non-custodial parent) earning the most income), who becomes the child support payer.

4) *Adjust base support amount for payment of health care premiums to calculate base support subtotal.* If the parents have to pay for health care coverage premiums out of pocket, this cost can be shared by the parties according to their incomes, and added to or subtracted from the base amount of child support. The percentage-of-incomes schedules in the formula manual supplement provide the percentages, and these can be used to allocate the net health care premium for the children to the parties. Page 19 of the manual explains this adjustment. After any adjustment for health care premiums, the remainder is the base support subtotal.

5) *Add any other child support obligations.* As explained before, child support pays for more than the cost of feeding, clothing and sheltering children; it also covers health care, child care and educational expenses. Parents can be ordered to provide health care coverage for the children, and extra amounts can be added to the total base support amount to pay for uninsured health care expenses and other costs.

More Information

The Michigan child support formula is explained in the Michigan Child Support Formula Manual issued by the state. The manual includes a text portion describing basic concepts and formulas and a supplement with extra material. The supplement has two sets of schedules: 1) percentage-of-incomes schedules showing parents' percentage shares of total family income 2) child support schedules for figuring base support.

The latest edition of the manual was issued in 2012 and went into effect on Jan. 1, 2013. The state used to revise the manual annually. But lately, revision has become irregular (the edition before the 2013 manual was issued in 2008, skipping the years in between). As a result, it's hard to say when the 2013 edition will be revised or replaced.

The state used to print and sell the manual. In 2002, it discontinued sales of the manual. The state provides a limited number of printed copies to friends of the court and libraries, including most law libraries. You may be able to examine a copy of the manual there.

The state's Friend of the Court Bureau also provides the manual online for free. It's accessible at the bureau's Web site at www.michigan.gov/courts, then to Administration, to State Court Administrative Office, to Friend of the Court Bureau, to Child Support Formula, then to 2013 Michigan Child Support Formula Manual (for the text portion of the manual) or to 2013 Michigan Child Support Formula Manual Supplement (for the supplement to the manual).

Health Care

Years ago, when medical costs were less, divorce judgments paid little attention to health care coverage for children. But these days, health care coverage is vital, and there are several ways the Michigan child support formula tries to provide it.

Health Care Coverage

According to paragraph #2 of the Uniform Child Support Order (FOC 10/52), one or both parents are required to maintain health care coverage (health insurance, HMO, PPO, etc.) when available at a reasonable cost. Typically, health care coverage is assigned to the parent with the best employer-provided coverage. When both parties have coverage, it's tempting to assign the obligation to both. But double coverage can create uncertainty between coverage-providers about which must pay the bills, delaying payments. On the other hand, sometimes it makes sense to split the coverage obligation between the parties. For example, one spouse may have good basic health care coverage but lack a dental benefit, which the other spouse gets in an otherwise mediocre health care package. In this case, the health care could be split up and allocated to the parties with the best coverage. Paragraph #2 of the FOC 10/52 isn't equipped to handle that kind of split coverage, so you would have to spell it out in paragraph #13.

Self-employed parents must provide individual coverage if affordable; self-employeds don't have to provide coverage they can't afford. Page 15 of the manual has guidelines for determining whether the cost of individual health care coverage is reasonable, and caps can be put on this obligation in paragraph #2 of the FOC 10/52.

As mentioned in 4), above, the out-of-pocket costs of health care coverage premiums should be shared by the parties according to their incomes. This cost can be added to or subtracted from the base support amount, as an adjustment, to calculate the base support subtotal.

Health Care Expenses

Besides the cost of health care coverage, the formula manual attempts to deal with the three remaining categories of health care expenses:

Routine expenses. These expenses include everyday items like vitamins, first-aid supplies, cough syrup, etc. They are included in base child support and aren't separately reimbursable.

Ordinary expenses. Ordinary expenses include known or predictable expenses not paid for by primary health care coverage, such as deductibles and co-payments. Page 28 of the manual has a chart, also reproduced below, estimating the annual and monthly amounts of ordinary expenses per child. (Note: The table amounts can be increased for extra uninsured expenses that are known in advance, such as orthodontia, special medical needs or ongoing treatment.)

You take the annual table amount budgeted for these expenses and insert this figure in paragraph #1 of the Uniform Child Support Order (FOC 10/52). You can take the monthly amounts and divide these between the parents according to their incomes (using the percentage-of-incomes schedules in the manual's supplement). The support payer's share is added as a separate line item to the base support subtotal in the child support box in paragraph #1 of the FOC 10/52; the recipient pays his/her share directly to health care providers.

Ordinary Medical Expense Averages		
Children	Annual	Monthly
1	$357.00	$29.75
2	$715.00	$59.58
3	$1,072.00	$89.33
4	$1,430.00	$119.17
5 or more	$1,787.00	$148.92

Extraordinary expenses. These are uninsured health care expenses over and above the annual amount of the ordinary expenses. The manual, on page 18, recommends that parents share these extraordinary expenses according to their incomes. These sharing percentages can be inserted in paragraph #1 of the FOC 10/52.

Child Care

The Michigan child support formula offers extra support for child care, which is added to total base support. To qualify for the add-on, a parent must obtain child care services from a babysitter or day care center because of: 1) work 2) an opportunity to look for work 3) education to prepare for work. Ordinarily, custodial parents use child care the most. But noncustodial parents may also need it during parenting time. Both can qualify for child care add-ons.

The child care addition is available to take care of children up to Aug. 31st following their 12th birthdays. The add-on can sometimes be obtained for older children when they need supervision for health or safety reasons.

Pages 19-20 of the formula manual explain the child care addition and how to figure it. Generally, you take the actual child care expenses, subtract any tax credits, subsidies or reimbursement available for them and divide the remaining net cost between the parents according to their incomes. The support payer-parent pays his/her share as an addition to the base support subtotal in the child support box in paragraph #1 of the Uniform Child Support Order (FOC 10/52).

More Information

As explained here, the Michigan child support formula has ways to cover ordinary and extraordinary uninsured health care expenses. But you want to obtain health care coverage and avoid uninsured expenses whenever possible. Look into some of these coverage options:

Medicaid (Healthy Kids). Children in low-income families should qualify for Medicaid (called the Healthy Kids program in Michigan), which provides full health care coverage. Children receiving Family Independence Program (FIP) payments automatically qualify for Medicaid. In Michigan, the family income ceilings for Medicaid are higher than those for the FIP, allowing children to get Medicaid even if they don't qualify for the FIP.

Children's Health Insurance Program (MIChild). All states now have special health care coverage for children from families without employer-provided coverage but who make too much to qualify for Medicaid. Michigan's program is called MIChild (pronounced "my child").

COBRA-coverage. A 1985 law, the Consolidated Omnibus Budget Reconciliation Act, or COBRA for short, can provide health care coverage. Immediately after divorce, COBRA allows you to obtain health care coverage for you and/or dependent children from your ex's employer-provided group plan (if the employer has 20 or more employees), which can last for a maximum of three years. What's more, you don't have to show medical insurability to get COBRA-coverage, so for example, you can get coverage immediately when you have high medical risks or pre-existing conditions.

One drawback to COBRA: You may have to pay the plan premiums (both the employer and employee shares) yourself. But fortunately, the premiums must be charged at group rates, which are usually lower than individual rates.

Michigan Prescription Discount Plan (MiRx). Michigan recently created this prescription drug discount plan for the same group as MIChild: low-income people without health care coverage but who don't qualify for Medicaid. The plan offers discounts averaging 20%.

Individual policy. Under the new Affordable Care Act, affordable health insurance policies should be available at state health insurance marketplaces or exchanges after Oct. 1, 2013. For more about the act, go to HealthCare.gov.

Health savings plans. These savings plans, similar to 401(k)s, include: 1) Health Savings Account (HSA) into which you (and your employer) can put pretax money and withdraw it later tax-free to pay for uninsured health care expenses left by a high-deductible policy 2) Health Reimbursement Account (HRA) funded by employers only, which can also pay for uninsured health care expenses 3) Flexible Spending Account (FSA) resembling HRAs, but whose unused balances revert to the employer at the end of the year.

Educational Expenses

The children themselves may have educational expenses, and these can be paid as another form of child support. For example, there may be private school tuition, or fees for music lessons, athletic instruction, summer camps, scouting and social activities.

If these expenses can be broken down into monthly installments, they can be assigned to the parents according to their incomes or in other percentages you choose, and added at "other" to the base support subtotal in the child support box.

6) *Subtract any social security benefit credit.* Social security retirement, survivor's or disability benefits paid to the children based on the support payer's social security earnings record can be taken as a credit against the payer's base support after any other child support obligations have been added to the base support subtotal. Page 21 of the manual explain this credit.

7) *Figure total child support in "tiered" format.* After the addition of any extra child support obligations to or subtraction of any social security benefit credit from the base support subtotal, you have the total monthly child support for all the minor children in the family. This figure goes into the child support box in paragraph #1 of the Uniform Child Support Order (FOC 10/52), and is the amount of support the payer must pay now.

But there's more to do if there are several children in the family. The Michigan child support formula requires the statement of child support for multiple children in a "tiered" format, showing both current child support and amounts for fewer children as each child becomes independent and leaves home. As a result, the child support calculations must be repeated for all children minus one, minus two, etc., down to one child. The friend of the court should give you these tiered child support amounts.

More Information

About the Healthy Kids, MIChild or MiRx programs, contact your local county health department or the **Michigan Department of Health and Human Services** at (888) 988-6300 or www.michigan.gov/mdhhs, then to Assistance Programs, to Health Care Coverage, to Children & Teens and choose either Medicaid (Healthy Kids) or MIChild.

About COBRA, go to the **U.S. Department of Labor's** Web site at www.dol.gov, then under Topics - Health Plans & Benefits, under Subtopics - Continuation of Health Coverage (COBRA).

About Health Savings Accounts (HSAs), go to:

• HSAInsider.com

• HSAFinder.com

Child Support for Third-Party Custody

When a third party has custody of one or more of the children, both parents may become child support payers—to the third-party custodian. Page 19 of the formula manual explains the calculation.

Departing from the Formula

The Michigan child support formula was designed to fit most cases. Nevertheless, the formula can't cover all situations. For exceptional cases, when application of the formula is "unjust or inappropriate," the court can allow you to depart or deviate from the formula and set child support at a nonformula amount. Pages 4-5 of the manual list some of the situations (children have special needs, parents are imprisoned, etc.) in which departure may be justified.

You can depart with or without the agreement of the defendant. Either way, you need the court's approval of the departure. The formula is designed to fit most cases, so courts are hesitant to allow departure. In fact, you must be able to show all of the following things before the court will approve departure:

- the child support amount specified by the formula for your case
- how your child support amount deviates from the formula
- the reason for the deviation; in other words, why the child support formula amount is inappropriate in your case
- the value of any property or other concessions made in lieu of support

To depart from the child support formula, in the Uniform Child Support Order (FOC 10/52), put in the amount of child support you believe is fair in paragraph #1, and check the box at paragraph #12. Then fill out the form entitled Uniform Child Support Order Deviation Addendum (FOC 10d). The form is not in the back of this book; however, it is available from the friend of the court or online. In the Uniform Child Support Order Deviation Addendum (FOC 10d), insert the Michigan child support formula amount of child support in your case in the box in paragraph #2a. Complete the form and attach it to the Uniform Child Support Order (FOC 10/52).

Reserving Child Support

As explained before, child support is based on the needs of the children and the incomes of both parents. When the defendant withholds financial information or has disappeared, you won't know his/her income, making child support difficult to figure. If this happened in your case, contact your DHHS caseworker, if you have one, or the department. The DHHS has special means for determining parental incomes and assets.

If all else fails and you cannot figure child support, you must reserve the support issue until later. In paragraph #17 of the Judgment of Divorce (TBP 4b), check the alternate paragraph box reserving child support (and/or alimony) and excusing filing of a uniform support order(s) because of the reservation. By reserving child support, you will be able to reopen the issue later when you catch up with the defendant. You must also reserve child support when there is only limited jurisdiction in your case.

Payment of Child Support

As explained in "Payment of Child Support" on page 24, child support is usually withheld immediately from the payer's source of income (typically wages or salary from an employer) and sent to the state disbursement unit

(SDU) for transfer to the support recipient or payee. The Uniform Child Support Order (FOC 10/52) provides for payment that way.

Immediate income withholding is popular with child support recipients and courts because it makes child support easier to collect. On the other hand, some child support payers dislike it because it creates more paperwork for their employers. They may want to bypass immediate income withholding and set up a different method of payment.

In some cases, it's possible to avoid immediate income withholding of child support and choose another method of payment. You can do this by opting out of the friend of the court system, either totally, partially or in a limited way. See Appendix C for complete opt-out information and forms.

Assigning Dependency Exemptions

As mentioned in "Will I Have Tax Problems from the Divorce?" on page 62, a custodial parent may claim dependent children as dependency exemptions on his/her income tax returns. However, the custodial parent can agree to assign these exemptions to the noncustodial parent. In a contested case, the divorce court can assign them to either parent.

For assignment, you need a special provision in your Judgment of Divorce (TBP 4). The assignment provision must order the custodial parent to release the dependency exemptions on the IRS's own assignment form, Release of Claim to Exemption for Child of Divorced or Separated Parents (Form 8332). After release, the noncustodial parent attaches this form to his/her income tax returns to claim the exemptions.

Form 8332 permits assignment of dependency exemptions annually, for several years, or permanently. From an assigning custodial parent's point of view, it's usually best to assign annually. That way, the assignment can be tied to payment of child support. And if the child support isn't fully paid by the end of the year, the custodial parent can withhold the assignment.

You must also decide whether the assignment can be modified after the divorce if circumstances change. A custodial parent will normally favor modifiability (because s/he can ask for cancellation of the assignment after nonpayment of child support); the noncustodial parent won't (because s/he wants assignment without linkage to support). Michigan law isn't clear about the modifiability of dependency exemption assignments. But generally, assignments tied to child support (an issue which is always subject to review and modification after divorce) are more modifiable than assignments which are part of property division (property division is usually nonmodifiable).

The assignment provisions below are identical except that the first example is part of child support and apt to be modifiable, while the second is linked to property division and tends to be nonmodifiable:

18. **Dependency Exemptions.** In addition to regular child support, defendant may claim the parties' children as dependency exemptions on city, state and federal income tax returns, beginning with the tax year [2009] and continuing afterward, under the following conditions:

(a) as long as defendant has paid child support ordered in this judgment in full by the end of the year, defendant may claim the parties' children as dependency exemptions for this year

(b) after full payment of child support, plaintiff shall release the dependency exemptions for this year by executing IRS Form 8332 (or similar documents) and delivering it to defendant

(c) if defendant has not paid child support in full by the end of the year, plaintiff shall not release the dependency exemptions for this year and may claim the exemptions for this year.

18. **Dependency Exemptions.** In addition to the regular property division, defendant may claim the parties' children as dependency exemptions on city, state and federal income tax returns, beginning with the tax year [2009] and continuing afterward, under the following conditions:

(a) as long as defendant has paid child support ordered in this judgment in full by the end of the year, defendant may claim the parties' children as dependency exemptions for this year

(b) after full payment of child support, plaintiff shall release the dependency exemptions for this year by executing IRS Form 8332 (or similar documents) and delivering it to defendant

(c) if defendant has not paid child support in full by the end of the year, plaintiff shall not release the dependency exemptions for this year and may claim the exemptions for this year.

Original - Court	2nd copy - Defendant
1st copy - Plaintiff	3rd copy - Friend of the court

Approved, SCAO	UNIFORM SPOUSAL SUPPORT ORDER (PAGE 1)	CASE NO.
STATE OF MICHIGAN **JUDICIAL CIRCUIT** **COUNTY**	☐ EX PARTE ☐ TEMPORARY ☐ MODIFICATION ☒ FINAL	Court telephone no.

Court address

Plaintiff's name, address, and telephone no.		Defendant's name, address, and telephone no.
	v	
Plaintiff's attorney name, bar no., address, and telephone no.		Defendant's attorney name, bar no., address, and telephone no.
Plaintiff's source of income name, address, and telephone no.		Defendant's source of income name, address, and telephon...

ADD SOURCES OF INCOME (EMPLOYERS) TO CAPTION

This order is entered   ☒ after hearing.   ☐ on stipulation/consent of the parties.

IT IS ORDERED, UNLESS OTHERWISE ORDERED IN ITEM 11: ☐ Standard provisions have been modified (see item 11).

1. **Spousal Support.** Spousal support shall be paid monthly through the Michigan State Disbursement Unit as follows:

Payer: DUDLEY E. LOVELACE	Payee: DARLENE A. LOVELACE	Amount: $ 200	Effective date: 9-7-2009

2. Income withholding takes immediate effect for those items payable through the Michigan State Disbursement Unit.

3. This order continues until the death of the payee or until the earliest of the following events:
   ☒ Date: _9-7-2011_   ☐ $_____ is paid.
   ☒ Remarriage of the payee.   ☒ Death of the payer.
   ☒ Other (specify all other events): _COHABITATION BY THE PAYEE WITH A MEMBER OF THE OPPOSITE SEX_
   OR MODIFICATION BY THE COURT.

☒ 4. For tax purposes, the payments will be deductible to the payer and included in the income of the payee.

☐ 5. Payments that must be paid directly to the third party (not to the payee) are listed below. (Payments to be made directly to a third party are not payable through the Michigan State Disbursement Unit or friend of the court.)

Type	Amount Per Month	Start Date	Pay to	End Date
	$			
	$			
	$			
	$			

(See page 2 for the remainder of the order.)

FOC 10b (3/13) **UNIFORM SPOUSAL SUPPORT ORDER, PAGE 1**   MCL 552.13, MCR 3.211

Approved, SCAO

Original - Court
1st copy - Plaintiff

2nd copy - Defendant
3rd copy - Friend of the court

STATE OF MICHIGAN	UNIFORM SPOUSAL SUPPORT ORDER (PAGE 2)	CASE NO.
JUDICIAL CIRCUIT COUNTY	☐ EX PARTE ☐ TEMPORARY ☐ MODIFICATION ☒ FINAL	

Court address

Court telephone no.

Plaintiff's name

v

Defendant's name

6. **Retroactive Modification, Surcharge for Past-Due Support, and Liens for Unpaid Support.** Support is a judgment the date it is due and is not retroactively modifiable. A surcharge may be added to past-due support. Unpaid support is a lien by operation of law and the payer's property can be encumbered or seized if an arrearage accrues for more than the periodic support payments payable for two months under the payer's support order.

7. **Address, Employment Status, Health Insurance.** Both parties shall notify the friend of the court in writing of: a) their mailing and residential addresses and telephone numbers; b) the names, addresses, and telephone numbers of their sources of income; c) their health-maintenance or insurance companies, insurance coverage, persons insured, or contract numbers; d) their occupational or drivers' licenses; and e) their social security numbers unless exempt by law pursuant to MCL 552.603. Both parties shall notify the friend of the court in writing within 21 days of any change in this information. Failure to do so may result in a fee being imposed.

8. **Fees.** The payer of support shall pay statutory and service fees as required by law.

9. **Prior Orders. This order supersedes all prior spousal support orders.** Past-due amounts owed under any prior support order are preserved.

10. **Property Settlement.** All property settlement (alimony in gross) payment obligations that are set forth in the judgment are not part of this order.

11. **Other: (Attach separate sheets as needed.)**

_____   _____
Plaintiff (if consent/stipulation)   Date

_____   _____
Defendant (if consent/stipulation)   Date

_____   _____
Plaintiff's attorney   Date

_____   _____
Defendant's attorney   Date

9-7-2009
_____
Date

Lester Jubbs
_____
Judge   Bar no.

CERTIFICATE OF MAILING

I certify that on this date I served a copy of this order on the parties or their attorneys by first-class mail addressed to their last-known addresses as defined in MCR 3.203.

_____
Date

_____
Signature

COURT USE ONLY

FOC 10b (3/13) **UNIFORM SPOUSAL SUPPORT ORDER, PAGE 2**

MCL 552.13, MCR 3.211

Regular Forms

Note: To remove the forms cleanly from the book, follow these steps: 1) keep the back of the book as flat as possible on a table or other hard surface 2) open the book at the form you want to remove and pull gently on the form at its perforated edge, keeping the back of the book flat 3) if the form won't pull away easily, take a knife and cut the perforated edge of the form around 1" at the top and bottom, and resume steps 1 and 2.

STATE OF MICHIGAN		CASE NO.
JUDICIAL DISTRICT **JUDICIAL CIRCUIT** **COUNTY PROBATE**	**SUMMONS AND COMPLAINT**	

Court address | Court telephone no.

Plaintiff's name(s), address(es), and telephone no(s).		Defendant's name(s), address(es), and telephone no(s).
	v	

Plaintiff's attorney, bar no., address, and telephone no.

SUMMONS | **NOTICE TO THE DEFENDANT**: In the name of the people of the State of Michigan you are notified:

1. You are being sued.
2. **YOU HAVE 21 DAYS** after receiving this summons to **file a written answer with the court** and serve a copy on the other party **or take other lawful action with the court** (28 days if you were served by mail or you were served outside this state). (MCR 2.111[C])
3. If you do not answer or take other action within the time allowed, judgment may be entered against you for the relief demanded in the complaint.

Issued	This summons expires	Court clerk

This summons is invalid unless served on or before its expiration date. This document must be sealed by the seal of the court.

COMPLAINT | *Instruction: The following is information that is required to be in the caption of every complaint and is to be completed by the plaintiff. Actual allegations and the claim for relief must be stated on additional complaint pages and attached to this form.*

☐ This is a business case in which all or part of the action includes a business or commercial dispute under MCL 600.8035.

Family Division Cases

☐ There is no other pending or resolved action within the jurisdiction of the family division of circuit court involving the family or family members of the parties.

☐ An action within the jurisdiction of the family division of the circuit court involving the family or family members of the parties has been previously filed in _____ Court.

The action ☐ remains ☐ is no longer pending. The docket number and the judge assigned to the action are:

Docket no.	Judge	Bar no.

General Civil Cases

☐ There is no other pending or resolved civil action arising out of the same transaction or occurrence as alleged in the complaint.

☐ A civil action between these parties or other parties arising out of the transaction or occurrence alleged in the complaint has been previously filed in _____ Court.

The action ☐ remains ☐ is no longer pending. The docket number and the judge assigned to the action are:

Docket no.	Judge	Bar no.

VENUE

Plaintiff(s) residence (include city, township, or village)	Defendant(s) residence (include city, township, or village)

Place where action arose or business conducted

Date _____ | Signature of attorney/plaintiff _____

If you require special accommodations to use the court because of a disability or if you require a foreign language interpreter to help you fully participate in court proceedings, please contact the court immediately to make arrangements.

MC 01 (5/15) **SUMMONS AND COMPLAINT** MCR 2.102(B)(11), MCR 2.104, MCR 2.105, MCR 2.107, MCR 2.113(C)(2)(a), (b), MCR 3.206(A)

	SUMMONS AND COMPLAINT
PROOF OF SERVICE	Case No.

TO PROCESS SERVER: You are to serve the summons and complaint not later than 91 days from the date of filing or the date of expiration on the order for second summons. You must make and file your return with the court clerk. If you are unable to complete service you must return this original and all copies to the court clerk.

CERTIFICATE / AFFIDAVIT OF SERVICE / NONSERVICE

☐ **OFFICER CERTIFICATE** OR ☐ **AFFIDAVIT OF PROCESS SERVER**

I certify that I am a sheriff, deputy sheriff, bailiff, appointed court officer, or attorney for a party (MCR 2.104[A][2]), and that: (notarization not required)

Being first duly sworn, I state that I am a legally competent adult who is not a party or an officer of a corporate party, and that: (notarization required)

☐ I served personally a copy of the summons and complaint,
☐ I served by registered or certified mail (copy of return receipt attached) a copy of the summons and complaint,
together with _____

List all documents served with the Summons and Complaint

_____

_____ on the defendant(s):

Defendant's name	Complete address(es) of service	Day, date, time

☐ I have personally attempted to serve the summons and complaint, together with any attachments, on the following defendant(s) and have been unable to complete service.

Defendant's name	Complete address(es) of service	Day, date, time

I declare that the statements above are true to the best of my information, knowledge, and belief.

Service fee	Miles traveled	Mileage fee	Total fee
$		$	$

Signature _____

Name (type or print) _____

Title _____

Subscribed and sworn to before me on _____ , _____ County, Michigan.
                                              Date

My commission expires: _____ Signature: _____
                              Date   Deputy court clerk/Notary public

Notary public, State of Michigan, County of _____

ACKNOWLEDGMENT OF SERVICE

I acknowledge that I have received service of the summons and complaint, together with _____

Attachments

_____ on _____
                              Day, date, time

on behalf of _____ .

Signature

STATE OF MICHIGAN Circuit Court - Family Division COUNTY	COMPLAINT FOR DIVORCE	CASE NO.

Plaintiff: ☐ Husband ☐ Wife

Defendant:

v

Plaintiff's name before this marriage:

Defendant's name before this marriage:

1. Plaintiff's residence: at least ☐ 180 days in Michigan immediately before filing of this complaint.
   ☐ 10 days in this county

   and/or

   Defendant's residence: at least ☐ 180 days in Michigan immediately before filing of this complaint.
   ☐ 10 days in this county

2. Date of marriage _____ Place of marriage _____

3. The parties stopped living together as husband and wife on or about _____

4. There has been a breakdown of the marriage relationship to the extent that the objects of matrimony have been destroyed and there remains no reasonable likelihood that the marriage can be preserved.

5. Children of the parties or born during the marriage:

   a. Minor (under-18) children:

   b. Adult children age 18-19½ entitled to support:

6. There ☐ is ☐ is not another Michigan court with prior continuing jurisdiction of minor children. The court with this jurisdiction is _____ case # _____

7. The wife ☐ is not pregnant ☐ is pregnant, and the estimated date of birth is _____

8. There ☐ is ☐ is no property to be divided; ☐ division of property is controlled by the parties' prenuptial agreement attached as exhibit 1.

BP 1a (1/16)   COMPLAINT FOR DIVORCE, 1st extension page to MC 01

STATE OF MICHIGAN Circuit Court - Family Division COUNTY	COMPLAINT FOR DIVORCE	CASE NO.

Plaintiff:

v

Defendant:

9. I request an ex parte order for:

   a. custody   legal custody to: ☐ plaintiff ☐ defendant ☐ joint
             physical custody to: ☐ plaintiff ☐ defendant ☐ joint

   b. parenting time ☐ reasonable ☐ specific

   c. establishing residences of children

   d. support for children

10. I request an opt-out from the following friend of the court services: ☐ all friend of the court services ☐ all friend of the court services except collection and distribution of support through the SDU ☐ immediate income withholding only

11. I request a judgment of divorce, and:

   a. property   ☐ award to each party the property in his/her possession
              ☐ divide

   b. change wife's last name to _____

   c. custody   legal custody to: ☐ plaintiff ☐ defendant ☐ joint
             physical custody to: ☐ plaintiff ☐ defendant ☐ joint

   d. parenting time: ☐ reasonable ☐ specific

   e. establish residences of children

   f. support for: ☐ children ☐ plaintiff ☐ defendant

   plaintiff/defendant earns_____monthly at_____and needs support

   plaintiff/defendant earns_____monthly at_____and can pay support

   g. other:

I declare that the information in my complaint is true to the best of my information, knowledge and belief.

Date_____   Plaintiff_____

TBP 1b (1/16) **COMPLAINT FOR DIVORCE, 2nd extension page to MC 01**

Approved, SCAO

STATE OF MICHIGAN JUDICIAL CIRCUIT COUNTY	VERIFIED STATEMENT AND APPLICATION FOR IV-D SERVICES	CASE NO.

1. Mother's last name	First name	Middle name	2. Any other names by which mother is or has been known

3. Date of birth	4. Social security number	5. Driver's license number and state

6. Mailing address and residence address (if different)

7. E-mail address

8. Eye color	9. Hair color	10. Height	11. Weight	12. Race	13. Scars, tattoos, etc.

14. Home telephone no.	15. Work telephone no.	16. Maiden name	17. Occupation

18. Business/Employer's name and address	19. Gross weekly income

20. Has mother applied for or does she receive public assistance? If yes, please specify kind. | 21. DHS case number
☐ Yes ☐ No

22. Father's last name	First name	Middle name	23. Any other names by which father is or has been known

24. Date of birth	25. Social security number	26. Driver's license number and state

27. Mailing address and residence address (if different)

28. E-mail address

29. Eye color	30. Hair color	31. Height	32. Weight	33. Race	34. Scars, tattoos, etc.

35. Home telephone no.	36. Work telephone no.	37. Occupation

38. Business/Employer's name and address	39. Gross weekly income

40. Has father applied for or does he receive public assistance? If yes, please specify kind. | 41. DHS case number
☐ Yes ☐ No

42. a. Name of Minor Child Involved in Case	b. Birth Date	c. Age	d. Soc. Sec. No.	e. Residential Address

43. a. Name of Other Minor Child of Either Party	b. Birth Date	c. Age	d. Residential Address

44. Health care coverage available for each minor child

a. Name of Minor Child	b. Name of Policy Holder	c. Name of Insurance Co./HMO	d. Policy/Certificate/Contract/Group No.

45. Names and addresses of person(s) other than parties, if any, who may have custody of child(ren) during pendency of this case

If any of the public assistance information above changes before your judgment is entered, you are required to give the friend of the court written notice of the change.

☐ I request support services under Title IV-D of the Social Security Act.

I declare that the statements above are true to the best of my information, knowledge, and belief.

_____   _____
Date   Signature

FOC 23 (3/13) **VERIFIED STATEMENT AND APPLICATION FOR IV-D SERVICES**   MCR 3.206(B)

Approved, SCAO

STATE OF MICHIGAN JUDICIAL CIRCUIT PROBATE COURT COUNTY	UNIFORM CHILD CUSTODY JURISDICTION ENFORCEMENT ACT AFFIDAVIT	CASE NO.

Court address | Court telephone no.

CASE NAME:

1. The name and present address of each child (under 18) in this case is:

2. The addresses where the child(ren) has/have lived within the last 5 years are:

3. The name(s) and present address(es) of custodians with whom the child(ren) has/have lived within the last 5 years are:

4. I do not know of, and have not participated (as a party, witness, or in any other capacity) in any other court decision, order, or proceeding (including divorce, separate maintenance, separation, neglect, abuse, dependency, guardianship, paternity, termination of parental rights, and protection from domestic violence) concerning the custody or parenting time of the child(ren), in this state or any other state, **except**: Specify case name and number, court name and address, and date of child custody determination, if one.

5. I do not know of any pending proceeding that could affect the current child custody proceeding, including a proceeding for enforcement or a proceeding relating to domestic violence, a protective order, termination of parental rights, or adoption, in this state or any other state, **except**: Specify case name and number, court name and address, and nature of the proceeding.

That proceeding ☐ is continuing. ☐ has been stayed by the court.
☐ Temporary action by this court is necessary to protect the child(ren) because the child(ren) has/have been subjected to or threatened with mistreatment or abuse or is/are otherwise neglected or dependent. Attach explanation.

6. I do not know of any person who is not already a party to this proceeding who has physical custody of, or who claims rights of legal or physical custody of, or parenting time with, the child(ren), **except**: State name(s) and address(es) of each person.

7. The child(ren)'s "home state" is _____ . See back for definition of "home state."

☐ 8. I state that a party's or child's health, safety, or liberty would be put at risk by the disclosure of this identifying information.

I have filled this form out completely, and I acknowledge a continuing duty to advise this court of any proceeding in this state or any other state that could affect the current child-custody proceeding.

_____   _____   _____
Signature of affiant   Name of affiant (type or print)   Address of affiant

Subscribed and sworn to before me on _____ , _____ County, Michigan.
                                         Date

My commission expires: _____   Signature: _____
                          Date

Notary public, State of Michigan, County of _____

MC 416 (3/08) **UNIFORM CHILD CUSTODY JURISDICTION ENFORCEMENT ACT AFFIDAVIT**   MCL 722.1206, MCL 722.1209

"Home state" means the state in which the child(ren) lived with a parent or a person acting as a parent for at least 6 consecutive months immediately before the commencement of a child-custody proceeding. In the case of a child less than 6 months of age, the term means the state in which the child lived from birth with a parent or person acting as a parent. A period of temporary absence of a parent or person acting as a parent is included as part of the period.

STATE OF MICHIGAN Circuit Court - Family Division COUNTY	DEFAULT Request, Affidavit, Entry and Notice of Entry	CASE NO.

Plaintiff (appearing *in propria persona*):		Defendant:
	v	

REQUEST

1. As shown by the proof of service on file, defendant was served with a summons and complaint on _____, but did not respond to the complaint within 21 days (28 days if served by mail or out of state).

I request the clerk to enter the default of defendant for failure to plead or defend as provided by law.

Date_____   Plaintiff_____

AFFIDAVIT

Plaintiff, being sworn, says:

2. Defendant is not a minor or an incompetent person.

3. Defendant's (non)military status:
   ☐ a. Based on ☐ my personal knowledge, ☐ attached military status report, defendant
       ☐ is not in active-duty military service
       ☐ is in active-duty military service, and ☐ has appeared and waived all lawsuit relief rights under the Servicemembers Civil Relief Act and/or MCL 32.517 (or similar military relief law from another state) in the attached appearance and waiver form.
       ☐ other:
   ☐ b. I am unable to determine whether or not defendant is in active-duty military service.

Date_____   Plaintiff_____

Subscribed and sworn to before me on _____, _____ County, Michigan

My commission expires _____ Signature_____

Notary public, State of Michigan, County of _____

ENTRY AND NOTICE OF ENTRY

The default of defendant is entered for failure to plead or defend as provided by law.

Date _____   County clerk _____

TO DEFENDANT: Please take notice of this entry of default against you.

PROOF OF MAILING

On the date below, I sent a copy of this Default to defendant by ordinary first-class mail at his/her address in the caption above, which is defendant's last known address.

I declare that the statement above is true to the best of my information, knowledge and belief.

Date_____   Plaintiff_____

TBP 2 (1/16)   **DEFAULT, Request, Affidavit, Entry and Notice of Entry**

STATE OF MICHIGAN Circuit Court - Family Division COUNTY	MOTION TO ENTER DEFAULT JUDGMENT OF DIVORCE	CASE NO.

Plaintiff (appearing *in propria persona*):

v

Defendant:

1. After entry of defendant's default on _____, I request the court to enter a default Judgment of Divorce granting the relief I requested in my Complaint for Divorce; ☐ and grant the following new/different relief _____

I declare that the statement above is true to the best of my information, knowledge and belief.

Date_____   Plaintiff_____

NOTICE OF HEARING

A hearing on this motion will be held in the courtroom of the judge assigned to this case, located at (place) _____ on (date) _____ at (time) _____

PROOF OF MAILING

On the date below, I sent a copy of this motion to defendant by ordinary first-class mail at his/her address in the caption above, which is defendant's last known address.

I declare that the statement above is true to the best of my information, knowledge and belief.

Date_____   Plaintiff_____

TBP 3 (1/16)   **MOTION TO ENTER DEFAULT JUDGMENT OF DIVORCE**

STATE OF MICHIGAN JUDICIAL CIRCUIT COUNTY	DOMESTIC RELATIONS JUDGMENT INFORMATION, PAGE 1 ☐ TEMPORARY ☐ FINAL	CASE NO.

USE NOTE: Complete this form and file it with the friend of the court (**do not file this form with the office of the clerk of the court**) when the first temporary custody, parenting-time, or support order is entered and when submitting any final proposed judgment awarding custody, parenting time, or support. Mail a copy to each party and file proof of mailing with the court (may use form MC 302, Proof of Mailing).

The information previously provided ☐ is changed ☐ is unchanged. (Complete only the fields that have changed.)

Date _____ Signature _____

Plaintiff Information	**Defendant Information**
Name	Name
Address	Address
Social security number / Telephone number	Social security number / Telephone number
E-mail address	E-mail address
Employer name, address, telephone number, and FEIN (if known)	Employer name, address, telephone number, and FEIN (if known)
Driver's license number and state	Driver's license number and state
Occupational license number(s), type(s), issuing state(s), and date(s)	Occupational license number(s), type(s), issuing state(s), and date(s)

CUSTODY PROVISIONS   sole, plaintiff = P   sole, defendant = D   joint = J   other = O _____
(must identify)

Child's name	Social security number	Date of birth	Physical custody P, D, J, O	Child's primary residence address	Legal custody P, D, J, O

SUPPORT PROVISIONS

☐ Support provisions are stated in the Uniform Support Order.
Medical Support provisions are stated on page 2 of this form.

FOC 100 (3/14) **DOMESTIC RELATIONS JUDGMENT INFORMATION, PAGE 1**   MCR 3.211(F)

STATE OF MICHIGAN JUDICIAL CIRCUIT COUNTY	DOMESTIC RELATIONS JUDGMENT INFORMATION, PAGE 2 ☐ TEMPORARY ☐ FINAL	CASE NO.

MEDICAL SUPPORT PROVISIONS: List the name of each insurance provider for the plaintiff and the defendant. Then enter the name of each child in this case who is covered by that provider and the type of coverage provided.

Plaintiff's Insurance Coverage

Provider name and address	Policy/Group no.	Cert. no.	Child(ren)'s name(s)	Medical	Dental	Optical	Other

Defendant's Insurance Coverage

Provider name and address	Policy/Group no.	Cert. no.	Child(ren)'s name(s)	Medical	Dental	Optical	Other

STATE OF MICHIGAN Circuit Court - Family Division COUNTY	PROOF OF SERVICE OF ORDER/JUDGMENT PAPERS	CASE NO.

Plaintiff (appearing *in propria persona*):

Defendant:

v

served the following papers in this case as described below:

1. On_____, I ☐ delivered ☐ sent by first-class mail to the friend of the court at its official address, these papers:
   ☐ Original Domestic Relations Judgment Information form for ☐ Ex Parte Order
   ☐ Judgment of Divorce

   ☐ Other:

2. On_____, I sent to defendant by first-class mail at his/her address in the caption above, which is defendant's last known mailing address, copies of these papers:

a. Interim relief papers:
   ☐ Domestic Relations Judgment Information form
   ☐ Ex Parte Order
   ☐ Uniform Child Support Order
   ☐ Other:

b. Judgment papers:
   ☐ Domestic Relations Judgment Information form
   ☐ Judgment of Divorce: ☐ Proposed ☐ Final
   ☐ Uniform support order(s): ☐ Uniform Child Support Order ☐ Uniform Spousal Support Order
   ☐ Order Regarding Income Withholding
   ☐ Other:

I declare that the statements above are true to the best of my information, knowledge and belief.

Date_____ Plaintiff_____

TBP 7 (1/16) PROOF OF SERVICE OF ORDER/JUDGMENT PAPERS

Plaintiff (appearing *in propria persona*):

v

Defendant:

Date of hearing_____   Judge _____

After the defendant's default, **IT IS ORDERED**:

1. **DIVORCE:** The parties are divorced.

2. **CHILDREN:** There are children of the parties or born during their marriage who are under 18 or adult and entitled to support.

3. **NAME CHANGE:** Wife's last name is changed to _____

4. **SPOUSAL SUPPORT:** Spousal Support is
   ☐ not granted for   ☐ wife. ☐ husband.
   ☐ reserved for   ☐ wife. ☐ husband.
   ☐ granted later in the judgment for ☐ wife. ☐ husband.

5. **PROPERTY DIVISION:**

A. **Real property:**   ☐ The parties do not own any real property.
   (Land and buildings)   ☐ Real property is divided elsewhere in this judgment.

All real property owned by the parties in joint tenancy or tenancy by the entirety is converted to tenancy in common, unless this judgment provides otherwise.

B. **Personal property:**   ☐ Each party is awarded the personal property in his or her possession.
   (All other property)   ☐ Personal property is divided elsewhere in this judgment.

6. **STATUTORY RIGHTS:** All interests of the parties in the property of the other, now owned or later acquired, under MCL 700.2201-700.2405, are extinguished, including those known as dower under MCL 558.1-558.29.

7. **BENEFICIARY RIGHTS:** The rights each party has to the proceeds or policies or contracts of life insurance, endowments or annuities upon the life of the other as a named beneficiary or by assignment during or in anticipation of marriage, are ☐ extinguished. ☐ awarded later in the judgment.

8. **RETIREMENT BENEFITS:** Any rights of either party in any pension, annuity or retirement plan benefit of the other, whether these rights are vested or unvested, accumulated or contingent, are ☐ extinguished. ☐ awarded later in the judgment.

9. **DOCUMENTATION:** Each party shall promptly and properly execute and deliver to the other documents to carry out the terms of this judgment.

10. **PRIOR ORDERS:** Except as otherwise provided in this judgment, any nonfinal orders or injunctions entered in this action are terminated.

11. **SUSPENDED FEES AND COSTS:** The previously suspended fees and costs in this case of _____ shall be ☐ paid by ☐ plaintiff ☐ defendant   to the clerk. ☐ waived finally.

12. **EFFECTIVE DATE OF JUDGMENT:** This judgment shall become effective immediately after it is signed by the judge and filed with the clerk.

Plaintiff: | v | **Defendant:**

IT IS ALSO ORDERED:

13. **INALIENABLE RIGHTS OF CHILDREN:** The children have the right to the love and affection of both parents. The parties shall cooperate during child-rearing to promote the well-being of the children and maintain strong parent-child relationships. The parties must also cooperate in carrying out the child-related provisions of this judgment.

14. **CUSTODY:** Custody of the minor children is granted as follows:

PL = Plaintiff   DF = Defendant   JT = Joint   3rd = Third party, named here:

CHILD'S NAME	DATE OF BIRTH	LEGAL CUSTODY	PHYSICAL CUSTODY

15. **PARENTING TIME:** Any parent without physical custody shall have parenting time as follows:
☐ reasonable   ☐ specific (describe specific parenting time later in this judgment)

16. **RESIDENCE OF CHILDREN:**

a. **Local residences.** A parent whose custody of parenting time of a child is governed by this order shall not change the legal residence of the child except in compliance with section 11 of the Child Custody Act, MCL 722.31;   ☐   After an agreement of the parties according to the act, and effective _____, the residence of the following minor children:

Names_____

shall be changed from their current residence with   ☐ plaintiff   ☐ defendant

at_____

to_____

b. **State residence (domicile).** The minor children's residences (domicile) shall not be moved from the state of Michigan without the prior approval of the court.

c. **Notice of change of residence.** The person awarded custody shall promptly notify the friend of the court in writing when the minor is moved to another address.

17. **SUPPORT.** Child support and any spousal support is/are provided for in a uniform support order(s) which shall accompany and be incorporated into this judgment.
☐ (Instead of the paragraph above), ☐ child support ☐ spousal support is/are reserved until further order of this court, excusing filing of a uniform support order for that support now.

Plaintiff: v   **Defendant:**

IT IS ALSO ORDERED:

This judgment ☐ resolves ☐ does not resolve the last pending claim in this case, and ☐ closes ☐ does not close the case, except to the extent jurisdiction is retained by law.

Reviewed by FOC:

_____

Date_____   Judge_____

STATE OF MICHIGAN JUDICIAL CIRCUIT COUNTY	UNIFORM CHILD SUPPORT ORDER (PAGE 1) ☐ EX PARTE ☐ TEMPORARY ☐ MODIFICATION ☐ FINAL	CASE NO.

Court address   Court telephone no.

Plaintiff's name, address, and telephone no.		Defendant's name, address, and telephone no.
	v	
Plaintiff's attorney name, bar no., address, and telephone no.		Defendant's attorney name, bar no., address, and telephone no.
Plaintiff's source of income name, address, and telephone no.		Defendant's source of income name, address, and telephone no.

This order is entered ☐ after hearing. ☐ after statutory review. ☐ on stipulation/consent of the parties.
☐ The friend of the court recommends child support be ordered as follows.
☐ If you disagree with this recommendation, you must file a written objection with _____ on or before **21 days** from the date this order is mailed. If you do not object, this proposed order will be presented to the court for entry.
☐ Attached are the calculations pursuant to MCL 552.505(1)(h) and MCL 552.517b.

IT IS ORDERED, unless otherwise ordered in item 12 or 13:   ☐ Standard provisions have been modified (see item 12 or 13):
1. **The children who are supported under this order and the payer and payee are:**

Payer:		Payee:

Children's names, birthdates, and annual overnights with payer:

Children's names	Date of birth	Overnights

Effective _____ , the payer shall pay a monthly child support obligation for the children named above.

Children supported:	1 child	2 children	3 children	4 children	5 or more children
Base support: (includes support plus or minus premium adjustment for health-care insurance)					
Support:	$	$	$	$	$
Premium adjust.	$	$	$	$	$
Subtotal:	$	$	$	$	$
Ordinary medical:	$	$	$	$	$
Child care:	$	$	$	$	$
Other:	$	$	$	$	$
SS benefit credit:	$	$	$	$	$
Total:	$	$	$	$	$

☐ Support was reduced because payer's income was reduced.

(Continued on page 2.)

FOC 10 / 52 (8/14) **UNIFORM CHILD SUPPORT ORDER, PAGE 1**   MCL 552.14, MCL 552.517, MCL 552.517b(3), MCR 3.211

STATE OF MICHIGAN JUDICIAL CIRCUIT COUNTY	UNIFORM CHILD SUPPORT ORDER (PAGE 2) ☐ EX PARTE ☐ TEMPORARY ☐ MODIFICATION ☐ FINAL	CASE NO.

Court address   Court telephone no.

Plaintiff's name	v	Defendant's name

1. **Item 1** (continued).

> **Uninsured Health-Care Expenses.** All uninsured health-care expenses exceeding the annual ordinary medical amount will be paid _____ % by the plaintiff and _____ % by the defendant. Uninsured expenses exceeding the annual ordinary medical amount for the year they are incurred that are not paid within 28 days of a written payment request may be enforced by the friend of the court. The annual ordinary medical amount is _____ .

Obligation Ends. Except for child care, or as otherwise ordered, support obligations for each child end on the last day of the month the child turns age 18. The child-care obligation for each child ends August 31 following the child's 12th birthday. The parties must notify each other of changes in child-care expenses and must additionally notify the friend of the court if the changes end those expenses.

☐ **Post-majority Support:** The following children will be attending high school on a full-time basis after turning 18 years of age. Therefore, the support obligation for each specific child ends on the last day of the month as follows, except in no case may it extend beyond the time the child reaches 19 years and 6 months of age: (Specify name of child and date obligation ends.)

_____

_____

2. **Insurance.** For the benefit of the children, the ☐ plaintiff ☐ defendant shall maintain health-care coverage through an insurer (as defined in MCL 552.602) that includes payment for hospital, dental, optical, and other health-care expenses when that coverage is available at a reasonable cost, including coverage available as a benefit of employment or under an individual policy
☐ up to a maximum of $ _____ for plaintiff.   ☐ up to a maximum of $ _____ for defendant.
☐ not to exceed 5% of the plaintiff's/defendant's gross income.

3. **Income Withholding.** Income withholding takes immediate effect. Payments shall be made through the Michigan State Disbursement Unit unless otherwise ordered in item 13.

4. **Qualified Medical Support Order.** This order is a qualified medical support order with immediate effect pursuant to 29 USC 1169. To qualify this order, the friend of the court shall issue a notice to enroll pursuant to MCL 552.626b. A parent may contest the notice by requesting a review or hearing concerning availability of health care at a reasonable cost.

5. **Retroactive Modification, Surcharge for Past-Due Support, and Liens for Unpaid Support.** Except as provided by MCL 552.603, support is a judgment the date it is due and is not modifiable retroactively. A surcharge may be added to past-due support. Unpaid support is a lien by operation of law and the payer's property can be encumbered or seized if an arrearage accrues in an amount greater than the periodic support payments payable for two months under the payer's support order.

6. **Address, Employment Status, Health Insurance.** Both parties shall notify the friend of the court in writing of: a) their mailing and residential addresses and telephone numbers; b) the names, addresses, and telephone numbers of their sources of income; c) their health-maintenance or insurance companies, insurance coverage, persons insured, or contract numbers; d) their occupational or drivers' licenses; and e) their social security numbers unless exempt by law pursuant to MCL 552.603. Both parties shall notify the friend of the court in writing within 21 days of any change in this information. Failure to do so may result in a fee being imposed.

7. **Foster-Care Assignment.** When a child is placed in foster care, that child's support is assigned to the Department of Human Services while under the state's jurisdiction and to the funding county while placed in a county-funded program.

(Continued on page 3.)

FOC 10 / 52 (8/14) **UNIFORM CHILD SUPPORT ORDER, PAGE 2**   MCL 552.14, MCL 552.517, MCL 552.517b(3), MCR 3.211

STATE OF MICHIGAN JUDICIAL CIRCUIT COUNTY	UNIFORM CHILD SUPPORT ORDER (PAGE 3) ☐ EX PARTE ☐ TEMPORARY ☐ MODIFICATION ☐ FINAL	CASE NO.

Court address   Court telephone no.

Plaintiff's name   v   Defendant's name

8. **Redirection and Abatement.** Subject to statutory procedures, the friend of the court : 1) may redirect support paid for a child to the person who is legally responsible for that child, or 2) shall abate support charges for a child who resides on a full-time basis with the payer of support.

9. **Fees.** The payer of support shall pay statutory and service fees as required by law.

10. **Review.** Each party to a support order may submit a written request to have the friend of the court review the order. The friend of the court is not required to act on more than one request received from a party each 36 months. A party may also file a motion to modify this support order.

11. **Prior Orders. This order supersedes all prior child support orders and all continuing provisions are restated in this order.** Past-due amounts owed under any prior support order in this case are preserved and paid at the rate calculated using the arrearage guideline in the Michigan Child Support Formula.

☐ 12. **Michigan Child Support Formula Deviation.** The support provisions ordered do not follow the Michigan Child Support Formula. The attached deviation addendum (FOC 10d) provides the basis for deviation and the required findings by the court.

☐ 13. **Other:** (Attach separate sheets as needed.)

Plaintiff (if consent/stipulation)	Date	Defendant (if consent/stipulation)	Date

Plaintiff's attorney	Date	Defendant's attorney	Date

Prepared by: _____
              Name (type or print)

Date	Judge	Bar no.

CERTIFICATE OF MAILING

I certify that on this date I served a copy of this order on the parties or their attorneys by first-class mail addressed to their last-known addresses as defined in MCR 3.203. ☐ I certify that I also served the Deviation Addendum (FOC 10d) with this order.

Date	Signature

COURT USE ONLY

STATE OF MICHIGAN	ORDER REGARDING	CASE NO.
JUDICIAL CIRCUIT	**INCOME WITHHOLDING**	
COUNTY		

ourt address   Court telephone no.

```
Plaintiff's name, address, and telephone no.




```

v

```
Defendant's name, address, and telephone no.




```

THE COURT FINDS:

1. The requirements for implementation or adjustment of income withholding
   ☐ have
   ☐ have not
   been met.

☐ 2. The proposed administrative adjustment of income withholding
   ☐ will
   ☐ will not
   produce an unjust or inappropriate result.

IT IS ORDERED:

3. Income withholding is
   ☐ discontinued.
   ☐ effective.
   ☐ effective in an amount pursuant to the Michigan Child Support Formula to pay current support and arrears.
   ☐ effective as follows:

_____   _____   Bar no.
Date   Judge

CERTIFICATE OF MAILING

I certify that on this date I served a copy of this order on the parties and sources of income by first-class mail addressed to their last-known addresses as defined in MCR 3.203.

_____   _____
Date   Signature

FOC 5 (3/08) **ORDER REGARDING INCOME WITHHOLDING**   MCL 552.601 *et seq.*

Testimony

My name is [full name], my address is [address], and I am the plaintiff in this case.

I was married to the defendant on _____ at _____ by a person authorized to perform marriages.
Date and place of marriage

Before the marriage my/[my wife's] name was _____.
Wife's former name

I filed my complaint for divorce on _____. Before I filed the complaint, I had resided in Michigan since _____ and in this county since_____.
Filing date
State residence County residence

As I said in my complaint, there has been a breakdown in our marriage relationship to the extent the objects of matrimony have been destroyed because _____ and there remains no reasonable
Brief facts to support grounds
likelihood that our marriage can be preserved because _____.
Brief facts to support grounds

The defendant and I have_____ minor children_____.
I/[my wife] am not now pregnant.
Names and ages of minor children

The friend of the court has recommended that I should have _____ custody of the children with
Custody
_____ parenting time to the defendant. S/he and I have agreed that this arrangement is satisfactory.
Parenting time

The friend of the court has also recommended that I receive _____ monthly in child support and I believe that this should be sufficient.
Child support

I am working at _____ and am able to support myself. As a result, no alimony is being ordered.
Source of support

0) We own some _____ that we have split between us. We have also agreed that the
General description of personal property
defendant is to give me _____ and I will pay off the debt on it.
Specific items of personal property transferred in judgment

1) We also own _____ worth around _____.
Description of any real property Value
We have agreed to _____.
Manner of division

2) I would like my former name of _____ back.
Wife's name change

3) My court fees were suspended when I filed this divorce. Since then, _____.
Current financial condition

4) Does the court have any questions?

Plaintiff (appearing *in propria persona*):

Defendant:

v

I served the following papers in this case as described below:

1. On_____, I ☐ delivered ☐ sent by first-class mail   to the friend of the court at its official address, these papers:
   ☐ Original Domestic Relations Judgment Information form for   ☐ Ex Parte Order
   ☐ Judgment of Divorce

   ☐ Other:

2. On_____, I sent to defendant by first-class mail at his/her address in the caption above, which is defendant's last known mailing address, copies of these papers:

a. Interim relief papers:
   ☐ Domestic Relations Judgment Information form
   ☐ Ex Parte Order
   ☐ Uniform Child Support Order
   ☐ Other:

b. Judgment papers:
   ☐ Domestic Relations Judgment Information form
   ☐ Judgment of Divorce: ☐ Proposed   ☐ Final
   ☐ Uniform support order(s):   ☐ Uniform Child Support Order   ☐ Uniform Spousal Support Order
   ☐ Order Regarding Income Withholding
   ☐ Other:

I declare that the statements above are true to the best of my information, knowledge and belief.

Date_____   Plaintiff_____

Optional Forms

Approved, SCAO

**REQUEST FOR REASONABLE
ACCOMMODATIONS AND RESPONSE**

Court name and address
Telephone number of ADA coordinator:

You should request accommodations as far as possible in advance of your court appearance or other court activity. To request accommodations, complete and return this form to the court at the above address. If you need help completing this form, contact the ADA coordinator at the above telephone number. To properly evaluate your request, the court may ask you for more information.

The ADA coordinator will respond to your request before the court appearance or other court activity. If your request is denied, you may request a review in accordance with the court's local administrative order. At your request, the court will provide you a copy of the local administrative order.

Today's date

APPLICANT INFORMATION (to be kept confidential)

Applicant is	☐ Witness	☐ Juror	☐ Attorney	☐ Party	☐ Other (specify)

Case name and number (if applicable)

Name	E-mail address

Address			
City	State	Zip	Telephone no.

1. What type of proceeding or court service, activity, or program are you attending (i.e., hearing, jury duty, mediation meeting, trial)?

2. On what dates do you need accommodations?

3. For what impairment do you need accommodations (for a sign language interpreter, specify ASL, CDI, or CART)?

4. What type of accommodations do you need?

RESPONSE TO REQUEST

☐ The request is **GRANTED**
    ☐ for the above matter or appearance,   ☐ from _____ to _____ ,   ☐ for an indefinite period,
        ☐ in whole as follows: (specify the accommodations)

        ☐ in part. As consented to by the applicant, alternative accommodations are as follows: (specify the accommodations)

☐ The request is **DENIED** because
    ☐ the applicant is not a qualified individual with a disability under the ADA.
    ☐ the request creates an undue financial or administrative burden on the court (as defined by the ADA).
    ☐ the request fundamentally alters the nature of the service, program, or activity (as defined by the ADA).
    The basis for this denial is: (Specify on separate sheet if needed. Include alternative accommodations offered but rejected by the applicant.)

The applicant was notified of the court's response   ☐ by phone   ☐ by mail   ☐ by e-mail   ☐ in person   on

_____   by _____ .
Date   Name

MC 70 (10/15) **REQUEST FOR REASONABLE ACCOMMODATIONS AND RESPONSE**   MCL 393.501 *et seq.*, 42 USC 12111 *et seq.*

Approved, SCAO

REQUEST AND ORDER FOR INTERPRETER

CASE NO.

Print the name of the court. _____
Court

If you have a court case and need an interpreter, complete this Request using the English alphabet. Then, date and sign it, and mail or give it to the court where your case is to be heard. If the court appoints an interpreter for you, the court may order you to pay for interpretation costs if you can afford to pay.

Request for Interpreter

I need an interpreter who speaks: _____
Language

Print your full name. _____
Full name

Print your mailing address. _____
Mailing address

Print your telephone number. _____
Telephone no.

Are you a party in this case, a witness, or another interested person? Check one.

☐ I am a party.
☐ I am a witness.
☐ I am an interested person (Describe your interest in the space below.)

I ask the court to appoint an interpreter so that I can fully participate in this case.

_____   _____
Date   Signature

Order Regarding Appointment of Interpreter

☐ 1. The request for an interpreter is granted.

☐ 2. The request for an interpreter is denied because: (Specify the reason[s] for denial.)

_____   _____   Bar no.
Date   Judge

Court Use Note: This completed and signed Request and Order must be placed in the case file. Bilingual versions of this form are available for informational use.

MC 81 (2/14) **REQUEST AND ORDER FOR INTERPRETER**   MCR 1.111(B), (F), (H)

STATE OF MICHIGAN JUDICIAL CIRCUIT COUNTY	CHANGE IN PERSONAL INFORMATION	CASE NO.

Friend of the court address

Telephone no.

Please type or print information. Complete only those sections that apply. You can only file changes for yourself or those minor children of whom you have physical custody. Use another form when making changes for more than one person. **You must sign this form and send it to the friend of the court.**

☐ for party and minor child(ren)   ☐ for party only

1. New Address and/or Telephone Number ☐ for minor child _____ no longer living with custodial parent

Name

Street address			
City	State	Zip	Area code and telephone number

I understand that by filing this change of address, it will be used to automatically update address information on any other child-support cases I have in Michigan. This change is effective for (check all that apply)

☐ all addresses you have listed for me.
☐ residence address only (where I live).
☐ an address that is confidential by court order and which remains confidential with this change.
☐ the single mailing address to which all notices and papers will be served.

2. Alternate Address
The court has entered an order making my address confidential under Michigan Court Rule 3.203(F). The following is an alternate address for the court, the friend of the court office, and the other party to use in serving me with notice and other court papers. I will retrieve all my mail regarding this case from this alternate address.

Street address	City	State	Zip

3. Name Change (Attach order changing name or certificate of marriage.)

New name

4. New Employer ☐ Employer information is confidential by court order.

Employer name	Street address		
City	State	Zip	Area code and telephone number

5. New Driver's License

Issuing state	License number	Expiration date

6. New Occupational License

Issuing state	Type of occupation	License number	Expiration date

7. New Social Security Number ☐ for you   ☐ for minor child _____

Name

Social security number

8. Health Care Insurance Provider

Provider name	Provider address and telephone number	Group number	Policy number

9. Other Information: (To be provided as ordered by the court.) (Attach separate sheet.)

Signature of party filing the change	Name of party filing the change (type or print)
Date of filing	Social security number	E-mail address

FOC 108 (3/13) **CHANGE IN PERSONAL INFORMATION**

Original - Court
1st copy - Applicant
2nd copy - Other party

3rd copy - Friend of the court
(when applicable)
PROBATE JIS CODE: OSF

STATE OF MICHIGAN JUDICIAL DISTRICT JUDICIAL CIRCUIT COUNTY PROBATE	WAIVER/SUSPENSION OF FEES AND COSTS (AFFIDAVIT AND ORDER)	CASE NO.

Court address	Court telephone no.

Plaintiff's/Petitioner's name	v	Defendant's/Respondent's name
Plaintiff's/Petitioner's attorney and bar no.		Defendant's/Respondent's attorney and bar no.

☐ Probate   In the matter of _____

NOTE: Requests for waiver/suspension of transcript costs or mediation fees must be made separately by motion.

AFFIDAVIT

1. I ask the court to waive/suspend fees and costs for the following reason: (check either a or b)
   ☐ a. I am currently receiving public assistance: My DHS case number is _____ .
   (MCR 2.002[C] requires the court to suspend payment of fees and costs.)

   OR

   ☐ b. I am unable to pay fees and costs because of indigency, based on the following facts:
   My average gross income is about $ _____ every ☐ week. ☐ two weeks. ☐ month.
   ☐ I am receiving unemployment benefits.
   ☐ I am not employed.
   ☐ I have a vehicle: Year: _____ Make: _____ Model: _____ Amount Owed: $_____
   The total amount in all my bank accounts is: $ _____
   Write down any other assets and how much they are worth. If you need more space, attach a separate sheet.

   I pay $ _____ in rent/mortgage every month. I pay $ _____ in utilities (water, electricity, gas) every
   month. I pay $ _____ for court-ordered child support. I pay $_____ for court-ordered _____ .
                                                                                                    specify
   Write down any other obligations and how much you pay.   If you need more space, attach a separate sheet.

2. The number of people living in my household is_____ .
☐ 3. I am signing this affidavit for a person who ☐ is a minor. ☐ has the following disability_____ .

_____   _____
Applicant signature   Name (type or print)

Subscribed and sworn to before me on _____ , _____ County, Michigan.
                                          Date

My commission expires:_____   Signature:_____
                          Date   Deputy clerk/Register/Notary public

Notary public, State of Michigan, County of _____

ORDER

IT IS ORDERED:

☐ 1. The applicant has shown by ex parte affidavit that he/she is
   ☐ a. receiving public assistance, and payment of fees and costs are waived/suspended pursuant to MCR 2.002(C).
   ☐ b. indigent and payment of fees and costs are waived/suspended pursuant to MCR 2.002(D).
   The applicant is required to notify the court if the reason for waiving/suspending the fees and costs no longer exists.
☐ 2. The application is denied.

_____   _____
Date   Judge

NOTE: This order must be served on the other party at the time the pleading is served.

MC 20 (4/14) **WAIVER/SUSPENSION OF FEES AND COSTS (AFFIDAVIT AND ORDER)**   MCR 2.002

INSTRUCTIONS FOR USING FORM MC 20, WAIVER/SUSPENSION OF FEES AND COSTS (AFFIDAVIT AND ORDER)

»» CAN I FILE MY LEGAL PAPERS WITH THE COURT FREE OF CHARGE?

When you file a legal paper with or are ordered to case evaluation, you are often required to pay certain fees. If you cannot afford these fees, you can ask the court to "waive" or "suspend" them using this form (MC 20).

»» FILING AN AFFIDAVIT

1. **Prove That You Cannot Afford to Pay a Filing Fee**

   You must show the court that you cannot afford to pay the fees. If you receive public assistance, you must give the court your DHS case number. If you do not receive public assistance, you must give the court information about your assets and obligations. An asset is something you own, such as money, a car, a house, or other property. An obligation is something you owe, such as rent, a loan payment, utilities, court-ordered child support, etc.

2. **Complete Form MC 20**

   After you prepare the legal papers you want to file with the court, complete form MC 20.

   If you are receiving public assistance, check the box in front of item 1a. Write in your DHS case number. Public assistance means you are receiving help from the Michigan Department of Human Services and/or are receiving federal social security income (SSI), which includes Medicaid (a DHS program). It does not include benefits such as veterans assistance (VA benefits) or unemployment. Do not check the box in front of item 1b. Gross income means before any deductions.

   If you are not receiving public assistance, check the box in front of item 1b. Check all the boxes that apply to you. If you are not employed, check that box. Write in all the requested information about your assets and obligations.

   Do not sign the form until you are in front of a notary public or the clerk of the court.

3. **Sign the Affidavit Under Oath**

   After form MC 20 is completed, sign it under oath in front of a notary public or a clerk of the court. You must bring your photo identification with you when you sign the affidavit. There may be a fee to have your affidavit signed in front of a notary public.

4. **Make Copies**

   After you have signed the affidavit under oath, make a copy of the completed form for your records. If your court case is a domestic relations case, such as divorce, paternity, separate maintenance, etc., make another copy of the completed form for the friend of the court office. If you are at the court when you sign the affidavit, you can ask the clerk of the court to make copies for you. There may be a cost to make the copies.

5. **File Form MC 20**

   Take or mail the original and all copies of this form (MC 20) to the clerk of the court along with any other legal papers you want to file. If your court case is a domestic relations case, such as divorce, paternity, separate maintenance, etc., include the friend of the court copy you made in step 4. If you mail the form, include a postage-paid envelope with your return address.

»» GETTING A SIGNED ORDER

When you file your affidavit with the court, the clerk of the court will give it to the judge. The judge will make a decision and will sign the order. The clerk of the court will keep the original and return a signed copy to you. The clerk of the court will send a copy to the friend of the court if you filed that copy.

You are responsible for sending a copy of the signed order to the other parties involved in the case.

STATE OF MICHIGAN JUDICIAL CIRCUIT COUNTY	DOMESTIC RELATIONS JUDGMENT INFORMATION, PAGE 1 ☐ TEMPORARY ☐ FINAL	CASE NO.

USE NOTE: Complete this form and file it with the friend of the court (**do not file this form with the office of the clerk of the court**) when the first temporary custody, parenting-time, or support order is entered and when submitting any final proposed judgment awarding custody, parenting time, or support. Mail a copy to each party and file proof of mailing with the court (may use form MC 302, Proof of Mailing).

The information previously provided ☐ is changed ☐ is unchanged. (Complete only the fields that have changed.)

Date _____

Signature _____

Plaintiff Information

Name

Address

Social security number | Telephone number

E-mail address

Employer name, address, telephone number, and FEIN (if known)

Driver's license number and state

Occupational license number(s), type(s), issuing state(s), and date(s)

Defendant Information

Name

Address

Social security number | Telephone number

E-mail address

Employer name, address, telephone number, and FEIN (if known)

Driver's license number and state

Occupational license number(s), type(s), issuing state(s), and date(s)

CUSTODY PROVISIONS

sole, plaintiff = P sole, defendant = D joint = J other = O _____
(must identify)

Child's name	Social security number	Date of birth	Physical custody P, D, J, O	Child's primary residence address	Legal custody P, D, J, O

SUPPORT PROVISIONS

☐ Support provisions are stated in the Uniform Support Order.
Medical Support provisions are stated on page 2 of this form.

FOC 100 (3/14) **DOMESTIC RELATIONS JUDGMENT INFORMATION, PAGE 1**

MCR 3.211(F)

STATE OF MICHIGAN JUDICIAL CIRCUIT COUNTY	DOMESTIC RELATIONS JUDGMENT INFORMATION, PAGE 2 ☐ TEMPORARY ☐ FINAL	CASE NO.

MEDICAL SUPPORT PROVISIONS: List the name of each insurance provider for the plaintiff and the defendant. Then enter the name of each child in this case who is covered by that provider and the type of coverage provided.

Plaintiff's Insurance Coverage

Provider name and address	Policy/Group no.	Cert. no.	Child(ren)'s name(s)	Medical	Dental	Optical	Other

Defendant's Insurance Coverage

Provider name and address	Policy/Group no.	Cert. no.	Child(ren)'s name(s)	Medical	Dental	Optical	Other

FOC 100 (3/14) **DOMESTIC RELATIONS JUDGMENT INFORMATION, PAGE 2** MCR 3.211(F)

<table>
<tr><td>STATE OF MICHIGAN
Circuit Court - Family Division
COUNTY</td><td>PROOF OF SERVICE OF
ORDER/JUDGMENT PAPERS</td><td>CASE NO.</td></tr>
</table>

Plaintiff (appearing *in propria persona*):

Defendant:

v

served the following papers in this case as described below:

On_____, I ☐ delivered ☐ sent by first-class mail   to the friend of the court at its official address, these papers:
☐ Original Domestic Relations Judgment Information form for ☐ Ex Parte Order
☐ Judgment of Divorce

☐ Other:

On_____, I sent to defendant by first-class mail at his/her address in the caption above, which is defendant's last known mailing address, copies of these papers:

Interim relief papers:
☐ Domestic Relations Judgment Information form
☐ Ex Parte Order
☐ Uniform Child Support Order
☐ Other:

Judgment papers:
☐ Domestic Relations Judgment Information form
☐ Judgment of Divorce: ☐ Proposed   ☐ Final
☐ Uniform support order(s): ☐ Uniform Child Support Order ☐ Uniform Spousal Support Order
☐ Order Regarding Income Withholding
☐ Other:

declare that the statements above are true to the best of my information, knowledge and belief.

ate_____   Plaintiff_____

<table>
<tr><td>STATE OF MICHIGAN
Circuit Court - Family Division
COUNTY</td><td>EX PARTE ORDER for Custody,
Parenting Time, Residence of
Children and Support</td><td>CASE NO.</td></tr>
</table>

Plaintiff (appearing *in propria persona*):

        v

Defendant:

Date of order_____   Judge _____

While this case is pending, **IT IS ORDERED**:

CUSTODY: Custody of the minor children is granted as follows:

L = Plaintiff   DF = Defendant   JT = Joint   3rd = Third party, named here:

CHILD'S NAME	DATE OF BIRTH	LEGAL CUSTODY	PHYSICAL CUSTODY

PARENTING TIME: Any parent without physical custody shall have reasonable parenting time.

RESIDENCE OF CHILDREN:

a. **Local residences.** A parent whose custody of parenting time of a child is governed by this order shall not change the legal residence of the child except in compliance with section 11 of the Child Custody Act, MCL 722.31.

b. **State residence (domicile).** The minor children's residences (domicile) shall not be moved from the state of Michigan without the prior approval of the court.

c. **Notice of change of residence.** The person awarded custody shall promptly notify the friend of the court in writing when the minor is moved to another address.

STATE OF MICHIGAN Circuit Court - Family Division COUNTY	EX PARTE ORDER for Custody, Parenting Time, Residence of Children and Support	CASE NO.

Plaintiff:		Defendant:
	v	

T IS ALSO ORDERED:

4. **CHILD SUPPORT:** Child support is provided for in a uniform support order which shall accompany and be incorporated into this order.
☐ (Instead of the paragraph above), child support is reserved until further order of this court, excusing filing of a uniform support order now.

5. **EFFECTIVENESS AND ENFORCEABILITY:** This order is effective when entered with the clerk and enforceable after service on defendant.

6. **OTHER:**

TO THE DEFENDANT:

NOTICE

7. You may file a written objection to this order or a motion to modify or rescind this order. You must file the written objection or motion with the clerk of the court within 14 days after you were served with this order. You must serve a true copy of the objection or motion on the friend of the court and the party who obtained the order.

8. If you file a written objection, the friend of the court must try to resolve the dispute. If the friend of the court cannot resolve the dispute and if you wish to bring the matter before the court without the assistance of counsel, the friend of the court must provide you with form pleadings and written instructions and must schedule a hearing with the court.

9. The ex parte order will automatically become a temporary order if you do not file a written objection or motion to modify or rescind the ex parte order and a request for a hearing. Even if an objection is filed, the ex parte order will remain in effect and must be obeyed unless changed by a later court order.

Reviewed by FOC:

_____

Date_____   Judge_____

TBP 5b (1/16)   **EX PARTE ORDER, page 2**

Original - Court
1st copy - Plaintiff

2nd copy - Defendant
3rd copy - Friend of the court

STATE OF MICHIGAN JUDICIAL CIRCUIT COUNTY	UNIFORM CHILD SUPPORT ORDER (PAGE 1) ☐ EX PARTE ☐ TEMPORARY ☐ MODIFICATION ☐ FINAL	CASE NO.

Court address

Court telephone no.

Plaintiff's name, address, and telephone no.		Defendant's name, address, and telephone no.
	v	
Plaintiff's attorney name, bar no., address, and telephone no.		Defendant's attorney name, bar no., address, and telephone no.
Plaintiff's source of income name, address, and telephone no.		Defendant's source of income name, address, and telephone no.

This order is entered ☐ after hearing. ☐ after statutory review. ☐ on stipulation/consent of the parties.
☐ The friend of the court recommends child support be ordered as follows.
☐ If you disagree with this recommendation, you must file a written objection with _____ on or
before **21 days** from the date this order is mailed. If you do not object, this proposed order will be presented to the court for entry.
☐ Attached are the calculations pursuant to MCL 552.505(1)(h) and MCL 552.517b.

IT IS ORDERED, unless otherwise ordered in item 12 or 13: ☐ Standard provisions have been modified (see item 12 or 13):
1. **The children who are supported under this order and the payer and payee are:**

Payer:	Payee:

Children's names, birthdates, and annual overnights with payer:

Children's names	Date of birth	Overnights

Effective _____ , the payer shall pay a monthly child support obligation for the children named above.

Children supported:	1 child	2 children	3 children	4 children	5 or more children
Base support: (includes support plus or minus premium adjustment for health-care insurance)					
Support:	$	$	$	$	$
Premium adjust.	$	$	$	$	$
Subtotal:	$	$	$	$	$
Ordinary medical:	$	$	$	$	$
Child care:	$	$	$	$	$
Other:	$	$	$	$	$
SS benefit credit:	$	$	$	$	$
Total:	$	$	$	$	$

☐ Support was reduced because payer's income was reduced.

(Continued on page 2.)

FOC 10 / 52 (8/14) **UNIFORM CHILD SUPPORT ORDER, PAGE 1**   MCL 552.14, MCL 552.517, MCL 552.517b(3), MCR 3.211

STATE OF MICHIGAN	UNIFORM CHILD SUPPORT ORDER (PAGE 2)	CASE NO.
JUDICIAL CIRCUIT	☐ EX PARTE ☐ TEMPORARY	
COUNTY	☐ MODIFICATION ☐ FINAL	

Court address

Court telephone no.

Plaintiff's name	v	Defendant's name

1. **Item 1** (continued).

> **Uninsured Health-Care Expenses.** All uninsured health-care expenses exceeding the annual ordinary medical amount will be paid _____ % by the plaintiff and _____ % by the defendant. Uninsured expenses exceeding the annual ordinary medical amount for the year they are incurred that are not paid within 28 days of a written payment request may be enforced by the friend of the court. The annual ordinary medical amount is _____ .

Obligation Ends. Except for child care, or as otherwise ordered, support obligations for each child end on the last day of the month the child turns age 18. The child-care obligation for each child ends August 31 following the child's 12th birthday. The parties must notify each other of changes in child-care expenses and must additionally notify the friend of the court if the changes end those expenses.

   ☐ **Post-majority Support:** The following children will be attending high school on a full-time basis after turning 18 years of age. Therefore, the support obligation for each specific child ends on the last day of the month as follows, except in no case may it extend beyond the time the child reaches 19 years and 6 months of age: (Specify name of child and date obligation ends.)

   _____

   _____

2. **Insurance.** For the benefit of the children, the ☐ plaintiff ☐ defendant shall maintain health-care coverage through an insurer (as defined in MCL 552.602) that includes payment for hospital, dental, optical, and other health-care expenses when that coverage is available at a reasonable cost, including coverage available as a benefit of employment or under an individual policy
   ☐ up to a maximum of $ _____ for plaintiff.   ☐ up to a maximum of $ _____ for defendant.
   ☐ not to exceed 5% of the plaintiff's/defendant's gross income.

3. **Income Withholding.** Income withholding takes immediate effect. Payments shall be made through the Michigan State Disbursement Unit unless otherwise ordered in item 13.

4. **Qualified Medical Support Order.** This order is a qualified medical support order with immediate effect pursuant to 29 USC 1169. To qualify this order, the friend of the court shall issue a notice to enroll pursuant to MCL 552.626b. A parent may contest the notice by requesting a review or hearing concerning availability of health care at a reasonable cost.

5. **Retroactive Modification, Surcharge for Past-Due Support, and Liens for Unpaid Support.** Except as provided by MCL 552.603, support is a judgment the date it is due and is not modifiable retroactively. A surcharge may be added to past-due support. Unpaid support is a lien by operation of law and the payer's property can be encumbered or seized if an arrearage accrues in an amount greater than the periodic support payments payable for two months under the payer's support order.

6. **Address, Employment Status, Health Insurance.** Both parties shall notify the friend of the court in writing of: a) their mailing and residential addresses and telephone numbers; b) the names, addresses, and telephone numbers of their sources of income; c) their health-maintenance or insurance companies, insurance coverage, persons insured, or contract numbers; d) their occupational or drivers' licenses; and e) their social security numbers unless exempt by law pursuant to MCL 552.603. Both parties shall notify the friend of the court in writing within 21 days of any change in this information. Failure to do so may result in a fee being imposed.

7. **Foster-Care Assignment.** When a child is placed in foster care, that child's support is assigned to the Department of Human Services while under the state's jurisdiction and to the funding county while placed in a county-funded program.

(Continued on page 3.)

Original - Court
1st copy - Plaintiff

2nd copy - Defendant
3rd copy - Friend of the court

STATE OF MICHIGAN JUDICIAL CIRCUIT COUNTY	UNIFORM CHILD SUPPORT ORDER (PAGE 3) ☐ EX PARTE ☐ TEMPORARY ☐ MODIFICATION ☐ FINAL	CASE NO.

Court address

Court telephone no.

Plaintiff's name	v	Defendant's name

8. **Redirection and Abatement.** Subject to statutory procedures, the friend of the court : 1) may redirect support paid for a child to the person who is legally responsible for that child, or 2) shall abate support charges for a child who resides on a full-time basis with the payer of support.

9. **Fees.** The payer of support shall pay statutory and service fees as required by law.

10. **Review.** Each party to a support order may submit a written request to have the friend of the court review the order. The friend of the court is not required to act on more than one request received from a party each 36 months. A party may also file a motion to modify this support order.

11. **Prior Orders. This order supersedes all prior child support orders and all continuing provisions are restated in this order.** Past-due amounts owed under any prior support order in this case are preserved and paid at the rate calculated using the arrearage guideline in the Michigan Child Support Formula.

☐ 12. **Michigan Child Support Formula Deviation.** The support provisions ordered do not follow the Michigan Child Support Formula. The attached deviation addendum (FOC 10d) provides the basis for deviation and the required findings by the court.

☐ 13. **Other:** (Attach separate sheets as needed.)

_____
Plaintiff (if consent/stipulation)   Date

_____
Defendant (if consent/stipulation)   Date

_____
Plaintiff's attorney   Date

_____
Defendant's attorney   Date

Prepared by: _____
                  Name (type or print)

_____
Date

_____
Judge   Bar no.

CERTIFICATE OF MAILING

I certify that on this date I served a copy of this order on the parties or their attorneys by first-class mail addressed to their last-known addresses as defined in MCR 3.203.   ☐ I certify that I also served the Deviation Addendum (FOC 10d) with this order.

_____
Date

_____
Signature

COURT USE ONLY

STATE OF MICHIGAN JUDICIAL CIRCUIT COUNTY	OBJECTION TO REFEREE'S RECOMMENDED ORDER	CASE NO.

Court address

Court telephone no.

Plaintiff's name, address, and telephone no. ☐ moving party		Defendant's name, address, and telephone no. ☐ moving party
	v	
Third party's name, address, and telephone no. ☐ moving party		

I object to the entry of the referee's recommended order dated _____ and request a de novo review by the court. My objection is based on the following reason(s):

_____
Date

Moving party's signature
_____

Name (type or print)
_____

NOTICE OF HEARING

A hearing will be held on this objection before _____
Judge

on _____ at _____ at _____.
Date   Time   Location

If you require special accommodations to use the court because of a disability, or if you require a foreign language interpreter to help you fully participate in court proceedings, please contact the court immediately to make arrangements. When contacting the court, provide your case number(s).

CERTIFICATE OF MAILING

I certify that on this date I served a copy of this objection and notice of hearing on the parties or their attorneys by first-class mail addressed to their last-known addresses as defined in MCR 3.203.

_____
Date

Signature of objecting party
_____

FOC 68 (5/10) **OBJECTION TO REFEREE'S RECOMMENDED ORDER**   MCR 3.215(E)

Original - Return
1st copy - Witness
2nd copy - File
3rd copy - Extra

STATE OF MICHIGAN	SUBPOENA	CASE NO.
JUDICIAL DISTRICT JUDICIAL CIRCUIT COUNTY PROBATE	Order to Appear and/or Produce	

Court address		Court telephone no.

Police Report No. (if applicable): _____

Plaintiff(s)/Petitioner(s)		Defendant(s)/Respondent(s)
☐ People of the State of Michigan ☐ _____ _____	v	
☐ Civil ☐ Criminal		Charge
☐ Probate In the matter of _____		

In the Name of the People of the State of Michigan.   TO:

If you require special accommodations to use the court because of disabilities, please contact the court immediately to make arrangements.

YOU ARE ORDERED TO:

☐ 1. Appear personally at the time and place stated below: You may be required to appear from time to time and day to day until excused.

    ☐ The court address above   ☐ Other:

Day	Date	Time

☐ 2. Testify at trial / examination / hearing.

☐ 3. Produce/permit inspection or copying of the following items: _____

_____

_____

☐ 4. Testify as to your assets, and bring with you the items listed in line 3 above.

☐ 5. Testify at deposition.

☐ 6. Abide by the attached prohibition against transferring or disposing of property. (MCL 600.6104(2), 600.6116, or 600.6119.)

☐ 7. Other: _____

☐ 8.

Person requesting subpoena	Telephone no.
Address	
City	State	Zip

NOTE: If requesting a debtor's examination under MCL 600.6110, or an injunction under item 6. this subpoena must be issued by a judge. For a debtor examination, the affidavit of debtor examination on the other side of this form must also be completed. Debtor's assets can also be discovered through MCR 2.305 without the need for an affidavit of debtor examination or issuance of this subpoena by a judge.

FAILURE TO OBEY THE COMMANDS OF THE SUBPOENA OR TO APPEAR AT THE STATED TIME AND PLACE MAY SUBJECT YOU TO PENALTY FOR CONTEMPT OF COURT.

Court use only
☐ Served   ☐ Not served

_____   _____   _____
Date   Judge/Clerk/Attorney   Bar no.

MC 11 (3/15)   **SUBPOENA, Order to Appear and/or Produce**   MCL 600.1455, 600.1701, 600.6110, 600.6119, MCR 2.506

PROOF OF SERVICE

TO PROCESS SERVER: You must make and file your return with the court clerk. If you are unable to complete service, you must return this original and all copies to the court clerk.

CERTIFICATE / AFFIDAVIT OF SERVICE / NONSERVICE

☐ **OFFICER CERTIFICATE**   **OR**   ☐ **AFFIDAVIT OF PROCESS SERVER**

I certify that I am a sheriff, deputy sheriff, bailiff, appointed court officer, or attorney for a party [MCR 2.104(A)(2)], and that: (notarization not required)

Being first duly sworn, I state that I am a legally competent adult who is not a party or an officer of a corporate party, and that: (notarization required)

☐ I served a copy of the subpoena, together with _____ (including any required fees) by
Attachment

☐ personal service   ☐ registered or certified mail (copy of return receipt attached)   on:

Name(s)	Complete address(es) of service	Day, date, time

☐ I have personally attempted to serve the subpoena and required fees, if any, together with _____
on the following person(s) and have been unable to complete service. Attachment

Name(s)	Complete address(es) of service	Day, date, time

Service fee	Miles traveled Fee		TOTAL FEE
$	$		
Incorrect address fee	Miles traveled Fee		$
$	$		

Signature _____

Name (type or print) _____

Title _____

Subscribed and sworn to before me on _____ , _____ County, Michigan.
          Date

My commission expires: _____ Signature: _____
          Date   Deputy court clerk/Notary public

Notary public, State of Michigan, County of _____

ACKNOWLEDGMENT OF SERVICE

I acknowledge that I have received service of the subpoena and required fees, if any, together with _____
                                                             Attachment

_____ on _____
                                   Day, date, time

_____ on behalf of _____ .
Signature

AFFIDAVIT FOR JUDGMENT DEBTOR EXAMINATION

I request that the court issue a subpoena that orders the party named on this form to be examined under oath before a judge concerning the money or property of:
for the following reasons:

_____
Signature

Subscribed and sworn to before me on _____ , _____ County, Michigan.
          Date

My commission expires: _____ Signature: _____
          Date   Deputy court clerk/Notary public

Notary public, State of Michigan, County of _____

MCR 2.105

STATE OF MICHIGAN	ORDER REGARDING	CASE NO.
JUDICIAL CIRCUIT	**INCOME WITHHOLDING**	
COUNTY		

Court address

Court telephone no.

Plaintiff's name, address, and telephone no.

v

Defendant's name, address, and telephone no.

THE COURT FINDS:

1. The requirements for implementation or adjustment of income withholding
   ☐ have
   ☐ have not
   been met.

☐ 2. The proposed administrative adjustment of income withholding
   ☐ will
   ☐ will not
   produce an unjust or inappropriate result.

T IS ORDERED:

3. Income withholding is
   ☐ discontinued.
   ☐ effective.
   ☐ effective in an amount pursuant to the Michigan Child Support Formula to pay current support and arrears.
   ☐ effective as follows:

_____
ate

_____
Judge   Bar no.

CERTIFICATE OF MAILING

certify that on this date I served a copy of this order on the parties and sources of income by first-class mail addressed to their ast-known addresses as defined in MCR 3.203.

_____
ate

_____
Signature

OC 5 (3/08) **ORDER REGARDING INCOME WITHHOLDING**   MCL 552.601 *et seq.*

Approved, SCAO

STATE OF MICHIGAN JUDICIAL CIRCUIT COUNTY	ADVICE OF RIGHTS REGARDING USE OF FRIEND OF THE COURT SERVICES (PAGE 1)	CASE NO.

friend of the court address   Telephone no.

. **Right to Refuse Friend of the Court Services**

  a. You have the right to refuse friend of the court services for custody, parenting time, and support. To decline friend of the court services, you must file with the court a motion requesting that friend of the court services not be required. You must attach a signed copy of this advice of rights to the motion. The court will grant the motion provided both parties agree and have signed this advice of rights and it determines that all the following are true.
    1) Under MCL 552.505a, neither of you receives or has received public assistance or requests friend of the court services.
    2) There is no evidence of domestic violence or of an uneven bargaining position between you.
    3) The court finds that declining to receive friend of the court services is not against the best interests of a child.

  b. If you already have a friend of the court case, you can file a motion to discontinue friend of the court services provided both parties agree and have signed this advice of rights and the court finds that all the following are true.
    1) Neither of you receives public assistance or requests friend of the court services.
    2) There is no evidence of domestic violence or an uneven bargaining position between you.
    3) The court finds that declining to receive friend of the court services is not against the best interests of a child.
    4) No money is due the governmental entity because of past public assistance.
    5) No arrearage or violation of a custody or parenting-time order has occurred in the last 12 months.
    6) Neither of you has reopened a friend of the court case in the last 12 months.

. **Friend of the Court Services (you will not receive these services if you choose not to use the friend of the court)**

  a. **Accounting Services**
    Friends of the court must collect support and disburse it within 48 hours. Friend of the court accounting services include: 1) friend of the court accounting for payments received and sent, 2) adjustments of support for parenting time or other credits, and 3) annual statements of accounts, if requested.

  b. **Support Enforcement Services**
    The friend of the court must begin to enforce support when one month of support is overdue. For friend of the court cases, child-support enforcement services include:
    • paying support out of tax refunds.
    • asking the court to order the nonpaying party to come to court to explain the failure to pay.
    • having unpaid support paid out of property the payer owns.
    • reporting support arrearage to a consumer reporting agency or requesting that the payer's license(s) be suspended.
    • collecting support by an income withholding order.
    If you choose not to receive friend of the court services, any existing income withholding source will be notified that the friend of the court is no longer responsible for income withholding. **The parties will be solely responsible for stopping or changing income withholding as the law allows.** The friend of the court will stop any unfinished collection actions.

  c. **Medical Support Enforcement Services**
    The friend of the court is required to recommend how the parents divide health-care expenses and to take action to collect the amounts that a parent fails or refuses to pay. When a parent is required to insure the children, the friend of the court is authorized to instruct an employer to enroll the children in an insurance plan when the parent fails or refuses to do so.

  d. **Support Review and Modification Services**
    Once every three years, persons with friend of the court cases may request the friend of the court to review the support amount. After completing the review, the friend of the court must file a motion to raise or lower support, or inform the parties that it recommends no change. It must also review support when changed circumstances lead it to believe that support should be modified.

  e. **Custody and Parenting-Time Investigation Services**
    For disputes about custody or parenting time in friend of the court cases, the friend of the court sometimes must investigate and provide reports to the parties and the court.

  f. **Mediation Services**
    Friend of the court offices must provide mediation services to help parties with friend of the court cases settle custody and parenting-time disputes.

  g. **Custody and Parenting-Time Enforcement Services**
    For friend of the court cases, the friend of the court must enforce custody and parenting time when a party complains that it is violated. Child-custody and parenting-time enforcement services include:

(See page 2)

OC 101 (3/13) **ADVICE OF RIGHTS REGARDING USE OF FRIEND OF THE COURT SERVICES, PAGE 1**   MCL 552.505, MCL 552.505a

STATE OF MICHIGAN JUDICIAL CIRCUIT COUNTY	ADVICE OF RIGHTS REGARDING USE OF FRIEND OF THE COURT SERVICES (PAGE 2)	CASE NO.

friend of the court address   Telephone no.

. **Friend of the Court Services (you will not receive these services if you choose not to use the friend of the court)** (continued from page 1)

  g. **Custody and Parenting-Time Enforcement Services** (continued from page 1)
- asking the court to order the noncooperating party to come to court to explain the failure to obey the parenting-time order.
- suspending the licenses of individuals who deny parenting time.
- awarding makeup parenting time.
- joint meetings to resolve complaints.

. **Michigan State Disbursement Unit and IV-D Services**

  a. **Michigan State Disbursement Unit (MiSDU)**
    If you choose not to receive friend of the court services, you may continue to make and receive child support payments through MiSDU. MiSDU will keep track of the amount paid and sent out. However, MiSDU cannot provide you with all the accounting functions the friend of the court provides. All payments made through MiSDU must be distributed according to the amounts due as required by federal law. When a payer has more than one case, federal law determines how a payment is divided among the cases. **Even if you choose not to receive friend of the court services, payments through MiSDU must be divided among all a payer's cases and distributed in the same manner as payments on friend of the court cases. You cannot discontinue friend of the court services if you want to use MiSDU unless you first provide to MiSDU all the information that MiSDU needs to set up an account.**

  b. **Your Rights Under Title IV-D of the Social Security Act**
    Title IV-D of the Social Security Act provides federal government resources to collect child support and it allows certain funding to be used for parenting-time and custody services. In Michigan, critical Title IV-D services are delivered by the friend of the court. **If you choose not to receive friend of the court services, you cannot receive most Title IV-D services.**

. **Public Assistance**

  Receipt of public assistance means receipt of any of the following benefits: cash assistance, medical assistance, food assistance, foster care, and/or child care.

ACKNOWLEDGMENT REGARDING SERVICES

Check below only if you do not want to receive friend of the court services. Then date, print name, and sign.

I have read this advice of rights and I understand the friend of the court services I am entitled to receive.

☐ I acknowledge that by signing below **I am choosing not to receive** any friend of the court services. I understand that before this choice can take effect, a motion requesting this choice and the other party's agreement must be filed with the court for approval. I also understand that the court may deny this choice if certain conditions are not met as stated in this advice of rights.

_____	_____
Name (type or print)	Name (type or print)

_____		_____	
Signature	Date	Signature	Date

If **you did not check the above box**, you are choosing to receive friend of the court services. **For the most effective friend of the court services**, you can request Title IV-D services by dating and signing below.

I request Title IV-D services through the friend of the court office.

_____	_____
Date	Signature

STATE OF MICHIGAN JUDICIAL CIRCUIT COUNTY	ORDER EXEMPTING CASE FROM FRIEND OF THE COURT SERVICES (PAGE 1)	CASE NO.

Court address	Telephone no.

Plaintiff's name, address, and telephone no.		Defendant's name, address, and telephone no.
	v	

Attorney: Attorney:

Date of hearing: _____ Judge: _____

Bar no.

THE COURT FINDS:

1. There is no evidence of domestic violence or of an unequal bargaining position between the parties in the case.

2. Granting the parties the relief they have requested would not be against the best interests of any child in the case.

3. The parties have filed executed copies of a form advising them of services they will not receive if their motion is granted.

4. Neither party receives public assistance.

5. No money is due the governmental entity because of past public assistance in the case.

6. No arrearage or custody or parenting-time order violation has occurred in the last 12 months in this case.

7. Neither party has reopened a friend of the court case in the last 12 months.

☐ 8. The parties do not want Title IV-D services and have requested that any existing Title IV-D case be closed. (Note: This box should be checked unless exceptional circumstances exist that entitle the Title IV-D case to remain open.)

IT IS ORDERED:

9. Subject to the provisions of item 14 below, this case is not a friend of the court case.

☐ 10. This case is not a Title IV-D case. (Note: This box should be checked if item 8 has been checked.)

11. The friend of the court shall not be involved in the enforcement, investigation, or accounting functions for custody, parenting time, or support in this case.

12. The parties are responsible for all enforcement and accounting functions for custody, parenting time, or support in this case.

(See page 2 for the remainder of the order.)

Do not write below this line - For court use only

FOC 102 (3/15) **ORDER EXEMPTING CASE FROM FRIEND OF THE COURT SERVICES, PAGE 1**

MCL 552.505,
MCL 552.505a

STATE OF MICHIGAN JUDICIAL CIRCUIT COUNTY	ORDER EXEMPTING CASE FROM FRIEND OF THE COURT SERVICES (PAGE 2)	CASE NO.

Court address   Telephone no.

Plaintiff's name	v	Defendant's name

13. Except as indicated below, there is no income withholding in this case, support will be paid directly by the payer to the payee, and the friend of the court shall terminate any existing income withholding. Should this case become a friend of the court case, the payer must keep the friend of the court advised of the name and address of the payer's source of income and any health-care coverage that is available to the payer as a benefit of employment or that the payer maintains, including the name of the insurance company, health-care organization, or health maintenance organization; the policy, certificate, or contract number; and the names and birth dates of the persons for whose benefit the payer maintains the coverage.

    ☐ a. Child support shall be paid through the Michigan State Disbursement Unit (MiSDU) by income withholding to the extent allowed by statutes and court rules; however, the friend of the court is not responsible for income withholding. The friend of the court shall notify the employer that it is no longer involved in the case and that any further information concerning income withholding will be provided by the parties.

    ☐ b. Child support shall be paid through MiSDU by the payer.

14. If child support payments are to be made through MiSDU by income withholding or otherwise, the friend of the court shall not close the friend of the court case until MiSDU notifies the friend of the court that it has been provided with the information necessary to process the child-support payments. There will be no accounting for support that is not paid through MiSDU.

15. The friend of the court shall open a friend of the court case if a party applies for or receives public assistance, a child is placed in foster care, or either party submits to the friend of the court a written request to reopen the friend of the court case. If this case becomes a friend of the court case for any reason, the following provisions shall apply.

    a. The parties must cooperate fully with the friend of the court in establishing the case as a friend of the court case.

    b. The parties must provide copies of all orders in their case to the friend of the court.

    c. The parties must supply any documents that a party to a friend of the court case is required to supply if they have not already done so.

    d. The friend of the court is not responsible for determining any support arrearage that is not indicated by payment made through MiSDU.

    e. Support is payable through MiSDU effective the date the case becomes a friend of the court case.

    f. The friend of the court may prepare and submit, ex parte, a uniform support order that contains all the statutory requirements of a Michigan support order as long as the order does not contradict the existing support order.

    g. At the request of the friend of the court, the parties shall complete a Verified Statement and Application for Title IV-D Services.

_____
Date

_____
Judge

CERTIFICATE OF MAILING

I certify that on this date I served a copy of this order on the parties or their attorneys by first-class mail addressed to their last-known addresses as defined in MCR 3.203.

_____
Date

_____
Signature

Approved, SCAO

STATE OF MICHIGAN **JUDICIAL CIRCUIT** **COUNTY**	**REQUEST TO REOPEN** **FRIEND OF THE COURT CASE**	**CASE NO.**

Court address   **Telephone no.**

Plaintiff's name, address, and telephone no.		Defendant's name, address, and telephone no.
	v	

Attorney: Attorney:

1. On _____ an order was entered exempting this case from friend of the court services.
     Date

I REQUEST that the friend of the court case be reopened upon filing of this request with the friend of the court office. Attached is a completed Verified Statement (form FOC 23).

☐ I request support services under Title IV-D of the Social Security Act.

_____   _____
Date   Signature

CERTIFICATE OF MAILING

I certify that on this date I served a copy of this request on the friend of the court and on the parties or their attorneys by first-class mail addressed to their last-known addresses as defined in MCR 3.203.

_____   _____
Date   Signature

Approved, SCAO

STATE OF MICHIGAN **JUDICIAL CIRCUIT** **COUNTY**	**AGREEMENT SUSPENDING** **IMMEDIATE INCOME WITHHOLDING**	**CASE NO.**

Court address
Court telephone no.

Plaintiff's name, address, and telephone no.

NOTE: MCL 552.604(3) requires that all new and modified support orders after December 31, 1990. include a provision for immediate income withholding and that income withholding take effect immediately unless the parties enter into a written agreement that the income withholding order shall not take effect immediately.

v

Defendant's name, address, and telephone no.

We understand that by law an order of income withholding in a support order shall take effect immediately. However, we agree to the following.

1. The order of income withholding shall not take effect immediately.

2. An alternative payment arrangement shall be made as follows:

3. Both the payer and the recipient of support will notify the friend of the court, in writing, within 21 days of any change in
   a. the names, addresses, and telephone numbers of their current sources of income;
   b. any health-care coverage that is available to them as a benefit of employment or that is maintained by them; the names of the insurance companies, health-care organizations, or health-maintenance organizations; the policy, certificate, or contract numbers; and the names and birth dates of the persons for whose benefit they maintain health-care coverage under the policies, certificates, or contracts; and
   c. their current residences, mailing addresses, and telephone numbers.

4. We further understand that proceedings to implement income withholding shall commence if the payer of support falls one month behind in his/her support payments.

5. We recognize that the court may order withholding of income to take effect immediately for cause or at the request of the payer.

_____
Date

_____
Date

_____
Plaintiff's signature

_____
Defendant's signature

FOC 63 (3/08) **AGREEMENT SUSPENDING IMMEDIATE INCOME WITHHOLDING**
MCL 552.604

Approved, SCAO

STATE OF MICHIGAN JUDICIAL CIRCUIT COUNTY	ORDER SUSPENDING IMMEDIATE INCOME WITHHOLDING	CASE NO.

Court address   Court telephone no.

Plaintiff's name, address, and telephone no.

v

Defendant's name, address, and telephone no.

1. Date of hearing: _____ Judge: _____

     Bar no.

2. **THE COURT FINDS:**

☐ a. There is good cause for the order of income withholding not to take effect immediately as follows.
    1) It is in the best interest of the child for immediate income withholding not to take effect for the following reasons:

    2) Proof of timely payment of previously-ordered support has been provided.

☐ b. The parties have entered into a written agreement that has been reviewed and entered in the record as follows.
    1) The order of income withholding shall not take effect immediately.
    2) An alternative payment arrangement has been agreed upon and is attached.

3. Both the payer and the recipient of support will notify the friend of the court, in writing, within 21 days of any change in
  a. the names, addresses, and telephone numbers of their current sources of income;
  b. any health-care coverage that is available to them as a benefit of employment or that is maintained by them, the names of the insurance companies, health-care organizations, or health-maintenance organizations; the policy, certificate, or contract numbers; and the names and birth dates of the persons for whose benefit they maintain health-care coverage under the policies, certificates, or contracts; and
  c. their current residencea, mailing addresses, and telephone numbers.

IT IS ORDERED:

4. Income withholding shall not take effect immediately.
5. Income withholding shall take effect if the fixed amount of arrearage is reached, as specified in law.

_____   _____
Date   Judge

FOC 64 (3/08) **ORDER SUSPENDING IMMEDIATE INCOME WITHHOLDING**   MCL 552.511, MCL 552.604, MCL 552.607

STATE OF MICHIGAN JUDICIAL CIRCUIT COUNTY	UNIFORM CHILD SUPPORT ORDER, NO FRIEND OF COURT SERVICES (PAGE 1) ☐ EX PARTE ☐ TEMPORARY ☐ MODIFICATION ☐ FINAL	CASE NO.

Court address   Court telephone no.

Plaintiff's name, address, and telephone no.	v	Defendant's name, address, and telephone no.
Plaintiff's attorney name, bar no., address, and telephone no.		Defendant's attorney name, bar no., address, and telephone no.
Plaintiff's source of income name, address, and telephone no.		Defendant's source of income name, address, and telephone no.

This order is entered   ☐ after hearing.   ☐ on stipulation/consent of the parties.

An order exempting this case from friend of the court services was entered on _____ .

(NOTE: If there is no order exempting this case from friend of the court services, form FOC 10/52 must be used.)

IT IS ORDERED, unless otherwise ordered in item 8 or 9:   ☐ Standard provisions have been modified (see item 8 or 9).

1. **The children who are supported under this order and the payer and payee are:**

Payer:	Payee:

Children's names, birthdates, and annual overnights with payer:

Children's names	Date of birth	Overnights

Effective _____, the payer shall pay a monthly child support obligation for the children named above.

	1 child	2 children	3 children	4 children	5 or more children
Children supported:					
Base support: (includes support plus or minus premium adjustment for health-care insurance)					
Support:	$	$	$	$	$
Premium adjust.	$	$	$	$	$
Subtotal:	$	$	$	$	$
Ordinary medical:	$	$	$	$	$
Child care:	$	$	$	$	$
Other:	$	$	$	$	$
SS benefit credit:	$	$	$	$	$
Total:	$	$	$	$	$

☐ Support was reduced because payer's income was reduced.

(Continued on page 2.)

	Original - Court 1st copy - Plaintiff	2nd copy - Defendant 3rd copy - Friend of the court

STATE OF MICHIGAN JUDICIAL CIRCUIT COUNTY	UNIFORM CHILD SUPPORT ORDER, NO FRIEND OF COURT SERVICES (PAGE 2) ☐ EX PARTE ☐ TEMPORARY ☐ MODIFICATION ☐ FINAL	CASE NO.

Court address   Court telephone no.

Plaintiff's name   v   Defendant's name

1. **Item 1** (continued).

> **Uninsured Health-Care Expenses.** All uninsured health-care expenses exceeding the annual ordinary medical amount will be paid _____ % by the plaintiff and _____ % by the defendant. Uninsured expenses exceeding the annual ordinary medical amount for the year they are incurred that are not paid within 28 days of a written payment request may be enforced by the friend of the court. The annual ordinary medical amount is _____ .

Obligation Ends. Except for child care, or as otherwise ordered, support obligations for each child end on the last day of the month the child turns age 18. The child-care obligation for each child ends August 31 following the child's 12th birthday. The parties must notify each other of changes in child-care expenses and must additionally notify the friend of the court if the changes end those expenses.

     ☐ **Post-majority Support:** The following children will be attending high school on a full-time basis after turning 18 years of age. Therefore, the support obligation for each specific child ends on the last day of the month as follows, except in no case may it extend beyond the time the child reaches 19 years and 6 months of age: (Specify name of child and date obligation ends.)

_____

_____

2. **Insurance.** For the benefit of the children, the ☐ plaintiff ☐ defendant shall maintain health-care coverage through an insurer (as defined in MCL 552.602) that includes payment for hospital, dental, optical, and other health-care expenses when that coverage is available at a reasonable cost, including coverage available as a benefit of employment or under an individual policy
     ☐ up to a maximum of $ _____ for plaintiff.   ☐ up to a maximum of $ _____ for defendant.
     ☐ not to exceed 5% of the plaintiff's/defendant's gross income.

☐ 3. **Qualified Medical Support Order.** This order is a qualified medical support order with immediate effect pursuant to 29 USC 1169. Further details, as prescribed by 29 USC 1169(a)(3), are stated in item 9.

4. **Retroactive Modification and Liens for Unpaid Support.** Except as provided by MCL 552.603, support is a judgment the date it is due and is not modifiable retroactively. Unpaid support is a lien by operation of law and the payer's property can be encumbered or seized if an arrearage accrues in an amount greater than the periodic support payments payable for two months under the payer's support order.

5. **Change of Address, Employment Status, Health Insurance.** Both parties shall notify each other in writing, within 21 days of any change in: a) their mailing and residential addresses and telephone numbers; b) the names, addresses, and telephone numbers of their sources of income; c) their health-maintenance or insurance companies, insurance coverage, persons insured, or contract numbers; d) their occupational or drivers' licenses; and e) their social security numbers unless exempt by law pursuant to MCL 552.603.

6. **Foster-Care Assignment.** When a child is placed in foster care, that child's support is assigned to the Department of Human Services while under the state's jurisdiction and to the funding county while placed in a county-funded program.

7. **Prior Orders. This order supersedes all prior child support orders and all continuing provisions are restated in this order.** Past-due amounts owed under any prior support order in this case are preserved.

☐ 8. **Michigan Child Support Formula Deviation** The support provisions ordered do not follow the Michigan Child Support Formula. The attached deviation addendum (FOC 10d) provides the basis for deviation and the required findings by the court.

(Continued on page 3.)

MCL 552.14, MCL 552.517, MCL 552.517b(3),
MCR 3.211

FOC 10a / 52a (8/14) **UNIFORM CHILD SUPPORT ORDER, NO FRIEND OF COURT SERVICES, PAGE 2**

Original - Court
1st copy - Plaintiff

2nd copy - Defendant
3rd copy - Friend of the court

STATE OF MICHIGAN **JUDICIAL CIRCUIT** **COUNTY**	**UNIFORM CHILD SUPPORT ORDER,** **NO FRIEND OF COURT SERVICES (PAGE 3)** ☐ **EX PARTE** ☐ **TEMPORARY** ☐ **MODIFICATION** ☐ **FINAL**	**CASE NO.**

Court address   **Court telephone no.**

Plaintiff's name	**v**	Defendant's name

☐ 9. **Other:** (Attach separate sheets as needed.)

_____   _____
Plaintiff (if consent/stipulation)   Date   Defendant (if consent/stipulation)   Date

_____   _____
Plaintiff's attorney   Date   Defendant's attorney   Date

Prepared by: _____
                    Name (type or print)

_____   _____
Date   Judge   Bar no.

CERTIFICATE OF MAILING

I certify that on this date I served a copy of this order on the parties or their attorneys by first-class mail addressed to their last-known addresses as defined in MCR 3.203.   ☐ I certify that I also served the Deviation Addendum (FOC 10d) with the order.

_____   _____
Date   Signature

COURT USE ONLY

Approved, SCAO

STATE OF MICHIGAN JUDICIAL CIRCUIT COUNTY	UNIFORM SPOUSAL SUPPORT ORDER, NO FRIEND OF COURT SERVICES (PAGE 1) ☐ EX PARTE ☐ TEMPORARY ☐ MODIFICATION ☐ FINAL	CASE NO.

Court address | Court telephone no.

Plaintiff's name, address, and telephone no.		Defendant's name, address, and telephone no.
	v	
Plaintiff's attorney name, bar no., address, and telephone no.		Defendant's attorney name, bar no., address, and telephone no.
Plaintiff's source of income name, address, and telephone no.		Defendant's source of income name, address, and telephone no.

This order is entered ☐ after hearing. ☐ on stipulation/consent of the parties.

IT IS ORDERED, UNLESS OTHERWISE ORDERED IN ITEM 8: ☐ Standard provisions have been modified (see item 8).

1. **Spousal Support.** Spousal support shall be paid monthly as follows:

Payer:	Payee:	Amount: $	Effective date:

2. This order continues until the death of the payee or until the earliest of the following events:
   ☐ Date: _____
   ☐ $ _____ is paid.
   ☐ Remarriage of the payee.
   ☐ Death of the payer.
   ☐ Other (specify all other events): _____
   _____

☐ 3. For tax purposes, the payments will be deductible to the payer and included in the income of the payee.

☐ 4. Payments that must be paid directly to the third party (not to the payee) are listed below.

Type	Amount Per Month	Start Date	Pay to	End Date
	$			
	$			
	$			
	$			

(See page 2 for the remainder of the order.)

FOC 10c (3/12) **UNIFORM SPOUSAL SUPPORT ORDER, NO FRIEND OF COURT SERVICES, PAGE 1** MCL 552.13, MCR 3.211

STATE OF MICHIGAN JUDICIAL CIRCUIT COUNTY	UNIFORM SPOUSAL SUPPORT ORDER NO FRIEND OF COURT SERVICES (PAGE 2) ☐EX PARTE ☐TEMPORARY ☐MODIFICATION ☐FINAL	CASE NO.

Court address _____ Court telephone no. _____

Plaintiff's name	v	Defendant's name

5. **Retroactive Modification and Liens for Unpaid Support.** Support is a judgment the date it is due and is not retroactively modifiable. Unpaid support is a lien by operation of law and the payer's property can be encumbered or seized if an arrearage accrues for more than the periodic support payments payable for two months under the payer's support order.

6. **Change of Address, Employment Status, Health Insurance.** Both parties shall notify each other in writing within 21 days of any change in: a) their mailing and residential addresses and telephone numbers; b) the names, addresses, and telephone numbers of their sources of income; c) their health-maintenance or insurance companies, insurance coverage, persons insured, or contract numbers; d) their occupational or drivers' licenses; and e) their social security numbers unless exempt by law pursuant to MCL 552.603.

7. **Prior Orders. This order supersedes all prior spousal support orders and all continuing provisions are restated in this order.** Past-due amounts owed under any prior support order are preserved.

8. **Other: (Attach separate sheets as needed.)**

Plaintiff (if consent/stipulation)	Date	Defendant (if consent/stipulation)	Date

Plaintiff's attorney	Date	Defendant's attorney	Date

Date	Judge	Bar no.

CERTIFICATE OF MAILING

I certify that on this date I served a copy of this order on the parties or their attorneys by first-class mail addressed to their last-known addresses as defined in MCR 3.203.

Date	Signature

COURT USE ONLY

FOC 10c (3/12) **UNIFORM SPOUSAL SUPPORT ORDER, NO FRIEND OF COURT SERVICES, PAGE 2** MCL 552.13, MCR 3.211

Approved, SCAO

STATE OF MICHIGAN **JUDICIAL DISTRICT** **JUDICIAL CIRCUIT** **COUNTY PROBATE**	**MOTION AND VERIFICATION FOR ALTERNATE SERVICE**	**CASE NO.**

Court address _____ Court telephone no. _____

Plaintiff name(s), address(es), and telephone no(s).		Defendant name(s), address(es), and telephone no(s).
	v	

In the matter of _____

1. Service of process upon_____ cannot reasonably be made
   as otherwise provided in MCR 2.105, as shown in the following verification of process server.

2. Defendant's last known home and business addresses are:

Home address	City	State	Zip

Business address	City	State	Zip

  a. I believe the ☐ home   address shown above is current.
                   ☐ business

  b. I do not know the defendant's current ☐ home   address. I have made the following efforts to ascertain the current
                                           ☐ business

    address: _____

_____

_____

3. I request the court order service by alternate means.

I declare that the statements above are true to the best of my information, knowledge, and belief.

Date	Plaintiff/Plaintiff's attorney signature

Address	Name (type or print) Bar no.

City, state, zip   Telephone no.

VERIFICATION OF PROCESS SERVER

1. I have tried to serve process on this defendant as described: State date, place, and what occurred on each occasion.

I declare that the statements above are true to the best of my information, knowledge, and belief.

Date	Signature

                             Process server (type or print)

MC 303 (3/11) **MOTION AND VERIFICATION FOR ALTERNATE SERVICE**   MCR 2.105

STATE OF MICHIGAN **JUDICIAL DISTRICT** **JUDICIAL CIRCUIT** **COUNTY PROBATE**	**ORDER REGARDING ALTERNATE SERVICE**	**CASE NO.**

Court address   **Court telephone no.**

Plaintiff name(s), address(es), and telephone no(s).		Defendant name(s), address(es), and telephone no(s).
	v	

Plaintiff's attorney, bar no., address, and telephone no.

THE COURT FINDS:

☐ 1. Service of process upon the defendant, _____ ,

cannot reasonably be made as provided in   ☐ MCR 2.105   ☐ MCR 2.107(B)(1)(b)   and service of process

may be made in a manner that is reasonably calculated to give the defendant actual notice of the proceedings and an opportunity

to be heard.

IT IS ORDERED:

☐ 2. Service of the   ☐ summons and complaint   ☐ other: _____

and a copy of this order shall be made by the following method(s).

☐ a. First-class mail to _____ .

☐ b. Tacking or firmly affixing to the door at _____ .

☐ c. Delivering at _____

to a member of the defendant's household who is of suitable age and discretion to receive process, with instructions to

deliver it promptly to the defendant.

☐ d. Other: _____

_____

For each method used, proof of service must be filed promptly with the court.

☐ 3. The motion for alternate service is denied.

_____   _____   _____
Date   Judge   Bar no.

MC 304 (9/09) **ORDER REGARDING ALTERNATE SERVICE**   MCR 2.103, MCR 2.105

ORDER REGARDING ALTERNATE SERVICE	PROOF OF SERVICE	
		Case No.

TO PROCESS SERVER: You must serve the copies of the order regarding alternate service and file proof of service with the court clerk. If you are unable to complete service, you must return this original and all copies to the court clerk.

CERTIFICATE / AFFIDAVIT OF SERVICE / NONSERVICE

☐ OFFICER CERTIFICATE	OR	☐ AFFIDAVIT OF PROCESS SERVER
I certify that I am a sheriff, deputy sheriff, bailiff, appointed court officer, or attorney for a party (MCR 2.104[A][2]), and that: (notarization not required)		Being first duly sworn, I state that I am a legally competent adult who is not a party or an officer of a corporate party, and that: (notarization required)

I served a copy of the   ☐ summons and complaint   ☐ other: _____

and a copy of the order for alternate service upon _____ by _____

☐ 1. First-class mail to _____ , on _____ .
                                                                          Date

☐ 2. Tacking or firmly affixing to the door at _____ , on _____ .
                                                                                      Date

☐ 3. Delivering at _____ , on _____ .
                                                                Date
to a member of the defendant's household who is of suitable age and discretion to receive process, with instructions to deliver
it promptly to the defendant.

☐ 4. Other: _____ , on _____ .
              specify   Date

I declare that the statements above are true to the best of my information, knowledge, and belief.

Service fee $		Incorrect address fee $	
Miles traveled Fee $			
Miles traveled Fee $		**TOTAL FEE** $	

_____
Signature

_____
Name (type or print)

_____
Title

Subscribed and sworn to before me on _____ , _____ County, Michigan.
                                                                          Date

My commission expires: _____   Signature: _____
                                Date   Deputy court clerk/Notary public

Notary public, State of Michigan, County of _____

STATE OF MICHIGAN ____ JUDICIAL DISTRICT ____ JUDICIAL CIRCUIT ____ COUNTY PROBATE	ORDER FOR SERVICE BY PUBLICATION/POSTING AND NOTICE OF ACTION	CASE NO.

Court address _____ Court telephone no. _____

Plaintiff name(s), address(es), and telephone no(s).		Defendant name(s), address(es), and telephone no(s).
	v	

Plaintiff's attorney, bar no., address, and telephone no.

TO: _____

IT IS ORDERED:

1. You are being sued in this court by the plaintiff to _____

_____ . You must file your answer or take other action

permitted by law in this court at the court address above on or before _____ . If you fail to do

Date

so, a default judgment may be entered against you for the relief demanded in the complaint filed in this case.

2. A copy of this order shall be published once each week in _____

Name of publication

☐ three consecutive weeks,

for ☐ _____ , and proof of publication shall be filed in this court.

3. _____ shall post a copy of this order in the courthouse, and

Name

at _____ and

Location

at _____

Location

☐ three continuous weeks,

for ☐ _____ , and shall file proof of posting in this court.

4. A copy of this order shall be sent to _____ at the last-known address

Name

☐ date of the last publication,

by registered mail, return receipt requested, before the ☐ last week of posting, and the affidavit of mailing shall be

filed with this court.

_____   _____   _____
Date   Judge   Bar no.

AFFIDAVIT OF PUBLISHING

Name of ☐ publisher   ☐ agent of publisher

Attach copy of publication here.

Name of newspaper | County where published

This newspaper is a qualified newspaper. The order for service was published in this newpaper at least once each week for three consecutive weeks on the following dates.

_____

Date _____   Affiant signature _____

Subscribed and sworn to before me on _____ , _____ County, Michigan.
                                          Date

My commission expires: _____   Signature: _____
                            Date   Court clerk/Notary public

Notary public, State of Michigan, County of _____

AFFIDAVIT OF POSTING

I have posted this order in a conspicuous place in the _____ courthouse and the

following places as ordered by this court: _____

_____

_____

It has been posted for   ☐ three continuous weeks   ☐ _____ continuous weeks   as ordered by this court.

Date _____   Affiant signature _____

Subscribed and sworn to before me on _____ , _____ County, Michigan.
                                          Date

My commission expires: _____   Signature: _____
                            Date   Court clerk/Notary public

Notary public, State of Michigan, County of _____

AFFIDAVIT OF MAILING

As ordered, on _____ I mailed a copy of the summons and complaint
                   Date

Attach mailing receipt and return receipt here.

and this order to _____
                      Name

at _____ .
   Address

The mailing receipt and return receipt are attached at right.

Date _____   Affiant signature _____

Subscribed and sworn to before me on _____ , _____ County, Michigan.
                                          Date

My commission expires: _____   Signature: _____
                            Date   Court clerk/Notary public

Notary public, State of Michigan, County of _____

Original - Originating court
Copies as needed
JIS CODE: NPC

STATE OF MICHIGAN JUDICIAL CIRCUIT PROBATE COURT COUNTY	NOTICE TO PRIOR COURT OF PROCEEDINGS AFFECTING MINOR(S)	CASE NO.

Court address

Court telephone no.

Name(s) of parent(s)/guardian(s)/plaintiff/defendant	Name(s), alias(es), and date(s) of birth of minor(s)

Case no. of other court

TO: County of _____
- ☐ Court clerk or Register
- ☐ Friend of the court
- ☐ Prosecuting attorney
- ☐ Juvenile officer

NOTICE:

1. ☐ a. A complaint/petition/motion was filed with this court that affects the minor(s) who is/are subject to the continuing

   jurisdiction of your court. A hearing on the complaint/petition/motion is scheduled for

   _____
   Date

   _____
   Time

   _____
   Location

   ☐ b. The attached order was entered on _____ .
   Date

2. The actions of the court in this matter may supersede part or all of the order(s) previously entered by your court as the best interests of the minor(s) require.

CERTIFICATE OF SERVICE

I certify that on this date I served a copy of this notice on the prior court by ☐ first-class mail. ☐ personal delivery.

_____
Date

_____
Signature

Note: If item 1a is checked, this notice must be mailed at least 21 days before the hearing.

Do not write below this line - For court use only

MCL 712A.2(b)(2), MCL 712A.3a, MCR 3.205, MCR 3.927, MCR 5.112

STATE OF MICHIGAN Circuit Court - Family Division COUNTY	APPEARANCE AND WAIVER OF MILITARY RELIEF LAW RIGHTS	CASE NO.

Plaintiff (appearing *in propria persona*):

Defendant:

v

Defendant says:

1. I am in the active duty of the following unit of the U.S. military:

2. I am currently stationed at:

3. I previously received copies of the summons and complaint for divorce and any other initial divorce papers in this case.

4. I make a general appearance and waive all lawsuit relief rights, including the right to request a stay or adjournment of proceedings, provided to me in this case by the Servicemembers Civil Relief Act (50 USC App. 501 et seq.) and/or Michigan's military relief law (MCL 32.517) (or similar military relief law from another state).

Date_____   Defendant_____

Request for Military Status Report

TO:

Defense Manpower Data Center
Attn: Military Verification
1600 Wilson Blvd.
Suite 400
Arlington, VA 22209-2593

RE:

Case name_____

Case number_____

Full name of defendant_____

Defendant's date of birth_____

Defendant's social security number_____

    I am the plaintiff in the divorce case above seeking a default judgment of divorce against the defendant. I must know whether or not the defendant is currently in the active duty of the U.S. military service, to comply with the Servicemembers Civil Relief Act and/or Michigan Compiled Law 32.517 or a similar military relief law from another state.

    Please respond by providing a military status report on defendant as soon as possible. A self-addressed stamped envelope is enclosed for your response.

Date _____

Signature _____

Name _____

Address _____

_____

Telephone _____

Military Locator Request

TO:

Army
Army World Wide Locator Service
Enlisted Records and Evaluation Center
8899 East 56th Street
Indianapolis, IN 46249-5301

Air Force
Air Force Manpower and Personnel Center
ATTN: Air Force Locator / MSIMDL
550 C Street West, Suite 50
Randolph Air Force Base, TX 78150-4752

Navy
Bureau of Naval Personnel
PERS-312E
5720 Integrity Drive
Millington, TN 38055-3120

Coast Guard
Commander
Coast Guard Personnel Command
4200 Wilson Blvd., Suite 1100 (CGPC-adm-3)
Arlington, VA 20598-7200

Marine Corps
Commandant of The Marine Corps
Headquarters, U.S. Marine Corps (MMSB10)
2008 Elliott Road, Suite 201
Quantico, VA 22134-5030

RE:

Case name_____

Case number_____

Full name of defendant_____

Defendant's date of birth_____

Defendant's social security number_____

Defendant's rank and service number (if known)_____

Defendant's last duty assignment (if known)_____

Defendant's last military address (if known)_____

I am the plaintiff in the case above seeking a divorce against the defendant. I request information about the defendant's *current* rank, service number, unit of assignment and military address. I need this information for service of the divorce papers, to satisfy the military relief laws and other reasons related to this divorce case. A self-addressed stamped envelope is enclosed for your response.

As the defendant's spouse, I ask for waiver of the locator request fee.

Date _____   Signature _____

                         Name _____

                         Address _____

                         _____

                         Telephone _____

Original - Court
1st copy - Applicant
Other copies - All appearing parties

STATE OF MICHIGAN

JUDICIAL DISTRICT
JUDICIAL CIRCUIT
COUNTY PROBATE

DISMISSAL

CASE NO.

Court address

Court telephone no.

Plaintiff's name(s) and address(es)

v

Defendant's name(s) and address(es)

Plaintiff's attorney, bar no., address, and telephone no.

Defendant's attorney, bar no., address, and telephone no.

☐ **NOTICE OF DISMISSAL BY PLAINTIFF**

☐ with
☐ without   prejudice as to:

1. Plaintiff/Attorney for plaintiff files this notice of dismissal of this case
   ☐ all defendants.
   ☐ the following defendant(s): _____

2. I certify, under penalty of contempt, that:
   a. This notice is the first dismissal filed by the plaintiff based upon or including the same claim against the defendant.
   b. All costs of filing and service have been paid.
   c. **No answer or motion has been served upon the plaintiff by the defendant** as of the date of this notice.
   d. A copy of this notice has been provided to the appearing defendant/attorney by ☐ mail ☐ personal service.

_____
Date

_____
Plaintiff/Attorney signature

☐ **STIPULATION TO DISMISS**

☐ with
☐ without   prejudice as to:

I stipulate to the dismissal of this case
☐ all parties.
☐ the following parties: _____

_____
Date

_____
Plaintiff/Attorney signature

_____
Date

_____
Defendant/Attorney signature

☐ **ORDER TO DISMISS**

☐ with
☐ without   prejudice. Conditions, if any: _____

IT IS ORDERED this case is dismissed

_____

_____

☐ This order resolves the last pending claim and closes the case.

_____
Date

_____
Judge

_____
Bar no.

MC 09   (4/14)   **DISMISSAL**

MCR 2.504

Approved, SCAO

| STATE OF MICHIGAN
JUDICIAL CIRCUIT
COUNTY | UNIFORM SPOUSAL SUPPORT ORDER
(PAGE 1)
☐ EX PARTE ☐ TEMPORARY ☐ MODIFICATION ☐ FINAL | CASE NO. |

Court address   **Court telephone no.**

Plaintiff's name, address, and telephone no.	v	Defendant's name, address, and telephone no.
Plaintiff's attorney name, bar no., address, and telephone no.		Defendant's attorney name, bar no., address, and telephone no.
Plaintiff's source of income name, address, and telephone no.		Defendant's source of income name, address, and telephone no.

This order is entered   ☐ after hearing.   ☐ on stipulation/consent of the parties.

IT IS ORDERED, UNLESS OTHERWISE ORDERED IN ITEM 11: ☐ Standard provisions have been modified (see item 11).

1. **Spousal Support.** Spousal support shall be paid monthly through the Michigan State Disbursement Unit as follows:

Payer:	Payee:	Amount: $	Effective date:

2. Income withholding takes immediate effect for those items payable through the Michigan State Disbursement Unit.

3. This order continues until the death of the payee or until the earliest of the following events:
   ☐ Date: _____   ☐ $_____ is paid.
   ☐ Remarriage of the payee.   ☐ Death of the payer.
   ☐ Other (specify all other events): _____
   _____

☐ 4. For tax purposes, the payments will be deductible to the payer and included in the income of the payee.

☐ 5. Payments that must be paid directly to the third party (not to the payee) are listed below. (Payments to be made directly to a third party are not payable through the Michigan State Disbursement Unit or friend of the court.)

Type	Amount Per Month	Start Date	Pay to	End Date
	$			
	$			
	$			
	$			

(See page 2 for the remainder of the order.)

FOC 10b (3/13) **UNIFORM SPOUSAL SUPPORT ORDER, PAGE 1**   MCL 552.13, MCR 3.211

STATE OF MICHIGAN JUDICIAL CIRCUIT COUNTY	UNIFORM SPOUSAL SUPPORT ORDER (PAGE 2) ☐ EX PARTE ☐ TEMPORARY ☐ MODIFICATION ☐ FINAL	CASE NO.

Court address   **Court telephone no.**

Plaintiff's name	v	Defendant's name

6. **Retroactive Modification, Surcharge for Past-Due Support, and Liens for Unpaid Support.** Support is a judgment the date it is due and is not retroactively modifiable. A surcharge may be added to past-due support. Unpaid support is a lien by operation of law and the payer's property can be encumbered or seized if an arrearage accrues for more than the periodic support payments payable for two months under the payer's support order.

7. **Address, Employment Status, Health Insurance.** Both parties shall notify the friend of the court in writing of: a) their mailing and residential addresses and telephone numbers; b) the names, addresses, and telephone numbers of their sources of income; c) their health-maintenance or insurance companies, insurance coverage, persons insured, or contract numbers; d) their occupational or drivers' licenses; and e) their social security numbers unless exempt by law pursuant to MCL 552.603. Both parties shall notify the friend of the court in writing within 21 days of any change in this information. Failure to do so may result in a fee being imposed.

8. **Fees.** The payer of support shall pay statutory and service fees as required by law.

9. **Prior Orders. This order supersedes all prior spousal support orders.** Past-due amounts owed under any prior support order are preserved.

10. **Property Settlement.** All property settlement (alimony in gross) payment obligations that are set forth in the judgment are not part of this order.

11. **Other: (Attach separate sheets as needed.)**

_____ _____   _____ _____
Plaintiff (if consent/stipulation)   Date   Defendant (if consent/stipulation)   Date

_____ _____   _____ _____
Plaintiff's attorney   Date   Defendant's attorney   Date

_____ _____   _____ _____
Date   Judge   Bar no.

CERTIFICATE OF MAILING

I certify that on this date I served a copy of this order on the parties or their attorneys by first-class mail addressed to their last-known addresses as defined in MCR 3.203.

_____   _____
Date   Signature

COURT USE ONLY

Plaintiff:

Defendant:

v

Local Forms
(for Wayne County only)

STATE OF MICHIGAN THIRD JUDICIAL CIRCUIT WAYNE COUNTY	CERTIFICATE ON BEHALF OF PLAINTIFF REGARDING EX PARTE INTERIM SUPPORT ORDER	CASE NO.

PLAINTIFF'S NAME		DEFENDANT'S NAME
	V.	

REVIEW BOTH SIDES OF THIS FORM BEFORE COMPLETING.
IF YOU ARE PRESENTING AN EX PARTE ORDER, COMPLETE THIS SIDE OF THIS FORM.
IF YOU ARE **NOT** PRESENTING AN EX PARTE ORDER, COMPLETE THE OTHER SIDE OF THIS FORM.
PLEASE PUT A LARGE 'X' ACROSS THE SIDE YOU ARE NOT COMPLETING.

_____I AM PRESENTING AN EX PARTE INTERIM SUPPORT ORDER FOR ENTRY, WHICH INCLUDES THE **FOLLOWING PREVISIONS:** (CHECK THE PROVISION AND/OR CIRCLE THE CORRECT CHOICE)

_____CUSTODY [with Names and Dates of Birth of minor child(ren)] MCL 552.15

    _____SOLE LEGAL AND PHYSICAL CUSTODY TO   *PLT / DFT*

    _____JOINT LEGAL, SOLE PHYSICAL CUSTODY TO   *PLT / DFT*

    _____JOINT LEGAL AND PHYSICAL CUSTODY

_____ADDRESS (NOTIFY FOC IS THERE IS A CHANGE) MCR 3.211 (D)(2)

    _____CHILD'S RESIDENCE

    _____PARTIES' RESIDENCE

    _____EMPLOYER'S

_____DOMICILE MCR 3.211 (C)(1)

_____PARENTING TIME MCL 722.27a

_____SUPPORT MCR 3.211 (D) & (E)

    _____PAYABLE THRU FOC

    _____IF MORE THAN ONE CHILD, IN FORM OF, e.g., "$100 For two children, $64 for one child… etc."

    _____IMMEDIATE INCOME WITHHOLDING

    _____STATUTORY FEES

_____HEALTH CARE MCR 3.211 (E)(3), MCL 722.27 AND .3.

_____NOTICE REGARDING OBJECTIONS REQUIRED BY MCR 3.207 B(5)

I CERTIFY THAT I AM PRESENTING A SUPPORT ORDER THAT AGREES WITH THE MICHIGAN CHILD SUPPORT GUIDELINES.

DATE_____   _____/_____ P _____
                        Attorney's or Party's Printed Name/Signature

Address_____

City _____ State _____ Zip Code _____ Telephone _____

A.   Please check the appropriate item(s), sign and serve the original of this certificate, the complaint (or counter-claim or petition) and an MSA 27A.659, MCL 600.659 custody affidavit upon the Court, the County Clerk, the Friend of the Court, and the other party. **A 'VERIFIED STATEMENT - FRIEND OF THE COURT' MUST BE SERVED ON THE FRIEND OF THE COURT AND THE OTHER PARTY. DO NOT GIVE THE COUNTY CLERK THE VERIFIED STATEMENT.**

B.   Provide the Office of the Friend of the Court with a copy of the **PROOF OF SERVICE** setting forth that each of the documents referred to in Instruction A have been served upon the other party.

STATE OF MICHIGAN THIRD JUDICIAL CIRCUIT WAYNE COUNTY	CERTIFICATE ON BEHALF OF PLAINTIFF REGARDING EX PARTE INTERIM SUPPORT ORDER	CASE NO.

PLAINTIFF'S NAME	v.	DEFENDANT'S NAME

REVIEW BOTH SIDES OF THIS FORM BEFORE COMPLETING.

IF YOU ARE **NOT** PRESENTING AN EX PARTE ORDER, COMPLETE THIS SIDE OF THIS FORM.
IF YOU ARE PRESENTING AN EX PARTE ORDER, COMPLETE THE OTHER SIDE OF THIS FORM.
PLEASE PUT A LARGE 'X' ACROSS THE SIDE YOU ARE NOT COMPLETING.

☐ I AM **NOT** PRESENTING AN EX PARTE INTERIM SUPPORT ORDER FOR ENTRY AT THIS TIME DUE TO THE **FOLLOWING REASON(S):** (CHECK THE REASON(S) THAT APPLY).

1. ☐ A prior order for support of the minor child/children is in effect:

    Name of County _____ Case Number _____

2. ☐ The non-custodial party is not the parent of the child/children named in the complaint and the complaint so states.

3. ☐ The Court lacks personal jurisdiction over the Defendant because the whereabouts of the Defendant are unknown. Service will be by publication.

4. ☐ The parties are presently residing together and the child/children are being adequately supported and there is no public assistance or application for public assistance pending.

5. ☐ I am the custodial parent and the other party is providing appropriate support for the child/children and there is no public assistance or pending application for public assistance pending.

6. ☐ The child/children are receiving Social Security Dependant Benefits as support.

7. ☐ The non-custodial parent is unemployed, receives Public Assistance or Supplemental Security Income (SSI) and has no other source of income. A request for a Friend of the Court child support investigation has been made.

8. ☐ The ability of the non-custodial parent to provide support for the minor child/children has not been determined. A motion for a temporary child support order has been filed.

9. ☐ Other _____

I CERTIFY THAT THE ABOVE INFORMATION IS CORRECT TO THE BEST OF MY KNOWLEDGE.

DATE _____ / _____ P _____

    Attorney's or Party's Printed Name/Signature

Address _____

City _____ State _____ Zip Code _____ Telephone _____

A. Please check the appropriate item(s), sign and serve the original of this certificate, the complaint (or counter-claim or petition) and an MSA 27A.659, MCL 600.659 custody affidavit upon the Court, the County Clerk, the Friend of the Court, and the other party. A **VERIFIED STATEMENT - FRIEND OF THE COURT MUST BE SERVED ON THE FRIEND OF THE COURT AND THE OTHER PARTY. DO NOT GIVE THE COUNTY CLERK THE VERIFIED STATEMENT.**

B. Provide the Office of the Friend of the Court with a copy of the **PROOF OF SERVICE** setting forth that each of the documents referred to in Instruction A have been served upon the other party.

STATE OF MICHIGAN THIRD JUDICIAL COURT WAYNE COUNTY	CERTIFICATE OF CONFORMITY FOR DOMESTIC RELATIONS ORDER OR JUDGMENT	CASE NO.

Penobscot Bldg. 645 Griswold Ave. Detroit, MI 48226   *313-224-5372*

PLAINTIFF'S NAME	v	DEFENDANT'S NAME

I certify the attached Order of Judgment as presented for entry to be in full conformity

with the requirements set forth by statute, **INCLUDING A PROVISION FOR IMMEDIATE**

INCOME WITHHOLDING (WHICH SHALL BE IMPLEMENTED BY THE FRIEND OF THE COURT).

THE PAYER'S SOCIAL SECURITY NUMBER AND THE NAME AND ADDRESS OF HIS/HER

SOURCE OF INCOME, IF KNOWN, UNLESS OTHERWISE ORDERED BY THE COURT, and with

Michigan Court Rules 3.201 and following and if applicable, includes all provisions of the

Friend of the Court recommendation or is in conformity with the decision of

_____ rendered on the _____ day of

_____, 20_____.

_____   _____
Date

Instructions: Please sign and present this certificate to the Court Clerk when the Order or
Judgment is presented for entry. If an ex parte interim order is being presented
to the Judge, please complete the "Certificate on behalf of Plaintiff regarding
Ex Parte Interim Support Order" and follow Local Court Rule 3.206.

#1225 (11/04) CERTIFICATE OF CONFORMITY FOR DOMESTIC RELATIONS ORDER OR JUDGEMENT

STATE OF MICHIGAN THIRD JUDICIAL COURT WAYNE COUNTY	CERTIFICATE OF CONFORMITY FOR DOMESTIC RELATIONS ORDER OR JUDGMENT	CASE NO.
Penobscot Bldg. 645 Griswold Ave. Detroit, MI 48226		*313-224-5372*

PLAINTIFF'S NAME	V	DEFENDANT'S NAME

I certify the attached Order of Judgment as presented for entry to be in full conformity with the requirements set forth by statute, **INCLUDING A PROVISION FOR IMMEDIATE INCOME WITHHOLDING (WHICH SHALL BE IMPLEMENTED BY THE FRIEND OF THE COURT). THE PAYER'S SOCIAL SECURITY NUMBER AND THE NAME AND ADDRESS OF HIS/HER SOURCE OF INCOME, IF KNOWN, UNLESS OTHERWISE ORDERED BY THE COURT,** and with **Michigan Court Rules 3.201 and following and if applicable, includes all provisions of the Friend of the Court recommendation or is in conformity with the decision of**

_____ rendered on the _____ day of

_____, 20_____.

_____   _____

Date

Instructions: Please sign and present this certificate to the Court Clerk when the Order or Judgment is presented for entry. If an ex parte interim order is being presented to the Judge, please complete the "Certificate on behalf of Plaintiff regarding Ex Parte Interim Support Order" and follow Local Court Rule 3.206.

#1225 (11/04) CERTIFICATE OF CONFORMITY FOR DOMESTIC RELATIONS ORDER OR JUDGEMENT

THE CIRCUIT COURT
FOR THE THIRD JUDICIAL CIRCUIT OF MICHIGAN
FAMILY DIVISION – FRIEND OF THE COURT

<u>ORDER DATA FORM-SUPPORT</u>
FOR SUBMISSION OF DOMESTIC RELATIONS ORDER FOR ENTRY INTO
Michigan Child Support Enforcement System (MiCSES) BY FOC

<u>NON-EX PARTE ORDERS</u>:

1.   Complete legibly and attach this form to the Friend of the Court (FOC) True Copy of the Order.

2.   Please note that the FOC worker will not review the order. If required fields are not completed (noted by asterisk *), the Order Data Form and the Order will be returned to you.

3.   Do not submit Orders with non-specific dates, such as orders that start support as of the date of sale of the marital home.

4.   If an order provides for different support amounts for different periods of time, complete an Order Data Form for each period. Label each with "1 of 'n', …, 'n' of 'n', in the upper right corner.

5.   The Judge's Circuit Court Clerk will forward the FOC copy of the Order, with attached Order Data Form, to FOC for entry into the MiCSES System.

<u>EX PARTE ORDERS</u>:

1.   Attach the Proof of Service if the Order is an Ex Parte Order. (The Order will not be entered into the MiCSES System unless the Proof of Service is attached.)

2.   Ex Parte Orders, with completed Order Data Form and Proof of Service, should be faxed or mailed to:

Order Entry Department   Attorney Window
3rd Floor, Penobscot Building   **or delivered to:**   2nd Floor, Penobscot Building
645 Griswold   645 Griswold
Detroit, Michigan 48226   Detroit, Michigan 48226
FAX: (313) 237-9290   FAX: (313) 237-9290

THE ORDER DATA FORM IS AVAILABLE FOR DOWNLOAD TO YOUR COMPUTER
OR FOR PRINTING
ON THE COURT WEBSITE AT http://3rdcc.org OR FAX LIBRARY: (313) 967-3662

Rev. 11/06/02

ABOUT THE NEW AND REQUIRED "ORDER DATA FORM-SUPPORT"

Friend of the Court, with the support of the Family Law Bench, has developed a data form, now called ORDER DATA FORM-SUPPORT (ODF-S), (formerly known as Fast Track Form) to assist the FOC in the task of loading the provisions of a support order into the Michigan Child Support Enforcement System. (MiCSES) It is now two pages.

A completed ODF-S must be attached to the FOC copy of any domestic relations order.

The old Fast Track form you have used was developed before and during the transition to the Michigan Child Support Enforcement System and is now obsolete.

Here are some features of the new form, as well as some practical considerations that should be noted when an order is being prepared for entry.

First, please note that it is the responsibility of the party submitting the order to the court for signature to enter all the relevant details of the new order into the ODF-S [ORDER DETAILS). The FOC worker will rely upon that information when loading the order and will not consult the attached order, nor any other previously entered order(s).

Second, the information required on page one, "ORDER DETAILS", of the ODF-S should be garnered only from the order attached. If the order results in a change in a certain element of the account, you check the relevant boxes and complete the relevant text areas.   If the order does not impact a certain element of the account, then you do not check those boxes and no change would be noted on MiCSES for that aspect of the account.

For example: the order modifies child support but not childcare. You would check the relevant boxes and enter the ordered amounts and dates into the text fields in the child support section. You would not check any of the childcare boxes. The worker will load the new child support, with its commencement date, and leave the childcare portion of the account as is.

For example: an order might provide for a certain cycle for one period of time, then a different amount for a subsequent period of time [for example, $10/wk from 04-01-02 to 05-31-02, then $40/wk from 06-01-02 until further order of the court]. You will prepare a "1 of 2" ODF-S (ORDER DETAILS) sheet for the '04-01-02 to 05-31-02 period' and a "2 of 2" ODF-S (ORDER DETAILS) sheet for the '06-01-02 until further order of the court' period of time. Only one copy of page 2, ODF-S (DEMOGRAPHICS) would need to be attached.

The only time an arrearage amount would be entered would be when the order, by its specific terms, sets a specific amount of arrearage for a date certain.

Again, the first page of the form (ORDER DETAILS) should contain the specifics of only the attached order.

The second page, DEMOGRAPHICS is also attached to the new order being submitted for entry. FOC will check and correct/update the account for any changes or errors. The information required is standard information you obtain from your clients. Your client's and the other parties' information should be on the verified statement initially and updated in your client file as you interact with your client and opposing counsel. Family Independence Agency account #'s, children's dates of birth and social security numbers, etc. are known to your clients and should be in your client files.

MiCSES has an automated Income Withholding Notice feature. The worker, as a part of the order loading activity that day, reviews the Demographics page and updates the employer, if necessary. Upon entry into MiCSES of a new support order, the system generates an Income Withholding Notice (IWN) that night, in batch, to the active employer. If the order specifies a certain $ amount to be wage deducted, that amount is loaded into MiCSES and the IWN is generated in that amount. If the order does not specify a certain amount to be withheld, the system calculates the guideline amount and the IWN is generated in that amount.

I believe that, especially if you download the template version of this form from the Website, you will find that it is very straightforward and quick to complete. The boxes and text areas, which are impacted by the order, are checked and filled and the balance of the choices are left blank.

ORDER DETAILS

STATE OF MICHIGAN
COUNTY OF WAYNE
THIRD JUDICIAL CIRCUIT COURT
FAMILY DIVISION

ORDER DATA FORM-SUPPORT

Re: SUBMISSION FOR LOADING
ATTACHED SUPPORT ORDER INTO
MiCSES ON FOC COMPUTER SYSTEM

THE ORDER WAS ENTERED ON:

_____

(DATE ON ORDER STAMPED BY JUDGE'S CLERK)

(PLACE LABEL HERE)

CASE #:

_____

_____

JUDGE

*INDICATES REQUIRED INFORMATION

CHECK ONLY THE BOXES WHICH APPLY TO PROVISIONS IN THE SUBMITTED ORDER

* PLAINTIFF NAME: *** DEFENDANT NAME:**

*THIS ORDER IS:
☐ EX PARTE (PROOF OF SERVICE REQUIRED)   ☐ TEMPORARY ☐ JUDGMENT ☐ MODIFICATION
*WERE CHILD SUPPORT GUIDELINES FOLLOWED?   ☐ YES   ☐ NO

*THE CHILD SUPPORT PAYER IS   ☐ **PLAINTIFF**   ☐ **DEFENDANT**   ☐ **NOT APPLICABLE.**

☐ **CHILD SUPPORT.** COMMENCEMENT DATE IS _____   ☐ **PAY DIRECT, NOT THROUGH FOC.**

* 5 CHILDREN PER WEEK	*** 4 CHILDREN PER WEEK**	*** 3 CHILDREN PER WEEK**	*** 2 CHILDREN PER WEEK**	*** 1 CHILD PER WEEK**
CHILD SUPPORT AMOUNT	CHILD SUPPORT AMOUNT	CHILD SUPPORT AMOUNT	CHILD SUPPORT AMOUNT	CHILD SUPPORT AMOUNT
$	$	$	$	$

☐ **INCOME WITHHOLDING:**   ☐ PROCESS AT GUIDELINE AMOUNT   ☐ PROCESS AT $ _____ PER WEEK

☐ **CHILD SUPPORT ARREARAGE:**
☐ PRESERVED ☐ CANCELED AS OF DATE: _____   ☐ SET AT $ _____ AS OF DATE: _____

☐ **CHILD CARE EXPENSES:** $ _____ PER WEEK, COMMENCEMENT DATE IS _____ ;
END DATE IS ☐ GUIDELINE DATE **OR** ☐ DATE: _____
☐ **CHILD CARE ARREARAGE:**
☐ PRESERVED ☐ CANCELED AS OF DATE: _____   ☐ SET AT $ _____ AS OF DATE: _____

☐ **ARREARAGE ADJUSTMENT:**
☐ DIRECT CREDIT IN AMOUNT OF $ _____   ☐ ADD ADDITIONAL OBLIGATION IN AMOUNT OF $ _____

☐ **MEDICAL INSURANCE IN ORDER.**
☐ **CHILD SUPPORT PAYER RESPONSIBLE FOR** _____ **% OF UNINSURED MEDICAL EXPENSES.**

☐ **PARENTING TIME ABATEMENT:** ____ **% PARENTING TIME CREDIT** AFTER ___ CONSECUTIVE OVERNIGHTS.
☐ **PARENTING TIME ORDERED: (CHECK ONE):**
☐ REASONABLE   ☐ SPECIFIC   ☐ SUPERVISED   ☐ RESERVED   ☐ REFER TO FAMILY COUNSELING/OTHER

*THE SPOUSAL SUPPORT PAYER IS   ☐ **PLAINTIFF**   ☐ **DEFENDANT**   ☐ **NOT APPLICABLE.**
☐ **SPOUSAL SUPPORT:** ☐ $ _____ PER WEEK, COMMENCEMENT DATE: _____ .
☐ PERMANENT   ☐ END DATE _____   ☐ **PAY DIRECT, NOT THROUGH FOC**
☐ **SPOUSAL SUPPORT ARREARAGE:**
☐ PRESERVED ☐ CANCELED AS OF DATE: _____   ☐ SET AT $ _____ AS OF DATE: _____

☐ **ORDER REFERS MATTERS TO DIVORCE INVESTIGATION/MODIFICATION FOR FURTHER INVESTIGATION.**

I CERTIFY THAT THE ABOVE INFORMATION IS TRUE TO THE BEST OF MY KNOWLEDGE, INFORMATION AND BELIEF, AND IS IN FULL CONFORMITY WITH THE REQUIREMENTS SET FORTH BY STATUTE AND COURT RULE AND THE DECISION OF THE COURT. (NOTE: FOC WILL NOT READ THE ORDER WHEN ENTERING IT ON MiCSES.)

DATE: _____   SIGNATURE OF ATTORNEY _____   BAR NO. _____

PLEASE PRINT:

_____
ATTORNEY NAME

_____
ADDRESS

_____
CITY/STATE/ZIP

_____
TELEPHONE NO.

FD/FOC 4002 (11/06/02) **ORDER DATA FORM-SUPPORT**

DEMOGRAPHICS

| STATE OF MICHIGAN
COUNTY OF WAYNE
THIRD JUDICIAL CIRCUIT
COURT
FAMILY DIVISION | ORDER DATA FORM-SUPPORT
Re: SUBMISSION FOR LOADING
ATTACHED SUPPORT ORDER INTO
MiCSES ON FOC COMPUTER SYSTEM

THE ORDER WAS ENTERED ON:
_____
(DATE ON ORDER STAMPED BY JUDGE'S CLERK) | (PLACE LABEL HERE)

CASE #:
_____

_____
JUDGE |

*INDICATES REQUIRED INFORMATION

CHECK ONLY THE BOXES WHICH APPLY TO PROVISIONS IN THE SUBMITTED ORDER

* PLAINTIFF NAME:	* DEFENDANT NAME:

* NAME(S) OF CHILDREN (OLDEST TO YOUNGEST)	* DATE(S) OF BIRTH	* SOCIAL SECURITY NUMBER(S)

(ADD ADDITIONAL CHILDREN ON SEPARATE SHEET)

NON-CUSTODIAL PARENT (OR FATHER IF JOINT CUSTODY)   ☐ PLAINTIFF ☐ DEFENDANT

* NAME:	* DATE OF BIRTH:	* SOC. SEC. NO.	HOME TELEPHONE NO:
* RESIDENTIAL ADDRESS:	* CITY, STATE, ZIP	OTHER TELEPHONE NUMBERS: ☐ WORK ☐ MOBILE	FIA/TANF N0.: NOW ACTIVE: ☐ YES ☐ NO
* EMPLOYER:	* EMPLOYER ADDRESS:	EMPLOYER TELEPHONE NO.:	EMPLOYER FED I.D. NO.:

CUSTODIAL PERSON (OR MOTHER IF JOINT CUSTODY)   ☐ PLAINTIFF ☐ DEFENDANT

* NAME:	* DATE OF BIRTH:	* SOC. SEC. NO.	HOME TELEPHONE NO:
* RESIDENTIAL ADDRESS:	* CITY, STATE, ZIP	OTHER TELEPHONE NUMBERS: ☐ WORK ☐ MOBILE	FIA/TANF N0.: NOW ACTIVE: ☐ YES ☐ NO
* EMPLOYER:	* EMPLOYER ADDRESS:	EMPLOYER TELEPHONE NO.:	EMPLOYER FED I.D. NO.:

I CERTIFY THAT THE ABOVE INFORMATION IS TRUE TO THE BEST OF MY KNOWLEDGE, INFORMATION AND BELIEF, AND IS IN FULL CONFORMITY WITH THE REQUIREMENTS SET FORTH BY STATUTE AND COURT RULE AND THE DECISION OF THE COURT. (NOTE: FOC WILL NOT READ THE ORDER WHEN ENTERING IT ON MiCSES.)

DATE: _____   SIGNATURE OF ATTORNEY _____   BAR NO.

PLEASE PRINT: _____
ATTORNEY NAME

FD/FOC 4002 (11/06/02) **ORDER DATA FORM-SUPPORT**